Books by John Ney

————————

WHITEY MC ALPINE

PALM BEACH

OX
(*for young people*)

THE EUROPEAN SURRENDER
A Descriptive Study of the American Social and Economic Conquest

THE
EUROPEAN
SURRENDER

THE
EUROPEAN
SURRENDER

*A Descriptive Study of the American
Social and Economic Conquest*

by JOHN NEY

LITTLE, BROWN AND COMPANY · BOSTON · TORONTO

LIBRARY OF CONGRESS CATALOG CARD NO. 78–108952

FIRST EDITION

Grateful acknowledgment is extended to the following for permission to quote from:

DEATH IN THE AFTERNOON by Ernest Hemingway, published
by Charles Scribner's Sons.

THE FRENCH by François Nourissier, copyright © 1968 by
Alfred A. Knopf, Inc.

THE EDUCATION OF HENRY ADAMS, by Henry Adams, copyright © 1946 by Charles F. Adams. Reprinted by permission of
the publisher, Houghton Mifflin Company.

DOWN AND OUT IN PARIS AND LONDON, by George Orwell,
published by Harcourt, Brace and World, copyright 1933 by George
Orwell. Copyright © renewed 1960 by Sonia Pett-Rivers. Reprinted
by permission of Brandt & Brandt.

Published simultaneously in Canada
by Little, Brown & Company (Canada) Limited

PRINTED IN THE UNITED STATES OF AMERICA

FOR MY FATHER

And also to the memory of his father, professor
of law at the University of Iowa; his uncle
Christopher, soldier and lawyer and
critic; and all the ghostly generations
of Iowans, both white and Indian,
who pondered the question
of Europe, the query
that came inevitably
from that flat and
philosophically
demanding
prairie.

"If the American is a barbarian — and all the world is agreed that he is, his own voice the loudest in assent — may I suggest that the European is even more so. When you see him cover his mouth as he excavates with a toothpick or removes prune pits (the shielding hand is supposed to disguise the operation, but actually makes it more obvious, of course), or eat toast with a knife and fork in order not to touch it with his hands, the American coarseness becomes almost refreshing. At those moments, European genteelness reverses the American certainty of four hundred years, and the Europeans are revealed as the true savages."

"And then there is the fear — Europeans have seen so much disaster that they always expect more. You knock on a European's door at the most innocent hour, three in the afternoon, and he can look up like a startled deer, not absolutely sure it isn't someone come to take him to jail. Fear is universally latent in Europe."

"When the American carpenter arrives on the job, he puts on one of those overalls with three or four dozen pockets and he has something to stick in each one. Then he hangs that balanced hammer in a special loop, and opens his saw case with the six beautiful saws inside, all different and all razor-sharp. His European counterpart puts on what looks like a discarded track suit, makes do with one rusty saw, and drives his nails in with the back of a crude hatchet. He doesn't have a hammer."

> — Fragments from a heated discussion among European and American diplomats at a cocktail party in Bonn in 1969. Interestingly enough, the three speakers quoted above were all Europeans.

CONTENTS

I
IN GENERAL

THE question is not whether dominance has occurred, but when it happened and what forms it has taken. The occurrence of the dominance is a boundary, a settled fact. To cross such a boundary by treating conquest and surrender as unresolved questions is not only a waste of time, but also distinctly anti-esthetic.

All Europe is Americanized and going to become more so, whether by its own hand or by that of the slightly enervated and befuddled teacher-parent. Each European country and each European regional and metropolitan subdivision is in the grip of the same principles and processes. The only legitimate — one is tempted to say the only honest — line of inquiry is into the form Americanization has taken in the various localities, what has happened visually and psychologically as a result of the highly active principles and processes.

Such a line of inquiry is admittedly restricted, but the subject itself is restricted, whether the restrictions are acknowledged or not. The writer cannot remind himself too often that the "big" questions have been answered. America has conquered, Europe has surrendered. Now the literary possibilities are almost exclusively descriptive, as on a trip through the Amazon jungles.

What is the visual and psychological form of the surrender in London? In Paris? In Rome? The writer must know what to listen for and what to look for: the timbre of the voices, not what they say; the tension of the fingers on their first automobile gear-shift knob, not who owns the factory that made the car; the exact appearance of the tired family in Rotterdam munching a still-novel TV dinner, not what is on the television screen. From an American standpoint, binding on both writer and reader, Europe is at pause, inactive in hiatus, going through a period of learning that no American alive can remember ever going through — if, indeed, any American ever did go through it.

Eliot's famous lines — "And I have known the arms already, known them all —/ Arms that are braceleted and white and bare/ (But in the lamplight, downed with light brown hair!)" — give incisive tongue to the odd combination of boredom and dormant sexuality that the American cannot help but feel when presented with this European pause; and the pleasurably defiant dishonesty he may feel in denying it may well be part of the sexuality. Muscular conjecture, hypothetical prose, the heavy feet of the Micheners, Galbraiths, Sampsons and Manchesters (heavy in different ways, but equal in oppressive weight), are not only tedious at this time but harshly unscientific as well.

This is not to say, of course, that there is not much to come, or that the pause itself is real for Europe. Europe imagines vast action and can't afford to imagine anything else; it is we Americans who must be responsible enough to remember that the opposite state prevails.

An American observer must be especially careful on that point. He cannot forget that although it will be years before the European Russell Baker steps forward to do a piece on Christmas in which it is called, among other things, the season of "a partridge in a plastic pear tree," the inevitability of his coming with his sophisticated synthesis means that until then European time is sheer filler from the American standpoint. The European present can only duplicate the American past; whenever it thinks it has caught up, it finds, like Achilles in Zeno's paradox, that America has moved on. Thus European time can only have meaning to an American if it is treated descriptively, if the appearance of the pause is given due precedence over its hypothetical causes and futures.

Applied to this book on the American-European relationship, the European "present" — the collective panorama of people and incidents — is viewed as taking place against the backdrop of a predetermined future. Because this European "present" is a pause, its future is already revealed, and it is not only possible but scientifically necessary for Americans to see it as a past, especially because it is a past of our own sloughing.

———

Colonization cannot be an isolated act, but is a result of resources, powers and confidences (and their lack!) produced, in turn, by psychological attitudes. In 1740, an arriving Englishman, suffused with expectation, strides down the wharf at Calcutta and instinctively drops his bags when he sees his first Indian. Just as instinctively, the Indian picks them up. Several hundred years later, in 1943, a two-hundred-and-fifty-pound American sergeant, calmly aggressive, enters a pub in London and instinctively (if obliquely) asserts his right to his first English girl. Just as instinctively, she complies.

The two instances are purely colonial in that both colonizees — the Indian man and the English girl — understand as clearly and believe as firmly in the colonizer's picture of himself as he does. The second instance is also an example of a former colonizer (England) becoming a colonizee, and it is necessary to realize that such reversals are commonplace — even concurrent on different levels, as shall be seen — but it is even more necessary to understand that all colonization flows from superior-inferior psychological relationships. Conversely, it cannot exist without them. In 1968, they are the ultimate basis for all the statistics in *Forbes* and *Fortune* and the rest of the business periodicals concerning the amount of American capital invested abroad, the number of European firms penetrated by American shareholders, and the other tables and indices of accrued tabulation. The statistical evidence tends to be considered a reliable recording of spontaneous generation — as real in *itself*, particularly among those who have had a hand in creating it — but such a view can hardly avoid standing as an admission of historical naïveté, if not historical ignorance. Statistics can only be, of course, a record of the present surface manifestations of the psychological past. In this case, that past has been very active and, in consequence, the surface has much variety and depth; but it is still only a surface.

Reliance on surface phenomena can lead to further errors, not the least of them the belief that any contemporary nation-group is capable of creating and maintaining a modern (American) technological society, and that the only reason the Americans are the leaders in such creation is that they have cast off certain arbitrary political and economic restrictions. According to this notion, Americans are not intrinsically different from Europeans at bottom or more adapted to technological activity, they have just had the good fortune (*sic*) to live in a country overflowing with natural resources and free of archaic political and economic practices. If the positions were reversed — if all the Americans were miraculously transported to Europe and all the Europeans to America — the master and servant relationship would be similarly reversed: the Europeans would be the masters and the Americans the servants.

The argument may be of service in the colonization process itself, but does not warrant serious consideration on its own. In sober fact, just the opposite is true. The Americans have taken over only because they are intrinsically different, and the restrictions have been peeled away as a natural result of that difference. If the geographical positions were reversed, the master and servant relationship would remain the same: the transplanted Americans would build Europe up and take charge of their former habitat in short order. Americans are the only people who *can* cope with (or put up with) technological living at the American level, so they are the only people who have it. And the European countries each have just that level of technological living of which they are capable. No more and no less, and not determined by any resource save the personal.

In dealing with that context, it is necessary to keep in mind the exact degree of mean national development. In England, for example, nearly all workers — even industrial workers — were paid in cash until very recently, and most still are. The atmosphere of payment was, and is, most important. The long line of shabbily dressed men, caps pulled low, inching along toward the paymaster sitting at a table covered with the small brown envelopes containing the week's wages in pound notes, silver and copper coins . . . the sullen, old-fashioned factory in the background, the endless bicycles awaiting their owners, the determination of the paymaster to enforce caste and the equal determination of the workers to accept it . . . all that, and much more, contribute to the formation of the average Englishman's technological capabilities and demands.

By contrast, American life is infinitely more complicated. Checking accounts, stock portfolios, personal life insurance policies and the rest of the typical worker's endless accounting and decision-requiring commitments are handled more or less successfully by the average man. At the present time, mean national development in Europe could not cope with such detail, and Europe is "behind" America to just the degree that the average European is behind the average American on an evolutionary scale-graph graded according to load capacity in terms of the individual as his own business enterprise.

And so, when Jean-Jacques Servan-Schreiber cries out that Europe must take its technological destiny into its own hands, the plea inverses priorities and possibilities. Scientifically speaking, his demand should be that the Europeans become different people inside. Without the interior changes, it is not possible to effect exterior changes. Thus, if there is an American lesson, it is that technological advancement follows psychological desire, adaptation and change. It cannot and does not happen the other way around.

Because of its wide circulation and acceptance, one cannot avoid evaluations of *The American Challenge*, Servan-Schreiber's analysis of contemporary and future American influence in Europe.

To begin with the opinions of others:

In his book on de Gaulle, John L. Hess, Paris correspondent of the *New York Times*, paints Servan-Schreiber as a pious ignoramus and dismisses *The American Challenge* as "not particularly profound or original."

A prominent American economist of my acquaintance goes further: "Hess's view of Servan-Schreiber himself may be open to question, but I think most responsible economists concur in his judgment of the book. It is execrably written, miserably organized, and reveals what I would have to call a touching trust in America and Americans. . . . It seems . . . little more than an interoffice memo, dashed off on a weekend, and I wonder if Servan-Schreiber originally intended it to go past his own staff. My own feelings on reading it were familiar enough — the initial incredulity that such lazy stuff could impose, could be read seriously by so many millions, and then the realization that it wasn't all that unusual in the mixture of shoddiness and general appeal. At that point, I was prepared to forget it as you forget *Portnoy's Complaint* or *The Valley of the Dolls,* what I guess you'd call the fictional counterparts, except that *The American Challenge* deals with an important subject, and, frankly, a poor book on an important subject can often be accidentally provocative and useful. I'm almost fond of it now."

A Swiss banker: "Already so out-of-date that only a public always credulous could accept it as contemporary."

My own feeling is that Servan-Schreiber performed a very real service, because until someone drew popular attention to the extent of American influence in Europe it was not possible to consider the causes of that influence seriously. He has pointed out that Europe is already Americanized and cannot avoid becoming more so; and he pointed it out at just the moment when Europe and America were ready to listen. So that fact is now established, and the settlement opens the door to more interesting and pertinent questions.

Now everyone agrees that Europe is Americanized — or colonized, if that is the more accurate term — but there is not agreement as to how and why it happened and what the future of the Americanization process is to be. There is not even a common understanding as to precisely what Americanization is, whether the stress should fall on the abstract control of foreign companies, or on the starkly visible putting of Europeans into Levi's, or on some more subtle and complicated aspect.

It is when he attempts to deal with those questions that Servan-Schreiber fails most conspicuously, and it is important to understand just how he fails. John Hess accuses him of being "subject to the vulgar error of post-hoc reasoning: Americans chew gum, Americans are rich — Q.E.D., one becomes rich by chewing gum." Probing a bit further, those errors come about because Servan-Schreiber himself is such a product of the Americanization that it is technically impossible for him to analyze it.

In *Death in the Afternoon*, Ernest Hemingway castigated Waldo Frank's *Virgin Spain* as "the unavoidable mysticism of a man who writes a language so badly that he cannot make a clear statement . . . I call [it] erectile writing . . . due to a certain congestion, or others, trees for example look different to a man in that portentous state . . . All objects look different. They are slightly larger, more mysterious and vaguely blurred." The amusing explanation of turgid prose as being the result of indefinitely sustained priapism is no more to be taken literally in Servan-Schreiber's case than in Waldo Frank's, but as symbol it is equally apt. Servan-Schreiber writes in a state of "excitement" so uncritical that he accepts anything any "qualified" American tells him. He reads *The Reforming of General Education*, by Daniel Bell, and says: "During the next 30 years our generation will see the advent of what Daniel Bell calls the 'post-industrial' society. We should remember this term, for it defines our future. It involves such fundamental changes that for certain industrialized countries life in the year 2000 will be as different from what it is today as our societies now are from Egypt or Nigeria." He reads the Hudson report and says: "In 30 years

America will be a post-industrial society with a per capita income of $7,500. There will be only four work days a week of seven hours per day. The year will be comprised of 39 work weeks and 13 weeks of vacation. With weekends and holidays this makes 147 work days a year and 218 free holidays. All this within a single generation."

Even the most dedicated American boosters are not so unquestioningly confident, nor so meticulously dogmatic. Servan-Schreiber's unqualified optimism reminds one that he is not an American but *Americanized,* and sees America much as Indian civil servants in pre-Gandhi India saw Great Britain.

His invincible naïveté leads, finally, to his grossest error, the one on which his whole argument is based: that Europeans can overcome the "American challenge" by a conscious act of will. This betrays such a misunderstanding of the origin of American power that one is inevitably drawn to refute it. As it turns out, the refutation is simple enough in itself, but the attempt to substitute a comprehensive answer to the question of that origin is not so easy. Eventually one arrives at the conclusion that Americans are on top because they are intrinsically different, because they have achieved mutation . . . but one only does arrive there after sifting through a number of other theories.

When all the world cries out that America has taken over Europe, it is not nearly enough to explain the takeover as the result of superior production methods, superior executive abilities, superior banking practices, greater "aggressiveness" . . . and so on. Even the commonest of common men know there has to be something more to it than that. Or something less, but certainly something more basic, more human.

Influence, like sex, has its moment, the split second in fresh, vivid colors when it comes down from the abstract and possesses the hearts and minds of those who do the influencing and, in turn, of those who are influenced. If such a moment is a result — and it is — it must be the result of a concrete rather than an abstract superiority.

In the early 1950s, for example, a prominent American motion picture company decided to make an epic film in Rome to take advantage of the cheap Italian extras for mob scenes. It was one of the very first and very biggest postwar epics to be made in Italy by an American company, and there were certain pioneering problems. From Hollywood came the American production chief, Maury Madder, a tiny man who smoked huge cigars and played gin rummy every night in the downstairs bar of the Excelsior Hotel. His production assistant, Giorgio Vellati, a personable Italian, was obviously a rascal. He was also something of a philosopher and fond of lecturing an American friend, Henry Fordyce, in the motion picture business, too, on how stupid the Americans were and how clever (*furbo*) the Italians. "We have been conquered many times in our history, dear Henry," he would say, "but we always conquer the conquerors because we are cleverer than they are." It was known that Vellati was making all he could as Maury Madder's production assistant — the opportunities were endless — and on one occasion he got so carried away with the cleverness of it all that he told Fordyce he would net $100,000 over and above his salary. A few nights later, Fordyce was playing gin rummy at Maury Madder's table at the Excelsior and another film producer kidded Maury about how his Italian help was stealing from him. At length, Maury said mildly that his company knew all about the stealing; that they had, in fact, anticipated it and entered embezzlement and pilferage figures in the budget when the picture's cost was being computed in Los Angeles two years before. More than a little curious, Fordyce asked what the Los Angeles figure had been on the production assistant. "One hundred thousand," Maury Madder said evenly and without hesitation, and Fordyce felt Vellati's position (and Europe's) crumble.

I have changed the names in the story, which was told to me many years ago by Henry Fordyce, but nothing can change the perfection of the illustration. One can't help but sympathize with Vellati, positive he had outwitted the Americans, but actually anticipated with crushing accuracy. Before he had even been hired — before anyone had known who the production assistant was to be! — one fat vice-president had turned to another in executive Los Angeles budget session and asked: "The Italian production man . . . Maury's assistant . . . how much will he swipe, Georgie?" And Georgie had replied, without a trace of concern: "Put him down for a hundred." A hundred, or two hundred, what difference did it make? The picture was going to save (and thus make) so much money by being produced in Italy that it didn't matter; but if one was going to be realistic about the advantages of filming in Italy, one also had to face the disadvantages, especially light-fingered production assistants. So poor Vellati, who thought he was such an individual, so special, had been figured out and catalogued with contemptuous ease by a man who was perfectly willing when they later met and chatted — for Georgie often came to Rome — to let Vellati think Vellati had done the outwitting.

One might search in vain for a finer example of the tremendous objective advantage Americans have over Europeans, of the very essence of their superiority. It is a superiority of wit, of pure intelligence; and it is very real, not abstract at all. The relationship between Georgie and Maury Madden, on one side, and Giorgio Vellati and all his friends, on the other, is the story of all American influence in Europe. Multiply it by thousands and spread it through every country and social level on the Continent and one begins to understand what has happened and how. The statistics come to life, the clichés about superior abilities and methods are lit from below and behind and one *sees* the participants as people, and the results as growing from their encounters and contests.

The influence has only occurred, after all, in human terms, where Americans and Europeans have actually touched each other, as in the tangents of elementary geometry. The tangential Madders and Vellatis have had to make the influence real by living through the countless incidents which have finally made the clichés possible; and it is only by ignoring the clichés and finding the life through the incidents that one can, at last, understand the influence as a generality. Without an appreciation of the particular, though, the general can't help but remain a mystery.

Even after taking into consideration the inevitable time lag between change and its recognition, the realization of American control in Europe seems extraordinarily tardy. Indeed, such recognition has only become acute in the last few years, but now it is not a challenge from America that Europeans have to cope with — or *will* have to cope with, to put it more severely — but the fact that the battle is over and the European sword long since broken over the European knee.

Perhaps there is always a delay between fact and its admission, in which case it is not surprising that eventual recognition of any fact should begin, as it has concerning American control in Europe, with the surface of the animal. It is not unhealthy in itself to draw attention, as American and European commentators alike have done, to the amount of American capital in Europe, the hordes of American businessmen, the transformation of Europe's economic and commercial and social life, and so on. What is disturbing is the inability, once that is done, to distinguish between the symptoms of a change and the forces which brought the change about.

After all, American businessmen and tourists did not arrive in Europe by accident. Nor were they successful in having their own way by accident. They represented — and continue to represent — the exploitation of very definite American rights, rights which were won long before they were born, and of which they are almost invariably ignorant. Not practically ignorant, for they have enough wit to see that they have a superior position and to use it to reap its rewards, but technically ignorant in that they are not familiar with the historical development of the rights which created the position.

When did the historical development start? One is tempted to peg it at the American Revolution, but no less an authority than Henry Adams would put it even further back in time. In writing in *The Education of Henry Adams* of America becoming a formal world power in 1898 as a result of the war with Spain, he said: "The sense of solidarity counts for much in one's contentment, but the sense of winning one's game counts for more; and in London, in 1898, the scene was singularly interesting to the last survivor of the Legation of 1861. He thought himself perhaps the only person living who could get full enjoyment of the drama. He carried every scene of it, in a century and a half since the Stamp Act, quite alive in his mind — all the interminable disputes of his disputatious ancestors as far back as the year 1750 — as well as his own insignificance in the Civil War, every step in which had the object of bringing England into an American system. . . . After two hundred years of stupid and greedy blundering, which no argument and no violence affected, the people of England learned this lesson just at the moment when Hay would otherwise have faced a flood of the old anxieties. . . . the sudden appearance of Germany as the grizzly terror which in twenty years effected what Adamses had tried for two hundred in vain — frightened England into America's arms — seemed as melodramatic as any plot of Napoleon the Great. He could feel only the sense of satisfaction at seeing the diplomatic triumph of all his family, since the breed existed, at last realized under his own eyes for the advantage of his oldest and closest ally [Hay]. . . . He could see that the family work of a hundred and fifty years fell at once into the grand perspective of true empire-building."

No one should fail to recognize it as a remarkable passage, least of all a contemporary American proconsul. Adams had the background, the access to state documents, the years of intimacy with national figures, the high native intelligence — the authority, finally — to talk of "bringing England into an American system," of England flapping into "America's arms," of "triumph," of "true empire-building," and make refutation difficult if not impossible.

It is not surprising that such statements would have seemed delirious to the Englishmen who passed Adams on the streets of London in 1898; or farfetched to most Americans of the age; or incomprehensible to Charles de Gaulle's father or Jean-Jacques Servan-Schreiber's grandfather. But it is remarkable that they are not articles of faith in our own day. Although the book in which they appear has been sanctified as one of the world's great autobiographies for over forty years and read by armies of students and scholars, the flat statements in which America is defined as the realization of formidably naked ambition — and the passage quoted above is only one among a great many — have been curiously passed over.

Adams claims that the colonial gentlemen who set the American Revolution in motion were well aware of its implications. They understood that if they won, they had to keep on winning; that if they were too advanced for England, they were going to be much too advanced for the rest of the world; and that the victorious little country was not going to exist in a vacuum — it was going to end up running the world unless it was superseded, not by a more powerful country but by a more sophisticated system. Which was unlikely, because England in 1775 represented the best the rest of the world could put up, the crowned champion of a tournament which had started with the Reformation. (And significantly for the future, a tournament in which Russia had not distinguished itself.) If the tender United States had superseded England as Fortune's darling, there was no need to worry about those already passed over. They had to bow in time as England had bowed: there wasn't even any hurry.

If there has been an American conquest, does it follow that there has been a European surrender? And even if there has been a surrender, isn't the conquest of more importance than the surrender?

At first, one tends to say "Not necessarily" to the first question and "Yes" to the second. But then one remembers that no conquest is ever complete without a surrender on the part of the conquered, and the American conquest of Europe is complete. The Normans were successful in England because the native Britons finally gave up and accepted them; the Moors were unsuccessful in Spain because the Spaniards didn't. Aztec legend prophesied the arrival of conquerors from the sea, so Cortez and his men had eventual surrender guaranteed before they landed.

Without surrender, ultimate colonization is impossible, as in the case of Vietnam, a relatively weak country which will *not* surrender and thus cannot be colonized. The choice between surrender and resistance is not dictated by manpower, material resources, or any other surface indicator, but is a psychological-sexual state of mind. Surrender is essentially the admission that something is lacking and that there is a willingness to take a chance on the conqueror being able to supply it. (The lack is the difference between the lives of the conquered and the conquering: what is left when the second is subtracted from the first, according to the arithmetical values of the conquered — not, of course, of the conquering.) Personified, surrender is the restless, lonely woman who lives by herself on a remote farm and keeps her restlessness from herself until the day she gazes, D. H. Lawrence fashion, from the rear porch onto the bare, sinewy back of the mysterious, self-sufficient drifter splitting wood for a meal. Her sigh, which carries clearly across the sunbaked yard, lets them both know that there is nothing left for her but to bow to him.

American conquest in Europe has been subtle and religious rather than coarse and military — in comparison to the Normans in England, the Spanish in the New World, and the Americans themselves on their own continent and in Asia — but the rules remain the same in that the conquest did not become a reality until Europe surrendered by admitting its lack and its need.

The surrender entailed the offering up of the material as well as

the psychological, and in 1900 Europe was filled with the accumulation of centuries. From the valley of the Loire to the mouth
of the Danube endless attics and storerooms were crammed
with ancient uniforms, letters, furniture, paintings and forgotten
dolls (the painted cheeks still bright under the gray dust); the libraries were loaded with unread books; the cluttered palaces
reeled under the sheer weight of possessions . . . all faded, all
worthless. But the living were still fabulously alive. Colette's Léa
was a ravishing, vital woman; her enormous lover, Spéleïeff, had
tremendous presence; the women's dresses were gorgeous, tantalizing; the men stroked their moustaches with assurance; the soft air
at Auteuil rang with real laughter: ". . . a fetching hat, a hat that
turned up on one side only, trimmed like a single sail to the wind
. . . her swan neck rising from a pleatless collar, a white and
rounded neck like the bole of a birch tree."

It may be said that the Europeans blew all that to pieces by themselves in the First World War, that it was destroyed before it was
"surrendered" to the Americans and the new way of life. But it may
also be claimed that the First World War was a fit of pique brought
on by an unspoken presentiment of death — as a ruined man will
throw away what is left of his money rather than let his creditors
have it.

In support, I recall Feliks Topolski, who had served with General
Anders's Polish forces in World War II, telling me a compelling
story about a vast collection of refugees in central Europe who had
slowly drifted into the mountains to avoid the advancing armies.
They finally ended up in an uninhabited valley, a hundred thousand pitiable wretches without food, their clothes in rags, all hope
gone. They composed themselves for death and were already dropping like flies when the American army discovered their existence
and ordered them saved. The enormous field kitchens were backed
up into the ghastly valley, the six-by-six trucks loaded with warm
clothing pulled up the narrow roads, and the individual soldiers
went toward them with candy bars and K-rations proffered. But, in

a strange moment for the western world, the tottering wrecks didn't reach out for sustenance. "They had given themselves up for lost," said Topolski. "They had seen that death, after all, was the end for which Europe had been yearning since 1914, and they had accepted it. Physical salvation was a very unwelcome distraction, and they didn't want it at all." Resistance could not last long, of course. "Such ghosts, without control of their future, had to accept deliverance. Not only because there was so very little choice, I suppose, between death and the American way of life, but also because nothing was theirs to decide any more. They had abandoned themselves to the mercies of Providence, and if Providence chose to send them K-rations instead of sweet sleep they had to obey. But in the moment of refusal it was very apparent that their desire — and that had to have been the desire from 1914, too — had been for annihilation, for an end to all and everything."

It is not so changed today. Watching the unguarded faces of Europeans in public places, one often senses that the human spirit is unwillingly present. There is a somber indifference to life in the present, and the implication that such life is only temporary; and Death, the preferred companion who is so barely offstage that the atmosphere is charged with his seductive appeal, seems not to have arrived recently but to have been there for a very long time. Death still seems to hang as heavy and as real in Europe as he does in the paintings of Breughel and Bosch. He is the anthropomorphic Death of plague and pestilence, a lively personality who was unaccountably left behind when the immigrants sailed across the Atlantic. Indeed, his absence from the New World heart may be the basis of all differences between Americans and Europeans.

Whatever the reason, though, the surrender had to become more conscious after World War I. What was left after 1918, and even after 1945, could not have been given up without a certain knowledge. The old religion, the old ways, the old prides . . . all were formally abandoned, and the lips — dry and cool, but also parted and receptive — were correctly offered. Technically, the surrender

was an acceptance of the situation as it really was. Europe admitted that it, too, found unabashed materialism more attractive than anything else. Pressed, it admitted that the old life had always been inferior. The picturesque peasant, the elongated aristocrat, the demonic artist, the country restaurant with sunshine playing through thick-leafed plane trees, the glorious chateau, the quiet square, the wonderful music, the Catholic and Protestant marvels, the nubile women . . . none of it had been enough. It was medieval, old-fashioned, slightly shameful, almost a fraud. Subtracted from the American way, it revealed an imposing lack; and when Europe felt the lack so keenly that life became unbearable, there was no choice except to embrace the American to get at the secret of his complacence. That embrace was the true moment of conquest, the moment of surrender at which conqueror and conquered assumed their official identities.

The high sexual moment for Europe as woman — and surrender is always sexual and female in general outline — came with the realization that there had been a passion for the conqueror from the first moment. The delay had been so unnecessary, so pointless, in view of the ultimate abandonment . . . which had turned out to be so unexpectedly delicious, so wholly satisfying. The realization brought a blush, a spasm of warm joy, the understanding that mastery had been ardently desired all those barren years. Embarrassing but also an added excitement, happiness and pretty confusion splendidly entwined.

The surrender was not, of course, to the Americans as flesh and blood, nor to the American way, but to the principles which rule the Americans themselves — as the Central and South American Indians finally surrendered to the religion behind the Conquistadors rather than to the men themselves.

And each European country surrendered in its own way and at its own time, both often quite different than popularly supposed. It is assumed, for example, that England gave in sometime between the wars, certainly not earlier than 1914; but there is a body of informed opinion which puts the date back to the late 1860s, just after the Civil War, when male members of the English aristocracy started marrying American heiresses. In popular mythology, the 1868 Duke of B——, with vast estates but pressed for money, married Katrina van Kappel, from New York, because she had fifty million dollars. It is after the marriage, in this view, that he finds out the money is controlled by relatives and bankers in America. Only the income will come to her and thence to him. American control of the capital means eventual American control of him and his issue and his peers and everything they own and influence. Instead of being a European man in control of an American woman, he is controlled by American men. The transformation from Heathcliff to Jeeves is instantaneous.

In actual fact, however, the Duke of B —— knew what was coming when he married Miss van Kappel. He knew it and he didn't care, because he was only too aware that America was already one-up on England and Miss van Kappel's gray eminences one-up on him. His marriage was a metaphor for his — and England's — surrender. The subsequent confusion came about because he didn't tell his countrymen what had happened, but went on pretending to all of them — thickheaded fellow aristocrats as well as the entire upper and middle classes and lower orders — that he was in control of his wife and her money and *her* countrymen. Unaware of the real state of affairs, by which they had been betrayed by their leaders, ninety-nine English men and women in a hundred went on with their confident assumption of superiority, making fools of themselves for over a half-century. The secret has been out since World War II, when the blinders were forever removed by the resident American army and the great majority of Englishmen of all classes surrendered to reality; but there are still small pockets of archaic faith, especially in the lower middle class, and the patient sociologist can occasionally turn up an entire English family — very rarely, a tiny set — that has not been enlightened and will not

believe the evidence of its own heart as long as the *Daily Express* says it isn't so.

Insofar as heredity is concerned, one cannot imagine Churchill without an American mother. Nor could the prime minister picked in 1940 have been without that sort of American connection. Churchill was, as has often been pointed out, too English to be true. Only a half-Englishman who had seen the reality at work in a hundred great houses — including the Blenheim Palace of his paternal relations — could have played the part of Englishman so perfectly to the American taste, and could have known so finally that it was the only audience that mattered.

Behind the surface puppetry, the harsh voices and fat cigars in Brussels and Madrid and Milan, the iron reality of the real conquest and the real surrender pull the strings. It is not surprising that the surface puppetry has received more attention than the iron reality; but now it has been studied to exhaustion and it is, perhaps, time to turn to the reality.

Casting back to Servan-Schreiber, one finds that he is not against Americanism in the general sense of the word — as a synonym for advanced technological living — but in a more restricted usage, as meaning American control of the technology in Europe itself. (This seems to be the growing definition — leading, naturally enough, to the growing dilemma of the new, modified resistance: how to have Americanism without America.) When he says Europe must mobilize against the American presence "as though it were war," he is only imploring his fellow Europeans to carry out the inevitable further Americanization themselves rather than allow the Americans to do it. It is a slim distinction, and one can almost hear Talleyrand snort: "As though that makes any difference!" Whether the Europeans can or can't carry out their own Americanization is not an essentially pertinent question, though, and serves as uncomfortable reminder that Servan-Schreiber himself is a reflection of the surrender. He is intensely Americanized — it might be said that he could not exist in his present form unless America existed exactly as it does — and one wonders if there is anything there except mirror reflection.

"If it were not for Vietnam, American business would be all over Russia right now, just as it is all over Europe. Russia would be asking for you today — they're asking the French to build them refrigerators and the Italians to build them automobiles. This is the great paradox of their technology; they can build Sputniks, but they can't build home appliances." This is a quotation from Servan-Schreiber in an interview printed in *Life* (May 17, 1968), and on first reading it sounds original. Technically, it *is* original in that Servan-Schreiber did not knowingly plagiarize such sentiments. But in actual fact, they have been commonplaces in American business for twenty years.

My brother, Edward N. Ney, president of Young & Rubicam, International, put it to me in his own words ten years ago: "When the Russians get enough money and the women there begin to want to look attractive and live in better surroundings and the men want them to have those things, and amenities for themselves as well, then nothing on earth will be able to prevent Russia from becoming like America. I really think that we will see the day when there will be American companies, advertising agencies — even brokerage houses — with Russian subsidiaries. It will be like America in Europe, but bigger. The market is there and it's only a matter of time. Actually, the greatest resistance to that future is not in Russia, where they haven't thought much about it and don't have preconceived blocks, but in this country, especially when you get off the East Coast. They have been talking anti-Communism in those places — the Middle West and the South, in particular — for so long that they've forgotten where the ball is."

Servan-Schreiber is speaking for himself and his analysis is primarily a contribution to debate; my brother's is an integral part of

American business and national policy. The difference is considerable. On balance, then, Servan-Schreiber is worth study as a reaction to conquest, but no more than any other significant reaction. It appears on time; it behaves according to prediction; and any serious study of the conquest and the surrender must pay attention to it as an artifact of value. Although far more intelligent — and certainly more scrupulous — than Giorgio Vellati, Servan-Schreiber has been just as anticipated by American business. My brother anticipated him by ten years; it is possible, even likely, that other, older executives knew about him twenty or thirty or more years ago.

Because Servan-Schreiber has been so anticipated — almost created — he does not understand that it is useless to exhort change by conscious will. Europe did not surrender capriciously, but only after a sense of lack became too enormous to resist; and Europe cannot take back — cannot rescind — that surrender like stopping payment on a check or renegotiating a contract. Only the slow arrival of another fact — different but equally enormous — could do that. Such a fact may begin to intrude tomorrow, or it may never come. But as of now the situation in Europe is hard and fast and can only change if the Europeans themselves change . . . as the early colonists in America changed. Not by consciously willing change, but by finding themselves with an entirely new will created by accident . . . by chance . . . by miracle. In weighing the situation, an American must keep this in mind. It is not to be expected that a European writing of American influence in Europe can understand the technical limitations and avoid transgressing them; but a serious American observer does not have such excuses. He must seek the basic *laws* of the colonization process, and keep the ephemeral surface of day-to-day activity firmly inside the framework of that search. Servan-Schreiber can afford to say, "Now it has happened," and stop there: but an American analyst is forced to go on to ask how and why.

The abstract questions — when and how will Europe resist, and so on — are not so important as the reality of the appearance. American influence in Europe is far more a fact than an idea, and demands to be treated as such. As a fact, it has definite life in appearances (psychological as well as physical, of course, and most often an amalgam of the two), and one of the aims of this book is to present those appearances as they *are*.

"I was trying to learn to write then," said Ernest Hemingway in the first chapter of *Death in the Afternoon* about his reasons for going to Spain in the early 1920s, "and I found the greatest difficulty, aside from knowing truly what you really felt, rather than what you were supposed to feel, was to put down what really happened in action; what the actual things were which produced the emotion that you experienced. . . . I was trying to learn to write, commencing with the simplest things, and one of the simplest things of all and the most fundamental is violent death. . . . I had read many books in which, when the author tried to convey it, he only produced a blur, and I decided that this was because either the author had never seen it clearly or at the moment of it, he had physically and mentally shut his eyes."

Once in Spain, Hemingway found the bullfight itself more engrossing than its violent deaths, but demanding the same scrupulous devotion to *seeing* what happened. In writing of the goring of an inept torero with whom "the crowd had no more sympathy . . . than with a suicide," he went on to say: "For myself, not being a bullfighter, and being much interested in suicides, the problem was one of depiction and waking in the night I tried to remember what it was that seemed just out of my remembering and that was the thing I had really seen and, finally, remembering all around it, I got it. When he stood up, his face white and dirty and the silk of his breeches opened from waist to knee, it was the dirtiness of the rented breeches, the dirtiness of his slit underwear and the clean, clean, unbearably clean whiteness of the thigh bone that I had seen, and it was that which was important."

He was right. The condition of the breeches and underwear against the "unbearably clean whiteness" of the thigh bone is the surface reality which gives the picture of the impulse to suicide far more clearly than any discussion of it. The problem *was* one of depiction and a correct image (Hemingway did not always understand that there may be more than one in any action sequence) was found and proper language was used.

American influence in Europe is also a problem of depiction. It may be based on an abstraction, and further abstractions may grow from it like quills on a porcupine, but it can only be comprehended through a selective portrait of its surface. In this it is not too different from bullfighting or suicide or any other activity which is susceptible to both physical and abstract interpretation. The only difference, in fact, is in usage: we understand that bullfighting and suicide can be approached through depiction of the act, but we do not always admit that influence can.

But influence is only carried through by people, the influenced as well as the influencers, and people and their actions are nothing if not depictable. The people involved may be acting out an idea, but, as with bullfighting, one cannot understand the idea except through its surface — in vulgar terms, one cannot understand bullfighting without seeing a bullfight — and it is the writer's task to see and depict those bits of surface which are significant and through which the reader can find his own version of the reality, abstract as well as physical.

In this light, it is anti-esthetic and sentimentally undisciplined to say that the analyst must attempt to find in the current excitements — the gold crises, the French strikes, the student upheavals — the connections between the events and the immediately unseen forces which made them inevitable. (Genuinely fundamental — and general — forces from the past are, naturally, another matter.) What is required is quite the opposite: a severe eschewal of contemporary "connections" and "unseen forces" and a determined concentration

[25]

on the physical and psychological presence of the event itself and the people themselves.

At the start, the observer knows nothing more than that it is these people who *are* the Americanization. The colonization is not an isolated fact, but an idea imbedded in flesh and bone and brain, as one sees it in the great European throng, a vast and disorderly crowd, a Vanity Fair of imported postures and attitudes. The conquerors are ponderously present, but it is the Europeans who still dominate the parade and fascinate the onlooker. They have abandoned the faith of their fathers and given themselves up to the tender mercies of the invaders, but they remain more compelling than their new models.

As one grows more familiar with the canvas, one begins to note that the reasons for the surrender — the weaknesses — are implicit in the bearings and actions and faces, all surface manifestations which reveal what has happened and why far more accurately than the more abstract indicators.

For if the American conquest is based on American strengths, the European surrender is based on European weaknesses, and in a study of Europe and the surrender, rather than America and the conquest, the emphasis must be on the weaknesses. It is an unavoidable emphasis, for it is only through those weaknesses that the footholds have been established and the colonization processes carried through. That certain strengths and charms remain in all European countries is not disputed, but a recital of them would be not only extraneous but distracting in a discussion of colonization. The business at hand is colonization, and its causes must be kept in as white a light as possible, with the rest left in sharply isolated darkness. The weaknesses must be examined — even probed — and all else left untouched. No other approach seems possible. In retrospect, one understands that no other approach *was* possible. When analyzing any failure — an unsuccessful military campaign, for example — one does not waste time on such minor victories as there may have been: only the losses are pertinent.

Also, concentration on the physical and psychological presences of events and people can only produce genuine results when the concentration includes the emotion produced in oneself. The dirtiness that Hemingway saw in the unfortunate bullfighter's rented breeches and slit underwear meant very little against a thigh bone laid bare by the bull's horn to reveal a mere "clean whiteness." It was only when that thigh bone became "clean, clean, unbearably clean," in his memory in the night, that everything snapped into final focus. "Unbearably" admitted the presence of emotion, for it could only be unbearable to the narrator.

The European weaknesses — examined in this book in England, western Europe and eastern Europe — which opened the doors to the Americans are ancient and sordid and pathetic. But the closer one gets to them, the more one sees that they do not stand alone. Against them and around them and forever mingled with them is one's own feeling of personal sadness and loss. . . . The American is inextricably involved with the vanishing Europe, and cannot help but respond to the desolation and loneliness of the end, the soft sense of death and finality put by the European Joyce with scientific precision as well as artistic perception in the closing paragraph of "The Dead," the last story in *Dubliners,* a passage which could serve as the epitaph for all Europe: "It had begun to snow again. He watched sleepily the flakes, silver and dark, falling obliquely against the lamplight. The time had come for him to set out on his journey westward. Yes, the newspapers were right: snow was general all over Ireland. It was falling on every part of the dark central plain, on the treeless hills, falling softly upon the Bog of Allen and, farther westward, softly falling into the dark mutinous Shannon waves. It was falling, too, upon every part of the lonely churchyard on the hill where Michael Furey lay buried. It lay thickly drifted on the crooked crosses and headstones, on the spears of the little gates, on the barren thorns. His soul swooned slowly as he heard the snow falling faintly through the universe and faintly falling, like the descent of their last end, upon all the living and the dead."

II

ENGLAND
The Colonizer Colonized

1

No nineteenth-century victim of British imperialism — not an Irish peasant or Boer farmer or Malaysian coolie or Indian servant . . . not even the haters who cursed the Empire and its Englishmen most eloquently and called down on it and them the wrath of an all-avenging God — not one, were they all raised from their dingy graves and given a look at modern England, could fault the calamities that have befallen the former oppressor. The subtle hater would not be satisfied with the mere physical and mechanical collapse of the Empire and the comfortable middle-class way of life. He would demand a terrible lesion of psychological and spiritual vitality, worse than anything he himself ever suffered, and he would be presented with a cup overflowing beyond his wildest dreams. In final delight, he would hardly know whether to cry out at the spectacle or abandon himself to vengeful laughter. Or get down on his knees to beseech the fates not to respond to another's prayer for his destruction as savagely as his own was answered in regard to England.

The English themselves are aware that there has been a disaster, but they think it is the loss of the creature comforts — the tea buns and the water biscuits: the worst of what has happened is that they cannot understand it has happened to *them,* and it is this pathetic incomprehension that awes their most implacable ill-wishers. Pathetic incomprehension is not, of course, confined to England. Visitors to the American Deep South before World War II found it in the faces of those who did not yet understand the reason for the grinding finality of the Civil War, especially in the generic William Faulkner face, with the unsupported pretentiousness terribly betrayed by the uncomprehending eyes. Such a face could not understand what had happened, or that it had happened because of Southern inadequacies, not in spite of Southern strengths. The Southern "aristocrat," his manner a haphazard blend of dubious gentleness and sudden belligerence, could not understand that there had never been an aristocracy in the South and that he was not the inheritor of a tradition but the inventor of a most awkward and ineffective posture. The North had swept into an abhorred vacuum, sucked in by a lack of genuine human activity on any level, and if that was too dismaying for the latterday residents to admit, then they had to create another version of the past and act it out in old tweed coats, rather ludicrous in their assumption of tragedy and rather repellent in their pathos.

The English pathos has something of that Southern sadness — all pathos seems related through the thespian rigamarole required to sustain it — but it has so much else in addition that the relationship is attenuated, and the analogy inexact. To cite just one difference, the English pathos is far more widespread; it crops up everywhere in England now, with the Beatles representing the culmination of a progressive gloom and the furthest reach of political collapse. Not, of course, the beginning of anything, as has been claimed by so many wishful persons who cannot imagine evolution as other than "constructive" in their own version of the adjective, but a defensive retrogression based on incomprehension — exaggerated personal eccentricities attempting to cover over, as in the South, a definite lack of understanding.

The key question, in view of the aims of this book, is how much of the present English situation is due to the American colonization and how much is the result of other forces and residual claims. An answer — even a temporary answer — can hardly be arrived at without some basis of analysis and comparison. England is the prime American colony, the definitive example, the star of the collection, and worth consideration in careful detail. Such consideration is practical in many ways: England shares a great number of the problems of the other colonized countries of western Europe, and a sizable percentage of what is true for her is also true for them and will not have to be gone into again in each separate instance.

The colonization of England can be loosely grounded on three general causes: (1) the national weaknesses. (2) The historical American opposition. (3) The economic-cultural vacuum created by World Wars I and II and the collapse of the Empire. These causes are related, but for expositionary purposes can and should be treated in separate sections.

The first, the national weaknesses, are exclusively English in origin and development, and might well have brought England down without America lifting a hand. But these weaknesses have dovetailed in startling coincidence with American strengths and have thus exerted a greater leverage than they would have on their own. They are, of course, intimately involved with the English historical process itself, especially over the past four hundred years. The swing from small nation to Empire to small nation, from Elizabeth I to Disraeli to Wilson, from feudal state to colonizer to colonizee . . . the entire record is dependent on English character in both triumph and collapse.

The second, the historical American opposition, began formally with the Revolutionary War and has continued its slow crunch to this day. It has the pace of chess, with the American brain and the American character against their English opposite numbers in relentless end game.

The third, the economic-cultural vacuum dating from 1918 and accelerating with each year, demanded the ascendancy of *some* alien way of life as relief from the indigenous loss of faith. The American way which has poured into this breach differs significantly from the historical opposition. The latter has grown from a deep taproot and adds a barely visible ring at lengthy intervals; the former is a surface torrent that has engulfed England in less than sixty years. To a considerable degree, the opposition has been submerged in the influx of the American way, but that influx could not have started to flow without the background of the opposition, and it is necessary to examine the two processes separately.

With the causes of colonization identified and investigated, it should be possible to proceed to an appraisal of individual American comment on England, personal as well as analytical and professional, and to hazard a few brief conjectures on the future. The whole should give some indication, by implication rather than direct statement, as to how much of modern England is purely English in origin and how much is the result of American existence, influence and power.

Descriptions of contemporary England, initial steps in forming the basis of analysis and comparison referred to above, do not pretend to be other than personal, but personal in the Baconian sense that there is nothing to rely on in any case except the personally observed. As depiction, this insistence concentrates on the refractions of the colonization processes and attempts to focus enough light on the visual and psychological aspects of those processes so that the reader can gain an active appreciation of what colonization actually looks like when made flesh. Without such appreciation, the entire subject cannot pass beyond the academic-abstract, and so it is most important that there be a picture of generous dimensions and strong colors.

(It should be pointed out that "England," "English," and "Englishman" are used throughout in the psychological but not technical sense of "Britain," "British," and "Briton." The latter set, referring to the inhabitants of England, Scotland, Wales and North Ireland, tends to connote physical placement rather than mental and emotional outlook, and is avoided here for that reason. An Edinburgh businessman of Scottish descent is, obviously, not an Englishman in the technical sense, but usually has far more in common with a London businessman of English extraction than he has with a Highland gillie. To call him and his London counterpart Britons is to intrude the technically correct at the price of the esthetically correct. They are both English in that they both work under English systems of response as well as nearly everything else, so the adjective is here used to include not only everything English *de jure* but also *de facto.*)

2

In late May, 1968, the surface entrance to England from the Continent lay through the Belgian and Dutch ports, the French strikes having cut off all egress from that country. Traveling from Switzerland, one took the Lorelei Express from Basel up the Rhine Valley and across the Netherlands to the Hook of Holland, near Rotterdam, and went on from there by boat to Harwich, in England. This is a business trip — a Swiss manufacturer has suggested a British company as a promising investment. They have a new patent in the electronics field and need capital to develop it. I, the American, am to receive a presentation and decide whether I wish to risk such capital (they have had to go afield because there are hazards) and advise other Americans with whom I am joined in a modest consortium to do so as well. The first stage of the trip is pleasant enough — the vineyards just coming in above Mainz, the Rhine clogged with barges, the Dutch landscape quiet and compelling in the late twilight — and then the mob pours off the trains at the Hook at half-past ten and England takes over.

At the entrance to the dockside buildings a narrow stairs, with a uniformed pair of pursers at the bottom to cater to the first-class passengers: "May I see your ticket, please? Yes, your stateroom is on B deck, the second turning to the . . . After you board . . . Have a pleasant voyage . . . Oh, how very nice of you to say so . . . We appreciate those who appreciate us. . . ." The formula dates from the days when only a fraction of England traveled; in

the swirling madhouse of exhausted refugees from the French confusion it is breathtakingly out of place. Passengers with reservations
are to be taken care of as in 1910 even if such treatment is mani-
festly impossible. National problems are sharply mirrored in the
vignette, and the English lack of flexibility, once such a source of
strength, is now only an embarrassing drawback.

The travel-grimed hands of lesser mortals clutch at the pursers'
sleeves: "I didn't have time to make a reservation . . . I couldn't
get through on the phone and neither could the travel agency . . .
What shall I do? . . . Will we get on the boat?" The pursers push
off the dirty hands with visible irritation: "My dear lady, it is not
our fault that the French have a strike. If you will kindly wait in
that salon until we have boarded the passengers with cabin reservations, we will see what can be done. We hope there will be room
for everyone." Consternation. If there is not room, who will pay for
the hotel room at the Hook? Who will pay for the telephone call to
the husband in Richmond? Who will answer for Baby's broken
booking with his pediatrician in Reading?

The pursers shake them off with an imperviousness that Dickens
would have found entirely contemporary and turn back to the important task of servicing the passengers with reservations. The first-
class passenger is kowtowed to everywhere in the world, but the
English serving class enjoys it with a fervor peculiar to the race.
The obsequiousness is relished; one suspects libido in the wrong
compartments.

The bedlam mounts, the formulas of 1910 are pursued in a gale
of hysterical movement and noise, with the doughty matrons and
fawning pursers pretending that this sea of disaffected humanity
does not exist. As late as 1944 this ability to blot out the unwanted
was, perhaps, still a national asset, still "thrilling" for American
newspapermen celebrating British pluck in the teeth of German
bombs. Now it is . . . pathetic — there is no other word. England
was built for war and now there are no more wars.

Blessed with both a first-class ticket and a reservation — most fortunate of men! — one postpones asserting them and joins the refugees in the "salon," a huge customs hall. Through the glass doors, the unhappy mob sees the last of the certified passengers board. Now their fate will be revealed. But there is further delay. The pursers whisper together in an anteroom, casting furtive glances at the seething crowd. At last one of them is given the unpleasant job and he delivers the bad news from a table:

"Ladies and gentlemen, there are no more cabin berths available, and all the seating in the second-class lounge will be occupied by other passengers, who, like yourselves, are traveling on second-class tickets, and who, also like yourselves, will have to sit up tonight, but who, unlike yourselves in this particular, got here first. There is seating in the first-class lounge, but we have the . . . um . . . difficulty — I should really say impossibility, goes right against company policy — of putting second-class passengers in the first-class lounge. So those of you who wish to get to England tonight will have to pay an additional pound for a first-class ticket."

Outrage! If the company can't supply second-class accommodations it has no right to levy an additional charge for putting second-class passengers elsewhere! Howls! Groans! To most of these people a pound means something and they are furious. (The foreigners are more furious than the English, who bleat without conviction, inured to arbitrary treatment from above.) But the purser is bored and tired now himself, and makes it plain that the decision is final. Resistance caves in, the wrinkled pounds are paid and the procession mounts the gangplank to the first-class lounge.

One secures one's own quarters, washes, puts on a clean shirt and goes to the dining room for a late supper. The first-class lounge has become a disaster area. Having paid the arbitrary surtax, the lower orders are spreading out with a vengeance. Mothers and babies and bottles, loose shoes, rumpled hair, intimate preparations for the night, grating accents . . . and through the shambles move the English first-class passengers, determined to see the lounge as peopled only by themselves or perish in the attempt. The Enchanted

Ground cannot become the Slough of Despond: pursed lips and a brisk discussion of the last visit to Glyndebourne will fend off such black magic. Again, one is forced to note that even the most dedicated attitudes become . . . pathetic.

One joins an elderly English gentleman over a good supper of lamb chops and beer and he spins out the familiar litany: "We have just spent three weeks in the Lowlands, and I must say I was astonished at the wonderful reception we got. Funny story about that — we were to stay with my wife's cousin, who's married to a Dutchman and has a beautiful estate near Amsterdam, and when we got to the station her Rolls was on hand to meet us . . . chauffeur in livery, the kind of thing that's practically disappeared in England, but, of course, we only won the war . . . Anyhow, we were with them for a week and it was Continental luxury at its best and then we left for Brussels and got off the train at the wrong station and General Slacton, my old comrade-in-arms, who was waiting for us in Brussels, had no idea what had happened and was waiting there with his car while *we* — this is really the joke — we had to *walk* about a mile from the wrong station to get a wheezing taxi to the right place. Walking out of the beautiful house that my wife's cousin has, transported to the Amsterdam station in all that pomp and circumstance, and then, a few short hours later, we're *walking* around in a Belgian village like a couple of gypsies. We had to laugh at ourselves — and so did General Slacton when we finally got together. From the sublime to the ridiculous sort of thing."

He is more impressive from a distance than close up. The teeth are very bad and he knows it (his hand flutters before them as he smiles), and the confidence is at a low ebb. His uncertainties are not particularly important in themselves, or even annoying — actually, he is diverting company — it is only when one thinks of England as a contesting participant in the political-economic climate of 1968 that he becomes irreversibly anachronistic. One remembers that one has known this type for over twenty years — the second-rank but acceptable public school, attendance at Oxford (a minor college, but, still, Oxford), a year in France at the end of World War I in a county regiment, a middling business career in the City between the wars, a long World War II all over the world, and the subsequent years of bewildering peace, a more difficult time, somehow, than the war and depression years. One has also known many other national types in the past twenty years, but they have all changed or adapted in some degree. This one has not. Whether he will not or cannot is academic: he has not, and a cruel natural selection puddles the hot tar around his feet.

After supper one passes again through the surreal lounge. The silver-haired old ladies cling to their chairs, islands of first-class respectability in a sea of unbuttoned grumblers, determined to "sit up a bit," because they have always done so. Nationals of almost any other country would not want any part of this lounge, but English insensitivity enjoys such challenges.

A discussion with the purser about the pound surtax is informative. "It's like this — it's like national patriotism, you might say. We can't throw away the chance of making money for our company because it's like making money for the country. All the same now, you might say. The old days are gone — when we could afford to be generous. England can't afford that any more." The propaganda has had an effect, but in a markedly ineffective way. Like a compulsive and spectacularly unsuccessful gambler who decides to move to a cheaper hotel to economize, England will survive the current balance of payments squeeze by picking up "the odd pound." One thinks of children selling homemade lemonade to augment the family income — and the mother's outcry when she discovers the expensive lemons have been sold below cost. Here, tonight, five hundred pounds have been collected and five thousand pounds of ill-will spent. The proportional deficit — one thousand per cent — is so huge that one realizes the English situation seems desperate to the English, perhaps far more so than is really the case: people do not grab so frantically unless the end seems very close.

[40]

One goes below to one's precious berth and sleeps for a few hours. First light comes at four and one rises to go on deck for the North Sea dawn. It is worth it — dirty spring clouds hang low over the sullen, gray-green water and bedraggled gulls announce the proximity of Harwich. Back inside the ship, one is drawn yet again into the lounge, now silent, the stricken figures sprawled and curled in desperate contortions. It is a set piece, like the famous crane shot of the Confederate wounded in the Atlanta railroad station in *Gone With the Wind,* and just as symbolic of the end of an era.

A multitude of images are evoked . . . the ribbon of the Victoria Cross pinned, as one has so often seen it, to a worn English lapel under a tight, small, birdlike face, the eyes tinged with moisture as the monarch is borne past, and the memory of wondering how the highest native emotion could be so shabby, an inadequacy carried through to the stiffened back and the poor old hands straight-fingered along the trousers . . . Shaw's soft, musical voice saying that English anger over the *Lusitania* sinking was within bounds until it was known that *saloon* passengers had been lost . . . the 1959 remark by an English bartender on the *Golfito*, a steamer on a regular run between Jamaica and England: "An Englishman turns into a different person when he travels first-class."

The first-class excitement still runs fierce and scarlet in the English heart (in despair, one often wonders if any other emotion can produce such heat), but can it overcome this scene? This shattered lounge, this gray morgue of the living, all of whom have lost all faith in the first-class scheme of things after being so carelessly mulcted last night, must be a sinister omen in any English dream — can the dream itself be stronger?

In a fragment of that English dream, Jerusalem and the Celestial City have always been an objective, but now, alas, Christian turns out to have been a toothy barrister on his way to Deauville. We are all confused and uncertain in our aims and methods, but the English confusions and uncertainties seem greater, and their aims and methods far cruder and more outmoded. One fears the difference

[41]

may be fatal, and Christian, adorned with golf clubs, wife with see-through blouse and private plane, may never get to Deauville after all.

An English friend, Simon Forster, has arranged a room at the Rochester Hotel, near Sloane Square. Both names are fictitious, as, indeed, are all those in this record where personal sensibilities are involved. The parody of the boat is continued. "The Rochester," says Simon, "is the only place I could get you into because of the Chelsea Flower Show. I know you don't want one of those tourist hotels — expensive tourist like the Connaught or noisy tourist like the Dorchester or vulgar tourist like the Hilton or middlebrow tourist like the Hyde Park and the Gore or queer tourist like the Cavendish. You want a quiet place where Irish peeresses and Suffolk landowners stay. That's the Rochester — undiscovered, but with all the amenities. You'll love it."

He was right, I do love it. The parody of the boat and the parody of London and the parody of all England is continued and refined and offered up without shame at the Rochester. One hardly needs to venture into the street — everything is here in Proustian microcosm.

English hotels of the first and second rank reflect many national weaknesses. At the Rochester, there has to be carpet on the floors, striped trousers on the concierge and iced champagne in the bar: but the carpeting is frayed at the edges, the concierge is useless in small matters, and the champagne is served with an oily pomp that suggests Blackpool rather than London. The Rochester is more the idea for a hotel than the realization and it is not atypical. From Claridges and the Ritz downwards, one has the feeling that the English hotel is a stage setting and everyone concerned, staff and guests alike, are acting for the benefit of an unseen audience. The English, surely the most self-conscious people in the world, must dread being in public beyond all other phobias — can there be any other explanation of the charades?

One tries to imagine the ideal articulated, as by the founder of the Rochester, presuming that such existed: "A small hotel, but with a strong dedication to Continental standards of service and food. For the discriminating Englishman, and Englishwoman." The class angle is rarely absent in such calculations, and tends to blur the actual carrying-out of the program.

Now the staff — unkempt and rather surly young Englishmen, and displaced persons from central Europe — snap furiously at each other over operational questions when they imagine the guests can't see them. And then turn on "the Continental standard" when attention focuses. The reception clerk seems unable to act on his own: any query sends him into a tiny anteroom where he argues in whispers with a stout woman in a shiny satin dress. He returns, hastily reassuming the air of a man who has only to clap his hands to command Daimlers and hold intercontinental jets at London Airport. "A member of the staff will be carrying out certain repairs — adjustments, actually — in the lower . . . down below . . . with the entire system, heating as well as hot water. The delay will be very short, however, no more than an hour . . ." The lady in shiny satin, eavesdropping, hisses from the door of her cubbyhole. He breaks off, waving his hands slightly, and moves to fresh conference with her. He is soon back, the accent wavering wildly between Clapham Junction and the Guards Club. "I am now informed the delay will be two hours."

In a taxi, riding to Wheelers, one remembers the sight, somewhere in Soho, years ago, of Ralph Richardson and Alec Guinness debouching simultaneously from different taxis. Both in trilbys, both full of themselves, both strangely reassuring in their innocent egotism. A London street band was playing "The Yellow Rose of

Texas" with tremendous gusto and equal innocence. The scene was so primeval as to be fresh to tired American eyes, and now . . . now the two actors and their orchestra seem as remote as Assyrians. One senses, with a cold pang, that London can be only nostalgic now.

This is to be a business lunch with Reeves and Harper, two directors of the English firm with the interesting patent, who promise to show me how I will make a great deal of money on a modest outlay. Reeves is forty, fat, and possessed of elaborate muttonchop whiskers. Harper is thin and Winchester and Oxford, smiles enigmatically as he toys with his hock, and has a stammer — infrequent and slight, but definitely artificial. They know their business, they have made money to date and they will make more . . . and yet, the investor hesitates. If the making of money is the sacred task — and these two are agreed with the Americans that it is — then the investor has to feel most secure with those who are most dedicated to that end. Reeves with his whiskers and Harper with his stammer seek to preserve an atmosphere of fun-with-business, but is it desirable? The American may have so much strenuous fun after he concludes his business that an observer should be pardoned for thinking he is interested in nothing save "relaxation," but when he is at business he is deadly serious. Reeves and Harper are not, any more than any Englishman will allow himself to be, and the investor wonders if they can afford such luxury.

After their competent but, perhaps, too charming presentation, they turn with relief to lighter topics. They have both been to America, and beneath the conventional disparagement one catches awe. The official screen of disapproval gradually disappears and they join in an antiphonal recital of American residential glories: ". . . Long Island . . . Palm Beach . . . Warrenton . . . Atlanta . . . Grosse Pointe . . . Beverly Hills . . . Pebble Beach . . . the parties . . . the grass . . . the girls . . . the drink . . ." Nothing as grand, one ventures, as Hatfield House or Chatsworth.

They reject that notion with rich scorn. "No heat! . . . too old . . . what do you do without servants? . . ."

Over coffee, we are joined by Gloinville, a Frenchman who is also interested in the venture, and Reeves summarizes our conference to him in very poor French. "It is fortunate that one of us does speak French," Harper confides to me with admiration, and I am reminded again that I have never heard an Englishman speak it properly. One would think that the race which can turn "Calais" into "Cally" and "ballet" into "bally" (both innovations rhyme with "dally") is essentially indifferent, but the English are fascinated with the language and can't resist taking it on whenever possible. It isn't that they are poor at French — we Americans are incomparably worse — but that they *think* they are adept.

Reeves and Harper have illusions, there is no blinking it, and one wonders idly how far they would not go in American industry. Conversely, how great is the advantage the Americans have over them in their own country because of the illusions.

They tax me with questions now. Am I a businessman or a writer? I am both, I tell them, and it is the truth. Business is my diversion, as some writers hunt big game. They are reassured — a man with residential roots in Palm Beach and Switzerland is above suspicion. There is much more to discuss on the proposition and we agree to meet this evening at the Rochester.

———

A quiet afternoon in the King's Road. The clothes on these young! At first one doesn't quite believe such harlequins against the dreary buildings. Bell-bottomed purple trousers, frilled shirts, silver bangles . . . but everything is of shoddy material, these Tiny Tims are as impoverished as the native original and as insecure as the New World namesake. They scurry along busily — do they have jobs? In America, the clothes would change the wearers; here they remain the same. Later, one hears the argument that long hair is not unusual because it has been worn in other ages. But it framed such different faces: one's mind flees to Van Dyke's portraits, to the young men of Botticelli and Raphael, even to Wright's glamorous study of Charles II. In modern England, it's the same pinched, twentieth-century Cockney face underneath, which is why one instinctively thinks of the Three Stooges when one sees the Beatles, and why one is sure they're wearing wigs.

The clothes and the hair are pathetic: one wonders if they can be anything but a reaction to colonization, a way of expressing a sense of loss. The faces are such a denial of the costumes, such a denial of sexuality, so dead. "They get plenty," Simon Forster says, "and they're always high. That's why old lechers like me are jealous of them." But Simon himself is drained, and his jaunty testimony is too wishful to be trusted. If the discordant young aren't enjoying Polynesian sensuality, then what — after all the noise — is one to believe in? He can't face the challenge to contemporary religion and genuflects with genuine piety.

But traditional American skepticism warns that these young are hurt and have done this to themselves to express the unhappiness and lack of order in their lives. It is a pseudo-revolt, and only proclaims the frustration that real revolt is beyond them. They hate having to know themselves incapable of true revolt — it is a more agonizing admission than sexual impotence — and express the hateful knowledge in what they have done to their persons. The colonization is already bearing bitter fruit.

At six o'clock, Reeves is munching potato chips in the bar of the Rochester. Harper's place has been taken by Ladrick, a creaking aristocrat whom one instantly likes. He is the racy, fifty-five-year-old London ruin — huge, florid, gray hair curling under trilby brim, dark flannel suit with immense side vents, red socks (a strange and anti-esthetic but beloved London custom) over suede shoes — who serves as a "director" of several dozen companies.

Younger sons of marquesses can almost always make a career of company directorship because of the automatic "And let's get some titles, too." Under their assumption of calm, Reeves and Harper are nervous, but Ladrick is not, and, in consequence, can afford to be amusing. He reminds me of David Tennant, a neighbor in the south of Spain many years ago. The sense of great but proper waste is the same, and I half expect that the evening will end in a wineshop with a dirt floor . . . the kind where Tennant spent so many nights reciting Milton in beautiful voice (he was once with the BBC), the tears rolling down his cheeks and the angular Humphrey Slater, a boon companion at that time, gargling away in the background about Freddie Ayer and logical positivism. But Tennant knew his business when he had to, and I am to find that Ladrick does, too.

It is a splendid evening at the Rochester. We make our contribution and are flanked by several others. To my right is the promised Suffolk squire, a squat bulldog of a man, and his wife and a younger woman, a relative who is being shown high life. He is the fully trained English husband, a testimony to female domination of such totality as to amaze an American, supposedly an expert on the subject. (Ladrick is later to say to me: "In every English family, of every class, the woman runs everything.") He never speaks. Literally. Lady Hermione, his wife, gives him an order from time to time ("Do push your chair round there, Henry . . . Do light Rosemary's cigarette, Henry . . ."), and he carries them out with cheerful alacrity, but in silence. For the rest, he smokes his pipe contentedly and gazes from one to another of the women as they speak. He is very trained, this bulldog, and he is very much the norm in England.

In his world, domestic social excursions are women's fun. The women chat as though alone, and the man is expected to be sufficiently amused by their wit so as not to notice his own removal from the board. Certainly Henry seems happy enough. The French (actually Corsican) maître d'hôtel, who doubles in the bar before dinner, greets Lady Hermione with elaborate insolence, and is given a rousing welcome in return. The playlet has been enacted before. "I will have a dry sherry, Armande . . . very dry . . . Rosemary, what will you have? . . . While you're thinking, why don't *you* decide, Henry?" Henry clears his throat, but he is far too slow. "Henry will have a gin and French," she says decisively to Armande. Henry closes his mouth and smiles in gratitude, saved yet again from expression.

Straight ahead, at the bar proper, stand five English storks in dark suits, discussing a new type of metal sash window. Drinks in hand, they sway and bend to each other with exquisite courtesy. The manner and setting suggest conversation on recondite cultural questions — Spenser's sincerity or Browning's worldliness — but, no, it is metal sash windows. These beautiful birds are *business-men,* and they are doing business after hours in the best American fashion. But where are the throat-constricting old-fashioneds and double martinis? The red faces and the hoarse demands that "We have it by Friday! Or else!"? How can business be done in modulated voices over Dubonnet (mangled into Dew-bon'ny) and Campari and soda?

"I *am* concerned just the . . . tiniest . . . bit about the curvature of the handle. Isn't there a chance — and no matter how remote, we must consider any and all possibilities, especially in view of the efficiency which is to be . . . um . . . so desired — that in bringing the tip of the handle so close to the . . . um . . . upright of the frame, there is a risk that a homeowner with especially fat thumbs might find his . . . thumb? . . . no, it would be the *index* finger, as the utilitarian usage has it, wouldn't it? . . . *mashed,* if that is the word, up against the . . . um . . . upright?" No one speaks for a moment, each face gravely considering. Then: "I think, Andrew, that your fears may be . . . um . . . unfounded. The . . . *clearance,* as I believe it is called, is . . . the engineers, I am sure have guaranteed it as adequate . . . and, in any case, wouldn't it be the *middle finger* that would . . . you know?" They all raise their right hands to chest height and manipulate imaginary handles, looking at each other hopefully over their twenty-five writhing fingers and trying to recall the clearance, a difficult task because only the engineers ever touch the actual product. The fingers are not fat, either, but bone-thin and extra-long, and they curl about as aimlessly as whippets' tails.

"The point is this," Ladrick is saying at our table, and he cuts to the heart of the matter incisively. Reeves is not really paying attention to him, and one realizes the weakness of the English caste system is more subtle than at first presumed. The old-boy presence — the inclusion of members of the peerage on company boards just because they are members of the peerage — is a poor system because birth is substituted for merit: but it becomes a deadly system when the substituters, like Reeves and Harper, don't believe in it anyhow. Those two could only look themselves, and each other, in the eye if they refused to have a title on the board. It is their own weakness in going along with "tradition" that has grown those facetious whiskers and led to that stammer. That Ladrick happens to be competent is only ironic: Reeves and Harper believe so firmly that all titled Englishmen are incompetent that they should get rid of him to save their self-respect. Without that self-respect neither they nor their country can ever succeed in modern business. The pretense — and they pretend to themselves as well as to me and all other Americans — that they believe in Ladrick is cowardly. As an investor, I cannot avoid knowing that Reeves and Harper are afraid to run their business as they think it should be run, a most damaging piece of information. And they are not exceptional — the caste system is still very much alive everywhere; and still ruinously expensive. In America, the company director may be a bore, but he is dedicated; in England, there are so many silly company directors that the job is dangerously close to acknowledged frivolity — an actor is considered more reliable.

At the next table, Lady Hermione is ordering dinner from Armande in her French, and has arrived at the selection of drink.

"*Champagne!*" she breathes, and Armande asks for the brand. "Henry," she says to her stolid husband, "*quelle champagne aime-je?*" Again he opens his mouth, and this time one is sure he will speak. The vocal cords flex, the sound starts up, but at the last split second (she seems to take desperate chances, but perhaps she really doesn't) she delivers the name herself: "Charles Heidsieck!" Her face is suffused with expectation: she might be saying, "My children!" It is the high point of *her* evening; the consumption cannot equal this excited dealing in sensual futures. One almost imagines that it is "*Charles* Heidsieck" instead of "Heidsieck" because the Christian name adds a final voluptuousness. Or it may only be for Armande's benefit — he and she exchange lavish glances, Madame de Stael and Benjamin Constant.

Our meeting breaks up inconclusively and Ladrick takes me to Buck's, a club of his.

"I belong to too many clubs," he says morosely. "And sit on too many company boards. By the way, this organization will make money."

"How do you know?"

"I just know. It has that smell to it."

Later he says: "I wasn't cut out to be a businessman. I should have been a writer."

"It's not as amusing as business."

"My God, wouldn't I like to write about what's happened to England!"

"How responsible for that do you think we Americans are?"

"A great deal and not at all. Not at all, because it's our own fault for imitating you. We imitate everything you do, especially at the top, people like Harlech." He looks at me carefully with tired eyes, but they have something of the strength of a forgotten England, too. "Harlech is the sort of man who can swallow the Kennedy myth," he says finally.

Myth? What does he mean?

"I'll say no more," he says. "Five children has Harlech — they ride motorcycles, model fashions, make films, marry into Carnaby Street, and stay with rich Americans in New York, where they earn their keep by being of a captive species, as parrots or Koala bears. If that is England at the top, how can the bottom resist? The day may come when *every* American has to have an Englishman on a stick in his 'living room' — the final status symbol."

We dine at L'Étoile and are surrounded with Americans.

"They were different in the old days," Ladrick says. "I liked so many of them then . . . Tommy Shevlin and Earl Smith (we called him the Earl of Smith), and all the rest of the OSSers during the war. Even poor old Hemingway. But those Americans weren't collectors, they didn't put us captive English in cages in their living rooms like . . ." He mentions a number of well-known Americans. "Cold pissers all," he concludes. "No heart for anything or anyone. Taking everything over, and we're helping them do it. It isn't the taking over, of course — it's their coldness, the lack of human warmth." He lowers his voice. "Look at this crowd, for example." He is right — the hard, suspicious faces of the Great Plains transported to New York and turned into "executives" stare cautiously about, learning by doing.

Later, over coffee, he says: "What the Americans do have, though, is an emancipated approach to industry. We English have always thought of it as shameful. I don't altogether mean the thing about going into trade. That is part of it, but there is a deeper certainty here that capitalism is wrong, something to be hidden. Dickens caught it, even Rimbaud caught it — did you know he was here twice in the 1870s? Lived in Soho and had odd jobs — even worked as a stableboy in Reading. He's a favorite of mine. People go on about Marx, but Rimbaud knew us better. We *are* capitalists, but we don't believe in it, so British industry has always been timid and uncertain. There are red faces and colonial accents six deep at the Savoy bar, all braying about business, but there isn't a real businessman in the crowd. Shopkeepers, yes; businessmen, no. You Americans are the businessmen because you have no sense of sin about it. Henry Ford, Howard Hughes — completely natural about doing it, like the Tahitians with sex before the white men came."

We share a taxi and he goes on: "Think of this, too. Fatuous old goats like Palmerston and Disraeli — would they have worked so hard to put it together if they could have seen how it would end?" He gestures out at Belgravia. "This was all private houses at one time . . . children, nannies, servants, filled with life, the residential envy of the world. Now the paint peels and six flats are extracted from each house. It's worse elsewhere — across the way at Notting Hill Gate, for example, where there are sixteen people in each flat and they all argue about whose night it is to take out the garbage. If our grandfathers could have foreseen it, would they have gone on? I don't think so. And if the present belittles their efforts, how much more does the future make any present effort unthinkable? There are no Henry Higginses left, you know, so David Hemmings, unlike Liza Doolittle, is a permanent condition."

He gets out in Eaton Square and moves majestically toward his own flat. "Thank God, Henry James never had to see it," he calls back with a laugh, the beautiful English voice floating anachronistically on the sullen, hyper-modern air.

I go on to Chelsea to meet Selwyn, a friend in publishing, who is nice and very earnest. He is accompanied by Montroy, a large, bald Englishman who has been married to two rich Americans and who goes to some pains to claim that he didn't like either one. He inveighs against their possessions and material greed, and says that now that he is back at his art (he plays the piano) he realizes how unhappy he was then. "I can chase young girls now, too," he says reflectively, "without getting a lot of black looks."

Selwyn tells me we are to go on to a party given by Berners, nephew of the owner of the firm Selwyn is with, and an executive there himself. Montroy says he looks forward to this, because Mrs. Berners appeals to him. "Long blonde hair and chubby little bottom," he says. "First time I went to the house I thought to myself, 'You need some piano lessons,' and I'm still hoping to give her some."

Selwyn is embarrassed by Montroy, but he is so shy that he obviously thought he had better bring along *someone* with an American connection. Montroy, with his two American marriages, is the best he can do.

We go in Montroy's car and there is talk about it, as there always is about any material possession in England. The talk may be facetious or disparaging, but it is never absent in the way it is in America, where a car is only a car. Here it is another piece of religious materialism; and Montroy, as a pianist with a car, is that much more devout.

Mrs. Berners, Gwendolyn, greets us and we are ushered into a small drawing room where a dozen young men and women — all between twenty and thirty — are sitting on the floor rather than in chairs. One recognizes well-heeled Bohemia with instant regret — the feeding on each other in the still air, charged with repressions — and resolves to make it short.

Berners is proud of his house and insists on showing me through it. It is small, arty, carpeted, striped-wallpapered and framed-pictured-in-the-bathrooms (three) — the sort of house of which there are so many thousands between Washington and Boston that they have become ultra-banal. In England, it is still a novelty, still wonderful.

We return to the party and one notes that its atmosphere, too, is several years out-of-date by the American calendar, although it is an authentic period piece: among many other models, Georgetown in 1952, the voices shrill in support of Adlai Stevenson, the young men from the Corcoran smiling knowingly, the pretty girl spoiling her looks with a frown as she attempts to follow what her companion is saying about Paul Bowles.

Gwendolyn gives the same sensation of the past revived. After Montroy's description, one expected something more of her — Yvette Mimieux with an English accent and two more inches on the hips — but she is amazingly ordinary. Dyed, lifeless blonde hair, squarish figure, fat legs, thick-skinned face, and she says "Super!" to everything. *Super!* Does smart young London say *Super!*? Yes, it does, and it seems to have no idea that that Americanism is as out-of-date in its country of origin as "Twenty-three Skiddoo!" Montroy's exaggerations are a reminder of earlier days in London, when one noticed for the first time the English tendency to lavish unwarranted praise on those about to be met for the first time. The national shyness precludes frank appraisals.

Gwendolyn, one must concede, is a waitress in a truck stop. And yet the room plays to her wildly. There are other girls in the room — there is even one very pretty girl — but all of them play to her, too. She doesn't even seem English — do they fawn because she, as the truck stop waitress, is the most authentically American?

In any case, one feels in the presence of a business truth. If the second-rate has to be touted as the best, then how can any grading system in any English field pretend to the slightest accuracy? What does this ultimately do to stock shares? Real estate values?

"We pride ourselves on being pretty close to the hippies," Berners says complacently as he nods toward a couple at the end of the room, happy to be able to show such evidence of civilized tolerance and sympathy. Under the complacence, there is feverish uncertainty — Berners doesn't know whether he's making a fool of himself for holding down a job while others play.

"How do you like Gwendolyn?" he asks unexpectedly, but one is prepared for the unexpected from Berners now.

"She's lovely."

"I guess I'm pretty lucky," he says, and, once more, one is stunned by the Americanism, best heard in a large Indiana backyard from a tractor salesman as he gazes fondly on a placid wife and four children caught in the faint light of the charcoal grill. Again, can this be smart London?

The object of his admiration jerks at her brief leather skirt with coarse hands, the fingernails bitten to the quick in the current young England fashion.

"I said I guess I'm pretty lucky," Berners says, ending the reverie and forcing a response, and one hastily agrees. Anything short of adulation, one feels, would be insulting, and Berners is already stretched to the breaking point.

The hour is late and Selwyn finally says he must leave. Montroy will stay on, so we depart by taxi. Selwyn, whose niceness never flags, has not an inkling that the Bernerses are a parody of life in New Canaan; he sincerely thinks they are original, in a variation of the English *hausfrau* saying, on her first visit to the United States: "Oh, you have Hoovers here, too!"

Preparing for bed, one realizes that very little changes in the English problem. After the war, there was also young England and it never had the price of a bottle of whisky. In a sense, it still doesn't, because England is basically a poor country. The American carelessness with money — often imitated, but never duplicated — just doesn't exist, even among the monied. It's not the cash, it's the attitude. *"Plus ça change, plus ça même,"* as Lady Hermione would put it. The problem never changes, but the solutions do, and the answer always seems to be more Americanization, no matter how dated.

―――――――

Next morning Simon Forster and I stroll the King's Road to see it in all its Saturday finery. To him it is the mysterious unattainable — the dirty girls are houris and the sad young men are to be envied because they don't work. To me, they are grotesque: not because of the clothes and the hair, but because of a terrible lack. They are missing something; they are people without a vital part. One begins to appreciate Ladrick's rather eccentric devotion to

Rimbaud as based on the assumption that Rimbaud, possessed of powerful vision, saw *this* England behind the surface of the 1870s. It is not a new direction, this England, but the butt end of colonialism, the ejection of the spent American shell casing.

We pass the Safeway supermarket near Sloane Square just in time to find Reeves leaving it with a large bag of groceries. He is in regulation Saturday-morning clothes, and, except for the flowing muttonchop whiskers (and even there, one wonders) could melt into Lincoln, Nebraska, with the assurance of a native son. To be such a perfect Nebraskan on Saturday undermines the authority of his weekday stance, and his diffidence announces that he is not unaware of that implication of derivative living.

He and Simon know each other — they were at Cambridge together — and exchange guarded English greetings. We are headed for the Phoenix for a drink — will he join us? He will, toting the groceries, even ten years ago an unthinkable burden in a public street for an Englishman of *any* social standing.

"The phonies have taken over the Markham," Simon says. "They all go there looking for Christine Keeler. So it's the Phoenix now."

It is crowded, as are all pubs in England on a Saturday morning, and the atmosphere is — it had to be — American. Young men in blue jeans and sweaters, young women in the same. There are English touches, and the older people still use native dress and customs, but it is not the England of a few years ago.

We leave at noon and Reeves asks us to his place. I accept; Simon, on the prowl, declines.

I am to learn that Reeves's grandfather was a landowner in Lincolnshire and lived a gracious life on twelve hundred acres. He had a fine Georgian house, and spent his years seeking various pleasures in various places, salmon fishing, mountain climbing, things like that.

Reeves himself has a flat in Knightsbridge and works hard all week. He and Mrs. Reeves — Jocelyn — are bright and cheerful together, and go on holiday two fortnights a year; to places like Davos in the winter and to places like Torremolinos in the summer. The flat is tasteful, if small. I am informed that two cars (a Riley and a Hillman) are garaged below; and there is an *au pair* girl for Baby Reeves. It would be good living in America; it is very high in England. And yet it represents a terrible comedown from Grandfather; and quite a comedown from Father, who was in the City and had a big house in Camden Hill.

The real rub is that Reeves and his Jocelyn must pretend that it is better than in Grandfather's day. This is one problem they do not share with Americans, who *are* better off than their grandparents were, except in very rare cases. If Reeves was tough-minded, he would laugh at the comedown and refuse to pretend he is better off. But then he would not be able to hold his job and enjoy as much as he has. Given his desire to live well, he can't afford to see himself as far below a former level. But those memories are so persistent! (He can remember riding about in Grandfather's chauffeur-driven Rolls, but has to coo over his own car as though it is the first he's ever seen.) So the pretense is really genteel-shabby under its shininess and he is essentially hangdog.

He believes in this new but less comfortable American-English world because he is afraid not to, and his fear is pervasive. Among other things, it undermines his efficiency in the business world in which he is trying to make his mark: he is pretending because he is afraid and he wants to succeed because he is afraid, but the fear shows through the pretense and threatens the success.

He wishes to discuss England and America, and I produce an article from the *International Herald-Tribune* of April 10, 1968, by Karl Meyer, London correspondent of the *Washington Post*. It is provocative, and its high spots are worth quoting, just as Reeves read them. The lead paragraph states the case: "If there were any doubt about it, the events of the past month have confirmed the degree to which Great Britain has all but legally become the 51st

[57]

state of the American Union." Strong words, and Mr. Meyer supports them by citing many evidences of the emotional and physical ties binding Britain and America together:

"It can be said without exaggeration that when America is wounded, Britain bleeds; that the British are as passionately involved with what goes on in Washington as they are with their own domestic politics; and that, in terms of identification, Memphis, Tennessee, is closer to the people of this country than Paris, France, or Bonn, Germany.

"An interesting measure of this involvement is the play that American news gets in the national press. In 14 of its last 25 editions, the pace-setting London 'Times' has led its front page with stories from or about America . . . What makes this emphasis on American news more striking is that it occurred during a very active period in British politics . . . A look at other publications shows the same tendency. Three of the four last covers of the influential 'Economist' showed the faces of Americans — Sen. Robert F. Kennedy, Richard M. Nixon and President Johnson. The trendy Sunday color supplements follow suit. . . .

"It seems impossible to turn on a television set without getting a filmed report on Vietnam, the racial troubles in the United States or the presidential campaign. . . .

"In talking with the British about their intense identification with America, four themes recur. The first is that through the United States this country can vicariously relive its own past as a world power. . . .

"A second theme is severely practical — the lively sense of dependency on the United States, particularly in economic terms. . . .

"A third theme is the obvious one of shared values — and also of shared problems . . . While no one is worried — yet — about a racial holocaust here, the news from America palpably quickens fears.

"Finally, there is the Kennedy leitmotif. The British were fasci-

nated by the late President and his memory has been suddenly revived in two ways. The candidacy of Sen. Kennedy has measurably
increased interest in U.S. presidential politics — every national
daily seems to have a team of reporters in America. And the murder
of Dr. King instantly evoked the anguish felt here in 1963. . . .

"All of this adds a note of irony to the debate under way as to
whether Britain is developing a presidential system. To the extent
that Britain feels itself a 51st state, it is already part of a presidential system — the American presidency.

" 'There is nothing going on in this country that is remotely as
important to our future as your election,' a British host said to an
American guest the other night. . . .

"In sum, one remark can be safely made about the British reaction to the multiple troubles that afflict the United States: The distance has been diminished, not widened, between America and its
anxious, unofficial and dependent 51st state."

Reeves's fingers tug nervously in his auburn whiskers as he reads.
When he finishes, he says: "Some good points, I suppose, but I
think he exaggerates."

"It's only journalism," I say.

"That's right," he says. "They'll say anything to stir up interest.
How do you happen to have it on you?"

"To ask Englishmen whether they agree with it or not."

"Well, I can say this . . ." he begins, and declaims for a full half-
hour, denouncing Mr. Meyer's fifty-first state talk so vehemently
that one can't help but marvel at how deeply he believes it. The
question is answered.

He is very warm, and I attempt to cool him off by talking about
our joint business interests. He explains the technical side of the
device very clearly and is himself again by the time we part.

Simon Forster takes me to a large cocktail party in the evening
and speaks of his own business career on the way.

"I have a great deal of responsibility now, and I suppose it breeds incentive." He is in advertising, my brother's field.

"That sounds familiar."

"It is," he says gloomily. "It's American business cant."

"That's what got us where we are today."

"Such balls — but everyone seems to be talking it now."

He tells me he is in love with a young girl whom he suspects of sensational promiscuity.

"Her minis have to be seen to be believed," he says. "Did I tell you what Lockridge [a mutual friend] calls miniskirts? 'The unwearable on the unbearable.' But that doesn't help me a great deal in this case. I went round there the other morning and she was having tea with an eighteen-year-old boy — boy her own age, all dressed up King's Road style — and he spoke to me in perfect Cockney. I just happened to know whose son he is and that he's at Eton. They all speak it there now. 'Where juh learn t'toh lah th'h?' he asked me, as though I spoke oddly. 'Same place you did,' I said, and she laughed, but I think I cut the older man figure."

"You might have to speak Cockney and grow your hair down the middle of your back — it's not much to ask for true love."

"If I could be sure it was permanent, I would," he says.

Ladrick is at the cocktail party and in excellent form.

"I've thought of a good way to say it," he says. "C. Aubrey Smith may have been a joke, but that doesn't mean the Beatles aren't, too."

"That's very good."

"I should write, I know it, but I'm so damned slow. Those things only come through at the rate of one a week."

"I'll quote you and make you famous."

"Would you? That would be marvelous, wouldn't it! Let me tell you some more then. I have a distant cousin — Hugh Grandell —

who is something called a colonel of a regiment. It's based in West Germany and I was in Berlin a couple of weeks ago and he was yelping at me to come see them and so I went. They — he and Jennifer and the children and so on — live in one wing of a decaying German manor house, and when I saw it I could only think: India. Those flat German fields and those well-behaved German woods, but it was all like it was fifty years ago in Simla except that everything had slipped and run, like a girl's mascara in the rain. Like those Tennessee Williams people in your American South. If I could only write! You see, the Empire created a new class — a piggy group of people who had to have their biscuits and keep all the stores (those endless chutneys and jams and marmalades and relishes — repulsive stuff!) locked up safely from the servants. And when the Empire went, they were left with those tastes and habits and no way of gratifying them on the old level. But they can't stop trying. People like John Osborne inveigh, but nothing really changes them. They've never heard of John Osborne, and if they did they'd think he was just envious, and perhaps he is. But I don't know of what because it's so rundown. They play at India in that sagging old manor house until . . . well, it's too much. The passion for *things!* Only now the things are all American. That's the point. I was no sooner there than it started. The house was buzzing because Major Arphlugmaster — some such American name — was condescending to take Jennifer to the nearest American PX that afternoon. 'We'll have *Gulf shrimp, Maine lobsters, Kansas City steaks!*' she sang to me, dancing around the room like Isadora Duncan, telephoning her friends to gloat. That night we ate the whole business — shrimp cocktails, lobsters, twelve-pound steaks — and the party (fourteen and all English) stuffed like Fiji cannibals. It was not only American but cheap, coming from the PX, so Jennifer was making up for all those skimpy meals she'd been serving the same people over the past couple of months. There she was at one end of the table, the skinny symbol of former glory in long dress and askew tiara, gobbling steak like a refugee from a concentration camp. Hugh the same at the other end, and the other guests in various stages of abandon in between. When it was over — and this is the terrible part — they all lolled in their chairs and had an anti-American debauch for an hour. Nothing American was any good. The shrimps and the lobsters couldn't compare with Continental *crevettes* and *langoustes;* the steaks were far inferior to 'good English' or French beef; Major Arphlugmaster was a hairy ape; the PX was an affront; everything American was awful and should be done away with. You see, they had all been taught that from birth, and then they found out it wasn't true and that they loved everything American. But after the gorging, there had to be a pretense that there had been no slobbering after American tastes and *things.* It hadn't happened: that mountain of gutted lobster shells was entirely imaginary. And I was sitting there thinking: it's not the pigginess that's so nauseating, it's the hypocrisy. But I suppose so many people have said that about us English already."

"You seem to have found a fresh form."

"I think you're just being kind. But look, here are you and I as possible business associates, and because of that I think about my own end of it — the end that Reeves and Harper and I have. And then I think of Jennifer and Hugh and realize we have no end at all. Because those people — that mentality — still dominate British business the way they do the British military."

"But you and Reeves and Harper aren't like that."

"You haven't met all our directors. No, I shouldn't say that, none of them are that silly, you're right. But business interlocks, as you know better than we, and there are questions of supply, of shipping, of a thousand and one things where a company finds itself dependent on some other company or organization where people like that *are* in charge. And that's where the trouble starts, and ultimately drags all the rest of us down."

Simon and I are at Churchill's late at night, and a well-known American Negro entertainer tells me: "Stay in a private house when you're here, that's my rule. You stay in one of those hotels, you get all that 'Yessir,' but no real service. I've stayed all over this town, and I guess those suites at the Dorchester are about the best, but I've been *cold* there, too, and couldn't get warm even after they worked on the heat the next day. But when it goes out at five in the morning and the rest of your party has goosepimples — that's when I ask myself, 'What am I paying for?' and decide to stay with those friends who say they can *guarantee* heat. Even then it doesn't always work, but it isn't costing five hundred dollars a week, either."

A Sunday. One lies abed and thinks of the colonization as coming from the British lower classes, and then spreading up. The lower classes were the first to be openly Americanized and they pass it on, along with their own accents. (Surely the most grating in the world. They sound to American ears as American accents sounded to British ears a hundred years ago. To contemporary educated English ears, they sound . . . but Simon has given me the answer. They sound beautiful. If Americanization is sacred, then the accent of the Americanizers — the lower class — is equally to be emulated.) And try as one may to find a better example of the process, the Beatles remain definitive. In Liverpool, a conscious decision to purvey American music, a profoundly American form of colonization in that if the music is swallowed so is all the rest. When England embraced the Beatles, it embraced America. Their rags-to-riches story was, in itself, intensely American — as are their later, exotic expenditures. Local pride and royal recognition came because honor was assuaged — England was to be Americanized by deputized Englishmen instead of American overseers. The hysterical counter-reception given the Beatles in America was for good and simple reason: England was to be like America! Another One! Joy! Love me, Ringo, because you've joined the team and brought

[63]

fifty million people with you! Even the American adolescents recognize the benefits of colonizing. The teen-age screech cuts through abstract theory and backs Wall Street up as Wall Street never dreamed youth could rise to the occasion.

There are those who will deny this and claim the Beatles this and the Beatles that (they have been compared with Mozart as composers), but there are always those who will deny reality. Reality is never generally acceptable: a girl goes next door to borrow some sugar and her mother smiles behind her back at a friend because they both know it isn't the sugar but the presence of the boy next door that draws her over. Naturally, the girl is not going to agree, nor is collective girlhood going to agree, but that does not change the reality. Nor would the Beatles agree, nor would the English lower class agree, nor would the rest of England agree, but that doesn't change the reality either.

The flat fact is that the Beatles and the rest of the lower class gave up on English models and began imitating America utterly, completely and finally. And the rest of England is imitating its lower class, which means they are imitating America secondhand. So the whole country is an imitation of America. If that isn't colonization, does the word have any meaning? And can any American businessman, even one who also writes books, afford not to know it? Is there one who doesn't know it, in one set of evasive euphemisms or another?

Of course there isn't. He couldn't make a valid business judgment on any level without knowing it. So he wouldn't last and would have to be replaced. The mere presence of an American businessman in England means he is aware of the situation.

In one's own case — the case of the investor and the company with the electronic device — if one didn't acknowledge that situation one would lose one's shirt. One shaves with that in mind, telepathically joined with the thousands of one's compatriots all over England.

I spend the day with company balance sheets, records, prospective offerings and other papers. The company seems sound, the device should make money. But I need expert corroboration. I know I cannot get what I want from an Englishman because the view will be English. It might be an honest and competent view, but it will be English, which means it will not take certain dangers into consideration . . . dangers that an American always has in mind.

So I call New York and speak with a friend who knows the field. I want to talk this over with an American electronics marketing expert who also has an engineering background. Does he know anyone in Europe who fits those specifications? He suggests two, one in Brussels and the other in Geneva. I call the one in Brussels and find he can't spare the time. The one in Geneva can. I shall have to pay dearly for his three days, but he shall be in London tonight and ready to start.

In the early evening, a long walk ending up at the Devonshire Arms, a pub in the Marloes Road. Five years ago, I lived nearby for two months and this was my local. There is an outside terrace, a pleasant place to sit and watch the bustle in the street. Across the way is a large hospital, and now the late sun warms its mellow reddish bricks to the exact shade that I remember; and the nurses' colorful habits add the same, somehow pleasing touch of official movement to the setting.

But inside all is different — and in a brief five years. Here was the public bar, a rough room once dominated by the working people of the neighborhood — like George, the ex-boxer who had a barrow on Kensington High Street. And given color by a few eccentrics — like Denis, an educated man with exquisite manners and a dedicated Marxist. He had been a flying hero in the Battle of Britain and bright things had been predicted for him after the war, but Marx changed all that. Now he lived in a furnished room and was happy enough to read the master by day and soak in the Devonshire through the evening. He was the most *amiable* Marxist I have ever known — even George, who looked like an American Indian and liked no one, got along with Denis. George kept his barrow somewhere in the vicinity, and trundled it down from the High Street each evening at seven, as punctual as Kant. Then he sat in the Devonshire until the ten-thirty closing, drinking a dozen strong brown ales, after which he made his way home, miles away across half London. No one ever saw him eat. He was extraordinarily generous and, unlike most old boxers, reticent about his career in the ring, although Denis told me he had once challenged for the British middleweight title. He had never been out of London — during the war he was a fireman — and felt no need to see or know any other place. He was, I think, the most English Englishman I have ever known, just as Denis was the most impersonally intelligent.

Now they are gone, and the public bar that once housed them for such periods each day is so changed that one knows they could not have sat in it. It has been completely remodeled and made far more "modern" than the saloon bar on the other side of the building, and is filled with lower- and middle-class English of all ages, all "casually" dressed. One might be . . . anywhere; there is a particular resemblance to bars like P. J. Clarke's in New York. But where are those who used to inhabit this public bar? They can't all be dead and gone. I walk around to the front and there, through a glass door, see the pitiful remnants of the band. No George and no Denis, of course, but three or four familiar faces. Five years ago, there would have been fifty of them coming and going in the big public room that was their own — old women in their crazy hats drinking gin together and talking about the racing results, taxi drivers and hotel porters in for a quick one, English navvies and Irish waiters, an occasional prostitute . . . the full range of lower-class London, perceptive, dignified and tough. Now they are four, and uncomfortable in a tiny cubicle; and when they are gone that room will be turned into something else.

But how does this dispossessed lower class support the conviction that it is the lower class that is Americanizing England? Quite easily — it is *their* sons and daughters who fill the new public bar, who have done the dispossessing. The Americanizing lower class dislikes old England in any form, but most of all in its own antecedents.

Technically, however, is this process (the young against the old) Americanization? No, to the degree that it would have happened anyhow. Yes, to the degree that it has been speeded up. But without American influence, would English pubs ever have been modernized? Would the new customers ever have been created?

One has to answer such questions entirely on one's own, because nowhere is society more reticent than on matters of social change. Ask a man how often he has sexual intercourse with his wife, and how, and he will be only too happy to tell all. Research by interview has proved it. (Masters and Johnson, the authors of *Human Sexual Response*, went further and showed that he will perform various acts, including masturbation, before other eyes just like any other higher ape.) But ask him when he stopped saying "beef up," or started saying "viable," and he will either go dumb or become aggressive. In neither reaction will he answer the query, even inadvertently.

Twenty years ago, for example, the American term "soccer" was unknown in England, where the game was always called "football." Today, many English newspapers have switched to "soccer," but no one is happy enough about the change to remember when it happened.

And also twenty years ago, the American asking for a "Scotch" in an English pub was met with a blank stare and then: "Oh, you mean a *whisky*." Under no circumstances did an Englishman then refer to his Scotch whisky as Scotch. He always asked for a whisky, and one soon learned to do the same.

By 1958, things had changed. Publicans had evidently grown

tired of straightening out thousands of Americans each year and now served Scotch when asked for Scotch without giving the whisky lesson.

By 1968, the inversion was complete. Even the English now say Scotch instead of whisky. In final perfection of reversal, if one asks for a whisky, the London publican looks blank and then: "Oh, you mean a *Scotch*."

And if one is so rash as to say "I can remember when one ordered a 'whisky,' and the word 'Scotch' was never used," the publican replies, with a cold look: "I don't know what you can be thinking of; it's always been 'Scotch' since I can recall."

And if one goes further and asks one's English friends about it, they are either equally sure it has always been as it now is, or very vague. Perhaps the reluctance to admit changes in social and verbal usage is part of the human reluctance to see ourselves as we are. (We can be talked into public masturbation only on the condition that we don't see ourselves doing it, that we can think of it as a contribution to "science.") And it may also be related to the fear of death. Changes in usage imply the passage of time, a hurried flight when they are brought to abrupt attention and the shadow of mortality falls across the question and must be exorcized by denial.

We are now in the midst of great business bustle. Frank, the American expert, sits in *his* room at the Rochester and bends everyone to his implacable will. He could have been predicted — flat face, flat jaw, flat voice, probably flat feet — and he eats up engineering studies and balance sheets like a garbage truck. After which he demands more. Reeves and Harper and Ladrick have all met him — once — and I can see they want no more. He looked them all over like John Wayne casing the habitués of a homosexual bar, and they are understandably irritated and resentful. And chastened.

Ladrick put it bluntly later: "Is Frank necessary?"

"I must have an expert opinion. I'm only an investor — I don't know any more about electronics and world markets for components than I do about aardvarks."

"But *Frank!* Doesn't he come in another model?"

"Do I have to answer that?"

"No, I suppose not. It's just that I thought I'd seen every kind of American you produce, but I've never run into a Frank before."

"They're special."

"I can see that."

Three days stretch into four, into five.

The great man completes his paperwork and is taken on an exhaustive tour of the company's modest factory. More calculations in purdah. We await his decision like condemned convicts hanging on a reprieve.

At last he summons me to his quarters, and the opinion is delivered. The gist is that the factory is hopelessly old-fashioned, the workmen and foremen worthless, the executive departments crying out for extinction, and the board of directors beneath discussion . . . *but,* the device itself is worth something and should command a good price on the world market. He suggests an outright sale.

"It's this way — if they try to produce it here with the setup they've got, there can't be maximum return. They won't make enough, or they'll make too many at first and lose heart. Then they won't put in quality control and so the finished product will be uneven and there'll be lost orders and they'll lose heart again. Then they won't understand how to market, how to find their biggest customers and hold them. Then there'll be the competition trying to get them to sell out. Or steal it if they won't sell. Add it all up and what do you get? The best program is sell it. ITT or someone like that. It would have to be an American firm to get the right price."

"Do you mind telling them what you've told me?"

"Hell, no, you're paying for it. I can put it all in a report, too, toned down and dressed up. I just wanted to let you know now what the. . . ."

"It's better in person, I think. Straight."

Ladrick, Harper and Reeves meet with us in a sequestered Rochester lounge. Frank tells them what he has told me, hardly changing a word.

The silence is thick as he finishes. They twiddle fingers and pencils and know he is right. No one can question Frank's efficiency.

"If we sell, you're out some money," Ladrick says to me.

"I'll make expenses and then a bit if you let me find the buyer and negotiate — a flat finder's fee."

"You'd be better off letting him do it," Frank advises. "An American can get more out of another American."

"But we don't want to sell!" Harper cries out in sudden emotion. "We bought this patent because we wanted to make the device. If we sell, we're just middlemen. Where does it leave the company? Where does it leave us?"

"Where does it leave England?" asks Ladrick.

"I've had enough of your sarcasm!" Harper says to him bitterly.

"Sometimes sarcasm is valuable," says Frank with unexpected tact. "It helps to remind you that business is a matter of self-interest, nothing else."

But Harper is not to be denied and shouts out like a boy: "I'm sick of hearing about 'self-interest'! I'm sick of hearing all this American dollars-and-cents brutality! You don't have any room for common decency, any of you. We promised Jenkins [the inventor of the device] when we bought it that we'd keep it here in England. If we sell it abroad, how can we look him in the eye? Come on, let's get out of here and leave these Americans to their everlasting calculations. We can do this on our own — we can get the capital we need here in England!"

He stands up, hands clenching, tears in his eyes. Reeves and Ladrick do not move.

"We tried to get capital here," Reeves says slowly. "We couldn't because it's risky. Someone else may produce a similar device and we'll be in trouble — paying for infringement suits, if nothing else. You know all that; nothing has changed."

Harper sits down again, and we talk on. After four hours, a compromise begins to glimmer. Frank concedes that if knowledgeable Americans were put in charge of two key departments — production and marketing — the company might be able to make a success of it. I announce that I shall abide by Frank's advice. Ladrick and Reeves give their support. Two hours later, Harper agrees. It is settled.

"You sure put me on the spot," Frank says later.

"What else could I do? I'm only an investor. I have to take someone's opinion."

"I hate doing business with these goddamned English," he complains, throwing his clothes into a small suitcase. "They're such a bunch of children. The only one worth *anything* is that Lord Ladrick. Did you see Harper? Ready to burst into tears like a little kid."

"Yes, I saw him. But aren't you forgetting your own rules? Who cares what one's partners are like if there's money to be made?"

"There must be an easier way. I never met an Englishman who wasn't a phony. They come in with all that talk, but they can never back up what they promise. Production! They always build *one* of anything — like their jets — and then expect a miracle. That Harper is so dumb he thinks all you have to do is call the company Sir Francis Drake Electronics and the whole world will come running! . . . And calling *us* money-minded! If we were really after the money, would we have laid it all on the table like that? S — t, no, we wouldn't. We'd have kept our mouths shut and said it was just great to make it, and then taken over after the company went bankrupt, and sold it with the whole price going into *our* pockets. That's what an 'honest Englishman' would have done if he'd been in our shoes. I tell you, these bastards are the . . ."

"You'll get used to them."

"Not me — I'm going back to Geneva where . . . what do you mean, 'You'll get used to them'?"

"Who do you think is going to be the American in charge here?"

"Oh, no, you don't! Why, I wouldn't stay in this country if you paid me ten times what I'm worth. I . . ."

I ask Ladrick if he thinks Frank would suit.

"Oh, my God," he says. "Does it have to be Frank? Harper thinks he's the ugliest American in Europe."

"He knows his field."

"How horribly all this is ending. America takes over another British company. Even the author-businessman turns out to be an imperialist octopus."

"Not of his own volition. I merely went through the motions and accepted the outcome. I did exactly what any other American investor would have done — hired an expert and followed his advice. You and Harper and Reeves made the decision. We were all involuntary, if you come down to it, controlled by outside forces, historical and otherwise."

"That sounds good, but . . . I wonder. Perhaps Harper has the right idea: go down with all popguns firing wildly."

"That's too babyish a solution for you."

"Yes . . . but I sometimes wish it weren't."

Departure is imminent, and things are more or less settled. Except for Frank. He is in Geneva, scorning the possibility of a new career as overseer, but calling every day to talk about it. I think he will accept in the end.

The last few days are easygoing. Ladrick attends the Thynne-Palmer nuptials and is still punchy next day at lunch. Thynne is Lord Christopher John Thynne, thirty-three, second son of the Marquess of Bath; Palmer is Antonia Palmer, twenty-seven, daughter of Lady Abel Smith, lady-in-waiting to the Queen. The ceremony was performed at Queen's Chapel, Marlborough House, and then, as Ladrick describes it, "The group weaved over to St. James Palace. So close, you know. The Queen graced the festivities, along with a horde of flower children from the King's Road, and the suave Mick Jagger, shirt open and carnation in hat. Sir Mark Palmer, the bride's beautiful brother, sported orange velvet trousers, a caftan adorned with flowers and bells on his bracelets. The Queen — well, I leave it to your imagination, saying only that never has a member of our stolidly Teutonic ruling family been seen against such a background. The plain German *hausfrau*, dressed as in Cologne for early morning marketing — sensible shoes, simple dress, playful but controlled hat — in the midst of the flower children, smiling at them indulgently, as one smiles at children splashing in the bath, not an inkling that they might not be so innocent. Or so little a threat to her. It was beyond the wildest dreams of the 'end of empire.' When that can happen in life, how can one think of writing? I abandon the idea; I see I was presumptuous. It was beyond satire. Not even Waugh could have handled it. (Did you know him, by the way? Nice man, and quite misunderstood in England, of course.) But do you see what I mean? I don't give a damn about the end of empire, or Elizabeth the Sixteenth or any of the rest of that drivel — I'm only talking about an historic moment. When we came to an end. You do see that?"

I said I did.

"The whole spectacle was so dominated by penury. Bath, father of the bridegroom, is hard up. He has to be, or he wouldn't have turned Longleat into a zoo to collect admissions. Or have become a male model in whisky ads. So the children are infected with money panic and fall prey to Chelsea, and we have the final scene wherein

Gin Alley takes over the wedding of the penniless peer. Tom Rake-
well goes broke and takes his Sovereign down with him. They go to
pieces together."

———————

Simon introduces me to his love, the hyper-youthful Gillian, who
speaks passable Cockney and wears more fringed buckskin than
Buffalo Bill in his prime. And her fingernails are bitten to the ever-
chic quick, so all fashion bases seem to have been touched. She is
emaciated; one thinks of the tubercular Mildred in *Of Human
Bondage.* Certainly Simon looks at her with eyes as uncritical as
those the hero of that book turned on Mildred.

Gillian speaks longingly of the Monkees. Do I know any of them?
Such fantasia is almost too much for Simon, who tries to change the
subject, and scowls at me when I tell her I don't know any of them
personally but understand they are marvelous boys and the sole
support of dozens of indigent relatives and worthy causes. She is
possessed of the primitive sentimentality one finds so often in the
modern young and nods her head in rapt approval.

As her head moves up and down in ritualistic regularity, the
fringe on the buckskin dancing in light counterpoint, one realizes
she is actively if crudely religious, like a Dunker or Holy Roller.
She has a vision of a promised land, somewhere near the Haight-
Ashbury and Beverly Hills and MacDougal Street and Park Avenue
— the stars pass in their Cadillacs, the Monkees wail all night, pot
and horse grow on every bush, Warren Beatty and Faye Dunaway
provide the art, and eight thousand Sidney Poitiers lean forward in
Dr. Kildare's clothes to tell her the poor and the needy have been
taken care of. (Under the innovations, the Beatles' *Yellow Subma-
rine* has the same ingenuous view of solutions to social and human
problems.) It is the modern English-European youth-dream of
America, a dream under the official one, supplanting the older notions of loose gold in the streets, and I am to meet with it everywhere, even in eastern Europe. Gillian is derivative American in

her fashionable half-wittedness; the cargo cult touches are a native contribution.

Simon sulks after she is gone. "I wish you hadn't encouraged her with the Monkees."

"What else could I do? I was only trying to please."

He concedes the point and brightens up. "She's lovely, don't you think?"

"Sensational."

He goes off into a lyric enumeration of her charms, ending up with a claim that she may very well become as important a figure as Baby Jane Holzer was. I am suitably impressed and we part on the very best of terms, better friends than ever.

I shall fly back to Switzerland, and have a farewell drink with Ladrick at yet another club of his.

"I give you the last act of the wedding," he says. "The aristocratic bridegroom was searched at London Airport as he left on his honeymoon and arrested for possessing drugs — something called amphetamine, presumably to flog spirits already drooping. By implication, the Queen takes a light view of the matter. Boys will be boys, especially if they're English lords of thirty-three."

"Simon Forster has reminded me that I met him several years ago. I remember an eager manner and ingenuous questions about Hawaii; he wanted to go there and become a photographer."

"Poor boy, anything to make a few shillings."

His last words are in the same vein: "We deserve all the Franks you send us."

"Frank isn't so bad."

"I know it. That's the point, isn't it? He's not at all bad. We are."

3

In retrospect, the trip seemed a reasonably formal presentation of English weaknesses, the doors through which the conquerors have poured. The piggy materialism, the inability to rise above gentility, the emotionalism, the aversion to efficiency and planning (and to intellectual activity in general), the pervasive eccentricity . . . all those and more had been offered up in revealing innocence.

"We are a primitive people with an industrial society superimposed," Ladrick had said, and one wondered if "primitive" was not the key adjective, the single weakness (especially where technological living is concerned) that underlies and guides the rest.

Insofar as Shaw is worth anything as a commentator on the English — and his credentials are more impressive than anyone else's — his conviction that primitiveness is the prime English characteristic is worth serious attention. The assertion runs through all his writing, and becomes explicit in numberless instances and characters. Stogumber, the bloodthirsty English chaplain in *Saint Joan;* Britannus, the solemn secretary in *Caesar and Cleopatra;* Tom Broadbent, the crude businessman in *John Bull's Other Island* . . . they are all primitive in the pinch. In essays like *Common Sense About the War,* written in 1916, he was even more direct, laying bare the primitive thought processes and procedural forms of the nation's leaders with surgical precision.

In *Back to Methuselah* (1922), he devoted a frankly propagandistic five-play cycle to the problem, which is treated with generosity. The primitiveness is put in terms of immaturity; he claims the English never grow up. But if they did, they would be more mature than any other race.

"In devising brainless amusements; in pursuing them with enormous vigor, and taking them with eager seriousness, our English people are the wonder of the world," says one character. "They always were. And it is just as well; for otherwise their sensuality would become morbid and destroy them . . . I tell you, what is wrong with us is that we are a non-adult race . . . The Irish and the Scots . . . although their lifetime is as short as ours, or shorter, yet do somehow contrive to grow up a little before they die. We die in boyhood; the maturity that should make us the greatest of all nations lies beyond the grave for us."

"Yes, that is it," says another. "I felt . . . we had the possibility of becoming a great nation within us; but our faults and follies drove me to cynical hopelessness . . . It is the highest creatures who take the longest to mature, and are the most helpless during their immaturity."

And another: "Ever since I learnt to distinguish between one English face and another I have noticed what the woman pointed out: that the English face is not an adult face, just as the English mind is not an adult mind. . . . Your maturity is so late that you never attain to it. . . . You are potentially the most highly developed race on earth and would actually be the greatest if you could live long enough to attain to maturity."

Shaw was not writing to hurt but to help, and because he was kind — surely a rare characteristic among professional dramatists! — his conclusions have a compelling authority. Certainly no one — Englishman *or* foreigner — ever brought to the "English problem" such a combination of brains, integrity and compassion. What struck Shaw as a young man and intrigued him for all his long life was the same thing that has struck generations of Americans in dealing with the English: the feeling that they are curiously retarded.

(The immense effort put into organizing the motoring competition from Britain to Australia, or the London–New York race — could any other breed or nation put such energy, in Shaw's phrase, into "devising brainless amusements . . . pursuing them with enormous vigor and taking them with eager seriousness"? There is much more indifference in the United States to an American on the moon than in England to an Englishman scrambling to the top of the Post Office Tower.)

This retardation — or primitiveness, or permanent immaturity — is found in all Englishmen, even the most notable. Winston Churchill's boyish conduct in the House of Commons is an embracing example. One feels the primitive in men as superficially worldly as Aldous Huxley, Harold Nicholson, Bertrand Russell, Harold Macmillan . . . there are very few exceptions. One wonders if it is a natural primitiveness or whether they are damaged through inheritance or in early childhood. Is something missing or has something been crippled?

Whatever the cause, the result is everywhere. One meets atypical nationals of other countries — non-American Americans, non-French Frenchmen, even non-German Germans — but never a non-English Englishman. (Many English are *anti-* English, like Ladrick, which is an entirely different matter. The non-national does not have the national manner; he is outside his origin. The antinational's posture is purely intellectual and he himself remains firmly inside national characteristics no matter how intense his fulminations against them.)

Eager tourists often find English eccentricity an appealing proof of English vitality and variety, and an argument for immaturity as a strength, but one regretfully concludes that they have deluded themselves on both counts. On close study, eccentricity comes out as no more than a symptom of primitiveness, and, as such, a deadly weakness.

Henry Adams's analysis of English eccentricity as a crippling burden is particularly pertinent. He devotes an entire chapter to it in *The Education,* and one can hardly approach the subject without deferring to his unquestionable authority, still unchallenged and unimproved sixty years after he wrote:

"For several years, under the keenest incitement to watchfulness, he observed the English mind in contact with itself and other minds. Especially with the American the contact was interesting because the limits and defects of the American mind were one of the favorite topics of the European. From the old world point of view, the American had no mind; he had an economic thinking machine which could work only on a fixed line. The American mind exasperated the European as a buzz-saw might exasperate a pine forest. . . . The American mind was not a thought . . . it was a convention, superficial, narrow and ignorant; a mere cutting instrument, practical, economical, sharp and direct.

"The English themselves hardly conceived that their mind was either economical, sharp or direct; but the defect that most struck an American was its enormous waste in eccentricity. Americans needed and used their whole energy, and applied it with close economy; but English society was eccentric by law and for the sake of the eccentricity itself.

"The commonest phrase overheard at an English club or dinner table was that So-and-So 'is quite mad.' It was no offence to So-and-So; it hardly distinguished him from his fellows; and when applied to a public man, like Gladstone, it was qualified by epithets much more forcible. Eccentricity was so general as to become hereditary distinction. It made the chief charm of English society as well as its chief terror.

"The American delighted in Thackeray as satirist, but Thackeray quite justly maintained that he was not a satirist at all, and that his pictures of English society were exact and good-natured. The American, who could not believe it, fell back on Dickens, who, at all events, had the vice of exaggeration to extravagance, but Dickens's English audience thought the exaggeration rather in manner and style, than in types. Mr. Gladstone himself went to see Sothern act Dundreary, and laughed until his face was distorted — not because Dundreary was exaggerated, but because he was ridiculously like the types Gladstone had seen — or might have seen — in any club in Pall Mall. Society swarmed with exaggerated characters; it contained little else. . . .

"The private secretary [Adams himself] . . . began by regarding British eccentricity as a force. Contact with it, in the shape of Palmerston, Russell, and Gladstone, made him hesitate; he saw his own national type — his father, Weed, Evarts, for instance — deal with the British, and show itself certainly not the weaker; certainly sometimes the stronger. Biassed though he were, he could hardly be biassed to such a degree as to mistake the effects of force on others, and while — labor as he might — Earl Russell and his state papers seemed weak to a secretary, he could not see that they seemed strong to Russell's own followers. Russell might be dishonest or he might be merely obtuse — the English type might be brutal or might be only stupid — but strong, in either case, it was not, nor did it seem strong to Englishmen.

"Eccentricity was not always a force; Americans were deeply interested in deciding whether it was always a weakness. . . .

"By natural affinity, the social eccentrics commonly sympathized with political eccentricity. The English mind took naturally to rebellion — when foreign — and it felt particular confidence in the Southern Confederacy because of its combined attributes — foreign rebellion of English blood — which came nearer ideal eccentricity than could be reached by Poles, Hungarians, Italians or Frenchmen. All the English eccentrics rushed into the ranks of rebel sympathizers, leaving few but well-balanced minds to attach themselves to the cause of the Union. . . . To most observers, as well as to the *Times,* the *Morning Post,* and the *Standard,* a vast majority of the English people seemed to follow the professional eccentrics; even the emotional philanthropists took that direction; Lord Shaftsbury and Carlyle, Fowell Buxton and Gladstone threw their sympathies on the side which they should naturally have opposed, and did so for no reason except their eccentricity. . . .

"This eccentricity did not mean strength. The proof of it was in the mismanagement of the rebel interests. . . .

"At that moment — the early summer of 1863 — the rebel party in England were full of confidence, and felt strong enough to challenge the American Legation to a show of power. They knew better than the Legation what they could depend upon: that the law officers and commissioners of customs at Liverpool dared not prosecute the ironclad ships; that Palmerston, Russell and Gladstone were ready to recognize the Confederacy; that the Emperor Napoleon would offer them every inducement to do it. In a manner they owned Liverpool and especially the firm of Laird who were building their ships. The political member of the Laird family was Lindsay, about whom the whole web of rebel interests clung — rams, cruisers, munitions, and Confederate loan; social introductions and parliamentary tactics. The firm of Laird, with a certain dignity, claimed to be champion of the English navy; and public opinion, in the summer of 1863, still inclined towards them.

"Never was there a moment when eccentricity, if it were a force, should have had more value to the rebel interest; and the managers must have thought so, for they adopted or accepted as their champion an eccentric of eccentrics; a type of 1820; a sort of Brougham of Sheffield; notorious for poor judgment and worse temper. Mr. Roebuck . . . was regarded by friends of the Union as rather a comical personage — a favorite subject for *Punch* to laugh at — with a bitter tongue and a mind enfeebled even more than common by the political epidemic of egotism. In all England they could have found no opponent better fitted to give away his own case. No American man of business would have paid him attention; yet the

Lairds, who certainly knew their own affairs best, let Roebuck represent them and take charge of their interests. . . .

"They [the rebel agents] were surrounded by cranks of the worst English species, who distorted their natural eccentricities and perverted their judgments. Roebuck may have been an extreme case, since he was actually in his dotage, yet this did not prevent the Lairds from accepting his lead, or the House from taking him seriously. Extreme eccentricity was no bar, in England, to extreme confidence; sometimes it seemed a recommendation; and unless it caused financial loss, it rather helped popularity. . . .

"The sum of these experiences in 1863 left the conviction that eccentricity was weakness."

If anything, both the extent of the eccentricity and the depth of the conviction have increased since Adams's day. Modern English eccentricity is not bizarre and striking, as in the mid-nineteenth century. It is drab, imitative and self-conscious, reduced to Reeves's whiskers and Harper's stammer, but it is more widespread. Englishmen with new money try to reproduce the habits of their former masters, and eccentricity is the most desirable characteristic of all — as sought after as philanthropic and cultural interests by recently affluent Americans.

It was not nearly so epidemic in the London of the 1860s, which contained, in addition to the eccentrics, many men of genuine ability and individuality. For purposes of comparison, Adams's descriptions of two are worth repeating:

"Monckton Milnes [Lord Houghton] was a social power in London, possibly greater than Londoners themselves understood, for in London society as elsewhere, the dull and ignorant made a large majority, and dull men always laughed at Monckton Milnes . . . and of course he himself . . . [challenged] ridicule with the indifference of one who knew himself to be the first wit in London and a maker of men — of a great many men. A word from him went far. An invitation to his breakfast-table went farther. Behind his almost Falstaffian mask and laugh of Silenus, he carried a fine, broad, and high intelligence which no one questioned. . . . In Parliament he made speeches, chiefly criticized as too good for the place and too high for the audience. Socially, he was one of two or three men who went everywhere, knew everybody, talked of everything and had the ear of Ministers; but unlike most wits, he held a social position of his own that ended in a peerage, and he had a house in Upper Brook Street to which most clever people were exceedingly glad of admission. . . . He was a voracious reader, a strong critic . . . but above all he was a man of the world by profession. . . . Not even Henry Brougham dared do the things he did, yet Brougham defied rebuff. Milnes was the good-nature of London; the Gargantuan type of its refinement and coarseness; the most universal figure of May Fair."

And John Bright, the Radical statesman: "He was a liberal hater, and what he hated he reviled after the manner of Milton, but he was afraid of no one. He was almost the only man in England, or, for that matter in Europe, who hated Palmerston and was not afraid of him, or of the press or the pulpit, the clubs or the bench, that stood behind him. He loathed the whole fabric of sham religion, sham loyalty, sham aristocracy, and sham socialism. . . . He could not act on the defensive; his mind required attack. Even among friends at the dinner-table he talked as though he were denouncing them, or someone else, on a platform; he measured his phrases, built his sentences, cumulated his effects, and pounded his opponents, real or imagined. His humor was glow, like iron at dull heat; his blow was elementary, like the thrash of a whale."

One cannot imagine such Englishmen in modern England; certainly they do not exist. Now London, and England, is devoid of both the generous aristocrat (Milnes), and the honest critic (Bright). What remains is *pastiche*, the imitation of a shallow notion as to what people were. Not even as they were back in the nineteenth century, but in 1910, or 1930, or, in extreme cases, in 1950. The water has got into the eccentricity in great quantity, but eccentricity is what it still is.

In the American vulgate, eccentricity is referred to as "an act," and the ordinary American is correct when he accuses the English of acting. He is wrong, though, when he thinks they act knowingly or maliciously; the acting is compensatory reflex, covering up the inner sense of inadequacy, as compulsive a disguise as that of the clown in his own high school class.

(A cultivated and clever American woman of my acquaintance, whose English husband died recently, has given me an illuminating personal view of this aspect of eccentricity as seen from close range: "The first impression I had of social England was that they were all theater people — you know how theater people in America twenty years ago had apartments in New York and places in the country near . . . oh, New Hope, Pennsylvania . . . and they were both filled with photographs in silver frames and second-class French period furniture and slightly frayed rugs and quite faded chintz and dogs and the women used a lot of lipstick and wore sweaters and smoked in a dramatic way and snapped out conversation like dialogue, in husky voices? They sat in the chairs in the sitting room — the ones with the very faded chintz — and held a dog or a cat, or had one on the floor near them, and wore rather tight sweaters, and the cigarette smoke was everywhere and their faces were pale, which accentuated the startling red of their mouths, and they ground out the cigarettes in the overflowing ashtrays — you knew the kitchen was untidy, too — and delivered all that terse dialogue, with the smoke from the last pull on the cigarette coming out with the words. Sometimes it was fun to see them doing all that. They were in the theater and how else could they have been? But no one would ever have dreamed of thinking them an American norm, not even the most unworldly American or foreign visitor. No upper-class American woman would have dared to prance around like that even if she had wanted to — her friends and her husband and her children would have made her life miserable. 'Who do you think you are, Tallulah Bankhead?' So imagine my astonishment when I came to England and was taken everywhere and found that what were supposed to be the nicest people were all what I had always called theater people. I had always heard English people were so stable, but the constant theatricality seemed frighteningly *unstable* to me. So *thin*, the chintz so *terribly* faded, the shabbiness of the theater dressing room — do you know what I mean? — in everything and everywhere. In time, I got over that, after I learned that the uncertainty under the falseness was so profound as to be a kind of dependability. I can't say that I ever got altogether used to an atmosphere where people were always playing a part, but I was very much in love with Roger — I was so sure he was different — and now . . . I just don't know. Isn't that awful? I was so sure at the time, and now I just don't know. Anyhow, I was sure then, and so the rest didn't make all that much difference. But I couldn't live in England after he died.")

Thus the lower-class assumption of long hair and exotic if shabby clothes is really no more than just another act. Perhaps the final act, but not out of the mainstream of English history. All other Englishmen have had their acts, the melancholy Three Stooges faces seem to say, so it's our turn now.

If all acts are pathetic (and pathetic in all details — faces, teeth, clothes, everything), then the latest English act — that of the lower classes — is no more (or less) pathetic than any other. They may well claim to be the final eccentrics, the last word in an English characteristic so strong that it can stand for English history in and of itself.

Students of English life have known for the past thirty years that the decay and collapse of the English caste system (if it ever comes!) might well result in the absorption of all castes into one caste. In polarized prediction, that would mean the entire country ultimately speaking either Cockney or Oxford English. In practical terms, it was agreed that the suburban twang of the middle class would triumph in typical English compromise. But now that is not at all certain. The lower class may well inhale the rest.

But no matter which class absorbs the others, eccentricity itself is the final victor. Whether in its own name or in any of the aliases to which it is entitled — immaturity, the revelation of something missing, the English silliness, primitiveness — it has overwhelmed England in a way that would have amazed even Adams. It is pallid, but it is everywhere. Generations of the downtrodden looking up at superior castes evidently decided that if they ever got "a bit" of freedom and movement, they would have their own "go" at that eccentricity that looked so tempting from below, and so it is only a watered-down continuation of all that has gone before.

It is claimed, and with good reason, that eccentricity harms no one except the eccentric. (It is a symptom of harm already done, "harm past," as Eliot would have put it, "rather than harm present.") Englishmen and visitors alike are free to wander through the strongholds of eccentricity without fear of muscular proselytism, which would be the case in America if eccentricity became the order of the day. In general terms, it is only harmful to England to the degree that England is a commercial entity, to the extent that she wishes to compete with America in the business world and can't. In Adams's day, the English aristocrat who couldn't get immediate respect and obedience from his own people (or from Americans) on the basis of his position was helpless. He had no further attributes to call on in enforcing his will, and ended up being laughed at. Today, all England is equally helpless because the eccentricity of the average man has been substituted for the aristocrat's former position. If an American will not be dominated by muttonchop whiskers and stammers (and what American could even if he wanted to be!?), then there is nothing else to throw in. Democratic eccentricity, the thinnest of defense lines, has been breached so often that it no longer exists as a pertinent weapon; it is only personal now.

English emotionalism is another child of English primitiveness and is also found everywhere. One may go so far as to conclude that all English actions require an emotional basis. In war, this is efficient, and for hundreds of years the English were unbeatable because of the depth of the emotional taproot on which the state depended. In peace, however, and especially in business, it is a drawback.

This weakness is epitomized in the insistence on the monarchy. ("As embarrassing to us as the Negroes are to you," said Ladrick. "We can't get rid of it, and it won't go away.") The mere existence of the British monarchy in 1968 implies the needed satisfaction of a primitive emotion, for the monarchy is not superimposed from above, but remains because the people demand it. It is a reminder that, as is the case with many primitive peoples, the English do not find their lives altogether possible, and must live vicariously through others in order to keep going. Americanization is shifting the focus of the vicariousness (the Kennedys, as Karl Meyer pointed out, run the Queen a very close second), but not diminishing its intensity a jot. Although the monarchies in other North Sea countries — Holland, Denmark, and Norway, for example — are indicative of similar weaknesses, there is an immense difference in degree. In England, the demand for vicarious living is infinitely greater, and is compounded with envy and a sense of incompleteness one does not find in Scandinavia, where the monarchies are commonly treated as only Graustarkian. Also, it is the size and pretension of England, in comparison to the smaller countries, that make its monarchy not only more atavistic but also more burdensome. Its large public moments — such as the investiture of Prince Charles as Prince of Wales in Caernarvon, where rooms with a view rented for over two thousand dollars for the day, and single windows for over five hundred — are too revealing in their delineation of the English people to be anything but deleterious for the country's reputation as a twentieth-century technological power. In England's present economic situation, the continued insistence on maintaining the monarchy as an indispensable diversion can only exacerbate the already strained relations she has with world business and finance.

Examples of emotionalism less obvious than the monarchy often give a greater understanding of its extent and depth. What American has not been subjected to the sudden rush of excited hero worship — the maundering, sentimental panegyrics to Jowett's scholarship, to "Max's" parodies, to the single-minded gallantries of Robert Scott, George Mallory and Howard Carter. For the written record, consider the *Encyclopaedia Britannica* (1966 edition) article on William Gladstone by Michael Foot, a former lecturer on politics at Oxford and the author of several historical critiques. Surely an educated man by definition, and yet his considered appraisal of Gladstone borders on the hysterical nonsense one finds in the British popular press:

"[He was] the greatest British statesman of the nineteenth century . . . As he grew older his face grew more formidable, with deep lines from beside the nostrils to the corners of the mouth . . . None who saw it soon forgot the flash of his dark eyes. . . . His truly extraordinary vigor far exceeded that of other men, and was coupled with no less extraordinary powers of self-control and an iron devotion to duty. . . . It was a simple sense of duty that took him into politics, a career . . . for which he was in some ways unfitted, not least by his tendency to believe that other men's motives were invariably as disinterested as his own . . . Political courage and personal magnanimity he had in abundance, and he was the most efficient administrator of his age. . . . He was combative by instinct, and combined a magical quickness of understanding with an unusually retentive memory and an inexhaustible fund of phrase; these qualities made him a fearsome adversary in debate. . . . Lord Acton . . . assessing for Gladstone's daughter in 1879 her father's standing among the world's statesmen of the past two centuries, concluded that 'in the three elements of greatness combined — the man, the power and the result — character, genius and success — none reached his level.'"

It is a boy's picture — the simple sense of duty, the fearsome flash of the dark eye, the slashing debater — and the qualities are those a boy attributes to his school's athletic hero. They can have no connection with a real man, much less with a real politician. No one would dare impute them to Lincoln, surely Gladstone's acknowledged superior in any conceivable comparison, or even to Churchill.

Contrast Foot's view with Adams's. On October 7, 1862, *after* the news of Antietam and Lee's retreat into Virginia had reached London, Gladstone made a speech in which he treated intervention on the side of the Confederacy as a *fait accompli*. "As Chancellor of the Exchequer, he was the Minister most interested in knowing that Palmerston, Russell, and himself were banded together by mutual pledge to make the Confederacy a nation the next week, and that the Southern leaders had as yet no hope of 'making a nation' [Gladstone had just made a speech claiming they had done exactly that] but in them. . . . Never in the history of political turpitude has any brigand of modern civilization offered a worse example. The proof of it was that it outraged even Palmerston, who immediately put up Sir George Cornewall Lewis to repudiate [Gladstone], against whom he turned his press at the same time. Palmerston had no notion of letting his hand be forced by Gladstone."

In the final cabinet fight over intervention, on November 11, 1862, Gladstone held out to the end for it, and also for a secret agreement with Napoleon III giving France a free hand in Mexico in return for *his* giving England an equally free hand in North America, and only quit when he found himself alone. Not even Palmerston and Russell would go so far. Adams was not to know this until Gladstone's own report of the meeting was published, many years later. At the time, he was ignorant. "The young student of diplomacy . . . knowing Gladstone and his lofty principles . . . would not doubt that Gladstone had violently denounced the scheme . . . [but he was to discover that] the only resolute, vehement, conscientious champion of Russell, Napoleon, and Jefferson Davis was Gladstone."

Years later, according to Adams, Gladstone confessed that his speech on the Confederacy had been a mistake: "I have yet to record an undoubted error. . . . I declared in the heat of the American struggle that Jefferson Davis had made a nation. . . . Strange to say, this declaration, most unwarrantable to be made by a Minister of the Crown with no authority other than his own, was not due to any feeling of partisanship for the South or hostility to the North. . . . I really, though most strangely, believed it was an act of friendliness to all America to recognize that the struggle was virtually at an end. . . . I did not perceive the gross impropriety of such an utterance from a Cabinet Minister of a power . . . bound to loyal neutrality. . . . My offense was indeed only a mistake, but one of incredible grossness . . ."

Adams's comments: "He [Adams] noted, without irritation, that Gladstone, in his confession, had not alluded to the understanding between Russell, Palmerston and himself; had even wholly left out his most 'incredible' act, his ardent support of Napoleon's policy, a policy which even Palmerston and Russell had supported feebly . . . but while Gladstone threw himself on the mercy of the public for his speech, he attempted no excuse for Lord Russell, who led him into the 'incredible grossness' of announcing the Foreign Secretary's intent. . . . 'I really, though most strangely, believed that it was an act of friendliness.' Whatever absurdity Gladstone supposed, Russell supposed nothing of the sort. Neither he nor Palmerston 'most strangely believed' in any proposition so obviously and palpably absurd, nor did Napoleon delude himself with philanthropy. Gladstone, even in his confession, mixed up policy, speech, motives, and persons, as though he were trying to confuse chiefly himself.

". . . granting in short what the English themselves seemed at last to conclude — that Gladstone was not quite sane . . . Their [Russell's and Palmerston's] senility was congenital, like Gladstone's Oxford training and High Church illusions, which caused wild eccentricities in his judgment . . . 'furiously earnest,' as Monckton Milnes said, 'on both sides of every question.'"

One need say no more than that Adams's is a different Gladstone.

It doesn't matter, really, whether it is the true Gladstone — the point is that it is an appraisal backed up by Adams's own authority as an observer and participant in the intervention question, by the authority of Gladstone's own "confession," by the claim that English public opinion at the time held Gladstone "not quite sane," and by Milnes's remark, very likely the most damning evidence of all. A considered appraisal backed with such weight can only be refuted with an equally considered appraisal backed with evidence of equal weight. Otherwise it stands, despite endless huffing and puffing on a lesser (boyish, or ill-considered and unbacked) level. The English inability to understand that the emotional counts for nothing in the long run is a fateful handicap. General English education is still based on textbooks and opinions that cling to the boyish view, the *England Über Alles* view of British history that is so contradicted by current revelations and events. Young Englishmen going into the world find such disparity between what they have been taught and the reality they must live with that they tend to distrust everything English from then on. They don't believe the cant, but they continue to parrot it, thus making themselves miserable as well as inefficient.

Strength seems to lie not in national hysteria and over-evaluation, but in just the opposite. No educated American would be so rash as to write of Daniel Webster (a fair counterpart to Gladstone, with many of the latter's specific weaknesses) as Mr. Foot has written of Gladstone. On the contrary, Webster is today regarded as more of a joke than he deserves to be. (He was a joke to Adams, too, but a subtle joke whose accomplishments had to be admitted along with his foolishnesses to get the full flavor.) The American lack of emotionalism has its drawbacks — a tendency to social barrenness, for one — but England's surfeit of it forever prevents the emergence of a competitive national intelligence.

In rebuttal, it may be pointed out that English debunkers like Lytton Strachey were certainly hard on sacred figures, but to the American such criticism is still boyish rather than considered. It is not flat and direct; it does not dispose of the subject for once and for all; it does not treat men and events in a way that claims authority until put down by equal authority. It actually prolongs debate, and opens the door to more discussion based on opinion. It is doubtful, for example, that Adams would ever have written a line about Gladstone, the Civil War or anything else unless he had been certain he was an authority on the subject — and then, one of only three or four — by virtue of possessing knowledge no one else had. He was not, in short, offering cheap opinion but extremely valuable information. The distinction is a difficult one for Englishmen to make, because the few who have firsthand information can't evaluate it because evaluation goes against their training. Put more crudely, they can't evaluate because evaluation is impossible to immature people.

So boyish opinion, pro and con, keeps rolling out by the carload. One has only to read what Churchill wrote and what was written for and against him to appreciate the paralyzing evenness of the product.

Even Englishmen of unquestioned genius reveal emotionalism under strain. In his novels, E. M. Forster is a master of objective situational and individual evaluation; but in *Two Cheers for Democracy* (the very title a return to childhood), he becomes shrill and shallow. Max Beerbohm had a lesser talent but kept it so rigidly under control that there was genius in the discipline if not quite in the work itself. But World War II brought out the inevitable lapse — his famous broadcasts from London were blatant sentimentality from a man who made his reputation puncturing just such silliness on the part of others. Such recidivism becomes even more striking when we conjure up comparable activity from men of genius of other cultures — Stendhal slobbering about French gallantry on the retreat from Moscow, Tolstoi mooning over the czar's "courage," and so on. If they had been English, they certainly would have. Just as, if Lytton Strachey had lived to see World War II, it is improbable that he could have resisted the urge to write eulogies of Churchill, Montgomery and the royal family as gushing as any he demolished in *Eminent Victorians* about "Chinese" Gordon, Matthew Arnold, Cardinal Manning and Florence Nightingale, and in *Queen Victoria* about that monarch. It is also quite possible that after the war he would have believed in a new "Elizabethan Age" by fiat, and in the superior efficiency of planes named after famous figures in English history — more stable, if also more anonymous, men than he made that mistake.

It is true that Americans are far from devoid of emotionalism. But in the pinch it is usually put down by the unemotional. In England there is no such safeguard. Also, as noted in the cases of Forster and Beerbohm and the hypothetical Strachey given above, there is a very curious English belief that succumbing to emotionalism under strain — war is the definitive instance — does not count. And that a man has the right — if not the obligation! — to assume the same sentimentality in later life that he scorned in older men when he was middle-aged. Americans suffer from these very human inconsistencies, too, but not to the same extent and not to the same level of national detriment.

The emotionalism and primitiveness is not confined to the ruling class or the literary class or any other privileged group or combination of such groups, but embraces all Englishmen. If anything, it is stronger at the bottom than at the top, as one can learn all too quickly by reading mass circulation English newspapers. Periodicals reflect their readers with close accuracy, and the picture of the lower and middle classes that one gets from papers like the *Daily Express, Evening Standard, Daily Mail, Daily Mirror, Daily Herald,* and *Evening News* (combined daily circulation of over 11,000,000 in a country of less than 50,000,000) taxes the imagination.

In these papers, the news of the day is sifted to find the English angle, which is then transmitted via a badly written, disorganized, inverted basic English washed through with gross sentimentality, adulation (overt and implied) of the royal family and aristocracy, and a special brand of British coyness. Everything else is omitted or subordinated to the vanishing point. The result is the thinnest of gruels — Twain would have called it "a grueled gruel" — a patronizing, insulting, drugged treacle that no race except the English could accept. It is frankly designed to pander to British weaknesses, and its cumulative effect is to undermine the intelligence and character of a people already dangerously deficient in those categories.

The writing is also deliberately bellicose, working in a rather sinister fashion on the British passion for violence and keeping the susceptible reader in a state of constant agitation. (Many of the techniques employed are described, in an entirely different context, in Dr. Eric Berne's *Games People Play*. The essential point of all such games — to excite and alarm others into a malleable state — is the same, carried out on a massive scale.) That passion used to be formally and legally indulged through large-scale wars; now it can only be served vicariously through the press reports. The material is eclectic — troubles in Aden, British subjects detained and imprisoned in foreign lands, racial and civil disorders in the United States and South Africa, and so on — but the inflammatory style is always at white heat.

(In the United States, only a few large dailies — the New York *Daily News* is the best example — follow this format, and at the most have a combined circulation of not more than 5,000,000 in a country of nearly 200,000,000 — a one to forty sales-population ratio in comparison to England's one to five. Also, the American counterparts are generally irreverent and often amusing, and, except for the bellicosity, are not truly the same on the other counts. There are no Suzy Knickerbockers in the English popular press, and not even any Walter Winchells.)

The prestigious English national papers — *The Times, Daily Telegraph* and *Guardian* (combined daily circulation less than 2,000,000) — are by no means free of omissions and distortions. Under the surface resemblances to the best American and European papers lurk strong responses to the emotional magnets; and careful readings reveal just as much inner excitement behind the elegant writing. In addition, there is the chronic addiction to reportage as opinion inviting more opinion: the heart of any controversial occurrence is always avoided because that would close it. This idiosyncratic prolongation nurtures a latent tendency to the same inconclusive attenuation among the readers of the best papers and further thins out an already alarmingly small group.

The United States, the new and diabolically mixed focus of British emotional life, naturally drives British commentators to extremes in all departments, as Bernard Levin pointed out in discussing the coverage of the 1968 Presidential election (*International Herald-Tribune*, October 1, 1968): "Once every four years (and at bad times in between) I get uncomfortably close to the conviction that the only qualification essential for a journalist who wants to write in a British newspaper about events in the United States is a total ignorance of America, preferably combined with a hatred of its way of life, an ineradicable envy of its prosperity and a bitter resentment of the knowledge that the life and freedom of every person in this country has depended for over 20 years on the willingness of the United States to defend us. . . . All of which really amounts only to a bit of friendly advice to Americans not to take too much notice of what they read in Britain about their country, and not to waste their time replying angrily that no reputable and serious American paper or television concern would dream of taking sides in a British election in the way in which so many British ones have been campaigning in the American one. 'We are,' said Harold Macmillan once in a moment of aberration, 'the Greeks in the Roman Empire.' Alas, we are not; these days we are only the ancient Britons, capering around naked except for the woad and not above telling Julius Caesar how to fight."

(One may well wonder whether Mr. Levin has not implied more than he intended. The English must maintain a fantastic picture of America because they must maintain a fantastic picture of themselves. England has never been able to see that America was and is the new thing — and thus technically beyond their comprehension and criticism — because that would automatically make England the old thing, and no country has ever been capable of such acid self-appraisal. When America's turn comes, it will show an equal appetite for fantasia, but its turn is not as yet and so the English have no choice, in purely human terms, but to go on pretending. This does not mean, of course, that the continued pretense is not a severe handicap, with the severity assured of increase because the handicap cannot be overcome. And so the prosaic facts — among them that American Negroes have an appreciably higher per capita income than Englishmen — will continue to be avoided.)

In sum, there is no press in the world as far down, and if the state of a national press reflects the state of national readership — and there is no reason to suppose it does not — there is no other nation as far down. The oft-criticized Communist press is supposed to be rigidly censored, but the remaining material is treated in a straightforward if dull style. In England, what is left after the censorship (esthetic rather than political, but, if anything, more stringent) is turned into excited babytalk. Also, Communist censorship is admitted in one way or another by Communist readers and appropriate allowance is made for it: but the English believe themselves to be marvelously well-informed — better so than any other people — which makes the reality that much more devastating.

Keeping the people tame by keeping everything from them is not, it should be emphasized, a plan originated from above. It is the people themselves who demand that treatment, and the newspapermen who want to keep their jobs soon learn how to administer it. In the innermost circles of the ruling class there is a faint, rather ugly suggestion of an awareness of deliberate manipulation, but more to ensure the survival of that class than to gratify a mere sadistic appetite. Those at the top want to stay there, as they do everywhere, and they are concerned lest the complete Americanization of England means they won't be necessary in the future. In traditional fashion, they are trying to work out a compromise whereby it will be America *and* the Queen *and* themselves. Hence the continuous propaganda for the ancient titillations.

The result is actually a closed state, and produces the marked limitations — in degree if not in form — common to any other closed state. No Englishman, for example, is really equipped to discuss the heart of any English social phenomenon, as those foreigners learn who ask for an explanation of the *why* of any class or institution. The faculty of social analysis has been stunted. And other faculties, on which other key functions depend, are similarly stunted. The consequences for a commercially ambitious state are . . . what they are.

In writing about France, Servan-Schreiber quotes Jacques Maisonrouge, the former French president of IBM-Europe, in a statement which is also apposite for England: "The French student, obliged to study very hard but in a very limited area in order to pass his exams or win his prizes . . . doesn't have the time to really think, and one is often astonished to see that this student, who reasons so well, has difficulty with practical problems of which he can't often understand the implications." The same thing could be said about the English student — indeed, in any discussion of American colonization, this comment should be kept constantly in mind as a prime factor for all Europe. It implies comparison with the American student, often woefully uneducated in terms of general cultivation as compared with his European counterpart, but well ahead in applied common sense. ("Splendidly automated and programmed," as Ladrick put it.) It is a common sense grounded on constant exposure to all the winds of a grotesquely open society. Without such exposure (and, very likely, such openness), the commonsense functions become stunted and even completely atrophied; and although a closed society can be more pleasant to live in, it cannot compete with America once those basic functions fall behind.

The lesson would seem to be that while a man can be emotional as well as highly cultivated, he can't let either characteristic — but especially his emotions — interfere with his common sense if he wishes to understand the "implications . . . of practical problems." To understand the practical he must *be* practical, and severely eschew emotionalism.

Such a lesson has never penetrated the fixed thought of those in England who do wish to challenge the American hegemony. They themselves are too emotional to see that it is the emotional that would have to go. The emotional and the immature and the primitive and the retarded. The problem is one of heredity and environment and education — far beyond the tiny area of hopeful "determination" by the present generation of Englishmen. It would necessitate the remaking of a people from the cradle — if not before! — a task so formidable as to seem impossible even to those few who might understand what was being asked.

It is this shadow of impossibility, I think, that is one's strongest general impression of modern England. One reaches it slowly and reluctantly, at the end of long and arduous investigation into what seemed at first a simple, mechanical question: why is there American influence in England? In the beginning, one was sure the answer had to lie around definite American strengths; but gradually one's eyes opened to English weaknesses as the root cause; and finally one stands awed at the effort required to exorcize those weaknesses, and the shadow of impossibility lengthens against one's personal wish that it could be otherwise.

Looking into the past for a hint of prescience, one discovers that many Englishmen of genius saw what was coming. Especially in English literature, where generations of writers as diverse as Blake, Byron, Shelley, Hardy, Butler, Lawrence, and Shaw have warned of a continuation of their present into a future. Either England would grow up, they said, or it would go down. England chose not to grow up, and Lawrence wrote the final account of that negation when he said: "Ours is a tragic age, but we refuse to be tragic about it." That was forty years ago, and so the tragedy is not recent and the shadow of impossibility does not itself seem so suddenly arrived as to be truly tragic. Pathetic, yes, but not tragic. It is pathetic, for example, that the "angry" generation in England tries to be different and ends up in the same grooves: but it is not tragic, because that generation was born to a level already depreciated; it did not fall. Put in terms of people, even Gladstone had more potential than Harold Wilson and Ted Heath; and Tennyson more than John Osborne and John Lennon.

In 1880, there was still latitude and room for movement, but from then on the noose tightened with dramatic speed. Less than fifty years later, T. S. Eliot had published *The Waste Land* and England had an epitaph, carved out, fittingly enough, by an American. ("Never forget that the poem is about England," an American critic has pointed out to me. "We'd like to think it refers to the whole world, and particularly the western world, but the emphasis and imagery are all on and about England. Those thousand lost golf balls were lost *there*, and the city that is celebrated as a symbol of paralysis is London.") The serious prophets of doom had written better than they knew, and were borne out in a way that would have been as distressing to them, had they lived to see it, as to anyone else.

If the feeling of the presence of the shadow of impossibility were only personal, one could afford to ignore it, but one finds in conversation with all American and most other foreign visitors to England that they, too, feel the same presence. Even the average tourists and businessmen come to the unhappy realization that there is, in their words, "something finished . . . something *over*" in the atmosphere. The ordinary visitor doesn't want to think such unpleasant thoughts — all he wants to do is enjoy himself and/or sell a few Hula-Hoops. He is, in fact, incapable of inventing such notions; they are forced into his consciousness by England and the English. It is they, alas, who scream inaudibly that the case is closed and that there is no point in going on, at least in the old way. They say it with their eyes, with their movements, with the set of their bodies and the tone of their voices — in every way except in so many words, and not even the most insensitive American can fail to get the message.

"You see those rows of chimneys in the cities like Liverpool, and you know that the only way this country could get modern would be to tear it down and start all over again," an American union official said to me after a three-month tour of industrial England. "Don't get me wrong — I like the place, and the people. But there's just no way they could get the *room* to make it modern without tearing it down. They live such . . . cramped lives in those little houses where they're all jammed together, they just can't *think* in modern terms."

The more I myself think of it, the more I recall Ladrick's references to Rimbaud, which I thought strained at the time but which seem quite unexaggerated now. If Rimbaud is known for seeing civilization as catastrophe, then England is Rimbaudesque. If Rimbaudesque also brings to mind nightmares, hallucinations, dissonances, the "it can't be happening" quality of unpleasant dreams, and so on, then England continues to qualify for the adjective on all counts. The melancholy is thick; the paralysis contagious; even the weather, in the summer of 1968, is the worst in memory or in the weather bureau records.

It is not a pretty picture, but it is even less attractive if unspoken; and if that were the only reason for being frank about it, one cannot avoid conceding that it is a sufficient one.

4

THERE is no reason to presume that the present English weaknesses are of recent origin. They are more likely of long standing, and existed in the days of success as well as today. Weaknesses do not prevent worldly success any more than they guarantee failure — the pendulum can and does swing through both.

England moved into an important place in Europe under Elizabeth I, and became the most influential and powerful of all European countries with the defeat of Napoleon, a little over two hundred years later. She held this position officially until the end of World War I, about one hundred years. In that century, the most powerful country in Europe was the most powerful country in the world, and England was magnified many times over in her empire.

Thus the past four hundred years of English history have been primarily capitalistic, and have seen the rise, crest and fall of England as a world leader. America has played a crucial part in English history for the last two hundred of those years or roughly half the span. In Part I, certain aspects of that presence were discussed in detail: Henry Adams's claims that his ancestors (and hence American foreign policy) had always had "the object of bringing England into an American system," and that the culmination of this work constituted "true empire-building," and that the American revolutionaries were well aware that after putting England into an American system they had to put the rest of the world into the same system in order to preserve what they had already won; and the surrender of the English aristocracy to American money and American ways just after the Civil War. In addition, as shall be seen, there was the inability of the English, the first Baconists, to keep that pre-eminence in the teeth of superior American Baconism.

In order to defeat England in the Revolution, the American leaders had to know England and Englishmen to the core. They had to be familiar with each and every weakness already cited, and they had to be clever enough to circumvent each and every one. In those days — and until very recently, in fact — the English ruling class waited, in any contest with another power, for the incident that could be turned into "outrage" and waved before the general populace. Once aroused, the English people were as solid and irresistible as ants, but they could only be so aroused through emotional (primitive) excitement, a fact the ruling class was quite well aware of. And knew quite well how to engineer once the pretext was available, as the French and Germans and other English foes discovered to their regret.

The colonists' only hope of winning was to get England to quit; they had not a chance in the field if they stirred up the full wrath of England against themselves. They had to make the war so dull, damp it down so far, muffle it so effectively, that the average Englishman could not excite himself or be excited about it, and would finally say: Let's stop.

The entire American campaign was grounded on a wager that the Americans knew the British character better than the British did (and immeasurably better than the British knew the American character) and could use that knowledge to maneuver the British as they wished. The wager was won so decisively that the Americans themselves were surprised at how accurate they had been. The English, of course, never suspected that they had been so predictable and predicted. They were aware they had been outmaneuvered, even beaten, but they never knew how it had been done.

When David outfoxes Goliath, he does more than win in a single time and place; he gains a permanent psychological advantage. Since 1783, all Englishmen have unconsciously felt themselves inferior to Americans in the generic, national sense (often to the exact degree that they consciously and honestly claim the contrary), and many have extended it, again unconsciously, to include themselves as individuals. After the Revolution, this feeling increased slowly but perceptibly until the Civil War, which gave it marked impetus.

(Adams's account of the Union diplomatic victory in London — peripherally referred to in previous quotations in this section — is one of the clearest and most engrossing stories of psychological warfare ever written. The English and American temperaments met in full, unrestrained clash — the English determined to support the Confederacy and thus divide and wreck the Union, and the Union determined to see that support as an act of war. Speaking and acting for England were Palmerston, the prime minister, and Russell, the foreign secretary. For the United States, Charles Francis Adams, the American minister in London (to whom his son, Henry, was private secretary), behind whom stood Seward, the secretary of state, and Lincoln himself. Behind Lincoln was the seasoned and formidable Union Army — this was September, 1863, two months after Gettysburg and Vicksburg — now the strongest in the world. If the ironclads were allowed to go from Liverpool to the Confederacy, wrote Minister Adams to Russell on September 5, 1863, the Union would have to believe it was done with the connivance of the British government. The letter closed by saying: "It would be superfluous in me to point out to your lordship that this is war!" Russell backed down; the South never got the ironclads. He had, according to Adams, "met wills stronger than his own, and, after persevering to the last possible instant, had been beaten. Lord North and George Canning had a like experience." It might be said that Russell backed down because of the Union Army: even with English help it was doubtful that the South could overcome such a force, and as a formal ally of that beaten South, England could expect to see Canada overrun by the Union in short order. But it is more probable that his reasons were purely psychological.)

After the Civil War, as has been pointed out, the British aristocracy gave up any hope of overcoming Americans and accepted the inevitable alternative: the Americans would overcome them. The surrender had elements of betrayal and dishonor (the continuing pretense to other, lesser castes that the opposite was the case), but these were so familiar to those betrayed as not to seem actual except technically.

The situation was not all that apparent, either. In 1865, the British Empire was approaching its zenith, a sprawling giant that demanded full attention from its operators. The American ascendancy, although fastened on a vital part of English life, was a frail and secret fact that might or might not be strong enough to persevere and grow. But by the end of the century it was increasingly in the open. In *The Wings of the Dove* (1902), Henry James, whose monumental work can be viewed as the story of European collapse and American takeover selectively refined into lasting art, is explicit: every major English character in the novel is an adventurer in search of money. It doesn't matter whether they have nothing (Lionel Croy) or a good deal (Mrs. Lowder and Lord Mark) or something in between (Kate Croy and Merton Densher) — they all feel they don't have enough. Millie Theale, the American heiress, has more than enough, and from the moment she arrives in London they are all after her like kites.

This was the turn of the century, the presumed pinnacle of British wealth and power, but the English are all represented as poor and grasping, a portrait which no one, to my knowledge, either British or American, has ever contradicted. It is significant that the portrait was executed by an American, and that in all British literature there does not exist such a study of a profoundly ubiquitous national characteristic. (It is equally significant, of course, that British literature has never produced an accurate portrait of an upper-class American. Americans can see the British whole — as in the English characters in Hemingway and Fitzgerald, to cite further literary support — but not the other way round, yet another American advantage when carried into commerce.)

Kate Croy is not a caricature from Thackeray or Dickens, but a beautiful and gifted woman who, notwithstanding what she has, can't resist reaching for Milly's money through her lover. It is the airiness of that money of Milly's, its unreality to Milly herself, that make Kate and her aunt reach for it. Milly has transcended money — even her poor American traveling companion, Mrs. Stringham, has gone beyond it in a way — but the English who are drawn to Milly have not. They cannot. The ancient materialism will not permit money to lie loose like that; they must reach for it because there is nothing else in life, under the elaborate pretense to the contrary, except money. And there is never, never enough. In the beginning of the book, Lionel Croy, Kate's father, is presented as an overt rascal, and Kate and the others as contemptuous of his utter lack of scruples; by the end, they have joined him. He didn't have enough because he had nothing; they don't have enough because there is nothing else. It is a marvelously done fable, but still as much of science as of art, as is demonstrated by the increase in the English certainty of "never enough" from that day to this. Ladrick even used the phrase in relation to the Grandells — Hugh, the colonel, a distant cousin, and Jennifer, his wife, the proper English matron who was so anxious to get to the American PX. "If they could only be content with what they have," Ladrick said. "But they can't — no matter how much there is, there's never enough. There never is for any Englishman. Never enough to stop wanting *things*, to go on to some other side of life. So sad, but that's the way it is."

Since World War I, the American opposition to England has declined in force simply because it is no longer necessary. After 1918, England was beaten; the opposition had served its purpose. The Englishman was no longer an equal; there was no point in fighting him. The new attitude would be quite different: the correct American would help the Englishman back on his feet by helping him become an American, the only way any proper American could think of to help friend or (former) enemy.

As has been noted, this Samaritanism was not altogether disinterested. World War I cracked English faith in England and produced an economic-cultural vacuum into which some other financial system and some other culture were bound to be drawn. By making themselves available, Americans made sure that no other system or idea would pick up such a plum.

Returning to the opposition itself, one can hardly resist asking what it came from. Everything else came from *it*, right down to the blue jeans on the latest Hayley Mills, and if one knew what it came from one would know all. The answer seems permanently elusive. The New World colonists became different, too different to answer the commands of English blood, the orders that came from home. And the difference made them resist, oppose and fight everything English until they had very nearly wiped their forebears from the face of the earth. That much is known. But the rest — the why and the how — remains mysterious. Even Adams can cast little light, although, characteristically, he comes closer than anyone else, as in this description of a trip back to America on the *Teutonic*, in 1892:

"Fate was kind on that voyage. Rudyard Kipling, on his wedding trip to America, thanks to the mediation of Henry James, dashed over the passenger his exuberant fountain of gaiety and wit — as though playing a garden hose on a thirsty and faded begonia. Kipling could never know what peace of mind he gave, for he could hardly ever need it himself so much; and yet, in the full delight of his endless fun and variety, one felt the old conundrum repeat itself. Somehow, somewhere, Kipling and the American were not one, but two, and could not be glued together. The American felt that the defect, if defect it were, was in himself; he had felt it when he was with Swinburne, and, again, with Robert Louis Stevenson, even under the palms of Vailima; but he did not carry self-abasement to the point of thinking himself singular. Whatever the defect might be, it was American; it belonged to the type; it lived in the blood. Whatever the quality that held him apart, it was English; it lived also in the blood; one felt it little, if at all, with Celts, and one yearned reciprocally among Fiji cannibals. Clarence King used to say that it was due to discord among the wave-lengths of the man-atoms; but the theory offered difficulties in measurement." ("Even when your point of view is the same, it is difficult to share it," an American journalist claims. "Even with a man like Malcolm Muggeridge, whom I admire tremendously, there is, I find, a final difference. You try, and they try, but there's a final barrier — a final atavism in them, I'm afraid — that neither side can break through.")

It may be that a century or two in the American wilderness had produced, by 1775, the advance on English immaturity that Shaw had pleaded for. Not, of course, the completed advance (or anything near it!), but a partial, even tiny step forward in a situation where an inch was to be as effective as a mile. The Elizabethan Englishman was a slave; the Englishman of George III was little better. Feudalism had evolved into a crude capitalism, but the mentality of the average Englishman was the same. He needed masters. He demanded them. The American of 1775 had taken another turning; he would not be that sort of slave. If we are all slaves in one way or another, he would be a slave in a way of his own making, but he was through with English slavery. The English themselves, though, were very far from through with it. Even in the palmiest days of the Empire, their slavery — the slavery that rests on the enslaved, that depends on the slave sincerely believing he is inferior to other men of his blood — flourished. It flourishes today, although it is weakened, unspoken and complicated. It has always been most apparent in its symptoms, like snobbism, but the symptoms give no real appreciation of the tenacity and depth of the weakness itself. The transference from a slavery to a tangible English ruling class to a slavery to an intangible American idea has not changed the English passion for slavery to *something*. That passion made them slaves to each other even as they conquered the world; today it is the basis of their prime ranking as colonizees. "Someone," Frank said with heavy contempt, "is always going to be on top of them."

(This characteristic of not being able to go against authority or give up respectability is nowhere better described than in George Orwell's *Down and Out in Paris and London,* not even in Dickens. His record of the docility of starving English tramps in the early 1930s lights up the historic inability of Englishmen to turn against or even criticize any sort of inhumane treatment from above. Orwell lived as a tramp himself and spoke from experience when setting down such incidents and comments:

"After dinner the cook set me to do the washing up, and told me to throw away the food that remained. The wastage was astonishing and, in the circumstances, appalling. Half-eaten joints of meat, and bucketfuls of broken bread and vegetables, were pitched away like so much rubbish . . . I filled five dustbins to overflowing with quite eatable food. And while I did so fifty tramps were sitting in the spike [the jail-like building where tramps were locked for the night or the weekend in return for charity meals] with their bellies half filled by the spike dinner of bread and cheese, and perhaps two boiled potatoes each in honor of Sunday. According to the paupers [he had been sent over from the spike to assist in the neighboring workhouse kitchen] the food was thrown away from deliberate policy, rather than it should be given to the tramps. At three I went back to the spike. The tramps had been sitting there since eight, with hardly room to move an elbow, and they were now half mad with boredom. . . . To pass the time away I talked with a rather superior tramp, a young carpenter who wore a collar and tie and was on the road, he said, for lack of a set of tools. . . . He criticised the system that makes a tramp spend fourteen hours a day in the spike, and the other ten in walking and dodging the police. He spoke of his own case — six months at the public charge for want of a few pounds' worth of tools. It was idiotic, he said.

"Then I told him about the wastage of food in the workhouse kitchen, and what I thought of it. And at that he changed his tone instantly. I saw that I had awakened the pew-renter who sleeps in every English workman. Though he had been famished along with the others, he at once saw reasons why the food should have been thrown away rather than given to the tramps. He admonished me quite severely.

" 'They have to do it,' he said. 'If they made these places too comfortable, you'd have all the scum of the country flocking into them. It's only the bad food as keeps all that scum away. These here tramps are all too lazy to work, that's all that's wrong with them. You don't want to go encouraging of them. They're scum.'

"I produced arguments to prove him wrong, but he would not listen. He kept repeating:

" 'You don't want to have any pity on these here tramps — scum, they are. You don't want to judge them by the same standards as men like you and me. They're scum, just scum.'

"It was interesting to see the subtle way in which he dissassociated himself from 'these here tramps.' He had been on the road six months, but in the sight of God, he seemed to imply, he was not a tramp."

". . . The idea that tramps are impudent social parasites . . . is not absolutely unfounded, but it is true only in a few per cent of the cases. Deliberate, cynical parasitism, such as one reads of in Jack London's books on American tramping, is not in the English character. The English are a conscience-ridden race, with a strong sense of the sinfulness of poverty. One cannot imagine the average Englishman deliberately turning parasite, and this national characteristic does not necessarily change because a man is thrown out of work."

The craving for respectability and the inability to give up middle-class values when all connection with them is forever gone are allied to the curious aversion to resisting authority because all resistance involves "scenes" and scenes are to be avoided at all costs.

These deepseated social inhibitions have proved particularly costly to the Labor Party and the socialists in England.)

In perusing English history, one cannot avoid wondering whether cruelty and colonization (passive as well as active) are linked. Leaving aside the aggrieved complaints of Irish and Indians and other foreigners, the conduct of Englishmen toward other Englishmen from 1066 on is very nearly unique in human history. The persecutions, the barbaric executions, the heads on pikes, the taking of lives for petty thefts, the treatment of the poor and of children . . . not the most savage of Asiatic despotisms can offer such a catalogue. But even more disturbing was (and is) the bland assumption that none of it was happening, that England was the most civilized and humane country in the world. The self-delusion of the classes administering the cruelties was far beyond anything mere hypocrisy could support; and the acceptance of those cruelties by the English people could not be explained except by a slave mentality. No other people in human record ever took so much from their masters without revolting — slave is a mild word for such unquestioning acceptance.

If England was as sick as it was — presuming that sadism and masochism are sicknesses — there is a question as to whether it has ever recovered; just as, conversely, if it is in the state it is today, the question is not whether something happened, but when. Could there have been any other result? And was there ever anything else?

An American Rhodes scholar of my acquaintance has put the same questions in a youthful but interesting fashion: "If England, as a country and a people, had always been as heroic, top to bottom, as always claimed, wouldn't the heroism have produced an heroic answer to the declining fortunes? What I mean is . . . if the whole Shakespeare-Wellington-Churchill syndrome had been what it was touted as being — if there had been anybody *there* for all those years — the poverty wouldn't have meant anything when it finally came. It wouldn't have meant anything to the aristocracy (we all know that true aristocrats are notoriously unaffected by adversity) or the lower classes (yeomen never cry) or anyone in between. But it doesn't mean nothing, if you'll excuse the double negative in the interests of communication. It means everything. English life today is simply nothing and English people are washed-out ghosts of what they are supposed to be. You should see it at Oxford. They're without shame. They seem to be saying: We did it for the jam, not the glory, and if there isn't going to be any jam, we aren't going to go on doing it. See what I mean? The grace, the beauty, the *élan*, the poetry, the bravery, the genius . . . they were never there. The semblance of them was there — mostly as propaganda for impressionable and ambitious foreigners — but the qualities themselves were never real to the English themselves. They *acted* them. If they had been real rather than propaganda they couldn't be dropped now, any more than a man or woman of true dignity can lose it entirely in a prison camp. I really loved England *before* I saw it. And the English. I'm English on both sides myself, but it was more than that. But now . . . this confessing of the fraud of years, this 'truth will out' attitude they have, sneering at themselves in straight self-denigration, picking through the picked-over garbage heap, telling you with their smiles that 'Shakespeare did anything for money, too,' admitting that it was all a game and that the game is over . . . it's too much for me. I may be soft or something, but I didn't know I could be so disillusioned . . ."

An American businessman on a plane adds another echo: "What I say about the English is this. They'd be all right if they had character. All this business about two wars is a lot of hot air. Plenty of countries have had more trouble, but they got on top of it. Look at Germany! France, too. France was in two wars, too, and even though I hate de Gaulle's guts, you have to admit that he did a lot for France. France and Germany didn't have half the resources in 1946 that England did — not a quarter — and look at them now. Where was Switzerland in 1946? Tell me that. Nowhere. And look at Switzerland now — the banking center of Europe. If England had only held onto the position they had in 1946, they'd be on top of the heap in Europe. Nothing more, just held onto what they had. If they'd had character, they would have. If they'd gone further and pushed ahead as much relatively as Germany or France or Switzerland they'd still be a great power. But they have no character, so they've gone down. Whining all the way about how mean everyone is to them and how tough they've had it. But the truth is that it all comes down to a lack of character."

And a Russian journalist contributes a final interpretation: "England was never Rome. She thinks she was, but she was not. She could not look as she does if she had been. She is too mean, too cheap. The Romans were grand and indifferent . . . like the Americans. No, don't smile, I'm serious. I have been to America and I have read *Moby Dick*. At bottom, the Americans don't care if they 'make it' or not, any more than the Romans did. All they want is to live on their own terms, and if they can't have that they will quit. The English will go on with any terms."

"The Americans may, too, when the time comes."

"Don't say that." He is as intense as Evtushenko. "I cannot believe that. They will commit suicide first, like Hemingway. To them all other peoples are barbarians, as they have to be . . . so why would they wish to go on living under the thumb of barbarians? Never. England would, though, as she does. Because the others were never barbarians to her. Am I explaining? The great imperial power now licks the American hand like a dog. Ridiculous! Paugh! More wag-tail with America than little countries that never had an empire, like little Denmark. There is no grandeur in an imperialism that can descend to such levels. Nothing Roman at all."

The historical American opposition was wonderfully assisted in its object by the English inability to push Baconism to further limits. Such Baconism — a practical, simple and acquisitive applica-

tion of the master's precepts — is defined on pages 164–165 as bowing completely to the marvels of the past couple of centuries (steam
and electric and atomic power, and so on), and carrying the revealed forces to their ultimates. The English were the first Baconians and led in industrial development until the middle of the nineteenth century, after which other countries — notably Germany
and America — wrested that lead from them. The aristocrat-serf
class structure had gone as far as it could by 1850; any further
"bowing to natural marvels" would break it. The ruling class was
face to face with the papal dilemma of the sixteenth and seventeenth centuries: they couldn't bow completely to the new discov-
eries and keep society as it was. Like the Catholic Church, they
chose to try to maintain the social equilibrium; and, also like the
Church, they lost their world leadership. The Church had lost to
England as the leader of the new Protestant world; England lost to
America as the leader of the new technological world. The discov-
eries on which that world was based were so far-reaching that a
complete bow to them necessitated a completely new people; only
the Americans were willing and able to supply such a bizarre com-
modity.

(A further detail of the similarity of the English-Catholic position is worth remarking. From 1600, the new English world forced
changes in the superseded Catholic world; and from 1850, the new
American world has forced changes in the superseded English
world. The social equilibriums which both the English and Roman
Catholic hierarchies attempted to bargain for turned out to be only
transitory.)

By 1918, as has been noted, the work of the historical opposition
was done. Whether because of "discord between the wave-lengths
of the man-atoms," the refusal to be slaves on a certain level, the
ability to bow more completely to natural marvels, superior "intel-
lect and character" (as the businessman quoted above would have
it), or other, more arcane reasons, the American had become a

different animal in the eighteenth century and from then on he had opposed all Englishmen and everything English. And he had finally triumphed.

The other side of his triumph, the slipping into the vacuum, began immediately after the Civil War. As the British ruling class moved away from belief in themselves, they moved to belief in Americans and American standards. Much of this was psychological and secret, but it had surface manifestations, including changes in fashion. "In its best days," wrote Adams, "Victorian society had never been 'smart.' . . . Nothing could be worse than the toilettes at Court unless it were the way they were worn. . . . Fashion was not fashionable in London until the Americans and the Jews were let loose."

The Anglo-American marriages were more obvious, and provided a beachhead through which American ways were funneled in easily at exactly the requested rate. This rate showed a slow but steady increase until the beginning of World War II, at which time, putting the situation as Palmerston would have, "the British ruling class was rotten with American influence." Waiting in the wings were the half-Americans like Churchill and Macmillan, whose careers over the next twenty years were to prove that only with American blood could one be entirely at ease at the top. Native Englishmen were never again to be altogether sure of themselves.

There was a faint trickle of Americanism downwards before 1918, but by and large the upper, middle and lower classes were still resolutely anti-American and still unaware that their betters had sold out. Those betters, of course, not only did not disillusion them, but went to some pains to hide the true state of affairs and to encourage delusions and anti-Americanism. This was not unreasonable or illogical. Their fathers and grandfathers had given up the leadership of the world to the Americans rather than destroy their own comfort, so comfort was what they had inherited. They had nothing else, and might as well hang on to it as long as possible.

But no secret can be kept forever, and the first great revelation came in 1936 when Edward VIII abdicated because he was so in love with an American woman that he couldn't live without her, and had to choose between her and his throne. The English people were stunned, and properly so, because they knew instinctively that no commoner of any other country (including England!) could have become more important to an English king than the English throne. Only an American could have managed it, and the abdication reeked of symbolic surrender. "Wallis Warfield had very little to her except the fact that she *was* American," an Englishman who was a participant in the abdication proceedings said to me recently. "The attraction was not sex, or wit, or anything else, really, except that American *will*. She saw no reason why she shouldn't have what she wanted, and neither did he, finally." The bride had reaped the fruit of hundreds of years of opposition and three-quarters of a century of infiltration. To the average American, it was only comic, but it came as a terrible shock to England. An American woman's will was more important than forty million Englishmen — was there any other way to interpret it? And that hadn't happened overnight, had it? Americans must have been of far more importance than had been dreamed, and for far longer, and to far more of the ruling class. It was a disclosure from which England was never to recover.

And after which was never to be the same. If the top was Americanized, the bottom was surely going to be Americanized, too, because what was good enough for the top was, by tradition, not only good enough but mandatory for the bottom.

At the bottom, it was easy enough, after World War I, to find out about Americans from the flood of motion pictures and popular music. The American dream poured into the new cultural vacuum, but there was still a need for the living model. In the lesser classes, however, it was not easy to get to Americans. How did one manage it? World War II, fortunately around the corner, provided them by the millions. They roared into England, found it ready and waiting, and responded to the best of their ability. Cultural colonization is nothing more or less than the sum of personal encounters, as noted in the example of the American sergeant and the English girl given in Part I, and here the sum was to be large enough to effect permanent change. Encounters with English men counted as much as (or more than) encounters with English women, and the grand total was staggering. Even where the emphasis was sexual, the cultural appetite was more basic and certainly more lasting. The English girl wanted the American because he was American, as Edward, her king, had wanted Wallis because *she* was American. Though the most obvious, the sexual encounters were far less numerous and far less important than the social encounters brought about in the business of day-to-day living. The real work was done by the American soldier invited to tea, the American soldier in the shop and in the pub and in the street and in the queue. No matter where he was, he exuded possession of a better, richer way of life, and the English who met him knew their superiors had reached for that life and saw no reason why they shouldn't do the same. He also put out a crudely dissembled shock at *their* way of life, and made them feel that what they did have was shabby and old-fashioned. The consequent embarrassment made them all the more determined to reach out for his way.

By 1946, the English lower class was as honeycombed as the ruling class. The middle class still resisted because the surrender had not been made official — they waited for word in black and white. The word never came. Instead, they were caught in a pincers between the top and the bottom and squeezed into submission by attrition.

The lower class of 1946 was won over, but it was already too old to effect great changes. Its children were a different matter. They were going to imitate everything American, and they weren't looking back. As the British in India and other conquered countries turned one class into imitation Englishmen and let them control the rest, so the Americans created imitation Americans (more by chance than design, it must be admitted, but no less completely) with the same result. Karl Meyer's picture of England as the fifty-first American state, far more interested in what goes on in America than in England, was only brought to reality by the young, postwar lower class. That class is epitomized for better or worse by the Beatles, who fall into clearer perspective if seen as the contemporary equivalent of the Indian civil servant of 1890, agitated and nervous in his western suit and high collar but determined to show his fellow Indians that an Indian can act like an Englishman. The real Beatle "message" is that an Englishman can act like an American.

On a colder level, postwar American control of political and economic England increased to just the extent that England was bewildered and uncertain in those fields, creating yet more vacuums. The bewilderment and uncertainty were a result of the war itself, another traumatic American revelation for England. In the beginning, the British war effort was efficient within limits and pleasingly heroic to the British themselves. But after Pearl Harbor, the Americans managed to take the war away from them by turning it into a production parade. "From the moment that the overwhelming industrial capacity of the United States could make itself felt in any theater of war, there was no chance of ultimate victory," wrote Rommel long before the end of the war. "Even if we had overrun the whole of Africa and the Americans had been left with a suitable bridgehead through which they could transport their material, we must eventually have lost the continent." What was true of Africa either was true or could have been true of everywhere else. In the end, it was apparent to all, Allies and Axis alike, whether they admitted it or not, that from the day America went to war the Axis was doomed with or without the participation of England, Russia or anyone else.

The smug and overwhelming fact of American production belittled the gallant efforts of all sides — the Russians at Stalingrad, Rommel in the desert, the Battle of Britain, even the Americans themselves in the Ardennes and at Iwo Jima — all drowned in a sea of supplies. For the English it was the last blow to emotionalism. They had had the war in perfect focus for themselves — Dunquerque and the RAF and El Alamein — and then it turned out it wasn't blood, sweat, toil and tears at all. It was fortunes made off defense contracts and black market gasoline and nylons for the girls and knocking off the Germans while the band played "Elmer's Tune." It was, finally, too much. Too much for the British leadership at all levels — military, political and economic. They had had such a dose of American power and American success by 1946 that the will to resist was no longer there. If America was that powerful and that successful, why fight it?

To the Englishman, "Why fight it?" implied a surrender of personal identity far beyond what the phrase meant to the European, who also had to adjust to the same feeling of helplessness. But where the European would fight to preserve as much of his national interest, share of the pie and individuality as possible, the Englishman's surrender was complete and unconditional. The difference was purely one of temperament. As natural followers, Englishmen in public life had always given everything of themselves to the national ideal. When the ideal cracked, they could not give a mere part of themselves to that which had cracked it. They had to give all; no lesser homage would have been possible. Neutrality was unthinkable.

The parade was complete. First, the ruling class; then the functional leaders — soldiers, politicians, administrators; and finally the bulk of the people. All united in the inability to turn on one's betters or challenge authority. As a people, they chose, naturally enough, to retain national characteristics rather than give them up in order to wage an uncertain struggle. The final disposition was almost painless: to him who must have a master it really doesn't make much difference who that master is.

The American businessman may huff and puff about England not doing as well in the postwar world as countries like France and Germany and Switzerland, but he forgets that he himself is more than a little to blame. He intimidated England, he made sport of its war, he crammed his superior technology down its throat, he sat in a cottage in Hampshire and smirked at the lack of tractors, he broke the spirit of its professional class . . . it was he, in short, who destroyed the icons of a nation of born worshipers and left them no choice except to fasten on him as the new idol, so he is not at all in a position to complain about their lack of resistance to him!

If there is material in modern England for writers of heroic caliber — writers like Dickens and Hardy and Forster — it lies in the inability of the officially dissenting groups to rise above their English heritage and fight as independent men. The heritage is one of subservience — subservience to Crown or class or outside influence: slavery at its worst and dangerously restrictive at its best — and no Englishman seems able to overcome it. The inhibitions which prevented discussion or even definition of the class system or any other fact of native control for hundreds of years are still sufficiently potent to block recognition of control from outside. As was noted earlier, the faculty of social analysis has been stunted. There is no *Theory of the Leisure Class* in English sociology, nor even *England's Ruling Families* or *The Class System*. "They can only talk about social reality if they can make it facetious," says my Rhodes scholar. "Like U and non-U. But they can't be serious about it — it always gets down to that Terry–Thomas–Searle–*Doctor in the House* boisterousness. You know an Englishman would never write a book like *The American Empire* — it would have to be a Frenchman, like Riencourt, or an American. The English just won't *admit* anything."

In politics, the British Labour Party was theoretically committed to a far sterner attitude toward America when it came into power in 1946 than the Tories had been, but it turned out to be even more of a lapdog. Attlee and Bevan, the prime minister and foreign secretary, were putty in American hands and ceded military rights in England (air bases, permanent camps, and so on) to America with a generosity that the Tories, acknowledged as the pro-American party, would have balked at. The pragmatic Americans could not help but realize immediately that the Labour Englishman, being English, had to have the same weaknesses as the Tory Englishman. And added to the usual weaknesses were the Labour Englishman's illusions that: calling himself a socialist automatically freed him from the limitations of the Tory Englishman; he was not really kowtowing to the Americans. He became the easiest of all to manipulate, and the colonization of England was far more damaging to him than to any other group because he had no idea what was going on. He was reduced to playing with power rather than exercising it, and by the 1960s had become an international joke. Figures like Harold Wilson and George Brown betrayed a paralyzed confusion bordering on the catatonic, comic to some but actually appalling. The humane intelligence of the Fabians of seventy years before had foundered on the immovable rock of English primitiveness.

The more informal but no less official dissenters have broken up on the same rock. Neither English youth in any guise — mod, angry, hip, straight, handsome, plain or fancy — nor English intellectuals, nor English dock workers, nor English of any other disgruntled persuasion, are able to shake the heritage and become effective.

Or as Ladrick put it: "We think the Beatles and Kenneth Tynan and the rest of our intellectual luminaries completely emancipated if nothing else, a far cry from the stifled Victorians. But under the 'brilliant' veneers, aren't they all only a collective extension of the grimmest constrictions of our English nineteenth century?"

American control of British foreign policy is unarguable. England follows the American line as firmly as Bulgaria follows the Russian line, and with much less consciousness of doing so. After World War II, Britain was incapable of independence or neutrality in the cold-war struggle between Russia and America, and the present situation grew out of that incapability. The French attempted independence and the Swiss neutrality, but the English were psychologically incapable of either. They had to have a master, and it had to be an American master because Russia was out of the question. Since the decision was made, there has been no questioning of American aims on the new, colonial level. This is often not apparent to foreigners, including Americans, who mistake residual criticism on the atavistic, empire level for true independence. The residual carping is reflexive and has no real meaning. (A high Foreign Office official can be amusingly anti-American over the weekend, but his house guests should not make the mistake of thinking he will be so in office decisions on Monday morning.)

In practical terms, this means that the collective English mind — and especially the collective English socialist, Labour, lower- and middle-class mind — cannot refuse the Americans anything if the request is put in terms of Anglo-American "security." That broad classification can be, and often is, stretched to include what would seem to be quite unrelated matters, the safety of American business interests in England and elsewhere among them. But perhaps true "security" *is* all-embracing. "Sometimes they embarrass us by going too far," an American diplomat has said to me. "As with Vietnam, where the official viewpoint, as put out in key administration speeches and the press, is often less conciliatory than our own — the *Express* and the *Daily Telegraph* can really go overboard. Which is when my Russian opposite number smiles his most knowing smile and I earn my salary."

There are, of course, political reactions to this situation reverberating all over the world. But most especially in Europe, where de Gaulle was on unassailable ground in claiming that to admit England to the Common Market is to let America in because England is America's creature. His further conclusion that this would be disastrous for Europe is debatable: America might decide that it would be in her best interests not to take over completely. This restraint, however, would be entirely voluntary, and reversible at any time. Even at that, the matter would not be altogether in America's hands. One of England's major passions in the days of power was the maintenance of a weakened Continent by playing off one European country against another. Nationals as prone to atavisms as the English might find that once in the Common Market they were unable to restrain themselves from starting up the ancient subversions even if instructed not to by the Americans. De Gaulle was not unaware of that danger, either, but neither are the Americans, in all likelihood, and they may well have been instrumental in keeping England out in order to prevent any unnecessary damage to the balancing out of world trade.

But sadly enough, one realizes that the Englishman who could see and write of the English inability to cope with the American would have to have overcome that inability himself and that seems to be impossible. No manipulation of a theory of probability would yield the possibility that not one of forty million people is capable of shedding ancient weaknesses, but such seems to be the case, extraordinary as it seems. The job is left to the American insofar as it is left to anyone, precisely where Henry James took it up nearly a hundred years ago. In that century, thousands of English writers have written but not one has touched the subject to a fraction of the depth that James plumbed in his first attempts, to say nothing of the descents in his major works. There is no reason to suppose the situation will change. Or even that the English will ever read James. "They don't have to have an official censor here," says my Rhodes scholar. "They do it themselves — even at Oxford, where they can read something without *reading* it, if you know what I mean."

5

IT should be plain that the English situation is not one from which anyone — but least of all an American — should derive pleasure. It has happened, and it was inevitable. Under ordinary circumstances, no one — and again, least of all an American — would wish to probe into what made it happen and find the root causes. But when the colonization of Europe becomes a topic on which analysis is solicited, the investigation of England, naturally the first European country to be considered, must be as searching as possible. If the trail leads to English weaknesses and deficiencies as being almost exclusively responsible for the American takeover, the discovery cannot be withheld or bowdlerized.

Nor can what may be called the darker side of the American strength be ignored. The conqueror is strong by definition, as judged in the immediate context of what he has overrun. But he is also human and subject to his own drawbacks. What Americans think of the rest of the world is pertinent to the colonization they have managed to accomplish, and what they think of England and Englishmen is particularly pertinent to what has happened in England. It would be reassuring to find that Americans are as generous and understanding toward the English as they should be. Some of them are. But others are not. Many lower- and lower-middle-class Americans have traveled abroad for the first time in the past few years, and their reaction to the lack of modern bathrooms in modest

English hotels, for example, is predictable. They do not choose to remember that the great majority of Americans over forty, a majority of which they are invariably a part, were born and brought up in exceedingly crude surroundings, and that a sobering one-third of contemporary America is materially "substandard." Middle- and upper-class Americans tend to be more polite, but the sneer is close to the surface, especially when the audience is exclusively American. The American ruling class is the most careful of all because its members have the most to lose if the show is given away altogether, but they, too, will smile when they feel it is safe.

The extent to which conscious American opinion of foreigners, especially of Englishmen, has helped or hindered American colonization is debatable. The colonization has been effected because of psychological differences, and the average American is as ignorant of what he really is (and really thinks) as the average Englishman is; and it is what he is, not what he imagines he is or what his opinions are, that has made the difference. Nevertheless, his opinions are full of information. He reveals himself through them in a backwards way, as he reveals other secrets in quasi-Freudian slips, and thus tells the listener much about the inchoate source of the colonial energy. And also much about the day-to-day business of colonization.

For these reasons, I think it pertinent and worthwhile to include here a collection of comments on England, Englishmen and English life from a mixed bag of Americans. They are all verbatim, just as they were said to me or as I overheard them. The reader should keep in mind that all these comments were made by people who are active colonizers in the sense that colonization is the sum of personal encounters; and that even un-American Americans find themselves supporting and/or extending the American way of life while in England. Also, it is only with other Americans that Americans are frank. (Under intense provocation or excitement they may let themselves go in front of or at foreigners, but such lapses are exceptional.) And lastly, even the most sincere Anglophiles seem to find that their inadvertent spreading of the American gospel (and its enthusiastic acceptance by Englishmen!) drives them, sooner or later, to seek the society of other Americans and let their hair down.

P.F.L., thirty-five, Harvard Business School graduate, executive director, large, American-run British corporation, has lived in England for six years with attractive wife and four children. Very serious, very concerned, exudes probity:

"I just don't know if we're doing the right thing. Will England develop the same symptoms that other countries have after we've taken over? As in Asia? The wild shirts hanging out? And the terrible discontent? The mobs smashing windows of American businesses, and insulting Americans on the streets? The span of peaceful American influence seems so short, and always followed by trouble. I just wonder if the American ways work outside America. . . .

"We Americans are tough, make no mistake about that. I mean tough in the brutal sense. Our own jobless at home have a certain look on their faces — you see it in the ghettos, black and white — and I'd hate to think the Europeans will get the same look. It's a *discarded* look: 'I'm finished,' it says. 'The company doesn't want me any more.' Capitalism is a terrible process under all the Timese, and we're so much rougher than the Europeans. I guess that's why we come out on top, but is it worth it? I mean, when we have to look at all those discarded faces? I don't want to see them here, but what can *I* do about it?

"You can see the current state of conditions in England as nothing new *or* you can see it as an incident in an irreversible decline and fall affecting the whole world. *I* see it as an incident in that decline and fall. Joan doesn't, but I do. I don't know what the kids think. Or will think, because they're too young now. England is an incident in world collapse is what goes through my head every day at the plant. There is nothing anyone can do about it. Overpopulated and overcrowded, she's going down as a preview for the rest of the world. Did you know that British roads are the most congested in the world? Fifty-five and three-tenths vehicles per mile of roadway, twice as much as the United States. Each British driver would have thirty-five feet of available space on the roads if they all got out there together. Of course they don't all get out together, but what if they did? You can't do much in thirty-five feet. We think we're overcrowded in America, but Britain is so much smaller that the situation is the worst in the world. I tell Joan that this is where it will crack. She doesn't agree — she thinks it will be Japan — but I'm betting on Britain, and I don't mean that to sound funny."

Chicago boulevardier, early fifties, high-color John O'Hara face, London-tailored suit with very narrow trousers and snug waist above flared lower jacket, New York hat, buttondown shirt with exaggerated curvature in collar flaps, Old Wykehamist tie, carnation in buttonhole, bourbon voice, overheard talking to friend at bar in O'Hare Airport, Chicago:

"We were there last year — I go every year to see my tailor, but I don't know what Flo goes for. She admits herself that she never buys anything. Just waits until she gets to Paris. We stay at Claridges, and I don't think it can hold a candle to the Ritz, in Paris. If I didn't have to see my tailor, I wouldn't even stop in London, that's how I feel about it. Now don't get me wrong, I know a lot of people like it — Bill Flaherty likes it, and I think the world of Bill's opinion on nearly everything (you know that because I know you do, too) — and I say: Good for them. It's a free country and they have a right to like England if they want. Just as long as they let me dissent. That's part of a free country, too. If you do go, though, let me tell you how to handle the cutters. You see, when you go to a good London tailor — I might even send you to mine if you promise to do it my way — you . . ."

P.A., in her sixties, distinguished educator and former dean at prominent women's college. Lifelong Anglophile:

"I suppose our enthusiasms were naïve before the war — we knew England had faults, but they seemed so minor next to her strengths. . . . English life is habit, and the habits used to be beautiful. Now the Americanization has made the old habits tawdry and cheap. . . . I never noticed the suspicion before — now they stare about in a restaurant like people who expect anything and everything to descend — clots of suspicious faces. Old women with beautiful white hair and then such pinched faces underneath. I swear they weren't like that thirty years ago. It must have been the war. All Europeans seem afraid now, and none more so than the poor English. . . . The class structure may have been unfair, but it was England. Its collapse has a great deal to do with the unattractiveness, and the feeling one has, especially abroad, that the English have gone down. The English on the Continent all used to be presentable. The lower class never traveled. Now they go everywhere; there doesn't seem to be anything else. I was stunned in Switzerland this summer. They had completely taken over Lake Lucerne — the dreadful voices, the awful young, the nauseating social behavior in which elderly women play at being girls and elderly men are the boys. Boisterous guffawing, messy. Not aggressively irritating, like comparable Americans, but so sad, so childish and unformed. . . . One is grateful for all England meant to one's own growth, but how can one feel a bond with these poor, grubby people? One weeps for what it was before. . . . I don't know, the day may come when American business will wonder whether it really wants England, just as England began to wonder if its colonies were worth the trouble. The imitation of America is so inept and has brought out all their foolishnesses so heartbreakingly. There can't be any future in it. . . . When I think of what it was like forty years ago, when I went to the Lake Country for the first time . . . I could cry . . ."

D.D.G., forty-two, lives in Geneva, permanent expatriate, man of the world, handsome, rich, shrewd investor, accomplished woman-izer, intelligent and lazily malicious:

"I had A—— N—— [the twenty-year-old daughter of an English earl] down here for a week, and after a few days I discovered that I was doing everything. She wasn't doing anything. Not because she wouldn't but because there was nothing there to put out in the first place. They have nothing to offer when you get right down to it. Nothing at all. None of them."

J.V.K., twenty-nine, American Negro, doctorate in sociology from Columbia, aspirant writer, married to an English girl and liv-ing in England while working on a book about American Negro leaders:

"I think that what strikes me very forcibly is the very sad quality of poor English life. The houses of the poor are so sad. So badly furnished, too. I might add that the houses of the rich are not in very good taste, either, compared with America, but it's the poor dwellings that make the deepest impression. I know Americans are poor — I don't think an American Negro from Harlem has to take a back seat to knowledge of poverty from anyone in the world — but it is a poverty of *possibility*. Even in Harlem there was always the chance that you could get out if you were good enough at a sport or had an angle or had an above-average I.Q. But the poor have no sense of *possibility* here. And that reverence for their 'betters.' The poor in America don't get down on their hands and knees like that, black or white. They couldn't believe it up at 125th Street. . . .

"And the way they talk. Do you realize that Cockney is actually babytalk. They say 'muvver' for 'mother,' for instance, just the way a baby does. They talk that way because they never grow up. When Jane and I first got married, I loved the way she talked, but then I met her family and listened to other English talk for a year and now I hate it. I am seriously wondering if all dialect speech everywhere in the world is not actually babytalk, and if it is that way in an unconscious playing-out of the inferior role as children. There are many obvious parallels in American Negro speech among the culturally deprived that I can vouch for. There are even resemblances to the completely undeveloped peoples I've studied . . . They think that if they don't say what's on their minds it doesn't count, a characteristic of all Stone Age peoples . . . smiling and offering, but also expecting . . . cargo cults . . .

"Jane's family is so very nice in a way, but why do they try to charm by being American? Trying to charm *me*, because I represent the great, wonderful place from which all blessings will flow. Sometimes I think I'm going crazy when we go over to their house. It's like America on a cracked record, blown up and distorted like in a funhouse mirror. Jane and I relate beautifully, but I don't know. What will happen when we have to go back to America? I tell her family how awful it is at home, how we Negroes are treated, how rotten American life is at all levels — I've even given them Jimmy Baldwin's books — but they just smile at me and pretend I'm kidding."

B.D., thirty-one, American divorcée living in Paris, beautiful, rich, bored:

"When I was younger I was wild about Englishmen. To have an English lover — that was my idea of heaven. Rex Harrison, David Niven, even Cary Grant, if you can still call him English. Well, I got my wish . . . more often than I like to think about . . . and what a letdown. Do you know that all Englishmen are deformed? I don't mean that way, although sometimes one wonders. I mean bones, skin, things like that. The teeth. And the feet! They all have deformed feet. All blocky and buckled up on top, as though they were bound in childhood like Chinese ladies. Have you ever noticed? There's a picture of Dickie Mountbatten — it was in *Life*, sitting somewhere with his shoes off — and he's got those feet. Dickie Mountbatten, the essence of charm, has those feet! Charles [an American suitor] is always going on about England — he has business there — talking about how antiquated it is. But who cares about that if they were only made right? I like them, but I just can't bear the way they're made any more so I haven't been *intime* with one in years. Frenchmen are nasty — and expensive — but I stick with them because they don't reveal all those ucky blemishes when they take off their clothes. Even Charles has to admit I'm right there."

F.J., in his seventies, American businessman of the old school:
"I'll tell you what Americans think of the English. Exactly nothing! To me the English are only funny, like Jews and Negroes are to those Italians. Did you ever see an Italian laugh behind a Jew's back? Or point out a Negro to his little boy? Talk about prejudice! No one is fit to open his mouth on the subject until he's gone to Italy. . . .
"I don't care who he is, an Englishman is only funny. . . .
"Yesterday, I heard an Englishman making fun of American business aggressiveness. He didn't know I was an American — we were in the bar at the Savoy and he was next to us — so I didn't say anything. But I was thinking to myself, 'And after what I've seen and had to pay for in the way of British hotel rooms, you could use a little of that aggressiveness, *old boy!*' Barbarians! I have nothing but contempt for them. That's what I think of them. Exactly nothing!"

Aging American entertainer, admitted homosexual, overheard talking to young American consular official, not an admitted homosexual but sympathetic to all minorities, at large cocktail party in London given by famous American hostess. English present, but not in his corner:
"What gets me is all this talk about leaving 'law and order' and 'trained civil servants' when they pull out of the colonies. They only leave nincompoops — I speak from dire experience, you are looking at a man who had the misfortune to buy a house in Jamaica while

there was still some law and order. And then our English friends pulled out, and there was nobody in charge but the junglebunnies. They wear those powdered wigs — you know? — but nothing is changed underneath. All that 'I wave a big stick at you, mon, and you lie down.' Trained civil servants, my sacred *gluteus maximus!* The English change them on the outside, but not where it counts, and when they're left on their own there's all that lovely accent on top, but the same old bongo-bongo underneath.

"And such prey for others. Yes, I know — and I know *you* know — those shifty-eyed Englishmen in soiled Daks. (Was there ever a more gruesome style in pants? With those two-foot bottoms flapping around the ankles?) in little offices just off the main office. Yes, I know they can still control up to a point, but don't forget they *are* controlled, too. . . . I don't think giving up the Empire was so great, they just couldn't think of anything else — They're junglebunnies themselves now. But weren't they always? That's what I was thinking in Jamaica looking at those fat black faces under those crazy wigs — is it any better with a white face underneath? Once you start thinking that way, London doesn't look any better than Kingston.

"We all howled when the American bauxite people moved in with their charming plans for tearing up the island, but the day came, I can tell you, when we were glad to have *some* sort of law and order. When the English leave, there's such chaos in those places that someone else from outside always has to take over . . . but the talk about leaving the trained civil servants still goes on. Can you tell me why? Yes, I know you can, because you have that clever-clever look . . ."

Big, bland American governor, friendly as a St. Bernard, more than ready to straighten everything out:

"You have to like people before you can get to know them. Like the English now — I always remember Harry Truman saying they ran everything here with a Privy Council for hundreds of years, and it was a pretty effective system, too. The Parliament was more or less window dressing, you might say, and all the real power was in the Privy Council. Well, then that changed and people started taking more control into their own hands, the way we do in America, but the English weren't as adaptable for that kind of democracy as we are, and they just haven't done as well without that Privy Council system. That's the cause of all their troubles, you might say. And I always try to keep that in mind when they get kind of fresh, the way they do. They talk anti-American and then they talk that U and un-U talk, and I just figure they're both faces of the same coin. They're jealous of us because we've got everything and so they fool around with U and un-U to cover it up. But what they really want is to get that Privy Council back. I only wish I could help them swing it."

C.A.M., thirty-three, American clergyman (Episcopalian), brilliant but eccentric, very nervous, sometimes incoherent. Living in England for no apparent reason. Exists from hand to mouth. Uses marijuana and LSD, but sparingly:

"Stood on Greek Street this morning feeling like a panhandler and someone asked me how I felt and I said like Henry James's illegitimate son. I suppose that's assuming the sins of the father with a vengeance, but I am sure that's where the trouble started, because James insisted we Americans were the innocent ones and the Europeans so anciently wicked and cynical, but he had it so reversed, good parishioners. Hawthorne could have enlightened him or he could have enlightened himself with a little elementary homework, but he didn't. He couldn't *see* any more; he couldn't see that every breath an American draws from birth to death is hypocritical. The American is *never* himself, and after a while there is no self not to be. He becomes the mask. It is the ultimate dishonesty, the final sin against God, the living of lives in which everything and everyone seems so evil that one has no choice except to believe oneself the same. A life of pure survival, all darkness, all false, but, of course, mechanically triumphant. We 'win' because we're the most dishonest people in a world where the Devil is triumphant. It's that simple. These poor English never have a clue, of course, any more than the rest of Europe does, because they don't believe in the Devil. My father, the esteemed Henry, did, but he didn't know where to pin the tail. So I say, on Greek Street, love thy father, but keep a sharp eye on his collected works. . . ."

L.L., American girl, willowy, sixteen, attractive in spite of herself, attends exclusive English finishing school:

"I sat there and read *The Rainbow,* by D. H. Lawrence, and it was so beautiful. And then I thought of what they have now, like John Osborne and Harold Pinter. Mr. Lawrence was *English,* and what they have now aren't English at all. They're either half American, and vulgar, like Mr. Osborne, or completely, like Len Deighton and Michael Caine. Just what my father sent me here to avoid. Even the little children are that way. They had a poll here, and those children voted for the people they most admired, and there were six Americans out of ten. And what Americans! Tommie Smith and Jackie Onassis and Jerry Lewis, and the rest about the same. All tied with God for the same number of votes! Doesn't that make a foursome, though? They never get to the kind you *could* make a case for, but stay with Jack and Jackie forever. And I sit in that room I have and look across the beautiful fields and read about Ursula, and moon around, and the English girls, the pick of the poor old realm, think it's because I miss America and my centrally heated sixty-three-room house in Greenwich and the thrilling vibration of the jet engines on my father's private plane. How could I tell them otherwise?"

F.F.O., fortyish, very small-time American in import-export, slippery and corrupt:

"I pay no taxes here in England. Fake books, the right answers, but no payoffs. They're too dumb, you don't need to. And too inefficient. Too lazy. London is wide open today. Anything goes. And there's always more money made when these socialists are in. My English colleagues pray they'll stay in, like bootleggers backing drys in the States. They just can't run this country. They don't know how to begin. Everything is a racket, and they stand there like the preacher's daughter. Pretty soon she tries it, too."

Memo from *Time* correspondent:
"*American woman on double-decker London bus* is title of this piece, written during coffee break and unsuitable for home office. When she gets on — it is the same bus I take to the office — there are no seats downstairs and conductor tells her there are seats above. She bridles, smirks, and says she can't climb those 'narrow little stairs.' He gently urges her to try: she refuses, little eyes and not-so-little jaw hardening. He finally asks English male passenger sitting downstairs to go upstairs so she can sit downstairs. English passenger is only too happy to oblige. She is still simpering as she takes seat, unaware that a woman of any other nationality would have been told to go upstairs or get off. I think this is end of incident, and turn back to my *Times*. But no, because as she plumps down next to English housewife she starts to talk: 'We just don't have this kind of bus back home — that's in Akron, Ohio? We have buses, but they don't have that place upstairs — second floor or whatever you call it. I could have gone up, though, if the stairs hadn't been so narrow. And the way the bus swayed. Why, I just don't know how you people do it, going up and down those stairs like that. I think it's just wonderful. I only wish I could do it. But what worries me is the idea of falling. My cousin, Jeff — he's in the fuel oil distribution field — fell last winter and broke his hip. In his own driveway! And he hasn't been the same since. That poor man . . .' Her voice booms on in the special basic American used by so many citizens of our United States in talking to benighted foreigners. She patronizes the entire bus with fabulous arrogance, but all the passengers act as though she is kindness personified. They would not accept such

condescension from any other race, and the extent of the exception made in her case is a crude but accurate indication of the extent of what we are pleased to call the American occupation. She treats them as inferiors: they find the treatment correct."

American drunk, name unknown, about thirty, in bar of Palace Hotel, Madrid. Well-dressed, upper-class accent, and regular features under the booze flush. Clever and vicious, but more than a little uncertain:

"I pick up the *Daily Telegraph* because I can't get the *Tribune* and what do I find? The full report from Chicago! *Violence!* British subjects bopped on the head . . . British outrage at American bulls, at America, at Mayor Daley, at terrible American character revealing itself, turds floating to top of American cesspool. 'Worse than Prague . . . worse than the Black Shirts . . . worse than Dachau!' [Long pause] Bulls—t! Do you know what I think? I think they're jealous! They're jealous because *they'd* like to be whacking people around themselves, like they used to, and they can't so they get wild when anybody else does. Ever hear an English woman say, 'My son is out in Aden,' with that faraway look in her eye? Talk about violence. And race hatred . . . you haven't seen race hatred until you've seen it in England. Every Englishman I meet complains about Negroes. And Jews. Met an Englishman right here two days ago and he said to me: 'When I was at Oxford, a one-armed Jew from the University of Chicago took over the Oxford Union — what do you think of that?' 'What do I think of that?' I said. 'Why, I'll tell you what I think of that. When I went to the beach at Torremolinos, a whole bunch of repulsive English sat down right next to me, and they all started to change their clothes on the beach, the way they do. Except that some of the women didn't change — they just sat around in their slips. Talking about the sons who were out in Aden. And they all complained about everything — the "midges" and the "rocks" and everything else they could think of. I finally had to move, and I was thinking while I picked up my stuff that I would have been much happier next to a one-armed Jew. What do *you* think of that?' He didn't think too much of it. I tell you, I thought we Americans were supposed to be so repulsive, but did you ever see the English on a beach? The women in their slips twittering about the 'midges' and the 'sons' in those goddamned voices that can drive you right out of your mind? I tell you . . ."

N.B., twenty-six, Smith graduate, unmarried, reporter who has worked for the *New York Times* and *International Herald-Tribune:*
"I don't think the English — or any other Europeans for that matter — understand that there is no spirit of compromise in the American businessman. Any more than there was in Genghis Khan. Think of what happened to the American Indian. As compared, for example, to the Indians the Spanish dealt with all over Central and South America. They intermarried and had a lot of cute little tan babies . . . Mexicans. Our businessmen are really the awful ones. 'Either become an American,' they say when they get in control of you, 'or get out!' Go to the Dorchester and look at them and listen to them! Then try to wake up England. Just try!"

H.L.H., forty-nine, high in American Foreign Service, married to very rich American wife who dominates him, a situation from which he takes refuge in didactic disdain:
"Think of Napoleon! He wanted to do something for Europe, clean it up. And who stopped him? England, the great reactionary. Always against anything constructive, always ready to undercut a new idea. If they get into the Common Market, do you think they'd really play the game? Not at all, because they can't join anything, become just another state in an organization. Any more than Israel could. They are incapable of submerging themselves. They can be dominated, as we dominate them, but they can't cooperate. . . . Talk about control — when there was any problem, we used to say:

Have Ike call the Queen and tell her what to do. And that isn't far from the way it's still done today, if you can follow the symbolism.

"Second Elizabethan Age! They took one look at the money in New York and the houses within a fifty-mile radius and they forgot all about the Second Elizabethan Age. Talk about being snowed . . . Churchill rolling around under the bench in the House of Commons looking for a jujube so he can take attention away from an Opposition speech. And someone dropping orange seeds down Mr. Robert Boothby's neck. What do you do with such babies? The Gentleman of the Black Rod beating on the door and the whole Parliament shrieking like schoolboys on the other side. They never grow up. . . . They're destructive! They can't do anything constructive. If they're let into the Common Market, they'll wreck it. If they're kept out, they'll wreck it. Out of sheer perversity and childish destructiveness. Europe can't win, because the Common Market can't win and the Common Market is the only chance Europe has. So *we* go on picking up the marbles. . . . Money! They'll do anything for money. They'll . . ."

J.H., noted Jewish black-humor novelist:
"Like I went to the Markham years ago, too — I made Tom Maschler take me there, we went on that damned scooter of his — and I sat there wanting to have a good time and all I could see was this chart, like something in an NYU embryo class — you know what I mean — where there's all this unattractive *fustiness* in the middle like a uterus and a few young nobles go there because it's their biological function to stake out new places. Then the girls follow them and the cocksmen follow the girls, and it's all very Pavlovian and in two weeks it's the new place. Pavlovian, but eighteenth-century Pavlovian, and that's the rub because these English will go anywhere to be where a lord is or has been recently enough. It's fun — and aren't we all fun people? — but it's such out-of-touch fun, like Run-Sheep-Run. . . . Like I said to one lord there, 'What do you think of Eliot?' and he said, 'Oh, a phony, I guess!' Then later

I said to him, 'Ask me what I think of Montgomery,' and after about an hour he got the idea and did, and I said, 'Oh, a phony, I guess,' and he was sore as hell. . . . Like you say, the Beatles are Americans, and I say to myself, 'Too glib.' But then they take me out to see Ringo and he's in a house full of TV sets and it's like Levittown. And then I snuggle up to these beautiful British chicks and all I get is 'fab' and 'smashing' and 'super' and 'groovy' (can you believe that Mick Jagger says 'groovy'? — well, he does) and then I get, like, a feeling I'm going backwards in time like a demented astronaut. It's 1939 and everyone who's no one is saying 'in the groove' and 'fabulous' and this beautiful girl fades right into the face of a junior at the University of Wisconsin in October, 1939, walking across the campus in his white buck shoes and thinking he's really from Princeton now that he's got them on. Have you ever walked through those October Wisconsin leaves? The kind they make for the weekend of the homecoming game? Don't tell me, it was only rhetorical. Anyhow, as Wisconsin to Princeton in 1939, so London to the USA in 1968 — same garbling of styles in same hope of belonging. . . . And back at the Markham, the young lord and I are now intimate friends because someone said, 'What do you think of Norman Mailer?' and we both said, 'Oh, a phony, I guess' at the same time, and it turns out we both speak from experience. It's like telepathy wins again and those big-game leaves are still falling in Wisconsin and Princeton is dead and buried and out in space they're singing 'Thanks for the Memory' and watching all the old Bogart films in drip-dry stay-prest space suits. . . ."

J.G.M., fifty-eight, American banker, blockheaded but efficient and dedicated:

"England has a future, and I think we should be careful not to lose sight of that fact in the day-to-day confusions and stresses of emotional thinking. Yes, they declined as a financial power, in the buying and selling arena. And we know why they declined. Their methods were too old-fashioned. And we know more. A certain type of man took over who might very well be described as the clerk mentality. What we would call definitely non-viable. They could not innovate. They could only follow. And they followed the wrong track. They followed the outmoded financial procedures of their former chiefs, the group often referred to as the 'old boys,' meaning, of course, that they were graduates of such-and-such a private school, which are called public schools in England, an interesting but time-consuming and roundabout way to say it. When those procedures broke down, they could not initiate new programs on their own. They had to look elsewhere, and they naturally looked to us Americans. They asked us what to do, and we told them. Frankly, we are still telling them. But it is a highly constructive dialogue and it is by no means a one-way dialogue. The English are intelligent and adaptable when they understand what is to be done and it is only a matter of time before they will have as efficient a financial community as we do. As efficient, but not as large. Whether they will ever be free of American influence is very, very moot. I don't know that they themselves would want to cut all ties and go it entirely alone. But who knows? I may be accused of incurable optimism, but I have always been very high on the English, and I'm pulling for them to go all the way."

6

ONCE the psychological basis of the colonization is understood,
the physical results — that one-ninth of the iceberg which is
visible — can be appreciated in proper perspective. The accumulated data then assumes a multidimensional meaning, and can even
be, within limits, informative and helpful. Included below is a brief
summary of such reportage from widely circulated sources:

Tad Szulc, in a lengthy report in the *New York Times*, November
24, 1967:
"All the well-known types of United States consumer goods are
available in Britain, in spite of the economic squeeze. In Paris, Lisbon, Bonn and Rome, there was an agreement with a London
report that 'some of these things have become so familiar that
American origins have been nearly forgotten by the public.'

"With an infinity of American products manufactured in Europe
with their own brand names under licensing arrangements or by
American-owned subsidiaries — automobiles, home appliances, cigarettes, soft drinks, detergents, cosmetics and foodstuffs to mention
only some categories — there is evidently a blurring of the line between the 'real' American and the European goods.

" 'When an Englishman buys a new Vauxhall, he is unlikely to
give any thought to the fact that Vauxhall is owned by General
Motors in the United States,' a correspondent reported.

"This blurring of lines is welcomed by both the American companies and the governments involved who, for basically the same reason, prefer not to call attention to the 'American economic invasion,' as a German editorial writer called it recently. The British Board of Trade is reluctant to provide figures on the United States capital investment in Britain and in British concerns."

The *Washington Post,* November 23, 1967, in an article on the rapid expansion of American banking overseas:
"The assets of American banks in Europe at the end of 1965 totaled $5.7 billion with three-quarters of this in England."

Reuters, in a February, 1969, feature on a British government handbook entitled *Mr. Average Briton:*
"His favorite food remains . . . baked beans in tomato sauce. In 1967 the British consumed more than a quarter of a million tons of baked beans, as well as vast quantities of pies. He could probably eat more beans, too, if he cut down on eating sweets. The British eat more sweets than any other people in the world."

UPI, February 13, 1969:
"About 17,000,000 Britons are toothless, disclosed today the Office of Health Economics."
This is nearly one-half the adult population, a staggering percentage for a western country.

Peter Osnos, in the *International Herald-Tribune,* January 15, 1968:
"London — In 1856, five partners in the New Brunswick, Maine, firm of J. S. Ford and Co. decided to open a vulcanized rubber factory in Edinburgh. This was the modest beginning of what has become known here as 'the American invasion.'
"The invasion — an uncharacteristically emotive term for the British — has been growing steadily in recent years until, by this Jan. 1 [1968], American companies:

"— had interests in virtually every British industry, including major shares of the car, computer, electronics, petroleum, drug, food and office machinery industries.

"— employed one out of every 16 British workmen.

"— manufactured 10 percent of all British goods for home consumption and produced 17 percent of the nation's exports.

"— represented 7 percent of the country's total industrial assets, an estimated cumulative investment stake approaching $6 billion. . . .

"There are well over 1,600 American-owned or controlled manufacturing companies in Britain. Just about every important name is represented: Esso, IBM, General Motors, Ford, Chrysler, Goodyear, Kodak, du Pont, Pfizer, Texas Instruments, Heinz, Procter and Gamble, Quaker Oats, Singer and many others.

"Britons bathe with Palmolive, shave with Gillette, use Tide and Ajax in the kitchen and bathroom and make-up with Max Factor.

"They have Campbell's soup for lunch with a Kraft cheese sandwich and wash it down with that uniquely American drink, dietetic Coca-Cola.

"Despite a trend in recent years toward investment in the Common Market countries, U.S. direct investment in Britain has been rising by about 10 percent a year.

"Prof. John Dunning of Reading University, a leading authority on American investment here, estimates that if present conditions continue — even taking into account the Jan. 1 measures — by 1980 between 20 and 25 percent of British industry will be in U.S. hands.

"Behind this expected growth is the fact that about 75 percent of U.S. capital is concentrated in several 'key growth' industries: chemicals, transportation equipment, and electrical and non-electrical machinery.

"The automobile industry, for example, is already 55 percent American-controlled. Last winter, Rootes Motors was taken over by Chrysler, joining Vauxhall, the General Motors subsidiary, and British Ford.

"It was generally conceded at the time that Rootes had little chance of survival without a substantial American boost. As Prof. Maurice Preston of Queen Mary College put it in the magazine 'New Society': 'The Americans are past masters of the business of making cars. We can't compare with them.'

"Ford, Preston pointed out, made £389 million ($934 million) worth of sales in 1965 compared with £233 million ($540 million) in 1959, shortly before it was taken over. Some 302,672 vehicles were exported in 1965 compared with 236,167 in 1959.

"Taking Preston's point a step further, Dunning said recently: 'American companies know how to do what British companies do, only better. Americans are more aggressive and more competitive. They have marketing and managerial expertise.

"As proof, Dunning cites a study he conducted for Dun and Bradstreet's magazine 'Business Ratios.' In the period 1961–64, American firms earned 51 percent more on every pound invested than did British companies. Between 1957 and 1963, they increased their sales by 80 percent compared with an increase of 23 percent by all manufacturing firms.

"The higher profits of the American firms Dunning attributes partially to the American business style and partly to the 'hidden subsidy' of enormous research and development programs in the parent companies. . . .

"On the whole, most Britons would agree that the nation has gained immeasurably from U.S. investment. Yet there is a feeling (true not only in Britain, but also in Western Europe) that somewhere the line must be drawn.

"There has been talk, increasing over the past year, of stricter controls on the Americans, particularly in export, research and development and personnel policies. But so far little action has been taken.

"In most cases, it is national pride coupled with a European aversion to American over-zealousness that lies behind the unease over American advances. 'Between your products, your techniques and your movies,' one British businessman intoned, 'we risk becoming just another bunch of bloody Yanks.' "

The Business Section, *Time*, September 27, 1968:

"One of the reasons for the improvement in Britain's balance of trade is the invasion of British business by U.S. businessmen. Few Britons would agree with that statement. But one who does — and is preaching it to anyone who will listen — is Joe Hyman, whose Viyella International Ltd. has grown into one of Britain's largest textile groups and most active exporters.

"Hyman has gone so far as to make a statistical study of his own. From 1950 to 1966, according to Hyman's figures, U.S. firms have increased their British investments 600%, from $840 million to $5.6 billion. Today, some 1,650 companies owned or controlled by U.S. interests provide jobs for 500,000 Britons, account for 10% of all British industrial sales — and are responsible for as much as 18% of British exports. 'There has been vociferous criticism of American enterprise seizing the so-called new "commanding heights" of our economy,' says Hyman. 'I can only observe that had it not done so, such heights might only have been molehills. Without this investment we would be in a parlous state.'

"Hyman also argues that U.S. companies and Stateside banks, which presently hold 14% of all British deposits, act as a spur to make Britons perform better themselves. A hard-driving industrialist who makes all of Viyella's management decisions, he is particularly impressed by American marketing and productivity. 'American businesses in Britain work back from the marketplace and simplify their plants,' he says. 'British businesses, through excessive product proliferation, are far less rational in their factories.'

"So far as Hyman is concerned, the British ought to take more lessons from the U.S. and try to restructure their business operations along American lines. . . . Hyman stoutly maintains that British socialism and nationalization are inconsistent. He says: 'To compare the remuneration of the lowest-paid operatives in American automobile businesses in this country with their equivalents in our nationalized industries is to make it appear that we have two nations in our midst, while in reality it is the difference between two systems.' "

Life magazine, November 11, 1968, in a feature on the soccer match between Manchester United and Estudiantes de la Plata, of Argentina, for the World Cup Championship:

"United's players were not about to shake hands and admit with hugs and kisses that the better team had won. They refused to trade jerseys, the traditional gesture of good will in international football. When the Argentines tried to take their hands, the English sullenly took them for an instant and sullenly walked away, heads downcast. But the best show of all was put on by United's goalie, Alex Stepney. He rushed up to Oscar Pachame, the Estudiantes' halfback, who was standing on the touch line trying to act like a champion and shake hands . . . Stepney . . . gave Pachame quite a shake — right in the face with the back of his hand . . . No wonder Estudiantes decided to quit England and refuse to play 'friendlies' against Arsenal and Birmingham City. The English had shown no grace . . . They were lousy losers."

Such examples of British bad sportsmanship have become commonplace in the past few years, and one wonders how often they were hushed up in the past.

The *Daily Express,* Britain's largest circulation newspaper, in a feature by Andrew Fyall and James Davies, November 25, 1968:

"Hundreds of thousands of families are waiting desperately, often hopelessly, for a new home in Britain today. They exist in atmospheres of neglect, in Dickensian environments of decay, for the blunt truth is that of the 15,500,000 homes in this country, only 9 million are regarded as satisfactory by modern standards. . . .

"Priority has to be given to families displaced by massive slum clearance programmes and there are nearly 2 million homes in this country unfit for human habitation. . . . For families trying to lead normal lives in hideous conditions, it is a national emergency."

Bernard Levin, in a feature in the *International Herald-Tribune,* February 4, 1969:

"There are industries — and among them are some of the most vital modern ones — in which American labor is two and a half times as efficient as British. . . . They have — in equipment, automation and industrial techniques — that much more mechanical aid to efficiency."

The *New York Times* story on "Britain's Economic Prospects," the Brookings Institution report put out in June, 1968:

"Sharp criticism was directed at British economic policies and many aspects of British life yesterday in a report on Britain prepared by the Brookings Institution of Washington, a non-profit research group.

"British education, medical service, public housing and research and development policies were subjected to severe criticism as were management and labor practices, fiscal policy, regional development policy and the incomes policy to avert wage inflation. The tone of comment was often sharp.

"Education becomes specialized and children are divided into academic and vocational courses of study at too early an age (usually at 11), the report said. Universities spend too much money educating too few persons. In addition, there is nothing 'unusual in the contribution of such education' to recent British growth.

"The National Health Service was criticized for an inadequate supply of doctors, poorly designed new hospitals and needlessly high drug payments. Subsidized rents for public housing were said to discourage labor mobility. Postal service was said to be good in quality but low in mechanization.

"Britain suffers from a shortage of engineers and a 'maldistribution of research and development activities,' the report said. It recommended reducing basic research and 'reducing the massive scientific inputs to the aircraft industry, where performance has not justified their continuance.'

"The report was prepared by 11 U.S. and Canadian economists under the direction of Richard E. Caves, chairman of the Harvard University economics department.

"The authors had harsh words for management and labor alike. Executives were criticized for tending 'to retain the civil service as their model and settle into a trustee role of gentlemanly responsibility that hardly conduces to rapid innovation.'

"The problem of British manufacturing was said to be 'the production of too many types and varieties, too little adapted to consumers' preferences.' Shortcomings were laid primarily to the 'inadequate quality of management.'"

The *International Herald-Tribune*, August 23, 1968, from London:

"Britain's leading independent economic forecasters today warned of an unemployment total of over 700,000 by the winter and a balance of payments deficit of nearly $1.44 billion.

"The gloomy news was contained in the August issue of the Economic Review of the National Institute for Economic and Social Research. The projected deficit — the difference between total payments to foreign nations and receipts from abroad — would be $84 million more than incurred in 1967."

Robert C. Toth, *International Herald-Tribune*, March 7, 1969:

"Not many years ago, Englishmen would get livid at each new sign of the coca-colonization of their country, whether it was chewing gum underfoot or ice in the whisky or a multi-billion-dollar takeover of British Ford by Detroit. Americanization seems to have lost its terror now, however. Not only do changes in traditional tastes (like the instant-coffee revolution) go largely unremarked, but there is an unreserved eagerness to have Americans put money in British industry. . . .

"American companies, according to Mr. Dunning [the Reading University expert quoted earlier], 'supply more than half the cars, office machines, sewing machines, earth moving equipment, domestic boilers, shoe making machinery, breakfast cereals, cosmetics and toilet preparations, vacuum cleaners, pens and pencils, razor blades, foundation garments and films produced in the United Kingdom, and nearly half the petrol and drugs sold to the National Health Service. . . .

"'. . . Britain has still not come to terms with the reality of the growing role of the multi-national company in the world economy and the way it can affect a nation state's sovereignty,' Mr. Dunning said in his study for the Political and Economic Planning Organization. The British people do seem to have come to terms with the Americanizing process, however. They no longer fight it. 'Ten years ago everyone was still upset about the Americans,' said one sociologist. 'But I don't know anyone in social research who is studying the subject now, which I suppose is one measure of its lack of force in our society. I guess we're just resigned to American domination.'"

Anthony Lewis, *New York Times*, May 13, 1969:
"Figures published today showed that Britain's trading deficit grew worse in April. It stood at $141.6 million. This depressing figure virtually killed hopes of bringing the country's international payments into surplus in 1969, as promised. Even worse, it suggested that the whole economic strategy since the devaluation 18 months ago had failed. The stock market took its worst slide since devaluation."

The bare bones of these items bring back one's own recent experiences in London. Behind the newsprint one sees the anxious faces

— Reeves and Harper in sharp relief among them — and remembers the strained moments. When the Brookings report mentions "the inadequate quality of management," one can refer to actual persons. "A trustee role of gentlemanly responsibility that hardly conduces to rapid innovation" — one can only imagine how Ladrick would have smiled at that stern description of the British executive's lazy conception of his job. Peter Osnos's report is a devastating summary of the extent of American economic penetration of England; and his statistics on the higher profits that American management makes with taken-over British firms exposes the reason British investors actually welcome such takeovers and why British lenders would rather loan to Americans than to Englishmen.

"The American TV series 'Peyton Place' will return to British screens following a storm of protests from angry housewives," reads an AP item from London dated September 6, 1968. "The series ended abruptly when the contract of the commercial TV company that presented it was terminated this summer. A new company, Thames TV, is bringing it back next month." If the British housewife cannot live without American soap operas, and the British investor is making money with American management, there would seem to be little likelihood of "stricter controls over Americanism" (Mr. Osnos's phrase) for some time to come.

Thus the story, one concedes, is being told constantly in periodicals (and even in some parts of some books) — but in a way that is only meaningful if one has already seen it at close range. Without firsthand experience, the ordinary coverage is neither amusing nor instructive, but tends to melt into the newspaper page and lie forgotten in the company of thousands of adjoining columns. Because only a minority of Americans have firsthand experience, the compromise would seem to be firsthand experience enjoyed vicariously (as attempted through this treatment) and then used as a fulcrum for prying out such nuggets as do come along in the periodicals every so often.

After all, again as Ladrick would have put it, "any fool can read a newspaper." Or a book full of statistics and mechanical details and theoretical opinions. The point is to be able to read them as reflections of a surface of which one knows the depths. One recalls Einstein telling a questioner who asked him a mechanical detail that he didn't keep that sort of thing in his head — when he needed it he looked it up in a book. Non-geniuses could profit as much — perhaps far more! — from the same approach. In my own experience, the fact that the new company putting on *Peyton Place* in England is called *Thames* TV is only truly real when I remember Frank saying: "Harper is so dumb he thinks all you have to do is call the company Sir Francis Drake Electronics and the whole world will come running." Without that recollection, Thames TV doesn't reach full stature.

And one finds significantly official corroboration of one's own observations when Professor Maurice Preston says (as quoted in Peter Osnos's article): "The Americans are past masters of the art of making cars. We can't compare with them," Professor Preston doesn't really mean we Americans make better cars. After all, a Cadillac can't compare with a Rolls-Royce. He means we market them better, and superior marketing requires a superior knowledge of human nature. He actually confirms the greater depth of American philosophical thought — an inescapable if initially surprising conclusion — and echoes Bernard Levin by saying, in effect: "We Europeans are the innocent barbarians and you Americans are the sophisticated civilizers."

When all analyses — one's own and others — are finished and committed to the page, the compelling memories of England remain, Ladrick chief among them. In him the old England stirred in lively if final energy, a spark still strong enough to escape the gigantic American snuffer. Shards of his gallant efforts keep returning at odd moments: "We taught all those silly old women to drink tea because there was so much of it in Ceylon and now we have to look at them forever. Some chickens and some roost, isn't it. . . . Wasn't it your Fitzgerald who said, 'Create a character and you find you've made a type'? So perfect for England — there was a certain human innovation: and then it went on for all time. . . . Heaven: where one never sees again an Englishman ordering a bottle of wine or hears one speaking French or handing out canards on the Germans. . . . Did I tell you that when Jennifer buys Levi's for the children at the American PX she asks for Levies — rhymes with bevies — and thinks the mispronunciation (after all, it is an American word) means she isn't really putting her children in American pants? . . ." One can't believe the Ladrick spirit will flourish in the England of the future. If there is a casual symbolism for that future, it can easily be found in the ordinary pop reactions. A photograph of John Lennon and Yoko Ono, the Japanese artist he says he loves. She is a hippie thirty-four to his twenty-seven, but he looks fifty, the long hair framing a face now drawn and tired and burned-out, oddly reminiscent of Lord Jim and the now-forgotten armies of English remittance men who used to lie awash in exotic harbor towns around the world. Yoko, next to him, has the contented smile of Babo in *Benito Cereno*.

And lastly, combining the Throne with past, present and future colonization, an item (*International Herald-Tribune*, July 22, 1968) in which the Duke of Edinburgh tells "an urban affairs conference that mankind is in a position to 'dominate nature' with synthetic materials and spare-part surgery, thereby rendering itself independent of God. 'It is not arrogant to say this. It is realism,' said the consort of the Defender of the Faith." The words, putting the American point of view with an extravagance that few Americans would dare, could have been spoken by a character in *The Loved One*. Hubristic Babbittry, the cornerstone of the American way, had achieved its ultimate British advocate. Symbolism could not be stretched further, and the future could not be improved on. The case, to put final comment in appropriate Americanese, was closed.

III

WESTERN EUROPE

The Present as Past

1

A PRELIMINARY EXPLANATION

In discussing American influence in Europe with me several years ago, T. S. Eliot emphasized a point which may well be the crux of the whole matter. "We must try to keep in mind," he said, "what modern Europe would be like if the United States had never come into being. If the American colonies had not chosen to revolt, but had remained within the British family of nations to this very day — a more boisterous but less snow-laden Canada — what would the effect have been on Europe? I should almost ask: what would Europe *not* be that it presently is? Until 1900, the influence was slight, but since then it has shown immense acceleration. It is not that Europe would be without automobiles and washing machines and the rest — I understand that many of the modern 'timesavers' were actually invented here — but they would be present in far smaller numbers and their presence would not have changed the whole style of European life.

"No, the American contribution has not been the gadgets themselves but a new notion of society, what many people are pleased to call a 'consumer society.' I gather that the credit for this invention belongs to Mr. Henry Ford, insofar as any single person can claim setting it in motion. To pay workers more so they can buy more seems simple enough, and certain persons may ask why no one in Europe thought of it. The answer is that no one *wished* to think of it for the very good reason that no one wanted to change the social structure of Europe to that extent. The emergence of a lower class that, as in America, would hold the buying of goods as man's highest activity was not to be desired. The dangers were clear — such a class would inevitably become all-powerful and overturn such Christian civilization as remained. The ancient and delicate balance between the various levels of European society would be swept away and the result would be, again as in America, a glumly pagan chaos.

"As we are painfully aware, this new paganism came to Europe in spite of the opposition of the European elite. The European lower classes are infected and in twenty or thirty years will be undistinguishable from their American models. And that means, of course, that in twenty or thirty years Europe as a whole will be indistinguishable from America. The American experience will be repeated exactly. The consuming class will become the only class, and it will rule such dissidents as remain with as little mercy as possible. We know from experience that this new class is exceedingly arrogant and will stick at nothing. The opportunity to consume has become the right to consume and he who would come between them and their bones should know the dangers he faces."

If he was correct in his appraisal, modern Europe is already Americanized to precisely the degree that the existence of America has pulled it from its own direction. Thus, it is quite possible that the European of 1968 would be far closer in outlook and way of life to the European of 1900 if America had never existed. It is even possible that the "consuming class" would never have arisen in Europe without the American example.

(It is certain that such a class could not have come to its present level without American participation in World War II and subsequent American resistance to Russia via the nuclear shield. Without such protection, it is quite likely that the slovenly inefficiency of eastern Europe would be the order of the day throughout the Continent, and Paris and London no better off than Warsaw and Prague. Consequently, it seems that America not only created modern Europe, but made — and makes — its continued existence possible. The child remains utterly dependent on the parent for its rapid rate of growth.)

Such American influence, such Americanization, is so basic and inchoate as to pale the more conscious aspects of colonization. On consideration, one is obliged to concede it as a fact — as the first and inescapable fact, so overwhelming that many otherwise important questions are snuffed out almost before they are formed. For example, many intelligent Europeans, following the Servan-Schreiber argument, would feel that Europe had re-assumed control of its own affairs if it raised its technological competence to a level equal or superior to that of America. But if Europe is already Americanized at its psychological and social roots, such a distinction becomes trivial. As does the idea that the decline of America, whether from internal collapse or external attack, would spell the end of the Americanization process. Just as modern Europe could not have come into being if America had never been, so the consumer-society Europe of the future does not depend on continued American existence any more than European Christianity in the Dark Ages depended on the continued existence of Rome. Russian control of all Europe would slow the process enormously but could not extinguish it or prevent its eventual triumph.

Thus one is rather embarrassed to find at the very outset that the entire subject can be viewed as closed if the view is confined to Mr. Eliot's fundamental point. On the other hand, it is too important a subject to be buried under any single truth, no matter how compelling.

The solution — or compromise, if that is the more accurate term — would seem to lie in an attempt to hold those two facts in as steady a balance as possible. Europe is already Americanized, but there is still much of importance to discover about the process. Abandoning the subject because it is closed in one sense would seriously diminish the understanding of a phenomenon of great significance.

It should be kept in mind that surrender and conquest are delicate subjects for the living, for those who must exist in ordinary proximity afterwards. And that one cannot avoid speaking of colonization with regret; it is unattractive just because it does always imply brutality on one side and timidity on the other. One can hardly help but wonder if it is not blatantly sexual at bottom; whether, if the colonizer is a type, the colonizee isn't, too. If so, the relationship between the two can be seen as a variant of the murderer-murderee, sadist-masochist, and man-woman pairings. Indeed, two psychiatrists have claimed to me that many people, European as well as American, subconsciously see America as a white man and Europe as a Negro.

However, it can — it should — be pointed out that in the end America may be only a duplication of Europe as failure, and thus, on another level, a colonizee to Europe as colonizer. This possibility applies with unusual force to the specter of American collapse, which seems in 1969 to be geared to a nineteenth-century European pattern of disaffected youth and endemic violence. As America colonized Europe technologically, Europe may be cross-fertilizing America with its own ancient compulsions to suicide, equally "tested" and equally irresistible. If this is what is happening, the balance would seem to be even in terms of superiority and inferiority. The legitimacy of such an hypothesis is not contested, but a thorough examination of it does not lie within the scope of this book, which is confined to American influence in Europe and so must deal with the conqueror triumphant abroad without inquiring into his problems at home. European influence in America deserves a book to itself, and it is to be hoped that it will appear before too long. Louis Heren's *The American Commonwealth,* in which he compares modern America to medieval England, complete with contests between powerful kings and rampaging nobles, is a promising if rather simplistic beginning. Strictly speaking, the colonizee must imitate with some consciousness; a coincidental duplication does not really qualify.

In any case, following Mr. Eliot's line, no matter what happens in America, the American influence in Europe will continue to have, as it has had to date, a life of its own. Like a number of other organisms in nature, the animal can exist without the head.

In my own experience, which includes that of all with whom I have discussed direct American control, it was far more apparent in Europe in the late 1940s and early 1950s than it is today. In those days, the Marshall Plan–ECA days, Europe was visibly poor and resident Americans of a different world. The American government distributed the money (ECA funds) to the deserving European companies, and American business stood by to supply needed goods and equipment in return for the same money. A Milanese textile firm, for example, could receive a loan for three million dollars in the morning to refit its ravaged factory and have the funds placed with an American textile-machinery manufacturer by five o'clock in the afternoon. In some cases, the orders were made before or at the same time as the ECA money was scheduled to be paid over, in which instances the check didn't have to go through foreign hands at all, but could be shifted directly from the American government to the American business. (In January, 1969, an aide to General Valdiva, one of the directors of the coup d'état in Peru in October, 1968, said, as quoted by the *New York Times:* "About 85 percent of foreign aid received by Latin America each year is in the form of interest-bearing loans, and 90 percent of United States aid never leaves that country." Europe was in the same position twenty years before, although I don't recall any European stating it so precisely.)

In those days, of course, many needed items were not available except from America, but even when a Continental printer, for example, could have bought a replacement press cheaper from England with his ECA check, there was pressure applied to make him see that it was only fair to spend it where he got it. "It goes without saying that with ECA money you do not buy except from American firms," was the commonsense refrain of European executives in those days, and the atmosphere of near-wartime jobbery was in the air. Coarse or not, that is the true atmosphere of privilege, and in those palmy days the American had only to speak to be obeyed in Europe. The Europeans still felt and acted like a conquered people — to them, ECA was merely an extension of the victor's prerogatives — and were only too ready to supply what was needed. The American's asparagus was carried to him in respectful hands, his sheets were ironed with care, and his mistresses were the cream of the very first sweep through the vineyards. He was not beloved, perhaps, but he was in charge and catered to — infinitely more so on the personal level than he is today. But no one *said* he was in charge then and everyone does now.

A statistical case, in terms of investment dollars and interlocking directorates and other indicators of economic control, can be made for those who feel that American penetration is greater today. And because of the current popularity of the position, the demand for such a case has created a brisk market for those who can supply it. But we have often found, to our sorrow as well as our confusion, that a statistical case can be made for anything; and statistical conclusions are doubly suspect when full data is not available. Today's penetration is fairly well documented at certain levels, but the 1945–1960 period, especially the 1945–1953 subdivision, is not, so there is no reliable basis for statistical comparison. Also, and more significantly, there are levels for which no statistics can or do exist.

In the end, the question of when American control was highest is a matter of opinion based on empirical observations, of which statistics are only a part — and a dubious part. In my view and in that of over ninety per cent of the European and American businessmen and independent analysts with whom I have discussed the question, direct American control is far less today than it was in 1945–

1953, and appreciably less than in 1953–1960. The popular view that the reverse is the case can be dismissed as yet another example of the truism that the public is always behind the times.

(Direct American control is not, of course, the same thing as Americanization, which is, as shall be seen, quite a bit more pervasive and lasting.)

Although startling, the delay in recognition is hardly abnormal; quite the opposite, in fact. When one recalls, for example, that capitalism had been in existence for hundreds of years before Adam Smith defined it in *The Wealth of Nations* — surely the classic example of observational delay — it is hardly surprising that American hegemony has been overlooked until now. In discussing the delay, a number of French and Swiss businessmen have claimed to me that Europeans can afford to be more conscious and critical of American economic controls now because they are so much better off. The theory implies that such criticism is brought out by prosperity, and the extent of the criticism becomes an accurate barometer of the extent of the prosperity, which did not reach the level at which criticism becomes mandatory until the 1960s. In the 1945–1960 period, Europeans just weren't sufficiently well-heeled to complain. They first (1945–1953) had to survive, and then to adjust to the possibility that the relative prosperity was not going to vanish overnight again. Since the economic-psychological corner was turned around 1960, the novelty of affluence has worn off, and, human nature being what it is, resentment of the American economic presence has set in.

There is much to be said for this view because it reconciles and explains the apparent contradiction between the 1945–1960 silence, when American control was greater, and the rising stridency of 1960–1968, as the control lessened. "People only notice what they can afford to notice," an Italian industrialist said to me recently. "After the war, Europe couldn't do anything about the American presence so we couldn't afford to notice it. Now we are stronger and can bring certain pressures to bear, so the matter has been opened for discussion. And I remember, too, that after the war America was our only defense against Russia, and for several years no one knew for sure that Russia would not try to overrun us. With such a danger, you do not ask too many questions of the only defense."

In an even more dramatic example of the human reluctance to think about what cannot be changed, a German-Jewish business-man pointed out to me that "the Allies could not dwell on the hor-rors of the German concentration camps, despite documented ac-counts, until the war had been won. In 1939–1945, the war took priority over everything else, as it had to. And from 1945 until about ten years ago, recovery from the war was of first importance in Europe. Again, it had to be. The extent of American influence was beside the point until that recovery was accomplished."

There are parallel examples in our own time, such as the recent reaction to Michael Holroyd's biography of Lytton Strachey, in which Strachey, Lord Keynes, and many other prominent English-men of the twenties and thirties are revealed to have been ardent homosexuals. Once the fact had been established publicly, a great number of letters appeared in newspapers and magazines from per-sons only too anxious to corroborate Holroyd, whose main source — correspondence between Strachey and Keynes — was hardly open to question, and to add further names from their own recollection. Rampant homosexuality in the English upper class between the wars is now accepted as a historical fact, but — and this is the only point of interest in a discussion of delay — it could not have been so accepted until now. The Strachey-Keynes letters could not have been referred to, let alone published, in 1925–1939. Nor could those who have now rushed forward with their own information have done so in that period with any more confidence than a Rus-sian could have spoken before 1953 of his experiences in a Stalinist prison camp.

In its review of the Strachey biography, *Time* (May 10, 1968) said: "Holroyd discloses that like Strachey, Keynes was a homosexual and a frequent rival for the affections of winsome young men; it was a proclivity that did not affect Keynes's later standing as one of the world's great economists." It did not affect that standing only because it was not known; and in time, now that it is known, it may have that effect after all, especially if his theories are superseded. In fact, the supersedure has already started. In the United States, Milton Friedman and the so-called Chicago economists claim that Keynes's theory of private investment and government spending being of more influence on economic activity than the quantity of money available does not work out, and they back up their views with impressive proof. In Britain, the Keynesian prescription for curbing consumer spending — devaluation, drastic reductions in public expenditures and a stringent budget — has failed. Ten years from now, the exploded Keynesian system may be dismissed as the work of a "nutty queer."

Because the extent of upper-class English homosexuality was known to so many heterosexual Englishmen, it can be claimed that their denial of the fact when speaking to the less well-informed indicated they were living in a coercive society. But perhaps even the people who knew it didn't know they knew it, or couldn't admit to themselves that they knew it, any more than Stalin's Russians could face what they knew. If the Strachey-Keynes correspondence had fallen, for example, into Evelyn Waugh's hands in 1933, would he have been able to do anything with it ("Duncan Grant is the full moon of heaven," Strachey wrote to Keynes on one occasion about a young man they were both interested in) in terms of his own artistic development, or would it have so depressed him in its sinister emptiness that he would have had to deny its existence to himself in order to go on writing at a more possible level?

Put another way, shall we find out in 1995 that the American upper and artistic classes were — *what?* — in 1960? In 1963, Jackie Kennedy's position in history seemed as settled as that of Penelope in legend, but five years later she married Onassis and much of the historical Jackie disappeared. The interesting question is how

[163]

much more could go, not only of Jackie but of so many other figures. We know that Lester Maddox and George Romney will be regarded as meaningless in future generations; is it possible that all the Kennedys and Truman Capote and Barbra Streisand might be reduced to the same insignificance?

Put in yet another but more immediate form, will we find out now that the economic-social control of another country is such a delicate subject that a painting of its real face in its own time is unacceptable? The reality of control is far more taboo than sex today, and to mention it at all is to tread on toes; to be specific about its actual appearance is to raise howls of denial based in part on the assumption that no one would be frank about such a distasteful subject unless he had a moral judgment to pass. As in any other taboo field, science and the disinterested observer are suspect.

Henry Adams was quoted earlier on the origins of American ambition and power. His views are deterministic as well as psychologically dramatic, and exceedingly relevant on both counts. Fortune's darling was beloved only because — and only as long as! — she represented Progress, which Adams defined as "the development and economy of Forces." In a chapter in the *Education* entitled "A Dynamic Theory of History," he goes on to say: "Further, it [a dynamic theory] defines force as anything that does, or helps to do work. Man is a force; so is the sun; so is a mathematical point, though without dimensions or known existence. Man commonly begs the question by taking for granted that he captures the forces. A dynamic theory, assigning attractive force to opposing bodies in proportion to the law of mass, takes for granted that the forces of nature capture man." (Anticipating McLuhan's pop "to the spoils belong the victor" by sixty years and in the round.) Nations and civilizations rise and fall almost solely in terms of their reaction to the forces revealed to them.

Christianity, for example, becomes the result of an economy in gods. "With the relentless logic that stamped Roman thought, the empire, which had established unity on earth, could not help establishing unity in heaven. It was induced by its dynamic necessities to economize the gods. . . . Good taste forbids saying that Constantine the Great speculated as audaciously as a modern stockbroker on values of which he knew at the utmost only the volume; or that he merged all uncertain forces into a single trust, which he enormously overcapitalized, and forced on the market; but this is the substance of what Constantine himself said in his Edict of Milan in the year 313, which admitted Christianity into the Trust of State Religions. Regarded as an Act of Congress, it runs: 'We have resolved to grant to Christians as well as all others the liberty to practise the religion they prefer, in order that whatever exists of divinity or celestial power may help and favor us and all who are under our government.' The empire pursued power — not merely spiritual but physical — in the sense in which Constantine issued his army order the year before, at the battle of the Milvian Bridge: *In hoc signo vinces!* using the Cross as a train of artillery, which, to his mind, it was. Society accepted it in the same character. Eighty years afterwards, Theodosius marched against his rival Eugene with the Cross for physical champion; and Eugene raised the image of Hercules to fight for the pagans; while society on both sides looked on, as though it were a boxing-match, to decide a final test of force between the divine powers. The Church was powerless to raise the ideal. What is now known as religion affected the mind of old society but little. The laity, the people, the million, almost to a man, bet on the gods as they bet on a horse."

After the simple religious unity of the Middle Ages was overwhelmed by material multiplicity, the Cross was doomed. "Except as reflected in himself, man has no reason for assuming unity in the universe . . . The *a priori* insistence on this unity ended by fatiguing the more active — or reactive — minds; and Lord Bacon tried to stop it. He urged society to lay aside the idea of evolving the universe from a thought, and to try evolving thought from the universe. The mind should observe and register forces — take them apart and put them together — without assuming unity at all. 'Nature, to be commanded, must be obeyed.' 'The imagination must be given not wings but weights.' As Galileo reversed the action of earth and sun, Bacon reversed the relation of thought to force. The mind was thenceforth to follow the movement of matter, and unity must be left to shift for itself. . . . For his true followers science always meant self-restraint, obedience, sensitiveness to impulse from without. . . . The success of his method staggers belief, and even today can be treated by history only as a miracle of growth, like the sports of nature. Evidently a new variety of mind had appeared. Certain men merely held out their hands — like Newton, watched an apple; like Franklin, flew a kite; like Watts, played with a tea-kettle — and great forces of nature stuck to them as though she were playing ball."

In this view, the Americans are nothing more or less than the most devoted Baconians. They were the first to bow completely (the English bowed first, but not completely, as has been seen) to the marvels of the past couple of centuries — steam power, electric power, atomic power, and so on — and the most religious in carrying the revealed forces to their ultimates. Conversely, and for purposes of perspective, one might say that among the industrial countries, the French are the most reluctant Baconians and have had to be dragged kicking and screeching through every stage of their development. The attitude is epitomized in de Gaulle, who may not represent all Frenchmen but who does stand for a goodly number or he would not have been in power at all. After three hundred years of evidence to the contrary, he still imagines that destiny can be commanded (rather than served), and huffs and puffs to impose his will in the most pathetically out-of-date style. (One is tempted to call the style Catholic, but the Vatican has long since abandoned such notions.) The results can be — as they were in 1968 — violent as well as comic.

If American international influence is considered in humanistic as well as deterministic terms, the same dedication is evident. The universal human appetite since the Reformation has been essentially materialistic and the problem of government how best to feed it. England became the most powerful nation in the world in the eighteenth century just because it responded most completely and effectively to this challenge; and its hegemony lasted until the late nineteenth century when Germany and America, but most especially America, developed their own, more effective responses. America finally won out simply because it offered the greatest material benefits to its own people, which, in turn, created a greater demand for those increased benefits in the rest of the world.

This contest — the word is exact — was carried on in relative obscurity until the winner was revealed. Then — roughly at the close of World War I — the establishment of a materialistic order of precedence became public knowledge. Since that time, the world's non-Americans have demanded American materialism in their own countries and regions. The demand has proved stronger than any diversions their harassed rulers have been able to think of — wars, appeals to dying cultural, family and religious customs, harangues on other values — and increases with time, intensifying an already powerful American world leadership.

The demand is, perhaps, rarely made in the name of America now. Indeed, the source may be forgotten, and the innocent on-looker may wonder how an Italian demand for Italian automobiles and washing machines intensifies American leadership. But the enactment anywhere of the proposition that the main business of people is to consume, and the main business of government and business to produce, supports and increases American hegemony if the accrued balance of many infinitesimal imitations is carefully weighed. The farther subsidiary consumption-production is carried, the more profound the subsidiary's understanding of what remains to be done and the more potent the leadership of the place where it has already been done. There is a parallel in the organization of the Roman Catholic Church, by which Vatican leadership is actually enhanced to the degree that Catholic nation-states can be allowed autonomy. The emulation and admiration of the relatively independent is a far sturdier prop than the admittedly slavish dependence of the undeveloped, and poor Bolivians are not worth so much to either Rome or New York as prosperous Italians.

So in the Adams consideration, the American advantage is the result of the work of two very different groups of men. First the revolutionaries, who were determined to force England into an entirely new political system, a plan which ran far beyond the popular notion of the Revolutionary War as the adjustment of colonial wrongs or even the founding of an independent state. After he saw England put into the American orbit, Adams felt that Europe, Russia and China would be drawn in in that order, with the smaller and weaker countries following them as a matter of course. By 1918, the year in which he died, only Russia and China were outside. Now, in 1969, China has been complaining for several years that Russia has been pulled in, which would seem to leave only China to come.

Of course, the non-American world has not been drawn into a political system as such. America as political theory died with the Civil War (again, according to Adams), and after that the system boiled itself down into an "enlightened capitalism" in which the American people were given relatively greater personal freedom to make and buy more material goods. Nothing more, but also nothing less. By a remarkably fortuitous coincidence, America was blessed not only with exceptionally able revolutionary leadership, but also with equally able Baconian captains of industry — Henry Ford as well as John Adams. The more efficient way of producing goods meshed smoothly into the more elastic political system; and the twin pre-eminence, in production as well as political theory, has proved irresistible.

The new political system came (and comes) down to giving people the personal freedom to do and have more of what they want; and it turns out that what they want — in Nigeria and Indonesia as well as in Cleveland and the slums of Liverpool — is an increasing number of goods and services. Thus America is the answer adopted by shrewd nationalists all over the world ("You want materialism? I'll give you materialism!") and will be the answer, no matter how paraphrased, until another *want* replaces the passion for the material.

It is thus obvious that American leadership is double-edged. In addition to the America that controls directly through economic imperialism, as in western Europe, there is the America that is the spiritual ruler in countries where very few if any American men of business operate, as in eastern Europe. In certain special instances — England is one — the dream and the reality are merged in a dazzling combination of octopus and iron maiden.

Naturally enough, one does not expect any of the players to be conscious of the development of their positions. Or even to realize that they have positions. In the lobby of the Hotel des Bergues, in Geneva, an American businessman clumps ponderously to the desk, the eyes filled with an uncertainty that does not bespeak the conqueror, the body slack and nearly devoid of tensile meaning, the voice cadaverous and hesitant, the large hands pathetically lifeless as they close on the registration pen — and an observer can hardly find Adams and Bacon and Jefferson behind this cored member of the *apparat* of world control. In fact, an observer can hardly believe that America — if this citizen is a fair example — can be controlling anything.

The businessman himself would agree. He is so much the result that the beginning must be a permanently sealed mystery. Picking up salted nuts later in the bar with one heavy hand and transporting a dry martini to rather pallid lips with the other, he would forever deny or be ignorant of his historical position should anyone be so rash as to suggest it to him. Even intelligent Americans have an animal aversion to being classified, and even the most lethargic recognize the danger signals.

But the observer's dismissal and the businessman's agreement (and denial) are predictable and beside the point. They cannot be otherwise. And no serious student of the question can afford to believe for a moment that they could be otherwise. Nor can he afford to doubt that if the development of the positions has been Baconian, the final Baconism lies in a dedication to the evidence itself and a determination not to be swerved. He walks Piccadilly, the Champs Élysées, Piazza Venezia — all clogged with cars at six in the evening now, the drivers pale in the monoxide haze, the supermarkets waiting in the nearly unattainable suburban distance — and realizes they wouldn't be as they are without the American example. He goes further and understands that modern Europe as a whole could not have happened without the American example. If America hadn't developed mass production and the consumer society, Europe might well be still mainly horse-drawn, gas-lit and long-skirted. The only question is to what degree. Humbling thoughts in the gray-greens of twilight in the Place de la Concorde . . . but also rather strange and touched with the thrill of discovery. The terrible power of America can hardly find more indelible testimony than in the possibility it pushed Europe's clock ahead a full half-century.

Once the indispensability and root power of America are appreciated, the popular — certainly the secondary — explanations of her successes begin to assume some life. Not a great deal, because they are so immovably secondary, but enough to win a temporary attention now that they have a base under them.

"Well, America is the most powerful country in the world," says the lower-middle-class English housewife in her inimitable twang, "so the Americans were bound to 'take over,' weren't they, like water seeks its own level. They're the only ones who can cope with it, aren't they, and that's the reason they're the ones who are doing it — the leaders, you might say."

What she says is true, in a way, and one is grateful for any reduction in complexity, but . . . the most lasting impression of her little speech is of the substitution of "like" for "as" in the American style, an error — if one can still call it that — of which she would not have been guilty ten years ago. Words as such fail, as usual, in the teeth of their capacity for inadvertent demonstration.

This housewife — or anyone else, on either side of the Atlantic — could go on to point out the surface American advantages that made takeover inevitable: the doing away (on a relative basis) with red tape; the superior political system and production methods; the willingness to submerge differences to achieve a common goal; the capacity for adventurousness in economic methodology; the refusal to be bamboozled; and the powers of anticipation (as demonstrated in the ability to delineate the characters and actions of Europeans — Giorgio Vellati and Servan-Schreiber are examples — long before they are called to center stage). All these obvious advantages mesh together (they are often indistinguishable) and support each other.

On the debit side, Europe exhibits the converses of the American strengths and then adds her own, original weaknesses. The conversity includes: red tape by the unlimited Dickensian reel — the armies of ill-fed clerks still pushing steel-nibbed pens in every government office step intact from the nineteenth century and are, perhaps, Europe's prime shock for the American visitor; inferior political systems (speaking technologically, of course) and production methods; the inability to submerge differences — the resistance to the Common Market and the continued existence of antiquated customs procedures are expected symptoms; and the timidity, as demonstrated, for example, in the inability of financial interests in the City of London several years ago to fight a company takeover by Reynolds Aluminum — the restrictive old-boyism of the City was disillusioning enough to the Englishman still trying to take his country seriously, but the incapacity for change was decisively disheartening.

The most damaging original weakness is emotionalism. In England, for instance, any enterprise of magnitude begun in the past twenty-odd years — the construction of new jet aircraft is the most striking example — has been invariably tied up with the Queen, Sir Francis Drake and other extraneous anachronisms. The English could not reduce the production of aircraft to a business and nothing else, so lost the market to the Americans who could. (Doing anything for the money is far closer to doing it for its own sake — the most efficient approach — than doing it for the Queen.) The English could never have had all the market, of course, but they could have had much more than they do. As has been noted, emotionalism led England to think it was capable of doing more than it could, so it ended up doing less than it should. In France, de Gaulle really believed that a French industry suffused with *la gloire* was a qualitative match for the American production juggernaut. In Germany, the *Vaterland* is an occasional distraction, and the rest of Europe has similar mirages.

European feudalism is almost as weakening as its emotionalism. I recall a young Italian aristocrat telling me languidly several years ago that the Italian government had just given him the exclusive right to import a kind of tubing into Italy. This Luchino was not a businessman and had not made any sort of bid on the franchise — it had been "arranged" by his relatives in the government and the Church to give him a strong income. He, in turn, leased his monopoly to a genuine importing concern which then imported the tubing, the ultimate price, of course, reflecting a large slice to Luchino. Thus in 1955, Italian business was paying an enormous annual tithe to the Italian nobility and its silent partner, the Vatican, a baroque financial arrangement unchanged from the late Renaissance. Such practices are supposed to have diminished in Mediterranean Europe in recent years, but that may well be a wishful supposition.

(They also exist in middle and northern Europe, and on a wider scale than commonly presumed.)

The enormous physical resources lying within the United States are often cited as yet another American advantage over Europe, but here one wonders. In the past twenty years, America has had increasingly to go abroad for raw materials, and could not now maintain its economic machine on purely domestic sources. The world's raw materials seem to end up in the hands of the most ingenious, and if Europe had been better adapted than America for the twentieth century, it is a near certainty that the American natural resources would have ended up under the European thumb, even if processed in America itself. (One recalls that Englishmen owned much stock in American businesses before the overseas holdings were sold off: if the sale had not been forced because of the war, etc., such a base could have grown to formidable proportions.)

In the end, it is not resources but intelligence that counts. America, shrewder on a broader base, and blessed with the awful leverage of anticipation, conquers by handling technology so much better. And holds onto the conquered territory by applying the necessarily ingrained ruthlessnesses and ingratitudes. In the last years of his life, this was forcibly borne in on Lord Keynes, who had given the United States Keynesian economics, an invaluable asset in the establishment of the American leadership. In human terms, he had the right to expect special consideration from America for himself and his country in the creation of the postwar monetary world, but the Americans with whom he had to work at Bretton Woods and elsewhere noted the absence of an acknowledged bill for services rendered and refused to pay off on hints and innuendoes. He was even treated roughly at the end by hard men with small eyes and flat voices who acted almost as though they knew about Duncan Grant being the full moon of heaven and felt, in their harsh puritanism, that such indulgences on his part severely limited his rights. Armed and ticking at close range, Americans can kill Europeans with their hardness, and Keynes only lasted through a few years with them. The gifted economist, so facile in his field, was not by any means prepared for the literal adaptation of his theories by those most able to derive benefit from them. The fact that no economic sleight-of-hand can cope with, let alone dominate, human grunt and grind came as a distinct shock to him. And if to him, how much more so to the ordinary European?

Try as one can to concentrate on the popular (secondary) explanations of American control, attention is always led back to the underlying (primary) advantages. With such advantages, the penetrations and takeovers were inevitable. Without them, the control would not have been possible, and the secondary explanations would not have become necessary clichés.

Above all, the observer of Europe must be empirical. If Americans are nothing more or less than the most devoted Baconians (empiricists), then an American writer can hardly help but appreciate himself as most effective when most in the national mold — when most empirical. He never forgets Adams's remark: "For his [Bacon's] true followers science always meant self-restraint, obedience, sensitiveness to impulse from without"; nor the statement of Bacon himself: "The imagination must be given not wings but weights." He guards against the American tendency to abandon Baconism when it does not serve a predetermined end, or to refuse to use it on American results as distinguished from American intentions. And he takes special care to follow any observation out to the end, to avoid the particular downfall of so many American writers who insist that only the emperor "of their choice" is unclothed.

The observer cannot afford to find anything in Europe except what he can observe; he loses all if he attempts more or less. Finely interpreted, the empirical method could yield the whole story from very little. If there were no other material, the European position could be deduced from the books already written on it, if they were treated — as Servan-Schreiber's has already been briefly considered — as part of the position itself. All that has happened and will happen is revealed in them, however inadvertently, and a conscientious "study of the studies" would give the same results as a close investigation of the breathing whole.

It should also be stressed that the resources of conventional reportage on America in Europe are exhausted, very much as they are everywhere else. The exhaustion is twofold: the ground has been covered and re-covered, and the method itself is bankrupt. The same outmoded reporters — heavy men, most of them, with deep voices and hairy forearms and eyes of surpassing indifference — have trudged back and forth across Europe and left its story strikingly untold. In article after article and book after book they have dozed along the familiar paths: tired interviews with public figures, hatfuls of smudged statistics, creaking anecdotes about the boredom of American business wives in Geneva and the coarseness of German executives in the Ruhr. They have lost the power of getting to the fundamental, of piercing to the human; the conqueror's reporters, and their native imitators, are as mechanical as his computers. What is needed, *in extremis*, is the fresh breath of the primitive. (Even a book as relatively well produced as *Anatomy of Europe,* by Anthony Sampson — published in Britain as *The New Europeans* — is depressingly banal. There is some relief here, though, in the unintended comedy between the lines of a British author who has no conception of the extent to which England has been colonized. He writes as though there is still a British presence and authority, and urges Europe to take his country into the Common Market for its "stabilizing influence." The idea that shredded England could stabilize anything is so fantastic that anyone proposing it seriously — only a very shredded native could be so rash — becomes a figure of memorable fun in his own right.)

Perhaps the most pertinent detail of the story about Maury Madder and Giorgio Vellati, cited earlier in "In General," is that it was known to nearly all Americans who later wrote about their countrymen in Italy in that period, and yet none of them used it. Similar examples from other European countries and times have been equally well known to nearly all Americans who have written anything about American influence in Europe since the war, and yet none of them use such material. They have preferred to remain with the surface and the unearned generalities. But, as noted above, they have run that reportorial technique to its end. Enormously powerful and disturbing thoughts and images have been released in the past few years and only a concern with the simple and the direct can now sustain prose writing as a rival to life itself. The hairy forearms move in vain now, if at all.

In a book such as this, there can be no attempt to classify American control ethically. The phenomenon is treated here only as a fact, with no pretense to moral judgment, even when such judgments can be implied from unavoidable associations. For example, one may point out, in discussing the Europe of 1950 by comparing it to contemporary South America, that in November, 1967, there was wide newspaper coverage of the possibility that the American government might cut off its aid program to a South American country if that country bought French rather than American jet aircraft with the aid; and that this is a current illustration of the former climate in Europe, except that in Europe in 1950 such a squabble might not have found its way into the newspapers. It may seem disparaging to the United States to draw attention to such details of modern political-economic life, and in that sense, a cursory reader may find a judgment implied. But the fact cannot be stated without that hazard — i.e., one cannot discuss the similarity between Europe in 1950 and South America in 1967 without running the risk of being misunderstood — and so there must be a certain dependence on the reader making an effort to keep intent in mind. In casual discussion, it is easy to say that American control is unattractive; but one must qualify that by adding that all foreign control is unattractive. Because such control seems to be a chronic necessity, the American version may actually be less unattractive than most if not all others. Thus the ultimate morality of the American control is debatable; its existence is not.

The resistance to Americanization is another matter, although at the present time it appears to be confined to conversation and relatively innocuous. The conversation is gathering momentum, but it is still conversation. As of the time I write (June, 1969), prices on the New York Stock Exchange show that American investment is betting that Europe cannot mount an effective resistance within the next five years. If the opposite were true, stock prices would have to drop in many key issues which are now dependent on maintaining the present position of American business in Europe and even increasing its influence. (Stocks might drop for other reasons, but they can only hold at the present level or go up if Europe remains under the American thumb.) Because the investment bet represents money, it is a more persuasive indicator of the future than all the talk and books to the contrary.

But it is not an infallible indicator by any means, especially for the future beyond five years. And it is not at all impossible that Europe, the western center of religious convulsions, will again be moved by forces beyond current imagination to take action against its situation vis-à-vis America.

Idle speculation about the future — often the most rewarding kind — makes one wonder if Europe will ever fight anything again. One drives through Lyons in the rain and realizes how completely its clock is stopped, how much more paralyzed than Pittsburgh or Detroit or Gary it is (they are still *becoming*), and how it could only come to life again if the frozen city were torn down and plowed under. With such feeble opposition one is sure, at least momentarily, that America, like Rome, will not be overturned from without. Technologically speaking, the rest of the world is composed of barbarians and incapable of the act. If and when it happens, it will have to come from inside the country.

In such an eventuality, Russia might fill the power vacuum by taking over; and to the extent that Russia is a European country it might seem Europe had triumphed over her old nemesis. But unless Russia and her western Europe substituted some other idea-method for the American philosophy of increased material consumption as the apex of human evolution (American production methods are not so important), America would rule from the grave, the spiritual leader enshrined in the dream, as, even today, modern India operates within an English framework although England and the Englishmen are gone forever.

The memory of English influence exists today in many countries which were never part of the British Empire, the residue of England's position as psychological world leader in the centuries from the Reformation to the American ascendancy. The victor's crown has gone from Rome (pagan *and* Catholic) to England to America — there are no others in the legitimate, two-thousand-year line. All other countries and regions in the west have always been psychologically subordinate to one of the three since the time of Augustus. For this reason, what one learns about England applies, in part, to all of Europe. And what one discovers about the Americanization of England applies, also in part, to the Americanization of each and every part of Europe. Thus much of what was previously pointed out about Americanization in England should be kept in mind as existing in each country treated in this section on western Europe, even if it is not repeated — as it cannot be — in each instance.

France, Germany, Italy (as distinguished from Rome), and other European countries have not been world leaders as the term is used above, but they have influenced each other in their several ways, and much of what is said about any one of them in this section on western Europe applies to the others, especially when the characteristic under discussion is European rather than regional or national. Thus there is a definite cross-accumulation of detail supporting and extending each individual section.

In practical terms, to return to the importance of adding one's own emotion to the physical and psychological presences, one must attempt to be accurate about those personal feelings. For example, the recent student riots in France and Italy and Germany are only clear when the emotional sense adds to the noise and blood a consciousness that they are *pathetic*. With perfectly predictable irony, the European student riots are an imitation of the American student riots (in obedience to the law that all American phenomena are to be imitated) without a clear understanding of the reasons for them. The rioting American student is protesting a system that prepares him for the American way: he feels it overprepares him, and he doesn't like the American way anyhow. The rioting European student has felt for some time that his universities are old-fashioned: that is, un-American. They prepare him for a life that no longer exists: that is, a pre-American life. But he wants to be trained for successful Americanism because, after surrender, common sense demands that the stronger magic of the conqueror be learned and mastered. The European student knows he does not possess a social sense and has no power of discrimination in the modern world — which is almost as bad as having no sense of money — and he wants to be taught those skills so he can participate.

Naturally, he doesn't feel and want and know all about his passion for Americanism consciously; he knows no more consciously than that he resents his universities. So when he learns that American students resent their universities, too, he unconsciously assumes that they are unhappy for the same reasons. Consciously, because he imitates everything American as a first rule of conduct, he knows it is time to riot.

Thus one *sees* the awkward arms heaving the paving blocks, but it doesn't end there because one also *feels* the pathos of the imitation based on a near-complete misunderstanding. No picture of the riot is clear unless that feeling is included.

The young French faces I saw at the Sorbonne and the Théâtre de France all shared bewilderment and childish hope, qualities which invariably bring out the grossest official and police brutalities. The brutalities were thus inadvertent affirmation of the pathos — full substantiation if one didn't trust one's own judgment. So, later, was the massive vote for de Gaulle. Humanity can't stand a general pathos, especially humanity in Europe, where the landscape is crowded with reminders of what happens when pathos takes charge, and where there is a current determination not to let it get the upper hand again. Not the least important reason is that pathos is un-American and interferes with the Americanization process.

"We Americans do so well, businesswise, where the more sophisticated appetites are already awakened," a high American executive declares. "Europe is the perfect example. And so poorly where they aren't, in the backward and undeveloped countries. Which is why Vietnam is such a disaster. If we were as intelligent in Washington as we should be able to afford to be, we'd *let* the poor countries go Communist and forget about them until they got tired of it and were ready to live a little. Or a lot. Once a country has gone through the Communist experience it never wants to try it again. All it wants is peace and quiet and good living. Everything we already have in America and that we can help them get. I'll go farther — if we were really as intelligent in Washington as we should be able to afford to be, we'd *urge* the Communist experience on the poorer countries. It's the foolproof way to make them into permanently enlightened capitalists. Instead of deciding to fight in Vietnam, we should have said, 'You can have it!', knowing the Vietnamese, north as well as south, would be as tired of it by 1980 as Czechoslovakia is now."

The same thought was put to me in another way by an American newspaperman, a friend who has spent much time in Vietnam. "You say national surrender is the admission that something is lacking and a willingness to take a chance on the conqueror being able to supply it. But neither the Viet Cong nor the North Vietnamese feel any lack. As Tom Wolfe would say: 'They just can't get excited by the American's button-down shirt with the sweet percale roll to it and start thinking that their own pajama tops look lousy in comparison.' Maybe we can make them think so someday, but I wouldn't count on it."

Such sentiments are not fleshed out insofar as Europe is concerned until the other side is heard from. "Capitalism is relentless in pursuit of profit," a young German Marxist says quietly to his girl as they discuss American business interests in Europe, and for him there is no more to be said. He sits in an old *bierstube* in Cologne, his scraggly beard lit through from behind by the spring sun reflected in the glaze on the fine wood ceiling, his girl picking idly at a matchbox as she listens, her melancholy eyes shaded by long sticky hair, and capitalism is relentless in pursuit of profit and there is no more to be said. Oversimplified or not, though, the Marxian view — as distinct from the views of those countries which espouse Marxism officially — is an interesting one and much of visual Europe supports it.

In the small towns of Switzerland, for example, one sees the solemn Swiss girls in tragic miniskirts and beehive hairdos and one realizes they are dressing as girls do in New York and Paris and London so that they can be there in their minds. Twenty years ago they were one with their village and its life and dressed accordingly. But now, schooled each week by the mass fashion media, they are one with Jackie Onassis and the international set, at least in their conscious dreams. They do not understand, of course, that their clothes announce a profound dissatisfaction with the life of the village; nor do they understand that it is schizophrenic to live physically in the village and mentally and psychologically in Hollywood and St. Tropez. The village is no longer real to its inhabitants, so it is dead, and the Marxist says America killed it. Because America spells death to such European order as did exist without substituting even such order as does exist in America, America is thus construed as responsible for the violence rising in Europe. The non-present villagers are no longer altogether real to themselves (the weapon that finished the village is just as effective on people), and their increased physical activity is not healthy movement but an aimless and violent restlessness symptomatic of a potentially psychotic condition.

Cutting the same material another way, the Marxist will say that the friction between America and the other capitalist countries of western Europe is a fulfillment of the master's prophecy that the capitalist countries can't pull together but must fall out and fight to the death. "The *Time* magazine avers for so many years that Marx is wrong," says the young German, "but then, suddenly, de Gaulle, the arch-bourgeois, turns on the USA and walks out of the NATO and tries to break the dollar and the rest. Unless a holy war against Communism appears — and Russia will not fall into that trap — the struggle over markets will force a war between the competing capitalist countries and Marx will be devoutly vindicated and the *Time* magazine forever discredited."

Even many of the non- or un-Marxists find Americans "hard." There is the technical hardness of the cost accountant ("European employers will often operate a business that is losing money for the sake of old and loyal employees — Americans have no such sense of obligation") and there is also the latent, racial hardness of the average American traveler, the hardness the young German referred to in Katherine Anne Porter's story "The Leaning Tower," the hardness of the type that first seems so simple and nice — the role Marlon Brando has played so often — the "boy" who comes in all smiles and turns out to be a seasoned sadist.

The hardness seems final to Europeans, and they do not realize it is not always the last word. They see the sharply creased robot take over their lives with stupefying assurance, and can't believe it has problems. Little do they dream what often lies behind at "home": the shrewish, adulterous wife; the son on drugs; the daughter pregnant and unmarried; the corporate infighting, feminine and implacable. They do understand that this mechanical man has come to them from a land replete with general worries — polluted air, poisoned food, rampaging Negroes — but they tend to forget that there are personal troubles, too. (And that only a very sick man could make himself into a robot; that such self-mechanization is invariably a symptom of profound sickness.) Perhaps that very morning a telegram has arrived to announce his daughter's suicide. Even now it is folded (neatly) in a pocket: he will have it with him when he makes arrangements to return this afternoon. His glacial self-control does not mean that he is entirely oblivious to what has happened, but that he is a good soldier in the service of his company and his country and will not allow anything to interfere with his duty. If and when the hardness dissolves and he breaks down and weeps like a baby, it will not be in front of his foreign customers and subordinates. He will, if he can, collapse where only other Americans — relatives, psychiatrists and hospital attendants — can see him. No prestige and no orders will be lost that way, and a sacred trust will not be violated. King Arthur's knights were not more dedicated to an ideal.

Perhaps what Europe fails most of all to understand about America is the greater complexity of American life. It is not simple or resolved, but more difficult; not primarily material, but idealistic and abstract. To adopt it successfully, Europe will have to give up much of its own basic materialism, if true materialism is understood as being inseparable from a sense of secure well-being — the French bourgeois locked in his dining room with his *Médaillons de Veau Pyrénéenne* on the table and his gold in the cupboard and his quiet street outside and his certain tomorrow beckoning. This is not the materialism of formal philosophy and ethics, but simply a devotion to material interests. Perhaps the difference should be explained further here, because the word will be used often and exact definition is desirable.

Philosophical materialism insists that everything depends on physical processes, and repudiates idealism, belief in God, free will and so on. Carried to systematic extremes, the theory shows flaws that Marx attempted to reconcile through dialectical materialism, in which man himself interacts with sensory perceptions rather than being little more than their container. Ethical materialism's first modern spokesman, Thomas Hobbes, claimed that the human will is simply the human appetite, which is chiefly dominated by fear and the drive to self-preservation. He drew man as an antisocial creature whose instincts and desires are all self-serving, a theory which has received much support recently from anthropological research. "The object of every voluntary act is some good to itself," was the way he put it, adding that "moral philosophy is nothing but the science of good and evil," and "good and evil are the names that signify our appetites and aversions."

As employed in the present text, the word "materialism" has a limited connection with ethical materialism, but little or none with philosophical materialism. A devotion to material interests, the definition used herein, is only a part — and a very small part — of the human appetites covered by ethical materialism, which is, after all, a comprehensive theory of man as a functioning animal. Ethical materialism offers an explanation for everything, including the entire range of emotions (pity, for example, is the surface manifestation of the fear that what happened to the pitied might happen to oneself, and charity is only the pleasurable exercise of power), whereas we are only concerned here with man's desire to have and to hold exterior material possessions and pleasures. In this sense, none of us can avoid being material up to a point; but after that point has been reached, individual, national and regional commitments vary widely.

Put negatively, we are materialistic to the extent that we have no other interest, especially no other religion. Official Christianity is not ashamed to admit that it stood between the western world and all-out materialism until it went bankrupt in the nineteenth century, after which its disillusioned children, being religious animals as well as materialistic animals, brought the same ardor to worship of the material that they had formerly given the unseen. This worship extends from Moscow to London to San Francisco, but it is dominated in America by capitalism, the official state religion, and in Russia by Communism, also a state religion. Europe has no such official religion and the obeisance to unrelieved materialism is complete.

The generality can be made specific in innumerable observations and comparisons. Contrast: an American woman's indifferent shopping in the assembly-line supermarket with a French or Italian woman's deference before an imaginatively stacked display of fruit in a small shop; a Swiss or German girl's care of her clothes with an American girl's carelessness; the anticipation an Englishman brings to his holidays with an American's boredom; and so on.

The crucial European objection to American life is that it is not comfortable — i.e., it does not give absolute precedence to material well-being. In the European scale of values, the small amenities of life are worth more than a superhighway, which is only a way of getting from one amenity to another. In America, the superhighway — or bridge or skyscraper — is more important than the amenities, which are only useful for killing time between movements. Successful American executives work like dogs; to a European they are unsuccessful because they have no time for pleasure. (My brother spends countless hours flying around the world; very few European businessmen would want to trade places with him. None would want to be Howard Hughes and live in seclusion in a hotel in Las Vegas, surely the most abstract and antimaterialistic of all the residences open to a very rich man.) Under European materialism, it is not the money but what you buy with it; under American capitalism, it is not what you buy, but the money. Capitalism is

[185]

work; materialism is leisure. Capitalism is abstract; materialism is concrete. Capitalism is wanting to be President even if it does shorten your life; materialism is an easy pace and plenty of holidays.

To an American, the automobile is a symbol and an ideal and an easily replaceable tool (the evaluation that reaches its apogee in Texans getting rid of Cadillacs when the ashtrays are full — the tool is replaceable if the ideal is not); to a European, the automobile is a valuable possession to be treasured and enjoyed. It is real to him and he lavishes care on it, and would be shocked to learn that it is only another abstraction in America. (European visitors to the United States are appalled by the gigantic automobile graveyards, not because they are ugly, but because of the disrespect shown to the material. Going the other way, American visitors are often amused at the sight of an entire European family washing the car with obvious affection.)

It is true that Europe is becoming less material and less comfortable and more abstract as Americanization increases, but materialism is still its primary religious emotion. Abandoning it, even piecemeal, is a traumatic experience for most Europeans because it means giving up a completely formed and successful web of existence perfected over hundreds of years and perfectly satisfactory until recently. American life is wildly speculative in comparison, each day fraught with unfathomable consequences, fortune and ruin behind every decision. To live it, one must be both more advanced and willing to put up with a greater regimentation. The Americans accepted those conditions before they built their technological empire; the Europeans have reached for Americanization without realizing what the conditions are. When the bill is presented, will they wish to pay it? Will they be able to pay it?

The existence of Europe had a good deal to do with American willingness to accept the disappearance of many native amenities as part of the price, because they could always slip out to Europe to enjoy them. But where will Europeans go if Europe becomes simi-

larly denuded? In fact, where will Americans go then? Africa?
China? Hardly.

American imperialism had such an innocent beginning — according to Brooks Adams it was merely an extension of the westward movement of the center of trade as determined by laws concerning population densities and new industrialization techniques
— that these latter-day penalties are quite a surprising shock. The
Mexican War, the push to the Pacific, the drive to the setting sun,
"westering" . . . the whole De Voto-Sandburg picture is suddenly
tainted and suspect. The romance is gone (not even John Wayne
can put it back) and the world is left with the image of an aging
and uncertain rapist sitting unhappily in the midst of polluted
wreckage. For Europe, the ancient but sprightly crone who has
been raped so often that one more assault can hardly matter, it is
not the violence of conquest that is disturbing but the question of
aftermath. Will she become just as inert as the conqueror? Does the
colonization mean any more than that when all the refrigerators
and cars and drugstores and LPs and blue jeans are said and done?
Europe is not asking such questions generally yet, but if she does
. . . ? . . .

In the shadow of the Colosseum, I once heard an American florist
describing his life in Los Angeles to a mixed European bag — an
Englishman, two Germans and an Italian. He was devoutly American, as sincere as a Grant Wood farmer, and they were sheepishly
prepared to bask in old-fashioned warmth from the New World.
But what came out — the endless recital of Weimaraner *Kultur* —
was beyond them. The Weimaraners themselves weren't too much,
but what about the Japanese fishing boat, converted into home in
San Pedro?

"We bought it very reasonable," he said, "and outside of putting
in a new teak deck and air-conditioning and a very small swimming
pool amidships and remodeling, we didn't have to do anything
structural to it. And we all pitched in and so did our friends, so it
didn't cost anywhere near what it would if it had all been

[187]

contracted out. It's big — two hundred and twenty feet — with thirteen rooms and the five baths, so we have all the room we need, specially when the kids come home on vacation. Jane is at Harvard taking her Ph.D. in English literature (doing her thesis on what they now think are the lesser-known aspects of general psychoanalysis of this Kafka as paranoid — I dunno, though, because she says he was a pretty nice guy and it seems a shame to disturb sleeping bones), and Bill is in the atonal school at UCLA. And it's good for moving around. We went to the South Seas and Australia last summer and might go through the Canal to the French Riviera next year. The dogs? Oh, they love living on board. You see, they're not ordinary . . ."

The sermon was not in his description of his life, commonplace by Los Angeles if not American standards, but in the four faces gathered close to his. Incredulity, sympathy and apprehension first played across them . . . and then they slumped into a dogged acceptance. If this was to be their future, too — and how could it be otherwise? — they had best be getting used to it. The conquest, the surrender, the present as history . . . all were so tidily gathered and presented in those faces. They were offering not only the story of the conquest but the event itself, and they were finely representative of their three hundred and fifty million fellows, all of whom have come or will come to the same moment in the same way.

2

FRANCE

"**D**E GAULLE is like Hitler," de Renville says to me morosely. "A born loser." It is the night of June 10, 1968, and we are in his beautiful apartment on the Île St. Louis. Through the open windows come the sounds of a city in turmoil, for the final student riots of the Paris spring are in full cry, centered in the Latin Quarter only a few hundred meters from where we sit.

De Renville (as in the section on England, names have been changed where necessary) is in his early fifties, a thin and elegant widower, a member of the inner circle of France's *haute société protestante*, and a very successful manufacturer of heavy machinery. We met last year in Turin through mutual Italian friends, and while I am in Paris I am staying with him and we are doing little things for each other. He is helpful to me with information concerning a new Dutch adventure in precious metals, and I am in the midst of introducing him to some American heavy-machinery people whom he wants to meet but not formally.

I have come to Paris to see the troubles at first hand. The Dutch adventure in precious metals, although very interesting, could have been postponed, but I discovered in England that one learns far more about a country if one doesn't have to ask direct questions.

De Renville and I and his compelling daughter Clothilde, who is twenty-two, charming, and as handsome as Capucine, have just come in from watching the Paris police put on an extremely hysterical exhibition. Finally turned loose by de Gaulle, they literally screamed with excitement as they overran the barricades around the Boulevard Saint-Michel and then beat the students with heavy truncheons and rifle butts. Along with the students, they attacked anyone who happened to be abroad in the Latin Quarter and one saw elderly men and women mercilessly clubbed. De Renville has official connections, and we were accompanied by a plainclothesman whose presence guaranteed safety. Without him, we would probably have been assaulted, and we are a bit ashamed of the official immunity we enjoyed.

The soprano whinnies of the gendarmes reminded me of a record Reginald Gardiner made many years ago in which he imitated train whistles from all over the world and pointed out their reflection of national characteristics. His French whistle, naturally enough, was high and feminine, and even in the midst of the head-knocking I wondered if the French could ever transcend the feminine and the hysterical. The students threw the paving blocks as women throw, the arms awkward and jerky, the aim uncertain. The whole business was pervasively female, in fact, and thus more pathetic than it would have been elsewhere. ("It was like watching a bunch of lesbians fighting," an American reporter said to me later in describing earlier melees he had seen. "I saw a big squabble at the Place Maubert, in May, when it all started, and if you closed your eyes you'd swear it was a bunch of dykes fighting over a new girl in town. Thousands of cops and students and not a man's voice in the whole crowd.")

The *hôtel* in which de Renville has his apartment is very old, and the rooms are large and beautifully proportioned. We sit now in the drawing room, listening to the sirens on the night air. And then de Renville suddenly says: "De Gaulle is like Hitler. A born loser."

He speaks very good American English — or English American — but I am rather surprised at the idiomatic epithet in de Gaulle's case. A born loser? One thought him so successful, in one way if not another.

"No," de Renville says, "he is a loser. You see, the great thing he could have done — the one great thing — would have been to unify Europe. He was the only one who could have done it, as France was the one country that could have done it. If he had loved France, he would have done it. But he really cares no more for France than Hitler did for Germany. Or either of them for Europe. He cares only for himself, only for his own paranoid ideas. And in the end, what is the result? The result of Hitler was to give Europe to the Americans, and the result of de Gaulle is the same thing. He has lost. He has lost France and he has lost Europe. At the end, Hitler was running from one crazy scheme to the next, just as de Gaulle does now — 'nationhood for Québec' and all the other mad plans."

He seems overwrought after what we have seen, and I wonder what Clothilde, sitting with consummate grace in the soft light, makes of what he has said. She divines the curiosity and says with a smile, "My father feels this so deeply because he is officially a Gaullist."

"What else could anyone have been in 1958?" he asks impatiently. "There was nothing else to do. He was the only choice. But once he had power, again like Hitler, he got all of us in so deep with him that he has been able to blackmail us successfully into doing what he wants. . . . After the war, the Germans who were close to Hitler said there was nothing they could have done about him and we all laughed. But now *we* are in the same position with de Gaulle and it isn't so amusing. We understand how it happened — little things that don't seem important, but as they add up they become a river and the current is too strong to resist. You know his remark about disliking the Communists but respecting them — presumably because they see through him — and despising all who believe in him, as we did. That is exactly how Hitler despised the Germans who believed in him. You see the cabinet leave the Élysée after a session with him and it is precisely like Germany in . . . oh, 1943. The same preoccupied faces, the same air of hav-

ing resolved to say something, to refuse something, and then finding out at the crucial moment that the courage to carry out the
resolve was not there."

"But de Gaulle is not Hitler," I say. "He has not gone beyond
accepted political behavior."

"That is true," he says. "And for most people it is the most important truth. But for some of us, it is merely . . . relative. De Gaulle
is like Hitler in that he is a buffoon. Both of them . . . buffoons
who tried to rid Europe of foreign control and failed because they
were not realistic about the foreigners or Europe or their own
countries. Don't you see?"

We discuss it rather listlessly and then de Renville goes to bed.
Clothilde and I have a nightcap and make plans for the next day. I
have to see some of the precious-metals Dutch near Bordeaux, and
she has suggested coming along as an interpreter. The Dutch speak
English, but she is restless.

"I would very much like to get out of Paris now," she says. "And
that is a lovely drive. We can have lunch at a good place in Tours."

We leave next morning in a new convertible Pontiac left for my
use by an American friend who has gone to Greece. The car is
rather out of place on French roads, but only superficially so, and
its comfort more than makes up for minor drawbacks. We have
lunch at Barrier, which is something more than a good place — a
marvelous *grillade au feu de bois* and a bottle of Château Montcon-
tour, a superb Vouvray. In Bordeaux, we stay at the Splendide, and
stuff ourselves there and at the Dubern, Château-Trompette, and
Réserve Etche Ona, just out of town. It is a greedy time, and in the
next two days the six of us (there are four Dutch) put away *oeufs
Mollet, aubergines* and *boeuf rôti*, all *à la Bordelaise, gratin de vo-
laille, sole au gratin comme en Gironde, écrevisses, lamproies,* and
foie de canard aux raisins, washed down with Lafite, Latour, Mar-
gaux, Haut-Brion, d'Yquem, Guirand, Couet, and other extraordinary *grands crus* of Bordeaux.

When I finish up with the Dutch, we start back by way of Auvergne, staying the night at an inn near Riom. The food is again amazing, as it is the next day near Nevers, in a country place where we lunch on *saupiquet Nivernaise,* sliced ham with a memorable sauce.

We are back in Paris that evening. The trip has been short but so crammed that it takes me some time to sort out the impressions. They are of various kinds: the scenery, as in Orléanais, Touraine, Poitou, Angoumois, Bordelais, Périgord, Auvergne, Bourbonnais and Nivernais; the food and drink; and, most of all, the conversation of Clothilde herself. French women are infinitely more interesting than French men, and Clothilde is the definitive example. In the long hours we spent together, I deliberately encouraged her to talk — about anything and everything, but especially about France itself. And she did, with the special combination of gravity and amused intelligence so characteristic of certain French women.

The combination — the French landscape, the French food and drink, and, finally, Clothilde herself, a scarf around her head in the open car, her beautifully civilized face framed against the background of the passing country — seems in memory a distillation of France itself. Certainly all the classic French glories were woven together to make it. The feminine presence was the indispensable ingredient, reminding one that Joan of Arc is the greatest of all French figures, and that France is represented in human symbol by Marianne, a woman of the people, in contrast to the American Uncle Sam and English John Bull, both men, both abstract and both ludicrous.

In the latter half of the twentieth century, such distinctions may be entirely imaginary, but in a way they are all we have. Clothilde and her food and her landscapes were France to me, as a meal cooked over a fire on the open range and shared with a cowboy are America to a foreigner. When the cowboy speaks, the foreigner listens. When Clothilde spoke, I listened.

Her analysis of French weaknesses, the topic on which I was particularly anxious, came in bits and pieces, mixed up with all sorts of other thoughts and comments. In remembering her conversation, I have had to eliminate a great deal for reasons of space, despite the pertinence and wit of all of it. What remains is not as she said it word for word — it was far too much for that —but the phrasing is very close:

You must understand, she began, that I am not terribly moved by France. I suppose that must have something to do with my conception of "greatness," a horrible word now that de Gaulle has so debased it, but still unavoidable. I don't think, you see, that France has ever done anything great in the real way, the way that many other countries have. The Italians have the Church, they invented it, and it is a sublime idea. If nothing else, the English invented an Empire, the Americans created modern life, the Russians did . . . something . . . with Communism. Even the Germans created a monopoly on music and "wickedness." All large undertakings, unique, not carried through by any other country. But France has never done anything absolutely unique. You may mention the cathedrals, but there are cathedrals all over Europe, especially in Germany: Cologne, for example, which is equal if not superior to anything in France. France is very much of the first rank, and has made so many contributions to the world, but they are all contributions relating to some idea formed elsewhere. Nothing absolutely unique, and I think all Frenchmen know this and are ashamed of it. I am not ashamed of it myself, but perhaps that is because I admit it. We are like gypsies, unable to stick to a vision, always falling back on the slightly illegal. So greatness, the thing we lack, is what we make such a noise about having. It is like the Italians with courage. . . .

Whatever the reason, most French have tremendous inferiority complexes, particularly the men. This is very much revealed in our art. It is hard to understand, for example, how a writer like Gide can be taken so seriously outside France as well as in. So much the "frog" in his pompousness. I often think the French intellectual the most stupid in the world, the least spontaneous and the most self-centered. The farce of Sartre and de Beauvoir! Of Lévi-Strauss! And then Sagan and Godard . . . and Camus, Robbe-Grillet, Sarraute, and the rest. So pretentious, so puffed up, so interchangeable. Not a bit less absurd than the netherworld of the Grandes Écoles, of "X" and "ENA" and "Sciences-Po," of the self-mesmerizing staccato conversations and the corkscrew written word, as in your friend Servan-Schreiber's very mortal prose. . . . The marvelous confidence of sublimely stupid people, with the tiny kernel of un-confidence eating at them — the realization that it is all very minor — at their very cores. French intellectuals are like French fashion designers at bottom — quite aware it is a swindle. . . . Even the most undeveloped American has more humility, and so more in the way of natural intelligence. The French are like people who are tolerated by other people after a larger game, so they think they really make an impression. No one ever tells them how silly they are because no one finds them that important. So they never know, except in a shadowy way from inside.

. . . Because they are so full of themselves, the French don't really know the world at all, another of their cherished illusions with no foundation. Even the English are more knowledgeable. . . .

And all because they are French: I am convinced it is racial. It is because they — we — are "frogs" (the Anglo-American word for us is a stroke), Latin and excited in any emergency. We have no inner self-respect, not even as much as the Germans, whom we are all taught to despise. We know we are not great and it kills us — or those of us who do not admit it. It is what kills de Gaulle, makes him so peevish. . . . We are aware that we have so little to offer, but we have to pretend we have so much. Quite the opposite of a country with true possessions, where the attitude is always that they have so little to give.

I think anyone can deduce a country from its intellectuals and its artists, and what kind of country could you imagine from someone like Godard? Modern films, modern art, the high rate of homosexuality — they are all symptoms of profound stupidity. If that were not apparent in any other way, it would be plain because of the egotism of the people involved. All very ordinary but all so sure they are clever. Godard, of course, is our prize, the apotheosis of pretending nothing is something. Such a childish inversion, but it is very French. Our artists are childish because we are, and so they give the clue to the rest of us. The hysteria of the police and the students in the past weeks, which you mention, is the same as that of Godard and the others. There is a link between stupidity and hysteria — and all Frenchmen approach things in a hysterical state. Even their calmness is the forced calm of the hysteric. Hysteria is our hallmark, in Godard as well as in de Gaulle. (They think they are so different and they are twins!) And hysteria means stupidity because intelligence demands serenity. The New Wave is as silly, precisely as silly, as the New Bourgeois, and is its reflection.

I find Godard the French equivalent of your Beatles trying to be good Americans. He is the Frenchman trying to be the good American, as is the whole tide of film directors, writers and artists. They are quick to point out that American film makers are their models, but just as quick to claim they are not American otherwise. They have no idea that their whole attitude is imitative, that they themselves are not able to do anything but imitate — the material isn't there for originality. When Godard says he admires Eldridge Cleaver, he thinks he is being original when it is really only exchanging one model for another. . . .

Do you know *The American* by Henry James? Good. You remember the picture of the French family — the de Bellegardes — but do you realize there is nothing in French literature to equal it? Not even in Proust or Stendhal, certainly not in Balzac or Flaubert or the rest. So penetrating, right down to the roots, to the deadness, the silliness, the envelopment in money, the theatrical actions. But you see, James came from a great society and so was able to see ours better than we can see it ourselves. He had the position and the temperament from which to view. No Frenchman has that, although it would never occur to a Frenchmen that he doesn't. To see any part of one's society, even the smallest, one must have full confidence in oneself, true confidence, purged of hysteria. But no Frenchman has such confidence, so nothing he says about himself and his society is accurate, in large matters or small.

It is the same in the revolutions. The Americans made a revolution and a change. So did the Russians, in a way. But the French Revolution is a joke. After a few years it turned into an adventure for an Italian, and a few years later France was back where she was before 1789. Except for the absence of a formal monarchy, everything was the same. And except for mechanical development, everything has remained the same. There have been no real changes. So France did not have a revolution in the sense that Russia and America did. But France has to think it did. So another killing illusion is added.

And when my father says de Gaulle is a born loser, I say then that de Gaulle is the perfect frog because France is a born loser, too. We have precisely what we deserve. Actually, we French are very stupid — a people who could be imposed on by de Gaulle's tricks would have to be — and because we are so naïve, de Gaulle is able to force either-or choices on the people which other nationalities (and races) would be too sophisticated to accept. The naïveté is responsible, too, for the lack of pragmatism. The French look at all those Americans and have no idea what they *mean*. It never occurs to them that something has *happened*. I find most Americans extremely unpalatable myself, but I always try to distinguish between their unattractiveness and their meaning, what their position makes our position. The whole world is after the wrong things, but some people and nations are better at getting them than others. . . . We do have the consumer society in France, but we are not really successful with it, and it has not been happy for us. It actually brings out our worst qualities — the Parisians are ruder, the provincials are duller, as frogs we are froggier, even our Jews are Jewier. As we go deeper into "consuming," we shall very likely become even more unattractive, nasty and stupid.

The French never understand that when foreigners make a fuss over our so-called elegance, they are only doing so to make money in their own countries off the French goods or "viewpoint" they are importing there. High fashion, for example, is only big business in America, so the buyers come here and make much of St. Laurent and Bohan and the rest. But the French designers are too naïve to see that, they must take it literally. They believe in what they do and have no idea they are being used. Even Cardin, who is the best businessman of the lot and has set up his own chain in America, doesn't see that it is not he imposing his styles but the Americans using him in ways he can't dream of.

[Later in the summer, Clothilde sent me a newspaper clipping about St. Laurent which read, in part: "During the student upheavals in Paris . . . he saw the girls and boys behind the barricades dressed carelessly but beautifully in pants, scarves and shirts. 'They looked beautiful because they are beautiful themselves,' he said. 'They don't need anything else.'" "Can you imagine calling those poor fools beautiful?" she asked in an appended note. "Their faces all distorted like monkeys in a rage — and their movements so shabby, so *imitative* of what they thought they should be doing. But St. Laurent is as half-witted as they are."]

. . . All the French young, my age, are so pious and pompous that one can not believe they are true. And the so-called revolutionists even more so than the correct ones. One cries out in France, if one is young, for reality, but one must be careful to cry out in private and never expect it from this crop. . . . There is a hill, in the Cévennes, near our family home, which is very private and where I have actually cried out in all my girlish impulsiveness — what did the birds think, I wonder? . . . It is as though the frivolity and ignorance of the intellectuals had finally seeped down into the young and made them all as limited as Sartre and Godard themselves. In the riots, the older intellectuals would visit the young occupiers of places like the Odéon Theatre and abase themselves in approved fashion before their creations, who were, in turn, groveling for the professional exploiters like Cohn-Bendit. Midget Frankensteins with their tiny monsters, and the monsters with their unscrupulous caretakers.

Not that it can last for long, of course. A country with such young people is not a good insurance risk for the future. . . .

The older generation is not much better, even when it is supposed to be, a vague state so well illustrated by Malraux and the "beautiful" Louise de Vilmorin. Malraux you know about, of course. The "dashing" Frenchman, an ex-Communist, now de Gaulle's Minister of Cultural Affairs. Always dashing. The kind of Frenchman who takes everything about himself so seriously, who really thinks he has played such a role in the world for most of his life. Perfect meat for de Gaulle, who turned him into a Gaullist as easily as one turns a glove inside out. Which didn't seem comic to Malraux himself at all, because he must see himself as someone with a perpetual "destiny" of his very own that no one can tamper with. He is really the exquisitely preposterous Frenchman, the kind foreigners smile at when they see them on the beach in the summer: little white fellows with potbellies and pince-nez, throwing medicine balls with their wives, getting in shape, showing the correct technique, doing all these things all at once. Not unrelievedly boring and beside the point, like Sartre and that crew, but comic. There is a difference.

And comic people get into comic situations. With other comic people. In Malraux's case, who became his feminine intimate, his mentor for all the things he had missed? Louise de Vilmorin, who else could have filled the bill? You do not know of her? You know the name, but very little else. Good, because true comedy can't survive wide currency. She is a figure from James, almost from *The American,* in her late sixties, like Malraux, but possessed of everything he does not have. She is a writer, of course — she writes what we French are privileged to call classic French — and her subject matter is love among the aristocrats. She is a Chevalier of the Legion and has won the Grand Literary Prize of Monaco. She has been compared to Saint-Simon, Stendhal and even La Rochefoucauld. She has also been compared, more realistically, to Madame de Lafayette, who wrote *Princesse de Clèves*, which many female French writers call the first "psychological" novel of love in French. But she is rarely compared to Colette.

She has a literary salon! At the Chateau de Verrières-le-Buisson, the ancestral seat, where it is a family "tradition" for her and her brothers to read poetry in the evenings. Not the occasional evening, but every evening. She is very handsome, although her teeth are bad, and she sings and paints and is considered a brilliant conversationalist. Her first husband was an Englishman, Leigh Hunt, and her second a Frenchman, Comte Paul Palffy. She "amusingly" claims to be related to Joan of Arc, whom she says was the great-grandaunt of Philippe-Victoire de Vilmorin, an illustrious forebear. Now — as you say in America — I ask you!

I don't mean to be unfair. She is really a very nice woman, and the world would be less without her. But the present age makes a mockery of her accomplishments. The encumbrances of the past, the French madnesses and notions and inadequacies are so rolled up and bound up in her that she has no chance. Literary evenings in ancient chateaux were once possible no matter what went on in the rest of France and the world. Now they aren't: the power of ridicule can reach everywhere, even if no one sees it or admits it.

Anyhow, there is the scene and in comes Monsieur Malraux, blissfully full of himself. And what happens? Why, he is swept off his feet, naturally he is swept off his feet. He has been going there for several years now and all Paris says they will marry if and when he can divorce his present wife. Malraux, our font of esthetic wisdom, drowns in the oldest cliché in France. The suave aristocrats eat up another boy from the provinces. They are so smooth, so fond of fun and games that they don't even smile when he praises his chief, a man for whom they have not the slightest respect because they know all too well his secret pliances. In any other country, the scene would be laughed at. In France, no one finds it unusual or comic, not even the intellectuals, because we are so ill equipped to see reality. We cloak everything to make it more dignified, to avoid allowing anything French to become nakedly absurd. We might go so far as to say "figures from Proust," and draw parallels between Proust's narrator and Oriane de Guermantes, but that is far too dressy. It is much rawer comedy, and the leads are infinitely more ordinary. But, as I said, no French person could see that today. Not even the so-called satirists, because this is a new age and we are so very much more obtuse. If they did smile, it would be overdone, exaggerated. . . . Only your Henry James could do the scene credit; after all, the figures are frozen and haven't moved since his time. Nothing has changed, and wouldn't they have been grist for his mill? Can you imagine him coming on one of those poetry evenings? The voices being strummed so melodiously by the most beautiful language in the world, then the sudden entrance of the compromised Minister of Culture, followed by the bland patronization of the stiff gentleman with a moustache, spiritual brother of the Marquis de Bellegarde himself . . .

. . . When Frenchmen sit around the table, it is not that they could be sensible if they chose, as Servan-Schreiber thinks, but that their egos, as with Malraux, keep them from doing anything together. . . .

. . . And our charm is so frayed, you know. I can remember hearing, when I was a child, a friend of my father's repeating the famous remark Cocteau made about Paul Radiquet. Cocteau was very jealous of the boy, and got very angry when he'd slip away to spend the night with a woman. *"Bébé est vicieux,"* Cocteau is supposed to have said, *"il aime les femmes."* The man who quoted it to my father added, "Isn't that typically French?" He meant that even if Cocteau was a homosexual, he was a homosexual in the French style, with the famous French "wit" no matter what. But I was sure, then as well as now — yes, I was a precocious child — that the remark wasn't meant to be witty. It was typically French, all right, but because of the parochialism rather than the wit. An American or English homosexual, like Oscar Wilde, might make such a remark in jest, but never a Frenchman. The Frenchman would mean it. . . .

She is brilliant and amusing, and for selfish reasons I am appreciative, but I find myself wondering where such ideas leave *her*. I put my concern as delicately as possible.

"What do you mean?" she asks rather suspiciously.

"Surely not many people your age, in France or out of it, look at things the way you do. What do you do for friends?"

"I don't have any," she says briefly. "But I am not a recluse. I go out a great deal. I see people in all society — after all, I am part of *Tout-Paris* — and I even make a small joke from time to time. But most of the time I keep my mouth very closed. That is not as difficult for a European, especially for a French girl, as for Americans. We have learned from the foreign occupations to keep our thoughts to ourselves, and under the glitter it is no different now than in any other occupation. And, too, we French always have something of the outsider in us — as Colette says that a Frenchwoman always feels she lowers herself with a foreign man, no matter how handsome or rich. We are a bit like gypsies that way. We have a history, we Frenchwomen, of thinking the rest of the world, including our own men, quite crazy."

"But very few Frenchwomen now think as you do."

"That is true, and so I suppose I must admit that I am more alone than I would have been in the past."

She looks at me with level hazel eyes, the lovely face luminous with character.

"You say France is nothing," I say, "but you omit yourself."

"That is only a compliment," she says.

I can say no more to her about her brave, if quixotic originality.

Her position seems precarious to me, and too much talk about it might make it more so in her own mind and cause her more trouble than she will have anyhow. Cause it sooner, at least. Even as she talked, I could feel an awareness of her own helplessness welling up in her, an awareness brought on by the subject matter itself. No one, especially one so young, can talk about such bleakness without beginning to wonder how it affects him. After forty, there is a balance in that one's own impetuosities — one's own life, in a certain way — have been lived. But a twenty-two-year-old girl has nothing behind her. It is all ahead. Or there is nothing ahead. Whom will she find to marry in what she considers a barren moonscape? What will she find to do if she doesn't marry? Not a job — what would be the point in going further into a society in which she doesn't believe? Even the nunneries, traditional refuges of unadaptable French aristocrats, are tainted for her.

Her proud head droops a little now against the moving fields as these things inevitably occur to her in the silence, and I am annoyed with myself for permitting her to talk so long.

But after the superb lunch near Nevers she cheers up, and from there into Paris is nothing more or less than a charming girl, talking and laughing without visible scars. I can only hope that she will always be able to come back to such innocent tranquility after wrestling with what she can't help seeing and knowing.

The Americanization process in France is schizophrenic. On the mechanical level it has achieved its own momentum, and leaves little to be desired from the most dedicated American viewpoint. As François Nourissier says in his book *The French:* "In the postwar years, the United States — in France people simply say 'America' — has been the great mirage on the horizon of French imaginations. Whatever the subject, whether films — thrillers, comedies, or Westerns; literature — Faulkner, Capote, or Frank Slaughter, depending on which public; the Paris–New York art tussle; architecture — Saarinen or Philip Johnson; whether it is a way of life or a folklore, Audrey Hepburn or General Motors, James Bond in the Bahamas or Jacqueline Kennedy in Gstaad or Seville; whether it is the New Frontier or the Bay of Pigs, beatniks or Vietniks, Sinatra or Bob Dylan, the growing mechanization of western man, Louis Armstrong, race riots in Little Rock, Watts, or Detroit, one thing is certain; French heads are full of America. . . . Whether it be in terms of our free-moving economy, the development of our social structure, fashions, or any one of other manifold forms of imitation, France more and more resembles the United States."

(To call Audrey Hepburn and James Bond Americans seems a slip, and perhaps it is technically, but certainly Bond is only an American detective with a British passport, and a very pale imitation of the originals. That the French think of him as an American is merely a tribute to their common sense.)

Unlike the English, however, the French are not so sheeplike on other aspects of the process. They are, in fact, deeply interested in how to have the Americanization without the Americans. The difference in outlook is purely racial and cultural. Official England, Teutonic and conscience-laden, feels that if America is "right" — that is, if the American way is the desirable way — it is completely right, and the colonizees are not in a position to argue with their admitted betters on any of the details. Official France, Latin and amoral, feels that no matter how completely the American way is adopted in France, Frenchmen still have the right, even the duty, to assert the national and individual interests.

Such resistance as official England does put up is unconscious, whereas the French are quite conscious in their criticisms. One can't imagine an English Servan-Schreiber warning his fellows against the American presence; and it is well to remember that Servan-Schreiber, as a former Gaullist deputy, is more official than otherwise.

The real question is which attitude is the more realistic, and the evidence would seem to favor the British position. At least they never have to retreat from an unrealistic posture of resistance, but the French often do. Such retreats leave scars because they are based on mistakes in judgment, and the scars are not confined to those at the top who make the mistakes. The entire country is affected, and the average Frenchman thus becomes more neurotic about Americanization than his British counterpart.

The English are cautious, and see no point in rushing into a resistance unless they are sure it will work. The French are more impetuous, and have a long history of rushing into adventures without sufficient consideration and preparation. The belief in Napoleon is a prime illustration: very few Frenchmen understood — or understand — that he *never* had a chance, human nature being what it is, to effect permanent changes in Europe.

And belief in de Gaulle has been equally impetuous and equally expensive. By no means did all Frenchmen support de Gaulle and Gaullism, even at the height of the general's popularity, but none can altogether escape identification with him. He didn't represent all Frenchmen, but he represented France as a whole, and no Frenchman can wholly repudiate him and his years of power without repudiating France herself.

Specifically, de Gaulle took France to war and lost. The war was psychological rather than military, but the defeat was just as crushing as 1871 or 1940. The war was against the tide of history and events, a fight in which France, a very minor country, strove for parity with — and occasionally superiority over — the two superpowers. The vote against de Gaulle's referendum was an admission that the war had been lost and the adventure ended; but the war would have been just as lost had the vote been in his favor.

Because the war was not literal, the term can be avoided, and it is naturally very much in the French interest that the participation of all France and most Frenchmen in the general's wild dream be forgotten. This may be immediately possible to a considerable degree, but in the long run the truth will out. And because it will, it is well worth examination now.

At first, the extent to which de Gaulle represented a widespread French hankering after unattainable glories is not apparent, because the fact that de Gaulle is not a typical Frenchman on the surface obscures his intimate bonds with the country and the people. One's initial reaction is that his eccentricities are entirely personal, and that he has very little in common with other Frenchmen. In *The French*, M. Nourissier corroborates this view by describing de Gaulle as "a Louis XIV with the manners of a bandit chieftain, brutal, good-natured, mocking, a hundred times more cynical or artful than his best opponents." And in *The New French Revolution*, a study of France's technological plans and possibilities, John Ardagh dismisses de Gaulle by ignoring him. Surely, then, he is a mere freak, with no significance as a clue to France or Frenchmen.

But as one learns more about the French, one realizes that he does represent his people and is thus of great importance. The French cannot achieve a technological revolution, merely a euphemistic phrase for becoming complete Americans, as long as they are French, as long as they have those characteristics which they share with de Gaulle and on which he has played so skillfully. M. Nourissier puts it very well in a passage directly following the one above: "This is how . . . he looked to the French in the long empty mirror in which they were accustomed to see themselves, and as such he offered them an inexplicable, flattering image of themselves, which they accepted with the gratitude of well-trained pet dogs." And again: "Most of France is Gaullist out of laziness, perhaps, but not so by chance. . . . If France is Gaullist, that is because she must be. She loves what *Gaullism offers her and the image of herself that it holds up to her.*" (The italics are mine.) The judgment recalls de Renville's comparison of de Gaulle to Hitler. As un-German as de Gaulle is un-French, Hitler used the same technique of offering his people an "inexplicable, flattering image of themselves, which they accepted with the gratitude of well-trained pet dogs"; and Germany became Hitlerian with the same passive inertia, "because she must"; and in the end Germany "loved what" Hitlerism offered her, and "the image of herself" that it held up to her.

It should be plain that any comparison of Hitler and de Gaulle does not need to contend that de Gaulle has undertaken, or would undertake, criminal acts against society. Hitler was a very clever demagogue in the European tradition as well as a criminal, and de Gaulle is also a clever demagogue in that tradition. What they have in common as demagogues is not negated by their other differences, profound as those may be. Hitler's basic appeal to the Germans lay in his ability to rationalize mass surrender to their darker passions. The essence of his message was: "If you want the rest of the world so much, why not take it? If you hate Jews so much, why not get rid of them?" And so on. He was contemptuous of his people at bottom and didn't really care what happened to them, as de Renville pointed out. De Gaulle has much the same attitude toward the French and has treated them similarly, although the passions are different and contained within a system the world finds acceptable; and the collapse of de Gaulle has not brought on — at least as yet! — a fiery catastrophe for France and the rest of the world. (However, without the American presence and support, he might have managed to bring Russia to the Atlantic, outdoing Hitler as professional purveyor of disaster.) In any case, the precedent of holding all nationals responsible in degree — moral if not legal — for their leaders' actions, the precedent established at Nuremberg, has some force insofar as France is concerned, and the world shall insist that all Frenchmen supported de Gaulle.

The fundamental characteristic that de Gaulle and Hitler share — and the one that would have brought Hitler low had he never broken a treaty, invaded a country, or killed dissenters and Jews — is their notion that nature can be imposed on by man, the anti-Bacon fallacy. As Adams pointed out, since Bacon was persuaded to "lay aside the idea of evolving the universe from a thought, and to try evolving thought from the universe," the idea of imposing on nature has been hopelessly out-of-date. If de Gaulle were ten times as clever as he is — and he is a very talented man — he would still fail to cope with the modern world from such a philosophical base.

Thus his resistance to America is not really effective at all, but as essentially hystero-comic as was claimed. To ordinary American eyes, and they are not always inaccurate eyes, he is as comic as Hitler. Hitler had a silly moustache and a wild oratorical style and plans that couldn't work and thought he was attractive. De Gaulle is equally odd physically, and equally pretentious and ridiculous in spoken delivery and phraseology. (*"Force de frappe"* and *"tout-azimut défense"* are stern reminders of how foolishly inadequate the French language can be in certain fields — as Clarence Day pointed out years ago in writing of his boyhood reaction to reading a French Bible and comparing the solid roll of such phrases as "Moses and his rod" to *"Moïse et son bâton."*) He also has plans that are equally unworkable and thinks he is just as beautiful. In the unspoken American view, de Gaulle and Hitler are both European clowns who tried to rid Europe of foreign control and failed because they were not realistic about either the foreigners or Europe. As non- or anti-Baconists, their insistence on mind over matter, and on the notions that destiny can be commanded and nature imposed on, are as fantastic as if they believed the sun went round the earth.

Pretentious persons are still often shocked at the memory of the average American's refusal to take Hitler seriously, to see him as anything but a joke, but perhaps the popular view disguised a deeper understanding of the situation. A man who believes in a discredited scientific system *is* a joke, no matter how much pain and misery he may inflict before he is bankrupted by his beliefs. The American refusal to take de Gaulle seriously is based on the same stark application of scientific evolution. "Even the kids laughed at Hitler when he got up and shook his fist and howled in crazy German," recalls an American sergeant in Frankfurt, "and I guess we all have been laughing at de Gaulle when he waved his arms and yelled about *la gloire* for the same reason. It's like those movies where the European professor works away at some nutty invention in his lab down in the basement and he's always blowing the whole building up and always going back to try again."

If de Gaulle's resistance to America was not effective, neither was France's, nor can it be now or in the future, for they are one and the same. And even with de Gaulle gone, the French would have to overcome the national predilection for hysteria (de Gaulle only reflected a national characteristic there) before any genuine resistance could be dreamed of. Add to that the necessity of becoming hyper-Baconian (more so than the Americans, for Baconism is the only yardstick now) and it can be seen that the road before the French, or any other aspiring European resisters, is really very long, and the more one thinks about it the longer it becomes.

What de Renville meant when he called de Gaulle a born loser was that the general should never have embarked on a resistance to people and methods he didn't understand. "It was so hare-brained," he says, "so slapdash. But he is very French in that. When a Frenchman doesn't understand something, or more particularly, when he feels a weakness or inferiority to something, he attacks it. People who act like that can't do anything except lose."

But de Gaulle did so very well for such a long time. How does one explain that? Of all responses, the most appealing came from a Yugoslav analyst in mid-1968, many months before the general was turned out: "It is easy to understand if you go much to the cinema. No, I do not joke. There is a scene that is played on occasion in the cinema where the cowboy has taken an oath not to kill more people or something like that, and a much weaker cowboy insults him and when the insult is accepted without striking back the weak cowboy goes further and offers more insults and the strong cowboy takes them all without a word. The weak cowboy does not understand the reason for his triumph over the strong one. He now thinks *he* is the stronger and many people who have been watching agree, because they don't know the real reasons either. I mean, of course, that the weak cowboy is de Gaulle. The strong cowboy who has taken the oath is America. America has not taken this oath for sentimental reasons but because she is locked in a life and death struggle with Russia for control of the world. De Gaulle, supposedly the American ally, suddenly decides to be 'independent.' America would like nothing better than to spank such a naughty child of an ally who doesn't understand the game that is being played. But she can't, like a mother, again in a scene we often see in the cinema, especially in the old days, a mother whose child misbehaves in public but who has to smile because people would think she was cruel if she spanked in a public place. France, the bad child who knows the mother's hands are tied, redoubles its tricks and sticks out its tongue at her and wee-wees on the grass and howls for another ice, and the mother can only smile like strangulation. If little France were Russia's child, Russia would spank and damn public opinion — I mean, of course, that Russia would invade France if France were Russia's ally and behaved in such a fashion — but that is not what America stands for, so she can't."

A Greek industrialist who spends half the year in France supported this view: "The Americans see Europe as either going under the American heel or the Russian heel and they are right. Certainly the Russians agree with them. The French think there is a middle ground and they are wrong. In the end, the world will be all America's or all Russia's — that is what the French can't see. Or can't believe. Or that every time they scrap with the Americans they only help the Russians. You'd think they could have seen that, because one of them — Malraux? — made that remark about someday there being only the Gaullists and the Communists left in France. What the French fail to understand, of course, is the depth of the American culture. America is not a young country, that's a myth. The American colonists came of old European stock and you have the oldest stable government — unchanged, I mean — in the world. All American decisions are the result of so much experience, so much patient analysis. In comparison, France is a child. And de

Gaulle — such a fraud! So uneducated, in the real sense. They say he is nineteenth century, but it is fake nineteenth century. *La grandeur!* Better *le ridicule!* He is incapable of seeing what is happening under his nose. He can't see that the rise of American power is the story of the twentieth century. Very well, it will engulf him. It rolls over him as he lays a wreath at Verdun, which is a very unimportant event in this century. . . . Ninety-nine Frenchmen out of a hundred, and that certainly includes de Gaulle, have an inflated idea of France's importance. The truth is that France is nothing, and has nothing to offer in the modern technological world. De Gaulle and the French either have to face that fact, as England faced it, or it will be taught to them by circumstances, which means with the buckle end of the belt."

An American diplomat commented on these opinions with characteristic national optimism after the Yugoslav and the Greek left the table at the Crillon at which we were talking: "I concur to a degree with your Yugoslav friend, but he forgets there is a third alternative to the triumph of either American or Russian influences — I mean a genuine United States of Europe. It's the only way. I mean it. I mean it's inevitable, isn't it? Everyone understands that possibility; everyone, apparently, except de Gaulle. We Americans support it as actively as we dare. But the old boy is against that, too. He's against American influence and against a United States of Europe, and that leaves only Russian control. Doesn't it? He thinks it leaves French control, but of course that's a myth. . . . It's been difficult, don't think it hasn't. He's given us some very bad moments with his policies, and he undoubtedly has been a great help to the Russians, who realize he's rather simple and play him for all he's worth. They know he doesn't understand the real game, and doesn't understand that he is only helping them when he undercuts us — our Greek tycoon is right there.

"What a position France could have now if he had chosen to opt for a federated Europe! They would have had the lead, they would have been the natural leaders. Now, if it ever comes, they'll have to take a back seat. But let's look on the bright side, for there is a bright side here. In the long run, we think de Gaulle is going to help us more than he hurts us. Surprise you to hear that? Look at it this way. He has represented the anti-American case as well as it can be represented, and he's lost. We knew he had to lose, that's why we gave him so much rope. He knows perfectly well that everything he's done — the flirting with Russia and the eastern bloc, the exclusion of England from the Common Market, the encouragement of French nationalism in Canada, the attempt to topple the dollar, the dismissal of NATO to the wilds of Belgium — would not have been possible for him if we had removed our military, nuclear umbrella. He has done everything from behind our skirts — I like the analogy of the naughty child, I buy it, even though it does make Uncle S. look like a transvestite — and we could not afford to repudiate him and push him out on his own because of Russia gobbling him up. So we had to eat it all, but now it's coming to an end. He will be gone soon and his policies will go with him. Our plan has been vindicated. We waited him out and ruined that brand of anti-Americanism for a very, very long time. The reaction will be entirely in our favor. He is going downhill now and he looks worse every day. I personally hope he tries to hang on to power until he's carried out, because he will end by discrediting *everything* he ever did, and most of it deserves to be discredited. But even if he departs tomorrow, the work is pretty well done. It takes a while for the reaction, you know, anyhow, but I'd say that in five to ten years the pendulum in France and the rest of Europe will have swung completely the other way. De Gaulle will be an unperson, about like Khrushchev in Russia."

We dined with de Renville, who said: "I am very cynical about you Americans. I saw what you did with Hitler. You knew you had a great booby and that he would be your entree into Europe — after his collapse, of course. You see poor de Gaulle the same way."

The American diplomat resented that and was not shy about saying so: "You have the cart before the horse. We were against Hitler on principle and we are against de Gaulle on principle. If we 'did well' in Europe after the war it had nothing to do with our getting into the war in the first place. The same is true of de Gaulle. We are against him, but we are not thinking about what happens after he is gone and discredited. We would actually prefer, to the extent that we think about it at all, to see you Europeans drop the whole nationalist farce and create a genuine third world force, a real United States of Europe, dominated and run by yourselves . . . It would be amusing if we were as cynical as you think we are, but we're not. Your own cynicism makes you think everyone else is. If you are too cynical to understand that a federated Europe is what we want, with no strings attached . . . well, you will only hurt yourselves with such cynicism."

The opinions above were all based on the assumption that de Gaulle's star was declining, for which the evidence was becoming stronger by the day. If it had been the star of an atypical adventurer, its movements would not have been important. But it represented France to a considerable degree, too, and so it was and is important. Whether de Gaulle had lost on his referendum vote or not, and whether he had decided to quit if he lost or not, there were and are forces at work in France and the world which would have brought him and his country down. If he were still in power — or even if he returns to power — nothing would or will be any different in the end.

When de Gaulle decided to resist American control, he — in distinction to the English — made it quite plain to his countrymen that that was what he was doing. And the majority of them made it equally plain, in turn, that they approved. It was a joint decision, with the prospect of joint rewards or joint penalties, even though tacitly arrived at. And it involved even those Frenchmen who did not approve, because any national adventure finally does touch every citizen whether he likes it or not.

If de Gaulle and France had resisted successfully, it would have been extremely interesting (many Americans would have welcomed a check, even a defeat, for the produce-and-consume philosophy), but it failed. The French mind and the French character and the French appraisal of human nature, including their own, were not strong enough — mature enough — to challenge the American mind, the American character and the American appraisal of human nature. In the American view, it is foolhardy to go into a fight unless one has a chance of winning, which chance depends on a careful analysis of the enemy's strengths as well as one's own. The Americans understood that the French were not capable of analyzing their own position, to say nothing of the American position, and knew the French could not succeed in what they were trying. Unworldly observers might think it cruel of the Americans not to have warned the French of this, but the Americans were not in a position to issue such a warning. In an extension of the Yugoslav's Wild West analogy, America was the sober cowboy with three aces showing and one in the hole, France the drunken trail bum with three kings visible. The sober cowboy knows he's the winner no matter what the drunken trail bum has in the hole, and if the drunken trail bum wants to bet all he has that's only his tough luck. A warning is out of the question because it goes against the code which insists that a man has the right to ruin himself without interference if he so chooses.

Incapable of analysis, the French were left with the choice of swinging blind or not swinging at all. Temperamentally they would rather swing blind than not swing at all (the British take the opposite view), so they swung blind and lost.

The loss is a definite one, the recession from a high-water mark on a number of key issues. At the beginning of 1968, de Gaulle had reached his peak, and commanded the maximum respect from those French who supported him. He had, in the popular mind, taken on the Americans successfully. NATO, their creation, was driven from French soil; the dollar was threatened and weaker than the franc; America's internal problems seemed much more discouraging than those of stable France; Britain, America's creature, was being successfully kept out of the Common Market and sabotage prevented there; and the idea of *détente* was providing an alternative to the either-America-or-Russia hegemony over Europe. Nine short months later, all that ground was lost and de Gaulle seemed defeated on every count. The Russian invasion of Czechoslovakia made the NATO decision look rash, and spoiled the *détente* possibilities. The French strikes and riots pointed up their own domestic difficulties; a run on the franc weakened it while the dollar was firming; and the rise of Germany made the exclusion of Britain from the Common Market seem a definite blunder — one which Britain and Germany together, with or without France, were determined to rectify.

By December, this accumulation of setbacks was being called the French malaise and was under discussion in America as well as in Europe, and there was considerable perplexity about what had caused it. For example, in three reports selected at random — a feature in the *International Herald-Tribune* of December 30, 1968, entitled "1968, France's Year of Crisis"; a long article in *Time*, January 3, 1969; and an article by John L. Hess in the *New York Times*, January 16, 1969 — it was unanimously agreed that although 1968 had been a difficult year for France, there was no reason for the gloom to be as extensive as it was. France was a rich country, and the economic indicators were actually quite promising. Why such unhappiness? Why such an internal loss of spirits?

Because France had fought a war and lost it. Mechanical troubles can only depress to a certain extent; it takes a psychological setback of major proportions to put people flat. The war against the Americans had been fought with every resource the French could command, and the loss was a violent shock. The later vote against de Gaulle was a mere reaction; he was actually finished in December, 1968, and could never have recovered, even if he had stayed in office for the rest of his term or longer.

("And don't think for a minute that the well-heeled French — bourgeoisie, haute bourgeoisie, aristocracy, all of 'em — didn't know they'd had a terrible shock," the American newspaperman quoted earlier says. "They took a real pasting on the gold squeeze against America, just for one example. De Gaulle practically *promised* them profits of fifty per cent plus when the lid came off the price of gold. After he had put the screws to the dollar by redeeming against gold. The whole damn country was in on it! He was the boss and they were all going to make a fortune. They were practically winking at each other, it was so much the sort of thing that a Frenchman with money goes for. They were drooling, I can tell you, and de Gaulle was drooling with them because it was something he could understand, too. So simple, such a fundamental way of making money. So they bought all the gold they could get, and the Americans ran around end with the Swiss and the other banking countries and gold went nowhere. Up twenty per cent and most of that at the beginning. No better than a fair stock, and it's been stalled for months now. Even if they make it tomorrow, it's too late, because it was supposed to have happened quickly. But the true madness was to have let it happen at all, not to have seen that if it was successful it would bring the whole system down, all over the world. It was the all-time shortsighted selfishness. Multiply it by the rest of his failures and you can understand why those people *know* they've taken a licking. The only people in France who don't know it, ironically enough, are the American correspondents in Paris — they've all been writing books about how 'right' de Gaulle has been about everything and what a 'wise statesman' he is. If it was New York, I'd say they were on the take, and sometimes I wonder about Paris.")

France attempted to carve out a larger share of world prestige and influence than international empirics felt she deserved and she failed. Some French, and not necessarily de Gaulle, would say she had been defeated by the Americans, but the Americans would very properly answer that she had gone down because she attempted to defy a natural order. That the modern "natural order" and America have become nearly synonymous may be suspicious, but until a more compelling order, based on a deeper obeisance to nature itself, takes over there is little ground for argument. Certainly France was not able to substitute a more profound world method and/or idea.

Victory would have united the country; defeat tore it apart. Pro-de Gaulle or anti-de Gaulle, the country as a whole had made a bet and lost it. The loss made France "wrong" and it is the losing of the bet and the resultant "wrongness" that is causing the trouble. If, in the teeth of the evidence, it is argued that France does not bet so intensively, the implication is that France is not all that nationalistic. But France *is* extremely nationalistic. Nourissier calls "the nationalist dithyramb" the greatest French ailment. "It contains, controls, colors and subsumes almost all the others," he says. "It is not only the first; it is also prime — fundamental. . . . Its manifestations are numberless. It affects sports, diplomacy, science, communications, artistic and literary creativity, technology. We French have got into the habit of talking about a victory in a ski meet, an art competition, or an auto race as if it were a challenge that French ardor, astuteness, and genius defiantly hurled at the rest of the world. France is forever finding herself confronted by the brute strength of Soviet barbell stars, the massive power of Detroit's big cylinders, or the blind power of dollar millionaires. Pluckily, she fights back with a mixture of fury, flexibility, irony, resourcefulness, and wild audacity. We are unbeatable little Davids facing all those Goliaths which the twentieth century has manufactured expressly to ruffle French pride. So, when a young girl or a horse or a cyclist manages to hold his or her own, perilously or pathetically, against the hordes of the rivals of France, our delirium knows no limits." If an athletic event can call out such hysteria, what depths are touched in a power struggle with another nation?

Then, too, there is the matter of temperament, of possessing a proper posture for both victory and defeat. The French are notoriously ill equipped for victory: they are even less ready for defeat. They cannot lose the bet and turn from the table without losing control, in the mythical English fashion, but must collapse in one way or another. The current depression is no more or less than the form this collapse has taken.

In retrospect, it seemed mad to many Germans that they had ever tried to fight the terrible American industrial machine; it is now, perhaps, beginning to seem mad to many Frenchmen that they ever tried to resist the deeper, ultra-Baconian American view. And under the leadership of a man who hadn't done his homework very well, not a lot better than Hitler had. And after accepting the American way completely on the Kleenex-supermarket-Sinatra level. France didn't resist Americanization, but did decide to fight on the monetary-military-political questions, where they insisted that there were alternatives to the American answers to those questions. But how could there be alternatives on those questions if there was no alternative to Americanization itself? How could the country that was right about jeans and rock be wrong about NATO? And conversely, how could the country with *Le Drugstore* on every available corner contest anything with the country of drugstore origin?

Formerly one felt that the French would not understand they had fought and lost until de Gaulle's reign ended, either by retirement, ouster or death. But the realization came while he was still in. The French suddenly decided that the orgy was over, and began to assess the extent of the psychological defeat. That defeat is also an American victory and hence part of the colonization process, but the Americans are still strong enough in most cases to avoid victory celebrations — the successful colonizer must be able to control his emotions. (*Time* was a notable exception: with characteristic jingoism and opportunistic hindsight, the vote against de Gaulle was heralded there as a triumph for the "new" France, the one that is "moving rapidly, almost visibly, into the age of mass-consumer, pop-culture society." In other words, becoming irrevocably American. *Time* is not wrong in its analysis, but *post hoc* and politically tactless. Quasi-official publications are not supposed to turn the

spotlight on fresh conquests.) Indeed, if the victory was symbol-
ized by de Gaulle's resignation, it did not receive all that much
notice in the bureaucratic beehives that formulated the policies
that ground de Gaulle up. There he was regarded as completely
extraneous, as of no more importance than a drunken window
washer, and so his disappearance means very little. There is definite consciousness in the State Department, naturally enough, but
even there the note of triumph is missing. No one can afford to say
now that they ever took him seriously.

"The Québec business was the last straw," de Renville says. "So
completely crazy — like Hitler and his secret weapons at the end of
the war. But I thought — and I was not alone — that the first truly
dangerous sign was his refusal to be serious about the hard facts of
economic penetration. He didn't understand that it was everything.
He thought something else, some miracle, would be stronger. An
aversion to economics betrays a very simplistic view, not of economics itself, but of human nature, and isn't it curious that all the
dictators have it. They don't realize that they are always beaten —
or would be if they lasted that long — by the other side offering
the world not a better cannon but a better economic system. It is
what people want more than anything else, at bottom. Napoleon,
Hitler, Stalin, de Gaulle, they all thought it was something else,
and they were all beaten by it. Even your Abraham Lincoln, who
was far more the dictator than people realize — or who, I should
say, had far more of the dictator's prerogatives — had no understanding of the economic realities of mid-nineteenth-century America. If he had lived, his fate would have been the same as the
others. The Reconstruction and the Gilded Age and Northern capitalism — the significant results of the Civil War — would have
killed him or driven him mad."

In defeat, France (and de Gaulle) have three choices. First, to
accept American leadership as completely as England does. Second, to join sincerely with the rest of Europe to create a third world
power, a genuine federation of Europe. Third, to betray Europe

(and America, by association) to Russia. Such a betrayal would stem from spite: rather than accept choices one and two, which put the seal on the defeat, the admission of setback would be avoided by substituting the illusion that France and Russia, great powers of equal rank, were taking destiny into their joint hands. Given the Russian and French flair for maladroitness, it probably wouldn't come to much, and the French might not intend that it come to much. It would more likely be deliberately muddled and botched, and only qualify as betrayal in a restricted, almost negative fashion.

(Either England or Germany, for example, could be the ostensible reason, as C. L. Sulzberger of the *New York Times* pointed out in his February, 1969, profile of de Gaulle: "If Britain and West Germany try to intrude the United Kingdom into the Common Market through the back door of the Western European Union (WEU), they will in fact only produce one thing: the threat of Franco-Soviet alliance. This is less unimaginable than it sounds. De Gaulle is obsessed with defending what he sees as France's 'independence.' . . . If de Gaulle really becomes convinced that West Germany is a danger to what he considers France's rightful place, he may conceivably want to consider alliance ties with Russia. Improvements in Franco-Soviet relations through commercial, economic and cultural exchanges aren't intended to lead to that conclusion; but they are obviously no barrier. The general recalls how much France and Russia suffered during World War II. The minute he feels Germany is becoming a big power, militarily, economically, politically or — above all — atomically, he apparently feels the only logical recourse will be another pact with Moscow. . . . If others forget, de Gaulle himself remembers that he reminded Stalin: 'We have the same interest in respect to Germany.'")

In any case, choices are rarely clear in national matters, so the strongest probability is a mishmash of the three, the emphasis depending on the future power of de Gaulle and the Gaullists. Elections are not the final word now: de Gaulle's future power, in or out of office, could range from nil to a great deal, as could that of the Gaullists, in or out. The short-term surface events in France, including de Gaulle's present condition, are not important; what matters are the long-term trends. De Gaulle could return to office tomorrow and nothing would really change, any more than it would if he ruled through a deputy or through clever opposition to a non-Gaullist incumbent, or gave up completely and retired to his memoirs.

But the tighter any Frenchmen forge future bonds with Russia, through increased trade and identification of political interests, the more unruly France will become. The memory of an old man warning against a Communist "takeover" in June, 1968, in near-paranoid excitement will clash in every subconscious with the spectacle of the same old man or his heirs cementing France to Russian interests. And any French triumphs claimed from now on without a balancing admission of defeat in the American adventure will have to contend with the average Frenchman's vague but indelible conviction that something did go wrong in that escapade. Any future dictator, de Gaulle included, may be forced to follow the classic line and find a diversion (French successes with Russia) to channel off attention from what has happened; but, just as classically, it won't work in the long run. In such a game, France will become so neurotic that when the dictator finally does go the country will expand into immediate vacuum, drawing in outside influence with irresistible suction. If nothing infuriates nature as much as a vacuum, nothing creates a vacuum like a dictator's departure. It may well be that this disaster is what de Gaulle saw coming and what led him to design his own downfall.

De Gaulle's departure, if it is genuine, will naturally leave a vacuum — not so powerful as if he had held on as long as possible and eased his smarts with a Russian affair, but still a definite suction. His successors will have to decide, and decide very swiftly, at which control they will aim that suction: all-out American, federated European, or Russian. If they abjure the choice, or leave it up to the people, all-out American will probably be the natural selection, as it usually is.

In the meantime, there will be thoughts of what might have been had de Gaulle remained in office, or of what still might be if he slips back in. On his 1969 trip to Europe, for example, President Nixon centered his visit on France and spent much time with de Gaulle and it seemed to a large part of the world that this meant de Gaulle had forced America to deal with him on his terms. The general boasted that he had, and the NATO allies muttered to each other: "We support America, and Nixon barely speaks to us. De Gaulle behaves like a cad and Nixon falls all over him. Then de Gaulle says to us, 'I take these Americans, who have not seen much of the world, to Versailles and show them the civilization of France, and they are so impressed that they do what I tell them.'" Nixon added corroboration with his maudlin praise for de Gaulle on landing in Paris (after the general had tried to get England to pull out of NATO on the eve of Nixon's arrival) and his social uncertainty. "Nixon looked like Chamberlain at Munich," an official who had a close view of both arrivals told me. "He treated de Gaulle like a lunatic of whom he was terrified, a lunatic who could wreck everything if he — Nixon — did the wrong thing."

But even if de Gaulle had been right, and Nixon actually that susceptible to French champagne and French blackmail (the Russian alliance), such parties would still be only window dressing. The American attitude toward France or any other European country is determined by the pace of American technology and the desire of Europeans to become Americans. What the United States President chooses to say to European leaders is immaterial; the magnetic attractions and tidal flows are unaffected. Johnson and de Gaulle were estranged, Nixon and de Gaulle seemed as thick as a couple of Kennedys — but neither relationship could change what is really happening by a jot. It was only another delusion of de Gaulle's that if he could get an American President to spend time with him and make certain verbal commitments he had gained ground and was cutting the necessary *bella figura* in the eyes of his people and the world.

It may even have been the delusion of a U.S. President that he could settle things with de Gaulle. But as many European heads of state have discovered, American Presidents are singularly evanescent persons. After returning to their own country and talking to their earthbound advisers, they usually forget what has been agreed to abroad in the glow of friendship and are very difficult to telephone from then on. American Foreign Service officials of my acquaintance were unanimous in predicting that the Nixon-de Gaulle match would go that way. "Nixon thinks he can handle de Gaulle," they said, "but he can't. When he learns that, he'll give it up just like everyone else has had to." Which would have erased de Gaulle's image as successful puller of U. S. Presidential noses and returned attention to what had been really happening all the time anyhow.

It was *conceivable,* of course, that de Gaulle would have been able to lead Nixon by the nose and achieve his subconscious dream of destroying the west. But such an outcome would have depended on Nixon losing his way in the American game — babying de Gaulle with promises until he was gone — and refusing to listen to those who tried to get him back on the track. It was possible, but unlikely, about as unlikely as the other extreme, Nixon leading de Gaulle by the nose. The middle course was by far the most probable.

The two French groups most opposed to de Gaulle and Gaullism have been the Communists and the young. Communist opposition is more theoretical than active, however, and there is much bitterness over Moscow's position. A high-ranking party official told me privately in 1968 that Moscow had "consistently undercut the French party. The worst part of that is not the undercutting, but that so many important French Communists go along with it. We are like a paralyzed rabbit between the Élysée and the Kremlin. De Gaulle has so much more influence in Moscow than we do because he has so much more to offer — France herself, after all — at a time when the control in Russia is becoming increasingly nationalistic and increasingly czarist and increasingly militarist. De Gaulle and the present military rulers in Moscow naturally get on well — they all believe in the same things."

The young are largely indifferent, as they are everywhere, but even indifference constitutes resistance to a man and a program based on patriotism. And indifference is also subtly pro-American, because it duplicates the mood of most American young. However, there is also a "conscious" French youth, of considerable strength and angry about everything. One of its leaders, who was active in the 1968 uprisings, told me then that "we laugh at everything old. To us, de Gaulle and the Communists and the bourgeois are the same because they are all old and timid. And under the thumb of money. Do you realize that de Gaulle is timid and dominated by the bourgeois? You should. Hitler was horrible, but he was total. He went past the middle class. German big business put him in and thought he could be controlled. But he threw them off and went on — did his own thing. De Gaulle was also put in by the bourgeois, but he was afraid to go as far as Hitler did, so he has remained in their hands. Do you know that is the story of all dictators who stop short of complete control? You should know it if you don't. I could actually respect de Gaulle if he had gone all the way. This way I can't respect him. He is too middle-class. He seems to be so active, but he only plays while others work. His activity is all on the surface. He is really doing nothing, just waiting for a big bourgeois to come in and tell him what to do. He is their tool, and he talks from the nineteenth century like all of their tools. To make the people fight, if not one thing then another. When he goes, France will leave the nineteenth century and enter the twentieth. We are that far behind. Because de Gaulle will not go against the rich and the semi-rich. It is not that he is anti-Marxist. He is pre-Marxist. He has never heard of Marx. I don't suppose you can imagine that. So he is a tool. . . .

"The Communists have forgotten everything. They only want to become respectable bourgeois. The membership only wants that, so the leadership has to want it, too. They are under the thumb of money as much as de Gaulle is. That is why they have so much in common with him, and why we see them as the same. Pigs. De Gaulle is a pig, and so is Rochet. They both want their food and their houses and their gold under the mattress. And the people who follow them are the same. Only we young are different.

"We know you foreigners laugh at France because France puts up with a pig-insult like de Gaulle. Now I surprise you — we young laugh, too! We know why the French put up with him. Because they are weak, inferior. They allow themselves to be imposed on, like the Germans did. We know you say, 'The very presence of that man means a weak people.' We agree! There is no more to be said. That is it. Now we wait our chance. We do not want you Americans either, don't forget. We don't want de Gaulle and we don't want the Communists and we don't want the Americans. We know all about your consumer society and the penalties it demands. What we want is freedom from all that. We want a completely socialized country working closely with a completely socialized Europe. And we will get it! We are going to make the great leap in this generation! We shall overcome all the others because they are dead. But we are not dead! We are alive! The rest of France is today on a crazy spree of buying — buying everything they can get their hands on. Because they know in their hearts that some sort of end is near and all that junk won't be worth anything. But we remain poor. And political! We know this is only the end of fascism. That is why the resisting students at Nanterre have pinned the Star of David on their clothes, to make identification with the Jews under Hitler, to make it plain that this *is* fascism and that we know it! But when this fascist state has disappeared, then we shall be able to remake France! Then we . . ."

De Renville, of course, is caustic about both the Communists and the anarchist young: "Poor France, sunk so low she might yet have to depend on the ignorant and the barbaric. Even de Gaulle is more palatable."

American comment on de Gaulle and France is not, perhaps, quite so illuminating as that on England. France is more mysterious, for one thing, and the language and cultural barriers are higher. Nevertheless, there is a generous amount of material and some of it is very instructive:

C.O.S., fifty-three, American expert on bread. In France to help French bakeries become "modern." (At their request, induced by some sort of subsidy.) I met the bread man, as one inevitably grew to refer to him privately, at Auteuil (racing was his one diversion), and was immediately so fascinated with him, and with him in France, that I spent several hours talking to him and saw him several times later. In a way — especially for one interested in the American-European clash — he had everything. The American who could come to Europe to work for the downfall of European bread and the triumph of the dreadful American substitute was surely a sinister figure. Especially if he sincerely believed he was spreading a proven gospel to barbarians. There were touches of Melville's lightning-rod salesman, of the infantile brashness of the Connecticut Yankee, of the tight-lipped missionary to the South Seas. From a cultivated European standpoint (I introduced him to Clothilde as a present, as one might send flowers), he was the distillation of the American savage. And yet, even in his grotesque occupation and self he preserved something of the quality that had led a small ex-colony to world control. The blind perseverance had something to do with it. To have been an American bread expert in former times was one thing, but to base one's whole being in 1968 on the assumption that American bread represented progress was another. No one believed in American bread any more, least of all the Americans, but he paid absolutely no attention. Hippies, riots, clever talk . . . nothing kept him from his appointed rounds. He was at once an illustration of the old determination and the mutation of that quality into monstrosity. And yet, on subjects other than bread, he was often shrewd and even original:

"You just can't imagine what I found when I first came over here. No quality control, no idea of cost accounting, they couldn't even get the delivery truck schedules straight! I could hardly believe what I saw. And personally, where I was living, the lack of decent facilities. I couldn't believe it. Now I know it's the same all over Europe, but I can still hardly believe it. They've never gotten out of the Dark Ages. . . . Well, this was my problem: the bread industry was in terrible shape here, but I couldn't let the men I had to work with know how terrible it was. They all thought of Americans as 'nice,' and I saw immediately that I had to continue that tradition. I had to be as nice as I was expected to be. Later I used to hear them saying things about America and then they'd apologize to me for being so hard on my country, and I'd think to myself, 'If you think that's hard, you ought to know what's going on in *my* head about *you* people. It's so "hard" you wouldn't even understand it. You think I'm nice, but I'm not nice at all.' But I had to pretend to be nice and still get the job done. It was like working with natives in Africa. Sometimes at night I'd wake up in a sweat, there was that much pressure on me. But I stuck it out, one year, two years, three years, and finally the light began to show at the end of the tunnel. They began to get the idea, they began to feel the rhythm, and now I'm close to the end of my time here. And so I say to you that if you're wondering in your own line if you'll ever be able to do anything with these people, remember my experience. It looked black, but it finally worked. There's hope if you're willing to work hard enough.

"But it's been an experience, and I never want to have to come back. It's changed me, I'll admit it. I think the biggest shock was not finding out how backward they are, how crude everything is, but that they don't know it. They think they're real countries and that they live on a par with us. They've no idea they're in relation to us about the same way Africa is to them. No idea at all. And when you get off the actual way of life, into their idea of themselves and the intangibles and art, they think they're much better than we are. I could hardly keep a straight face when I figured out that they were thinking they were better than I was. Of course, I never let on by so much as a wink that I knew that, but it took my breath away all the same. That was when I thought to myself, 'All right, you think you have something, but you've had to get me over here to teach you how to make bread and how to sell it in the modern way, and so you're admitting you need me. I don't need you at all, and when I leave I'll never think about you again, but you'll be carrying what I taught you as long as you live.' And they will, too, and their children after them."

B.D., American divorcée living in Paris, beautiful, rich, bored, already quoted on the English as lovers:

"I like the French because they still resist America. Even when they go modern. When the rest of Europe goes modern, it's all *Ladies' Home Journal* — you know, like those young German marrieds who have the apartment and the car and the baby and the table settings. But the young French won't imitate the American middle class. Even when they're middle-class themselves and have no money. Oh, they imitate, all right — but the jet set, my dear. You see the young French insurance clerk and his wife setting off for a weekend and it's Brigitte and Gunther. Perfect down to the last detail — they're not speaking to each other. Getting ready has taken too much out of them. After all, he's had to transform himself from insurance clerk into playboy, and she from housewife into playgirl. The baby is dumped with *Grand-mère* and they climb into the tinny little sports car and adjust their shades and stick their jaws out with just the right amount of sullen glamour and head for the Alps or the Riviera and hope they still have jobs when they get back. It's pathetic, of course, but it's not middle-class. If they're going to imitate, they'll use their *own* models, thank you."

Pudgy Southern senator in his suite at the Ritz in late 1968:

"What I go for about de Gaulle is that none of these minority groups can get on top of him. You take the Jews — they say boo and everyone else in the world is afraid of them, like we are at home. But they don't scare him: he just says no more weapons after they went into Syria and blew up all those planes at the airport." His wife whispers in his ear. "I mean the airport in Lebanon. At Beirut. Then he had those riots with the students and the workers, and everyone said he was finished, but he just turned around and made a plus out of it. When it was over, he was stronger than ever because he brought it right down to a vote — who wants riots and who doesn't? Now you tell me who's going to say they want riots? Five per cent? Ten per cent?

"That's what none of *our* politicians understand. We have all those riots and sit-ins by nigras and students and everyone falls down in front of them. Why, if we had a de Gaulle — if Lyndon Johnson had been a de Gaulle — he'd go on television and say it was all Communist inspired — which it is, because who else benefits from it? — and it had to stop and if it didn't stop there'd have to be military action to stop it . . . and the whole country would stand up and cheer. Maybe twenty per cent wouldn't, but I can tell you that you can go a long way in politics with eighty per cent behind you. Lyndon could have stayed in forever if he'd done that, but he just didn't see it. I guess that's the difference between a great man like de Gaulle and us little old boys from down South."

He tosses back a shot of excellent bourbon and his wife smiles at him benignly. There is a good blaze in the fireplace of their sitting room, and it does seem a long way from the cotton fields. "But I don't know why that should be true," he muses on. "I don't know why *some* American from somewhere, North or South, can't be as good a politician as this de Gaulle, and not believe in nigras or young people or Jews, just in running a country right. By God, we used to, because we invented politics when you come down to it! Now all we care about is whether Jews and young people and nigras believe in *us*." He takes a furious pull on his cigar. "They say this Nixon will be different, but I don't believe it. He just doesn't have the . . ." He pauses and gestures helplessly at the coolly elegant walls.

Fagin-like American encountered late at night at the Brasserie Lipp. Sixtyish, long dirty fingernails, long dirty hair, yellowish-white beard on dirt-caked face, filthy clothes, eating his *choucroute garni* with his hands:

"Of course, the people who run things here know America is much better, but they don't want the common people to find that out, and that's where you get so much of the friction from. Like when it came out about the French government telling French students that they'd be liable for the draft in America if they went there to study. There was a big fuss about it here in Paris early in sixty-eight. I remember because I was living in a sleeping bag under the Pont Neuf, but I was keeping up with everything — what else can you do in the libraries? You go in to get warm and then you read. It's human nature. . . . Anyhow, the American Embassy denied that French students would get drafted if they went to America, and everyone was talking about it. The simple truth was that de Gaulle and his pals didn't want the young French elite to go over there and find out how we live. You know, when you drive up the Hudson from New York, or over through Connecticut or out to Long Island, not where all those housing units are but where you go for miles and miles through sections where people with money live. Your mansions, your manor houses, your estates, thousands of them, hundreds of thousands of them, and then you find out there are just as many around every city in America — Chicago, St. Louis, Atlanta, Dallas, Houston, Los Angeles, San Francisco — and the idea of the wealth of America begins to pile up and up and up, and all of a sudden France looks pretty shabby and pretty small. And the smallest thing in it is the idea by a bunch of Frenchmen that they can keep the truth away from their people. That's the undemocratic way they have over here, even when they're pretending just the opposite.

"They're afraid of America! They're afraid of what we have, of the truth about what we've done. I've found that out. But they get a lot of help on that from their own people. You couldn't keep the truth about a better way of life a secret from Americans even if it wasn't in America — Americans don't care about national boundaries where good living is concerned and they'll go anywhere to get it — but these people are so crude that it's easy to fool them. At first I thought it was because they were fooled from the time they were born, but then I figured out it's because they're so egotistical. Only the young ones, what you call your impressionable age, can get over there and admit what they see. And that's why they tell them fairy stories about the American draft grabbing them. The American draft! Why, my God, I'm an American who was eligible in two wars and I wasn't drafted, and if they didn't want me why would they want a French kid who can't speak English and is probably engaged to some swell girl anyhow? That's life, but it's not conscription."

A.W.W., thirty-eight, kindly and erudite American scholar, currently doing research in Paris:

"It is so difficult to keep holding two thoughts about France, but one must if one is to understand and enjoy the place. Holding two thoughts always reminds me of Fitzgerald, and then the subtle denigration of everything French that pervades his books, especially *Tender Is the Night*. It is a fair case, in a way, what one may call the frog details — the hair-oil aperitifs, the hair-oil singers, the hair-oil speech, the whole range of hair-oil culture, Latin and ridiculous to northern eyes. In our own day it is worse, if anything, than in Fitzgerald's time — now we have the French young who think themselves so beautiful, and the Belmondo admirers who swoon over a ludicrously smug hair-oil type. 'But he has such a lower-class body,' my wife said to me when he disrobed in a movie we saw recently, 'all twisted and the legs are too short.' She doesn't understand that people can't afford to see those differences any more. Especially the Belmondos themselves. . . .

"At any rate, I hope you don't think I am unaware of French drawbacks when I claim that we still have much to be thankful to France for. Because I think we do. France is awful, but America is awful, too, and the French are among the very few people in the world who think and say so. De Gaulle may be a terrible person, but he has resisted us, and we are very much to be resisted. He may even have resisted for the wrong reasons — the aggrandizement of the French bourgeois — but does that matter so much? Leaving aside all his nasty motives, he still hates us for a very good reason: we have dehumanized life. We are a nation of things, and no matter what else de Gaulle is he is not a thing. He may not even be consciously aware of how he sees us — I rather doubt he is, in fact — but it is the basis of his anti-Americanism, all the same. There are many people who resist Americans because Americans are things — including many Americans who have not already succumbed, I am happy to say — but not many world leaders, and that is why I consider him valuable. And France valuable. If there is ever to be a turning point in this American dehumanization of America and the world, of this turning everyone into things, then there will have to be a resistance, and I see France as the center of that resistance. So no matter her faults, and I am aware of them, I support her. And I supported de Gaulle, too, and would again, no matter his faults, and I think I am also aware of them. It is a fragile hope, this resistance, but we must believe in something. So when Sargent Shriver was appointed ambassador to France, I saw the irony of it — of sending *him* to de Gaulle — but I also saw the possibility in it. There we had, at last, a genuine confrontation — the cards were on the table. We could only pray, and I did pray . . . but evidently my prayers weren't good enough."

R.F., fortyish, American construction worker, self-educated, shrewd, antisocial, on train from Paris to Frankfurt:

"What I always try to notice is the difference between what they tell us and the way things really are. Like you take at home the John Birch Society says it's either us or the Russians, one or the other will end up running the world, and everyone laughs and says isn't that just too crazy. And then you get over to Europe and you find out that's what all the Europeans believe. The only ones who believe Europe could make it on its own are the Americans. The Americans who will swallow anything, that is, not these smart American diplomats of ours. The diplomats believe just what the Birchers believe, but they don't want us common people to know that. And then, with all of them in the same bed as the Birchers and hollerin' that they aren't, they have the face to say that this de Gaulle wrecked the idea of a Common Market. How could he wreck what no one believes in anyhow?

"The only reason we want England in the Common Market is to take over, and everyone knows that, too. But when de Gaulle tries to keep England out, everyone says he's being so unreasonable. It just shows you how people will say and do anything if they can't get what they want.

"De Gaulle reminds me of the story about the Jew who wanted to get into a country club that wouldn't take Jews and then when they changed their minds he decided he didn't want to join a club that would take Jews. I mean, he keeps telling these French people they're so great, and have so much stature, and then he shows he doesn't think they're anything by the way he has to treat them. He must have a hell of a time when he wakes up in the morning trying to remember which is which — whether France is great and it's wonderful to be alive, or whether France is terrible and it's a pain in the ass to have to take care of fifty million kids who need a strong father. . . . These European countries like France can get along all right until they get that first little whiff of prosperity and then they fall apart. They get that little economic miracle and then they start to wake up and notice the rest of what's wrong and the trouble starts. Like the man says, a little technology is fatal. Because after they get a little, they see for the first time the distance that's between them and us Americans and they crack up. They were better off with nothing and they know it. At least they didn't know what they didn't have."

Retired American general: "You don't begin to appreciate the French unless you've seen them close up in war. I've been so privileged in both world wars, and in Africa and Asia, and I can say in all sincerity that they are the greatest jokes. The Italians are worse from the military view only, but the French are lots funnier in other ways. . . . When I first saw them in 1917–1918, I knew there had to be something very wrong behind all that insecure impertinence, but it wasn't until we invaded Europe in 1944 that I began to find out how deep the wrong was. Their contribution to the invasion was only token, of course, and we let them go into Paris first because it was their city. But then you found out they actually believed they had liberated France with our *help*. De Gaulle believed it because he was their *Führer*, but the rest of the professionals believed it too, without such a vested interest. You couldn't talk to them about it; it was like arguing with women or certified lunatics. They couldn't face the truth of 1940 so they took refuge in hysterical fantasy.

"I did research on it and found that it all dates from 1871. The hurt and shame were so deep after the Germans trounced them then that they dreamed up the idea that French *élan* was worth more than weaponry. Napoleon had said, 'The moral to the physical is as three to one,' and they forgot that he was assuming physical parity with the enemy. From 1871 until 1914 they overlooked the physical and concentrated on morale, the *offensive à outrance*.

When Germany attacked, they counterattacked in Lorraine with their First and Second Armies — nineteen divisions — and they were badly beaten on August 20 at Morhange-Sarrebourg. Morale didn't work against the power of German defensive weapons, but it took them years to face that. In a way, they never faced it. They all still believe in that French *élan* — in peace as well as in war — and in a pinch of any kind they can only hold on to common sense for just so long before they lose control and revert to it.

"Isn't that exactly what has happened politically? By 1950 it was very clear that it was going to be a contest of time between Russia and America, a question of which system could outwait the other. Practically all of Europe understood it that way and sat back to wait it out. But not the French. They didn't have the nerves for that kind of fight, so they broke ranks and lost control and reverted to the old *élan.* When they do that, you have to watch out. They get more female than women and they'll take you right down with them if you get too close. That's what they damn nearly did to us and the rest of Europe."

Pertinent reportage on France from various sources. First, to illustrate the recondite depth of the Americanization, a quotation from a feature by Mary Blume, "French Take Heart Over 'Les Majorettes,'" in the *International Herald-Tribune*, October 16, 1968:

"To the French, there is nothing more basically, more risibly, American than drum majorettes. Now, like so many things that are basically, and risibly, American, majorettes have become part of French life. There may be as many as 1,500 majorettes in France, according to Guy David, leader of *Les Majorettes de Paris.* Small towns that used to have marvelous, noisy amateur bands now prefer majorettes to the local *fanfare.* 'Every little village has its majorettes,' Mr. David says. 'It has become an epidemic.' For his girls Mr. David has designed and copyrighted a uniform that is traditional but slightly more emphatic than the American ones. His uniforms are red with white shakoes and sateen capes and large gold epaulettes. The girls' skirts are shorter than in America and so, alas, are their legs. 'The French have shorter, thicker legs and there's nothing to be done about it,' Mr. David said. They also tend to have two left feet and an inborn objection to doing anything in unison. It's hard to manufacture a majorette in France."

In *The French,* François Nourissier puts his finger on three specific French ailments. Except for the first, they are not generally known or recognized outside France, but they are all relevant to an appreciation of Americanization:

"Just as a hankering for fascism constitutes a kind of tradition in French political life, anti-Semitism occupies a place in our collective unconscious that has not changed much in seventy-five years. . . . All French anti-Semites, with the exception of some violently anti-German nationalists, stood behind Pétain and the French Nazis. And if the racial laws (decreed by Germany but carried out by French officials) and anti-Jewish persecutions were possible, if they did not rouse an indignant reaction throughout the country, that was because of the passivity, the toleration of crime, that corrodes the conscience of the middle classes in France. The yellow Stars of David caused no feeling of shame. . . .

"One must never forget that even quite well-to-do French people have lived for a long time in surroundings that were ugly and uncomfortable almost to the point of squalor. (It is a revelation to visit apartments in Paris with an eye to buying one. You discover crumbling walls and a simplicity bordering on poverty, which are acceptable to people who in other respects live well.) . . . There is always a touch of shame in the haste with which a Frenchman shuts his door. The house and its furnishings — the background of daily life — are a kind of vague, unavowable family secret. . . . He will hesitate to return it [foreign hospitality] when the opportunity presents itself. He would be humiliated to have to expose a style of life unworthy of his guests, his own means, and his self-esteem. Foreigners who find us so little hospitable and who complain about how difficult it is to get to know French families should never forget that this shame is real and, in most cases, justified. . . . Vacations, weekends, restaurants, a car — for the Frenchman these are the contemporary signs of luxury. But the home, the daily habitat, reveals his embarrassment and his acceptance of neglect and *laisser-aller*. . . .

"It is hard to find anywhere else in Europe such disregard for and neglect of the vestiges of the past, and such a daily assault on taste, as is exhibited so widely and with such impunity in France. . . . the Frenchman sacks and botches ('modernizes' and 'embellishes'), remodels, fragments, and destroys what was once the proud setting for French life. . . . Whether the Frenchman is setting up a café, modernizing a shop, renovating a house, or building a shed, he perpetuates a kind of outrage. Ninety-nine out of a hundred Frenchmen lack not only a sense of beauty but also common sense. . . . The sudden wealth of the last few years and the availability of new materials (plastics and cheap, mass-produced items) have multiplied the manifestations of ugliness both in quality and virulence. Villages in undeveloped regions, long preserved from desecration because they were underpopulated and poor, have succumbed in the last decade to roughcasting their walls in ultramarine or canary yellow, to 'bold new' town improvements, and flashing lights. Shops that had resisted a hundred years with their charm intact . . . are now, thanks to flourishing business, transformed in six months into juke-box joints or public lavatories of 1930. If to the crimes against the past you add the aberrations tolerated in the name of the present . . . you will understand that while French beauty has become increasingly anemic since 1850, it may well have been mortally wounded in the last ten years. Rhapsodized in our schools, our textbooks, by our propagandists and by ourselves, this august entity has had it. Here and there it is already dead and everywhere it is dying."

L'Hôtel is a period restoration of the place in Paris where Oscar Wilde spent his last days. It is very fashionable, very expensive and has been very much publicized. However, it suffers from the endemic carelessness to which Mr. Nourissier refers, as pointed out in this amusing feature by Naomi Barry in the *International Herald-Tribune*, November 8, 1968, which could stand alone as a picture of a very large part of modern France:

"Sunday lunch: 'Let's eat at the place everyone wants to see.' That means L'Hôtel at 39 Rue des Beaux Arts.

"The decor is very precious, well-researched and unmistakably cost a fortune. People wander around in an unending procession inspecting everything as if they were on a tour of the Duke of Bedford's. A tent ceiling and a series of overhead infra-red lamps warms up the garden, making it possible to eat there during all seasons. The big feature is the long *table d'hôte* where anyone can eat family style, provided there is a place. A special 35-franc *prix-fixe* is reserved for this table only. Otherwise, every other table is *à la carte*. There was no room at the *table d'hôte*.

"Never mind, the strangers at the long table did not seem to be having fun. The formula, fine in a bistro, appeared awkward and unnatural in L'Hôtel's carefully evoked atmosphere of *Petite Marquise*. Besides, downstairs was a suite of deliciously arranged small intimate dining rooms. Elaborate 18th-century bouquets filled the vases. The tables were set with blue and white Limoges porcelain and antique crystal glasses.

"But so many details were grotesque, we simply burst out laughing. In the pink linen cloth was a hole big enough to insert a thumb. The foot of one of the wine glasses had been a third broken away. The napkins were paper. Soft quality paper napkins may cost a lot of money in France, but they will never make a suitable marriage with Limoges. The door to the serving pantry was permanently open, providing a still-life composition of Mess. In one of the small dining rooms, a romantic hideaway with two tables, a huge television set was blaring full force. Since nobody was there having a TV dinner, eventually we turned off the set. The headwaiter was negligently dressed in a washed-out pistachio shirt. He wore no tie and the buttons gaped in the front. Hadn't he ever heard of a turtleneck for playing casual? Offstage, he dropped something in a clatter and the word *merde* rang out strong and clear. It was almost too predictable.

"The *à la carte* menu has four main dishes: lamb chops, veal chop, *côte de boeuf* and T-bone steak. There was no T-bone steak. Our lunch for two consisted of the following: A small serving of crab salad presented in a hollowed half-green pepper and an *oeuf en cocotte* with caviar. There were seven grains of caviar, just enough to be counted present. The egg was quite cold. Main course was a *côte de boeuf* for two. We shared a single portion of nut cake. Between us we also had a total of three Scotches, 3 coffees, ½ bottle of Vittel. No cheese, no wine. The bill was a healthy 150 francs, a little over $30. On our way out, we took another look at the garden dining room which has elicited so much singing praise in the last few months. The diners had gone but the side tables were forlornly covered with the debris, even though the sightseeing types were still meandering around."

A letter in the *International Herald-Tribune* praising the attractions of France is quickly rebutted by another (September 14–15, 1968), from a Dr. R. Bellizi, putting the majority view of residents:

"Sarah Judson's letter cannot be left to stand without some comment. It would appear that she has never enjoyed the *effort* it takes to live in France. A recent 25 per cent increase in the price of bread, massive unemployment and the coming increase in taxes . . . are far better illustrations of what is going on than the 'dramatic landscapes and breathtaking art treasures' of Auvergne. Behind these landscapes are inadequate housing, lack of indoor plumbing, no sidewalks, and cow dung to adorn the front of a house — charming, if you are passing through. I challenge Sarah Judson to go to one of these quaint villages and pass the supreme test of trying to make a phone call to someone in the next village.

She might find out more if she read the French papers; she would surely not if she watched the state-controlled TV (the poorest in Europe). The French people are once again called on to endure the 'French miracle.' However, they too wish they were 'passing through.' "

Mary Blume's account, in the *International Herald-Tribune*, January 25–26, 1969, of the French National Library, gives a fair picture of French bureaucracy:

"The nerve center of this great library [the Bibliothèque Nationale] is its ground floor reading room, an ill-lit domed chamber with murky murals to which only scholars who have the proper credentials, two photos and three francs have access. Access gained, the nightmare begins. The scholar presents his card at the entrance and waits to be assigned one of the 358 seats. He may wait over an hour. Then he descends to the catalogue room, a curiosity not only because of the rudeness and antiquity of its staff (Cornelia Otis Skinner, who has since switched libraries, swears that the section chief was an ancient Gaul), but also because there is no catalogue, properly speaking.

"An alphabetical catalogue was indeed started in 1896 but is not yet finished (if you are doing research on Wincklemann or Zwingli, best wait until the year 2000). Many books that should be under 'anonymous' were given whimsical attributions by a former cataloguer and so are unfindable. It is, says one French scholar, easier to get a French work through the Library of Congress or the British Museum than from the Bibliothèque Nationale.

"Books cannot be removed from the library, of course. Nor is there much hope that the BN's hours will be extended; a curator has stated that if the library were open later, the books would wear out too quickly! For many Americans, spoiled by the Dewey decimal system, it is all too much (one American scholar, fleeing the reading room, realized she had left her coat behind and refused to go back even for that)."

And for those still under the impression that France is a temperate nation compared to the United States and Sweden, this AP item of February 10, 1969 (italics mine):

"Alcoholism kills more people in France *than in all major West-ern industrialized countries put together,* a World Health Organization survey showed today. France also registered the highest rate in fatalities from cirrhosis of the liver, which is frequently caused by excessive drinking . . . Per 100,000 population, the French alcoholism death rate was 12, compared with the United States' 1.4 and England and Wales' .1. In the cirrhosis death rate, France led with 34.2 . . . The United States rate was 12.8."

A selected bag of retrospective de Gaulle items, starting with this statement at his semi-annual press conference on September 9, 1968, in reference to the spring riots:

"I was waiting for things to become clear. In the eyes of the nation, I waited for that moment to act like a great man."

The remark is really more pathetic than megalomaniacal. One's immediate reaction is embarrassment for a man who could say anything so cheap and still believe he could be great.

De Gaulle's spitefulness and distortion of truth are well known. Here is another example of both, as exhumed by Don Cook, *Washington Post,* September 12, 1968. At the press conference cited above, de Gaulle had declared that France was not invited to Yalta and that he had refused to attend a subsequent private meeting with Roosevelt because he felt he was being ordered to.

"A check of the records at the U.S. Embassy in Paris now turns up a document which shows conclusively that an invitation to President Charles de Gaulle to attend the Yalta conference in 1945 was discussed by President Roosevelt's envoy, Harry L. Hopkins, with the then French Foreign Minister, Georges Bidault, and turned down. . . . The embassy records contain a cable from the then-U.S. Ambassador to France, Jefferson Caffery, to the State Department in Washington dated Feb. 2, 1945 . . . 'Bidault tells me that he told General de Gaulle you [Harry Hopkins] said President

Roosevelt would like to see him before he returns to the USA. De Gaulle replied that he would be delighted to meet President Roosevelt before he returns to the USA. . . . Bidault tells me also that it is his opinion now that it would be better not to invite General de Gaulle to join this big three conference.' . . . Clearly there was a discussion of an invitation with Mr. Bidault and the Foreign Minister turned it aside before it was ever presented to General de Gaulle. This has enabled General de Gaulle to claim repeatedly, as he did at his Monday press conference, that France 'was not invited' to Yalta. The Caffery message also cast a different light on General de Gaulle's prideful recounting last Monday of how 'I refused to attend the talks to which . . . Roosevelt had summoned me.' It shows that General de Gaulle through his foreign minister accepted Roosevelt's invitation to a foreign meeting after Yalta, to which the American President responded by proposing a talk aboard an American cruiser in Algiers Harbor. General de Gaulle then snubbed Roosevelt by refusing the meeting at the last minute after having accepted it secretly in advance."

De Gaulle's fantastic illusions as to his influence in the outside world — increasing as he grew older and the influence itself declined — were pointed up in this piece by Ronald Koven in the *International Herald-Tribune*, September 21–22, 1968, concerning the meeting between General de Gaulle and former governor William Scranton of Pennsylvania, the personal emissary of Presidential candidate Richard Nixon:

"The unusual length of the meeting, an hour and 15 minutes, was considered a definite sign to the Gaullist faithful of where the general's secret heart lies in the U.S. election. . . . By contrast, when former Gov. George W. Romney of Michigan, then a candidate for the Republican nomination, came through Paris in January, General de Gaulle declined to see him. The French considered him a loser. According to Raymond Tournoux, a top French de Gaulle expert, the general is absolutely convinced that his personal dealings with top American public figures play an important part in U.S. domestic politics. In his recent book, 'The General's Tragedy,' Mr. Tournoux quotes General de Gaulle as saying: 'France is tremendous in America. Nixon and Rockefeller make their publicity around the fact that I had them to lunch or for a private talk . . . Johnson's first official act as President was to say that I would go see him in Washington. Johnson needs me for re-election. He was only too glad to be able to announce a piece of good news to the American people.' (The general did not go.)"

The flirtation with Quebec was a combination of spitefulness and delusion. The AP item below, September 24, 1968, indicates the lengths to which de Gaulle was willing to go in that combination:

"Prime Minister Daniel Johnson of Quebec Province will be received in Paris next month with the honors usually reserved for a visiting head of government, a spokesman at Quebec House disclosed tonight. These protocol arrangements seemed certain to deepen the quarrel between France and the Canadian federal government over Quebec's future."

Prime Minister Johnson died unexpectedly and so the drama of treating a provincial Canadian minister as the head of an independent government never came off. The intent was very much there, however, in all its overt animosity.

There is an irradicably comic side to de Gaulle, as there is to all European dictators. It is overshadowed in most instances by his more publicized characteristics, but occasionally it stands alone, as in this item from the *International Herald-Tribune*, December 19, 1968, where the aging autocrat had to find a place for even Marielle Goitschel's pants in the French mythos:

"If gold medals were given out for personality kids, French Olympic ski champion Marielle Goitschel would have won another one today at the lunch President Charles de Gaulle gave for all the French Olympic winners. She outshone everyone there, apparently including the general himself.

"It started from the minute her car pulled up into the Elysée Palace courtyard. She astonished the *Gardes Républicains* with a few swerves of the car, as if to remind everyone that her specialty is the special slalom. Miss Goitschel, who is as well-built in the cross-wise direction as in any other, jumped out dressed in a black pants suit in the same spirit if not the same size as the one Brigitte Bardot once wore to the Elysée.

" 'This is the third time General de Gaulle is receiving me,' she said in the doorstep. 'And the emotion I felt the first time was dissipated long ago.' But she added diplomatically that 'I'm proud to be at his side.' All went well at the lunch. The general gave a little speech in which he said he admired sports champions because 'You are the people who struggle, who fight.'

" 'Your example is spreading,' he said. 'It contributes to the renaissance of our great and beloved country.' Marielle made the general bare his soul on everything from his favorite sports to the monetary crisis. To hear her tell it afterward, she asked if he minded all the questions and he answered: 'No, no. Please go right ahead.' What about those pants you were wearing? asked a reporter. Wasn't General de Gaulle surprised by them? 'No, he told me, "Athletes are athletes, and in France we are always in the avant garde in fashion." ' "

And in this bit from a story by Ronald Koven, *International Herald-Tribune*, January 15, 1969, following the Israeli raid on Beirut airport:

"The raid . . . enraged General de Gaulle. The magazine Paris-Match and others quoted him as saying: 'Destroying (French-made) Caravelle airliners with French helicopters: they could at least have used American helicopters!' "

De Gaulle's idea that French machinery remains "French" no matter to whom it is sold is almost as charming in its naïveté as it is comic. But at the same time, the notion that machinery is national — a variant of the pathetic fallacy — put him at a terrible disadvantage in the international business field. Can one imagine the

American robot-executive in business or government thinking that a steam shovel sold to Ghana was still "American"?

De Gaulle has not lacked critics, and his weaknesses have been pinpointed by experts. Five examples are given below: Willy Brandt, the *Neue Zuercher Zeitung,* the *New York Times,* a letter to the *International Herald-Tribune,* and Senator Vance Hartke, of Indiana:

Willy Brandt, in a story by John L. Hess, *New York Times,* February 4, 1968: "Foreign Minister Maurice Couve de Murville summoned the West German Ambassador today to explain what his Foreign Minister had said about President Charles de Gaulle. . . . The West German news agency DPA had quoted Mr. Brandt as telling a Social Democratic meeting in Ravensburg last night that 'the deep-rooted Franco-German friendship, particularly among young people, will in the end be stronger than the rigid un-European thoughts of a head of government obsessed by power.' "

The *Neue Zuercher Zeitung* (Zurich), as quoted in the *International Herald-Tribune,* November 26, 1968: "Having recently declared that a devaluation of the franc would be an 'absurdity,' de Gaulle was clearly unable to rise above his own shadow. With his refusal [to devalue] he has virtually turned his back on the West's monetary solidarity."

The *New York Times,* as reprinted in the *International Herald-Tribune,* June 4, 1968: "The Gaullist election effort to run against the Communists is an attempt to cash in on a self-fulfilling prophecy.

" 'Tomorrow, in France, there will remain only the Communists, ourselves and nothing,' André Malraux predicted almost two decades ago. General de Gaulle, making his first postwar bid to regain power, had combined his negative vote in Parliament with that of the Communists in an effort to block, then tear down, center government in France.

"The attempt failed. But in recent years every effort has been made by the Gaullists to polarize French politics again — to destroy the center and force the center-left into alliance with the Communists. The aim has been to create the bogey needed to bring out the middle-class vote for Gaullism. . . .

"During ten years in power, the Gaullist government progressively has become more remote from the French workers and youth, who are communism's chief recruiting ground. The dismissal of eight ministers in the cabinet reshuffle just completed is an admission of gross mishandling of the grass-roots protests at the beginning of the recent unrest.

"The great political need in France is to reconstitute the vital center that can provide the country with an adequate spectrum of alternatives to the policies of the extreme Left or Right. Gaullist efforts to turn the National Assembly into a rubber stamp, to limit debate, to rule by decree, and to manage news on the state-run radio and television networks have led France's Socialists and left Catholics to seek any ally, including the Communists, to oppose Gaullism.

"The tragedy of General de Gaulle is that the longer he holds power the more he destroys his own objectives. Forcing the nation repeatedly to choose between de Gaulle and chaos — instead of solving the problems that produce unrest — has given France de Gaulle and chaos. His search for grandeur abroad has progressively weakened France's influence in the world. His attempt to break the dollar has sapped the strength of the franc. And the campaign he is now waging against French communism is more likely to increase than to reduce Communist strength in France."

Letter to the *International Herald-Tribune*, December 25, 1968, from Donald A. Bailey: "In his Friday contribution to his very fine series on Eastern Europe, C. L. Sulzberger correctly attributes to Karl Marx the comment, in Marx's words, 'that all facts and personages of great importance occur, as it were, twice.' He . . . forgot to add: 'the first time as tragedy, the second as farce.' Mr. Sulzberger is, of course, speaking of the German, then the Russian, invasions of Czechoslovakia. It is interesting, however, to remember that Marx, in his 'The 18 Brumaire of Louis Bonaparte,' was writing about Napoleon III, whose coup d'état of 1851 was a re-enactment of the earlier coup by the great Napoleon. It is interesting, because it leads one to wonder what Marx would have said about a third occurrence of a greatly important fact or personage. For it is surely obvious that the third Napoleon (to number according to facts and not to fantasy) is the present president of the French Republic. In all three cases, one can see as predominant characteristics at least two important features: a paradoxically reforming conservative, with the reform either bluster or belated and the conservatism ever present; and the representation of oneself to all easily frightened elements of the population as the 'party of moral order.' Napoleon III and the present president also have in common a romantic enthusiasm for nationalism under whatever form it may be found, and a very costly concern to build up a handsome but worthless military power. My own feeling is that this third occurrence is happening as a tragi-farce."

Senator Vance Hartke, Indiana, as quoted in an AP item, December 2, 1968: "The blame for France's 'economic and fiscal disaster' rests entirely on President Charles de Gaulle, Senator . . . Hartke . . . said today. . . . He said General de Gaulle must end his 'autocratic absurdities' if he expects to regain full Western cooperation. 'De Gaulle,' Sen. Hartke said, 'is the author of his own economic and fiscal disaster. He brought it all on himself. He kicked NATO — meaning the United States — out of France and, as a result, he automatically cut his nation off from $300 million to $500 million annually in direct dollar payments for the maintenance of scores of military bases. It is now clear that this huge dollar income was a kingpin in France's economic structure.' "

In the business world, the material comes thick and fast. Below is a pair of newspaper items which indicate the awkward position into which de Gaulle got France:

First, from the AP, September 16, 1968: " 'The profit-starved auto industry of Europe is due for a shake-out,' *Fortune* magazine said yesterday. It quoted chairman Giovanni Agnelli as saying 'eventually there will be three American companies, and one British. The rest will wind up together — as one or two companies.' *Fortune* said that only by such consolidation would the 'fragmented European industry gain the economies of scale necessary for successful competition' in an increasingly tough market.

"Fluctuating demand is familiar enough to U.S. auto makers, *Fortune* said, but it is a 'new and thorny problem for European companies long buoyed by a seemingly insatiable demand for cars.' Now that there are fewer first-time car buyers, the sales growth and profitability of European car manufacturers have tapered off. At the same time, tariff cuts have intensified competition. The American companies in Europe will, of course, be the subsidiaries of General Motors, Ford and Chrysler. If Mr. Agnelli's prediction comes true, the British survivor is likely to be British Leyland . . . Continental survivors might be the merger products of German Volkswagen with Daimler-Benz, and in France Peugeot with Renault, and Italian Fiat with French Citroen.' *Fortune* said that 'large-scale mergers among the European companies appears to be the only answer to the American challenge' of Detroit's Big Three."

Second, a headline in the *International Herald-Tribune*, October 11, 1968: "France Vetoes Plan for Fiat to Buy Interest in Citroen."

In the first item above, the case is put. Europe's automobile manufacturers must merge to fight the American challenge. In the second, the predictable French reaction: de Gaulle would not allow a merger which permits a foreign company to control a French company. The true weakness of his position lay in its unfairness: he would not mind a bit if a French Agnelli proposed taking over an Italian firm. He was not against mergers but against playing the cards as they are dealt. He did not see that in the long run France would have its share of control in any European federation. He could only take the short-term view of all or nothing, and one must finally concede that the adjective "bourgeois" is inescapably appropriate. (The merger was later approved. The French said on their terms, Agnelli said on his. No matter which, the net result was the same: France fought the inevitable once again and lost.)

The three items below present the same psychological climate from a different but related position. In the first and second, the need for English computers — and hence for England — in the EEC is established. The third shows the lengths to which England and the rest of Europe is preparing to go should Gaullist France continue to try to thwart the inevitable.

Washington Post, October 31, 1967: "The European Common Market today took its first step toward closing the technological gap with the United States. But the six almost tripped over the question of moving ahead without waiting for Britain to join the European Community. . . . Most attention is being given to cooperation in data processing and in air and water pollution. It is unclear, however, exactly what can be accomplished by the six with data processing since the only indigenous computer industry in Western Europe is in Britain."

New York Times, by Lloyd Garrison, March 29, 1968: "France Is Alarmed over the Inroads of U.S. Computers — The merging of British computer companies into a giant, Government-backed corporation has sparked fresh talk here of bringing the British into a joint European effort to stave off the threat of total conquest of the Continent by the United States computer industry. . . . Many leading French financial writers have echoed widespread sentiment here [in Paris] that only cooperation on a European scale can match America's head start in the computer field. *Le Monde* put it this way: 'Isolated efforts of one firm or one country have no chance of breaking the American grip,' and it added that if directors of the Plan Calcul [de Gaulle's answer to the American challenge] did not team up with the British and other European computer makers, then individual French companies might take the initiative on their own.

"Despite all the talk of computer cooperation here, a number of economists remain skeptical that a European approach can be hammered out. These observers point out that three years ago Frank Cousins, then Britain's Minister of Technology, was ready to share all of his country's computer expertise as a symbol of British sincerity in entering the Common Market. The offer was declined by President de Gaulle, largely on the grounds that the British were so far ahead in the field that France's retarded industries would become totally dependent on British techniques without developing any of their own. . . .

"But there is doubt here that the British can match American sales and marketing techniques in the competition for future European buyers. This will be an uphill battle. I.B.M., for one, already has more than 30 years of sales and maintenance experience on the Continent. . . . With Britain's apparent determination to go it alone, observers here predict a revival of Franco-German discussions to join hands in face of both the American and now the British threat. But to these same observers, a counter-move in this direction is already too late."

Donald H. Louchheim, in the *Washington Post*, October 15, 1968: "Britain called on France's Common Market partners today to circumvent President Charles de Gaulle by establishing a new framework for European unity and an enlarged community for economic and military cooperation on the Continent. In a speech to the Western European Union here, Lord Chalfont, who has spearheaded Britain's recent efforts to win entry into the Common Market, conceded that France has 'effectively blocked' the British bid. But he said: 'We are not content to sit about idly until it can be opened again. We are ready to act now with our friends in areas outside the immediate purview' of the six-nation Common Market. 'If any country is not prepared to join in concerted action now,' he said, 'those of us who are prepared to move cannot afford to waste any more time.' Lord Chalfont's speech appeared to signal a major new British thrust to outflank the French with an end run around

Gen. de Gaulle's Common Market veto. It coincides with mounting frustration and exasperation among France's Common Market partners over what they regard as Gen. de Gaulle's inflexibility and intransigence."

And a last item which is an adequate, if oblique, summary of the whole position:

Richard M. Cohen, *Washington Post,* December 5, 1968: "Former UN Ambassador George W. Ball called yesterday for an end to the 'special relationship' between Britain and the United States which, he said, impedes Britain's entry into the European Economic Community. Citing the recent French monetary crisis as an indication of French weakness, Mr. Ball said that Britain must begin to turn toward the European continent to balance the 'leading role' West Germany will play in a post-de Gaulle Europe."

It is a remarkable statement. After years of official American denial that a special relationship exists between Great Britain and the United States, an American who should know says that there is such a relationship. De Gaulle, then, has been right all these years: there *is* a special relationship and to let England into any European community is to let America in. His opposition to English entry has been realistic.

Mr. Ball makes the admission because of pressure — the specter of West Germany as the most powerful nation in Europe. Something must be done about that, even if it necessitates conceding that de Gaulle's opposition has been based on a reality.

From de Gaulle's point of view, that is all there was to it. A prominent American shows that even Americans are human where their interests are concerned. Forced to choose between admitting a secret and West Germany, Mr. Ball chose the admission, and de Gaulle hoped he was the first of many.

But, unfortunately for de Gaulle, there is much more to it than what de Gaulle saw. To begin with, the admission is double-edged. There is a special relationship, says Mr. Ball, and it should be ended, but its termination is expected to open the EEC door to England. Thus it is difficult to accept the admission without opening the door. De Gaulle always tried to have it both ways in such a situation, but he never managed to. And the harder he tried, the less he usually got.

Then he lost more because he misread the motives. It is true that the special relationship exists, but not in the way de Gaulle thinks. To him a special relationship is an arrangement between knowing people who can deliver what they promise; between Richelieu and Louis XIII, between Marlborough and Prince Eugene, between Stalin and Hitler, between himself and . . . no matter if he had never achieved such an understanding, there was always tomorrow. He did not understand that the "rulers" of America and England are neither sixteenth-century manipulators, seventeenth-century soldier-statesmen, or twentieth-century despots. They are Baconists, men who look for the inevitable and bow to it. They have nothing in common with the strong "personalities" of the past or with those who have tried (with considerable lack of success) to resurrect such autocracy in the present. America and England don't have a special relationship because they are clever and wish to impose their joint will on everyone else, but because such a relationship was inevitable, the way the vacuum pulled. Now it may be beginning to tug another way with enough strength to pull the special relationship apart. If that happens, there will be no Anglo-American "regret," because it was not personal in the first place. The special relationship never took precedence over applied Baconism, which is what de Gaulle never understood. He saw the special relationship but he did not see that it was impersonal, only the result of a religious dedication to Baconism. The bowing to the inevitable was, and is, what he should have paid attention to, not the direction of the bows. He has imagined sentimental ties where he should have seen it was only business, without which connection Englishmen and Americans could see each other eaten up without a qualm, and without lifting a finger in assistance.

In a way, one can find de Gaulle a very touching figure. Not as the fictitious strong man, but as the very poignant weak man, hopelessly handicapped by outmoded theories of his past and present. He is like a crippled child reading the novels of Sir Walter Scott in an industrial slum and then trying to find romantic beauty in the street, or the village eccentric trying to build his own flying machine. There is a superficial similarity to Don Quixote, but much less resilience and far more grim pathos. And when he attempted to make his own special relationships with other heads of state — those special relationships which no longer exist because they run counter to the produce-and-consume groundswell — no one knew where to look. Not those next to him, not the recipient of the attention . . . no one. It was too embarrassing, like an old woman dressed for a party in a frock from the early 1900s. One is haunted by the idea of his actually saying, "I waited for that moment to act like a great man."

And the embarrassment extends to France and all Frenchmen. Not to the same degree, of course, but there is a touch everywhere and in everyone. The ugly houses of which they are ashamed, the bad taste in building, the premature decomposition of L'Hôtel, the majorettes with the legs that are too short . . .

They have resisted the Americans, but they are none the less Americanized for that. Because the resources (human rather than material) were not there in the first place, the ultimate Americanization may be grosser and more far-reaching than elsewhere, even in England. Particularly if nations pay for their mistakes in resisting America by having to accept an accelerated Americanization pace. Behind the crumbling wall of France's ideological resistance appears the outline of a surrender of startling proportions — in time, France may even supplant England as the showcase, the jewel of the empire, with Frenchmen believing as intensely in this wonderful new religion, *Baconisme*, as they now do in unrelieved materialism. "There was a day," they may say with wry, Gallic smiles, "when we Frenchmen believed unrestrainedly that men could impose on nature. Not only that Frenchmen could, but that all men could. And it was not only the old men, like de Gaulle, who believed it: even the young progressives did, even those who first sought to lead us out of the wilderness, figures like Servan-Schreiber. Those were wild days for France, days of spleen and confusion, days almost impossible to imagine now."

Such realism is well in the future, though, because the national belief in controlled destiny is still triumphant. The disease approaches a climax, but the end is not in sight, although in late 1968 and early 1969 there are significant symptoms, many of them more meaningful than de Gaulle's resignation. Long before he left, the French army made plain its distress over his Israel policy, and went so far as to wish openly for the return of American tactical nuclear weapons. France finds it doesn't have the money to continue in Euratom after the year's expensive adventures, a small but illustrative example of her inability to support any pan-European project for long, even on the financial level. Crumbling psychologically, France demands special privileges from her disenchanted partners, and the EEC acts to force her to fulfill a pledge not to exercise export subsidies, a pledge she has no shame about breaking as she becomes increasingly indifferent to legal obligations. She also makes a childish scene over a WEU meeting in London, in February, 1969, and boycotts that group for refusing to knuckle to her demands; and then goes so far as to propose to Britain that they join in setting up an organization to supplant the Common Market, a group to which Britain would be admitted if she got out of NATO.

The tempo of eccentricity becomes more frenzied, and it destroys more than de Gaulle's possession of immediate office. He is, after all, no more egotistic than his countrymen — that is why they have supported him — and they joined him in a dance so abandoned that it can't be turned off entirely just because he has suddenly left the floor. He didn't care if the orgy meant the end of European unity and ultimate American control, and his people didn't either. He may be able to walk out on the party, tone down his insolence and act as though there never was an orgy, certainly not one of his choosing. But his people weren't acting. It was real to them and it still is, and thus the French egotism — the most prominent national weakness — shows every sign of having the power to deliver the Continent as well as the country.

In any settlement, France — and Europe — will have to live with the consequences of de Gaulle and the fragile philosophy of "Gaullism" long after de Gaulle is dead. In addition to breaking the spirit of his own people by leading them into a lost battle, he managed to delay the formation of a European federation for so many years that America was given what may well be an insuperable lead. The reign became polished burlesque slapstick — the anti-American reincarnation of Joan of Arc, Cross of Lorraine in hand, nightcap on head, candle in hand, bare feet on cold floor, promises to lead his people to independence and ends up as Uncle Sam's secret agent. In his last few months in office, de Gaulle may have seen, at last, just what he had done and how perfectly he had betrayed France. The true hero would have made a public confession ("I was ensnared by my own ignorance and arrogance into delivering us to the Americans . . ."), but de Gaulle, with characteristic weakness and malice, may have deliberately provoked personal defeat on the unnecessary referendum, leaving the Gaullists holding the bag and himself safe at home. The masquerade may work for the moment, but time will not resist the temptation to see him plain. If Hitler stands unchallenged in the view of the Americans, the prime beneficiaries, as the grand betrayer of Europe, de Gaulle's grip on a close second place seems secure.

———————

In late October, 1968, a telegram from de Renville informs me that Clothilde is dead, and I go to France for the funeral. In Paris, de Renville tells me she killed herself with poison. He is overwhelmed, but insists he is not surprised. "I knew it was coming," he says. "She made it very plain she thought there was nothing for her. Feeling as she did, it would have been surprising if she had gone on living. I tried to dissuade her, of course, but without much conviction. She knew I didn't have much more hope or appetite than she did, and I couldn't have deceived her on that point if I had tried." He talks on, barely under control.

From Paris, a melancholy party goes south to the family stronghold in the Cévennes, where she is buried. We stand in the small graveyard in a hazy autumn sun, everyone avoiding the usual bond of sympathy. If she had died by accident or from illness she would seem gone, but as it is she is uncomfortably present and we are all disconcerted and embarrassed.

On the way back to Paris, de Renville is finally silent and I am left to my own recollections. I remember a party at the Île St. Louis apartment in the summer, mostly young people, at which the girls were secure enough to avoid current fashions and even those who didn't were attractive enough to carry them off. The girls wove their special brand of French magic over the proceedings, the ancient, gypsyish intimacy — as Clothilde had put it — between themselves which shuts out all foreigners and admits only French men. Which sounds wonderful for the French men except that they can only be admitted if they retain their limitations. Clothilde, who didn't believe for a moment in such a provincial game, nevertheless entered into it with consummate skill, always clever enough not to draw attention to herself. And besides, it was art, it was entrancing for those privileged to attend the performance, and she was too sensitive to art to withhold her own participation and spoil the tableau. But beneath the gallant performance was a definite and sinister beating of wings, the dashing of a delicate bird against the bars of its elegant cage. She was sure there was something outside the French experience and she was determined to get out of the cage and have it. If she could not escape, she would perish. Very well, she had not been able to escape and she had perished.

"You see," she said to me at the party, in the full hearing of a young princess with a sharply cut bow of a mouth and eyes full of indolent confidence, "we French always get what we want." And the young princess was so overcome with the propriety of this remark that she almost nodded in agreement; only the iron strands of exceptional breeding sustained her. But Clothilde's impersonation was as false as it was perfect.

"There was never anything here," she had said to me in the afternoon before the party. "Never. Diane de Poitiers, Francis I, the endless gallery of monarchs, aristocrats, great men, subtle women . . . there has always been something lacking. We have never been in the avant garde of the psyche, not really. There are things we have never felt, and I can't stand that lack in myself. I must get out, get free, feel what there is to feel, serve what there is to serve. I would rather be an American and have a chance, no matter how awkward, than be French and have no chance in the midst of sureness."

"You have a great deal," I told her. "It is foolish of you not to realize that. And even more foolish to think you can transplant yourself successfully into a completely alien culture."

"You can say that," she said. "You're on the other side of the fence."

"You're very young," I said. "You'll feel differently when you marry."

"That's just it," she said. "Who can I marry? Frenchmen aren't men."

"We Americans aren't any better."

"You can't dispute French leadership there," she said sadly. "Especially if you're a woman."

She had sounded very young, almost ordinary, but now she was dead by her own hand, so she had supported her sentiments and raised them to maturity.

"Such an action is supposed to be mysterious, but there is nothing mysterious about it in Clothilde's case at all," de Renville says bewilderedly when we are back in Paris. "I knew how she felt and what she would do and she did it." He has borne up well, but the import of what has happened is now beginning to bear in on him. I stay for a few days to see him over the worst of it, and he tries to talk of other things. Only occasionally does he say anything about her, and then briefly: "She was so very beautiful. I already miss having such beauty near me. . . . She was quite correct in what she did, always, but I do not accept her final choice for herself. . . . She was very French, although she didn't think so, and she gave the lie to her own judgment that France had never been anything. Underneath the breakdown, the Americanization, what you call the resistance and ultimate surrender, there is a French presence, the presence that always was. It may be rare now, and it may soon become extinct, but it was always there. It was in Clothilde, and she didn't know it, wouldn't understand that it was what made her different."

("When the old lunatic quit," de Renville wrote after de Gaulle's resignation, "I wondered if that would have made a difference to her. But it wouldn't have. He was a symbol of what we are, and we are the same with or without him. That is why he is really of no importance in the end. Just another haphazard French attempt at grandeur, and we always fail there because we don't know what real grandeur is.")

Symbol of France or just a French girl, Clothilde remains a pervasive memory, coloring even the dullest recollections and facts about France. Not long after coming back to Switzerland from Paris, I sat one morning in a café in Zurich reading an account by Henry Tanner of the *New York Times* of an interview with André Malraux. At first, only the exquisitely egotistic belief in personal destiny, the rampant "Frenchness," came through: "Malraux often faces unfavorable comparisons between his revolutionary past and his present role as a patriotic pillar of the Gaullist establishment. In *Anti-Memoirs* he recalls telling General de Gaulle that he, Malraux, had 'married France' during the Resistance. He was asked what he meant by this, and whether it was not a break with his previous allegiances. 'There is a crucial point which you must well understand,' he replied. 'I married France in her agony after her defeat . . . General de Gaulle, on the other hand, was, if not a nationalist, at least a traditionalist with respect to the nation. What he defended in vanquished France were the same values he defended in the victorious France of 1914. As for me, if I am asked, "Have you changed?" I say undeniably I have, but only on one point. And this is that, when I was thirty years old, I defended essentially the proletariat. *Bon.* But with the second World War, I substituted France for the proletariat. That's absolutely true. . . . But, *attention,* I have never been a member of the Communist party. So there were no previous engagements that could have been broken. I was president of the World Committee for Anti-Fascism. But I did not give up my anti-Fascism when I defended France, since I defended her against Hitler. . . . And then there is another point, which concerns my own psychology, and that is my commitment to revolution stemming from Indochina. That is to say that the absolutely crucial element in my life lies in my anti-colonialism.' . . . Malraux . . . talked rapidly, racing to keep up with the torrent of his ideas, puffing a cigarette, coughing frequently and punctuating his talk with exclamation marks thrown at his visitor in the form of *'attention'* (mind you), *'bon,' 'alors,'* and, in almost every sentence, *'n'est-ce-pas?'* "

Bon, alors, attention, and *n'est-ce-pas?* indeed. For one occupied with trying to analyze the depth of the French weakness in order to be able to estimate the speed of the Americanization process, this seemed a prime clue. The French Minister of Culture, by reputation one of the most remarkable men in Europe, talks like a music-hall Frenchman. If this is Malraux, Disneyland-on-the-Seine can't be far behind! Through his words I could see the ardent march of the future — the fifteen hundred drum majorettes with the short legs melting into the tens of thousands with the long legs, all on their way to the stadium for the Friday-night high school (pronounced 'igh es-kool') football game under the lights . . . hamburgers grilling in a million backyards . . . two-fisted martini drinking at the Café de Bordeaux — a surrealistic panorama, all sharp edges, quick movements and harsh voices. And then, without warning but quite naturally, I thought of Clothilde's serene face, luminously reproachful. "I have more of a right to laugh at poor Malraux and at poor France than you do," her presence seemed to imply, "because I laugh at him and at my country for a higher reason and on a higher plane. And I paid a higher price for the privilege." The point must be conceded. Her priority does not invalidate the rest, but it puts it in a different perspective. Such probity does not mean that France won't go to the symbolic guillotine, but that she will take something with her that the colonization will never reach. It will be gone, and gone forever, but it will not have been violated.

3

ITALY AND THE MEDITERRANEAN

G IOVANNI AGNELLI, who runs Fiat, has become (in early 1969) Europe's most persuasive advocate of European unity. His argument is Servan-Schreiber's — European unity would reduce the scientific and technological gap between the United States and Europe, and a federated Europe would then be the world's third great power — but because of his position his voice carries more weight than Servan-Schreiber's. In a world that adores the Kennedys, he who has everything commands more respect than he who has merely a lot. (One can hardly imagine the people clamoring for bankrupt Kennedys.) Servan-Schreiber is rich, a successful magazine publisher and political-economic commentator, and dashing: but Agnelli is the richest man in Italy, the country's leading industrialist, and twice as dashing — after all, he was once a full-time playboy. Servan-Schreiber is well known, but Agnelli has been the subject of a *Time* cover story. Servan-Schreiber's espousal of European unity came when the subject was still controversial: Agnelli's advocacy means that it has become a majority desire, only waiting for de Gaulle to leave the stage.

Even presuming it all happens — and it has progressed far enough so that possibility is real for everyone — there are nagging questions. If Europe finally achieves some sort of unity — in the 1970s, or 1980s, or even in the 1990s — and the new federation does attain equal (or superior) economic and political standing with the United States, and equal political standing with Russia (long since surpassed economically), people everywhere will tend to claim that an important event has taken place: Europeans are independent! But will that really be the case? Will anything that stirring have actually happened? Will Europeans be truly independent? Or will they only have achieved Americanization without the Americans?

The crucial point is that the push to European unity is not really a push to a *European* ideal. It is an artificial desire, one which did not exist — except as the admittedly impossible dream of a handful of visionaries — before the Americanization process began. It is not a passion for unity per se (the visionary dream), but a negative desire for material parity through unity, a plan in which unity is only the means to parity. The passion for genuine unity would leave Europe intact, but the negative desire wants technological parity no matter the cost in terms of European culture. The reduction of the technological gap between the United States and Europe will also bring about a corresponding reduction of the cultural gap between Americans and Europeans. The elimination of the technological gap, the proclaimed goal, will also result in the elimination of the cultural gap, the stripping away of the last vestiges of Europe from Europeans. Then they shall be indistinguishable from Americans, for identical technologies today demand identical societies as their base, and identical societies demand identical individuals.

This has already been demonstrated in the United States, where the produce-and-consume society has broken down the regional differences once thought to be eternal. There are still differences between Atlanta, Georgia, and Providence, Rhode Island, for example, but they are a fraction of what they were thirty years ago, and it is difficult to distinguish either city from a "neutral" urban area like Cincinnati. In their day, the South and the Northeast were less Americanized than most of Europe is today, and their ultimate surrender to the rest of the country was actually more reluctant.

When it became apparent that the people in both those regions wanted to be Americanized more than they wanted to retain their native ways, the once-lofty argument degenerated into the question of who would do it and make the money. Businessmen from the industrial East and Middle West (the West did not become part of the "true" America until more recently) were ready to come in: in fact, some were already in, just as they are in Europe today. At the last moment, the locals decided they would prefer to keep the profits at home, and so the latterday Americanization of regional America was carried through by Southerners and New Englanders who had become Americans — i.e., producers and consumers. (As Charles Francis Adams, Henry's great-nephew, became head of Raytheon Corporation, in Boston. Henry himself, it will be recalled, had nothing but scorn for post-Civil War American plutocracy, the forebear of produce-and-consume.)

The visitor to America does not find much significance in the fact that the reluctant regions were Americanized by locals instead of those from other states and backgrounds. Neither do most Americans. The overwhelming fact is Americanization itself — who cares who did it or who made the money out of it? Who even remembers? I rather imagine that in time no one will remember or care who Americanized Europe. Today it seems of some importance, especially to those who will make the money out of it, like Agnelli, but tomorrow? . . .

The European may point out that the South and Northeast are technically part of the United States and thus have a different position than any European country, no matter how Americanized such a country might become. The fact is, though, that political affiliation means very little and degree of technological development means everything. A proper produce-and-consume American has much more in common today with his German or Italian opposite number than he has with unadjusted Americans. In 1860, the American South was part of the United States on paper, but in truth it was quite distinct because it had a different economy and

[263]

was in a far cruder stage of development than the rest of the country. If Europe should reach technological parity with the United States in . . . 1989, for example . . . then Europe would be part of the United States in truth if not on paper. Europeans would still give lip service to some sort of European political leadership just as Americans have a formal political focus in Washington, but the distinction would be of no real meaning. For all practical purposes, Europeans and Americans would then be citizens of one country, for technological parity forces parity on all other levels — cultural, political . . . even moral. Thus the Agnelli–Servan-Schreiber idea that Europe will become a third entity through technological parity is naïve; it could only do that through technological superiority, which is by no means impossible, although even the most sanguine Europeans seem to stop short of such a prediction at the present time.

There is more than a hint of the Emperor's new clothes about the whole struggle. Agnelli, the pan-European of limitless money, charm and energy, is going to join with the other Agnellis, great and small, all over Europe, and squeeze out a genuine federation in order to pool Europe's resources and produce an Americanized Europe free from American control. But in order to do that, what forces have had to be set in motion! Agnelli's mother was half-American; his wife's mother altogether so; and he speaks flawless English. On the surface, he is dashingly European, but his ideas, the thrust of his mind, the way he sees the world, are all completely American. His belief in the produce-and-consume society could not be faulted by any American, not even Henry Luce himself, were he still alive. Agnelli *is* an American, one finally concedes, and when that becomes apparent one begins to wonder how fine the distinctions are being drawn.

If Agnelli had to become an American (a process which started before he was born) in order to grasp the idea that the only way to save Europe from American control of its coming produce-and-consume society, which will turn all Europeans into Americans anyhow, is for Europeans to control it, how is the end result any different from what it would have been under straight American supervision? In Agnelli's field, does it really matter to the average European whether Detroit takes over the European automobile industry or whether the Agnellis put together such a perfect imitation of Detroit that they take over the European automobile industry? In either case, the result will be the same, not only on the surface but as far down as one cares to dig.

If Agnelli's grandfather had migrated to America and taken Fiat with him and made it as big as Ford and General Motors combined and left it to Agnelli (just as he did leave it in Italy) and Agnelli arrived in Europe to take over the European automobile industry — would he look or sound one whit different than he does? Would he have a different program? Would it make the slightest difference to anyone that he was American rather than Italian? Does it make any difference today that he is technically Italian rather than American?

Not a bit. He is Americanized to his backbone. And he is not alone. When Gaullism is finally pronounced dead, Agnelli will join with the others in Europe who are equally Americanized, his peers in the emerging Continental Baconism, and they shall do their very best to make Europe a single state and bring it to technological parity with the United States. As converts, they shall be even more zealous than those born to the faith. But in no event should their technical lack of United States citizenship beguile the interested observer into thinking that they averted the Americanization of Europe. They will do — and are doing — just the opposite. Already Americanized themselves, they are more anxious than their mentors to spread the gospel. The only difference between them doing the job and the Americans doing it is, as Twain would have put it, "the honor of the thing." They shall make a great deal of money, but they would have made just as much working for American proconsuls, because American policy would have insisted that the profits stay in Europe to keep priming the pump.

If imitation is the sincerest form of flattery, the sincerity of the Agnellis is beyond question. In addition, they are capable, industrious, and patient — all the American virtues are theirs and they have even managed to cut down on such specific American weaknesses as drink and prolixity. It would seem that they cannot fail in their appointed task of unifying Europe. But as shall be seen, they are up against formidable opposition, and may fail in spite of their best efforts. In that case, however, the American machine in all its supranational privilege will be available to do the work anyhow. So it is difficult to see how the Americanization of Europe can be stopped. If Europe remains nationalistic and divided, the Americans will do the job; if that threat forces Europe to drop its prejudices and federate, Europeans will do it. Insofar as Americans desire the Americanization of Europe, how can they be disappointed? Even if they don't do it themselves, the Agnellis stand ready, already Americanized in a surrender of all-enveloping proportions and more than anxious to exact the same fealty from their peoples.

(Amusingly enough, it may well be that instead of European unity bringing about technological parity, technological parity may bring about unity, in the spirit of the old Bob Hope quip, "Powder the eggs and start the war." Thus formal unity may be an ultimate result rather than a cause, and be brought to fruition *by* Americanization rather than in spite of it. In support, one notes that it is the completely Americanized Europeans — the Agnellis and Servan-Schreibers — who are the most ardent pan-Europeans. It was said earlier that true equality would have to come through an inner change, and they clearly demonstrate how it looks when it happens. The new, American Europeans have been produced — in small numbers, granted, but they are already the leaders — showing that the laboratory experiments have been as successful, as "exciting," as the production of any other strain from test-tube research. The process may, in consequence, be farther along than first suspected. To the degree that Europe is already Americanized — and that is considerable — the inertial velocity is gathering and there may be less distance to travel than commonly supposed, although such assumptions become highly speculative.)

Nevertheless, there are ways in which the American wishes can be thwarted. Nationalism and the entrenched aristocratic interest are still potent — de Gaulle speaks for both positions on occasion, although he is too eccentric to follow either line consistently — and both are gathered in and propelled forward by the Catholic Church, which still looms large and persuasive on the European landscape. Italy is naturally the place to study the Church, and it is also the place to study the related phenomena of aristocracy and nationalism, which can be found in clearer and more refined examples in Italy than anywhere else in Europe. Italy, then, is a rewarding field, finely representative of the Mediterranean; and its greatest creation, the Church, remains a dynamic force throughout all Europe. So much so, in fact, that one can scarcely understand Europe without some understanding of the Vatican.

The Vatican's great strength is based on the fulfillment of psychological need. Europe has only been unified twice, and Rome did it on both occasions, first with the legions and then with the Cross. Ennui and the barbarians broke the first unity, and technology and the Protestants the second. The memory of the first unity was superseded by the second, but because there has not been a third, the memory of the second is still alive. Even the most obdurate Protestant in northern Europe remembers that he comes from stock once Catholic, and that Europe was once one in the bosom of the Church. He will not go back to the Church, but he would very much like to have the comfort of unity again, so the Vatican and Italy play a double role in his subconscious. As a Protestant, he despises "the Catholic nonsense" and "the shiftless Italians": as a rather lonely human being, he is drawn in race memory to the cool mystery of the Vatican and to the Italians as former masters. He says he comes to Italy to see art treasures, but one suspects that it is really a comprehensive evasion for all that disturbs him beneath the surface.

In his nostalgic yearnings, the European Protestant is quite different from the American Protestant. The latter freed himself from hankering after the lost Catholic unity by inventing a genuine Protestant unity, materialistic and technological but none the less religious for that. Even American Catholics are Protestants in the religious moment of truth, the choice between being Catholics or Americans. Rome and the Church have none of the appeal to the American imagination that they do to the north European, and good American Protestants are always puzzled and disappointed to find their European co-religionists so atavistic.

If the American unity is the true end of the Reformation, the inability of European Protestants to achieve the same end would seem to mean that the Reformation has been abortive in Europe. And if abortive, Rome is still in charge, in a subtle, negative way, all over Europe. For example, the existence of an official aristocracy and an established church in England automatically guarantees that the similarities between England and Rome shall always outweigh their differences. An English duke will always have more in common with an Italian prince than with an English man of business, and a cleric in the Church of England more in common with a Roman Catholic priest than with a Methodist parson. The English duke is joined in his close relations with the Italian prince by noblemen from Scandinavia, the low countries and Germany. The relations are cemented by intermarriage and the result is a supranational network not a great deal different than it was before the Reformation. (What makes Europe different today from what it was then is the rise of the middle class, not changes at the top.) This network has survived for a long time, and it hopes to go on surviving. It has been the only unity Europe has had for several hundred years — from the Reformation until the arrival of the Americans — and it very realistically sees from the American example that there would be no place or need for it in a completely Americanized Europe.

The aristocratic network is closely involved with nationalism, which may seem paradoxical at first, but not when one realizes that nationalism keeps Europe from uniting and rendering the supranational aristocracy useless. From the aristocratic viewpoint, nationalism is an invention to keep the masses busy, to divert attention from themselves.

And all aristocratic-nationalist sentiment in Europe ultimately looks to the Vatican as its capital. This is as true of the staunchly Protestant Danish baron as of the ultra-Catholic Austrian count, because the Dane's Protestantism is abortive. It does not serve him in life's highest matters — money, power, control of the future. For those he has to revert to a dependence on the older faith even if he does not formally embrace it.

The American in Europe is usually ignorant of this buried current. But not through his own fault, because it is not all that obvious to the average European either. Because it isn't obvious — and it is very much to the aristocratic interest that it not be — most Americans and many Europeans make the mistake of thinking it no longer exists. The American meeting Count G —— in Austria feels the correct attitude is friendly condescension. He accepts the title and the kiss administered to his wife's hand as just another brace of European anachronisms, like the churches and the narrow streets. If he has to do business in Austria, he may discover that the aristocrats stick together and have influence, but he rarely realizes that they are part of an international order with great power in Europe. After all, they often do not realize that themselves, so how can an outsider? Nor does the American understand that the aristocracy is not a detached class wielding its power in spite of indifference or opposition from other classes. If that were the case, the aristocracy would not be of great importance. But by merely allowing the aristocracy to exist, those other classes give tacit support to the system. It is only when an American finally pierces through to this that he sees the gulf between himself and all Europeans. Not only the aristocrats but all, even his opposite number. He and that opposite number may look almost exactly alike in their suits and wives and cars and houses, but the fact that the opposite number sanctifies the aristocratic principle (blood is different and can be inherited) by allowing it to continue in his country, whether he himself believes in it or not, separates them over an unbridgable chasm.

Knowledge of that chasm, while rather a burden in some ways, can be positively helpful in educating the American to European reality. He sees, for example, that the disorganized confusion of the European shop is not due to willfulness or blind chance, but is at least partly the result of a chain running from the shopkeeper through his middle-class landowner to the aristocrat and the Vatican. It is not in the Vatican's interest to make shopping easy, and that iron suggestion is made into potent innuendo by national aristocracies that don't see easy shopping as in their interest either, and the innuendo ultimately reaches the lower classes with the force of law. And in the case of the American businessman, such whispers are often the cause of his own failure to carry through what had seemed so certain.

(In the old America — the one that ended with World War II — the aristocratic blood-principle was officially infra dig. It existed, but only in secret pockets along the eastern and southern coasts. No proper American acknowledged another American to be his superior unless the other American had more money. Since the war, the aristocratic principle has enjoyed a mild vogue — although rather hugged to death by being dragged into the open, in the American fashion, as with the Kennedys — but the country still remains basically anti-aristocratic. And probably will continue to remain so, because wide acceptance of the aristocratic principle would mean giving up the produce-and-consume principle, or at least cutting it down considerably, which most Americans are unwilling to do. Faced with a choice between Kennedys and consumption, Americans will probably always choose the latter. But nothing is certain in this changing world and even those priorities may be reversed in time.)

When the Americanization process started in Europe, it ran most smoothly in the north, where the abortive Protestant movement was most ready for some kind of unity. Such opposition as there was came from the Protestant aristocracy, which had, as has been seen, a unity of its own with other aristocracies. As the process moved south into the Catholic countries, the opposition increased. France balked, Austria dragged its feet, and Italy stirred uneasily. As the Americanization accelerated, European aristocracy began to remember its origins, as it always does in time of crisis, and looked to the Vatican. What would the course of action be?

On the evidence to date, it seems that the Vatican has not yet decided. Its immensely long life as a human institution is based not only on a fierce tenacity but also on not doing anything until absolutely necessary. It has seen so very few threats mature into dangers that its first line of defense is, very properly, to do nothing, to wait until the threat goes away, as nearly all threats have. The Vatican has time, and time is a decisive weapon. It has worked for the Church in nearly every challenge for twenty centuries, including that of Communism. The only failure has been the Reformation, if it is a failure, because the Vatican refuses to see any defeat as permanent, even when the evidence is overwhelming.

The question now is whether Americanization (as distinct from American Protestantism, if the distinction can be made) can be outwaited. Also, can the Americanization of Europe be completed, whether by Americanized Europeans or Americans, without a final Americanization-Vatican contest of wills? Europe was once completely unified under the Church. It is still partially unified through the Church by way of the aristocracy. Won't that unity have to be broken before the new unity can stand forth in triumph? One way or the other, Catholicism is the only unity Europe has had since the sixth century; but two unities can't exist in the same place at the same time, so won't the influence of the Vatican have to go if Americanization is to be complete? And isn't there already a recognition of this in the European subconscious — as in the Vatican's recent and rather panicky insistence on obedience regarding its rulings on contraception and other matters, and the restless refusal by large blocs of European clergy to give that obedience? Isn't the resistance prompted by recognition on the parish priest level of the fact that the laity is drifting away in alarming numbers? And where can they be drifting except to Americanization, the alternative religion?

For the Vatican, Americanization can be seen as a modern, isolated phenomenon, or as the natural outgrowth of Protestantism. In the latter interpretation, America must be cast as the arch-villain: without the American creation of a genuine Protestant unity, the abortive European revolt might well have collapsed long ago and returned the flock to the fold. In that view, the Americanization-Vatican contest becomes the America-Vatican contest, the final act in the drama that began with Hus, Luther, Zwingli, Calvin and the rest. In any case, though, the question is one of time.

In the late fall of 1968, I go to Rome and have an opportunity to test the climate. It is a business trip, but I hope to have an opportunity to ask a few of the above questions, however indirectly. The questions are difficult ones, not only because of the natural taboos but also because so very few people have knowledge rather than opinion in the field. One exception is Lorenzo Moradonia, an old acquaintance and new business associate. (As in earlier sections, names have been changed where sensibilities are involved.) Lorenzo has impressive credentials — he is a prince, a member of one of Rome's oldest and most influential families (the ancestral tree is strewn with cardinals and boasts ties with several popes), and he is intelligent. His wife is American: the number of Italian aristocrats who have married American women is extraordinary. And not only in our own time — the custom is a hundred years old, and a remarkable percentage of titled Italians have American mothers, grandmothers, or great-grandmothers. Interestingly enough, many of those women were from the less ostentatious regions of their native land: for example, the mother of Princess Marella Caracciolo di Castagneto, Giovanni Agnelli's wife, was from Peoria, Illinois. Not Philadelphia or New York, but Peoria. She met and married Prince Filippo, Duke of Melito, while visiting Italy; one is rather charmed at the picture of jaded Latin dukes being drawn so irresistibly to prim young ladies from the Middle West.

Lorenzo's wife has contracted his Christian name to Larry, and everyone calls him that now, even his oldest Italian friends. "I don't care at all," he says. "It is part of the times. 'Larry,' 'il weekend.' 'wheesky-soda' — all part of the same process." He and his American-born *principessa* and their two young sons live in an immense palace in Rome. "It is like the Adams family," he says. "Not those New England Adamses — the TV Adamses. I am the husband and Elizabeth is Morticia and we live in the haunted *palazzo*. But it is very interesting, because — as you may have noticed — the Adamses were the only happy family on American TV. I hate to go out, at least during the day, so I just lie around and make money and dream." Larry speaks perfect American. He is also tall and fit and darkly handsome. And indolent. "I am so lazy," he says. "I am what the Milanese mean when they talk about lazy Romans. But they can afford to be active — they are so stupid. It is very enervating to be intelligent." He *is* intelligent. Even his hobbies call for intelligence. He is a noted amateur archeologist and historian, and has written a little book on the Italian historical method as perfected by Guicciardini and others. Elizabeth plays up to him in the Roman fashion, and the two boys — twelve and fourteen, tall and blond — are not unwilling to complete the tableau as it moves from one dazzlingly frescoed room to another.

"Let's stay here," Larry says, dropping into a chair. "If we go out, we'll only hear Italians boasting about how clever they are. When they are really so stupid, of course. So I, who am really clever, stay at home and waste time."

We discuss the business project that has brought me to Rome. Larry wants to invest in desalinization plants, but, with characteristic secrecy, doesn't want his presence known, so there will have to be a lot of Swiss subterfuge. In one of our breaks from the table piled with papers in his lavishly baroque study, he says, "Business is all very well, but I think so much about the old days. No, that is not quite right. The old days, and the old incidents, but in relation to this time, the present." He looks at me with quizzical intensity. "Let me explain. It is a matter of precision. After the war, I had many girls, but who didn't? I was in love so often, but so was everyone else. Nothing made it different then, but what I think about it makes it different *now*." He pauses and scratches his head as we stroll a dim, frescoed corridor. Two maids in starched uniforms pass and he waits until they are gone. "Here is an example. I was in love with an actress for a while and it was very serious. She was beautiful and had much character and she used to tell me wonderful stories, although I didn't appreciate them at the time. One day she told me that her father had been arrested during the war on some charge or other, and she went to see Ciano to ask that he be released. And Ciano agreed to do that if she would sleep with him, and she agreed to do that. In Ciano's own office, of course. 'It was the custom,' she said. 'You went there for a favor, and he just pointed to the couch in the corner.' Well, I didn't believe her — it seemed too trite — but of course I didn't say so at the time. But now . . . here's the point . . . now I do believe. Not so much in the story — what difference does the story make? — but in the reality of her and me and the father and Ciano. The whole business as *Italian*. Do you see? The beautiful Italian actress telling her lover the trite story, possibly altogether false, and the lover not believing, and the father and Ciano peering over both our shoulders and approving because she is telling the expected story and I am having the expected reaction. It is the limitations I see now, the very Italian limitations. I suppose we are all trapped, but in different ways. That is my way. And that is why I remember her, and remember her story and find it wonderful now."

It seems the opportunity to mention my own curiosity about certain Italian matters, and I do so. He is immediately enthusiastic.

"I could tell you so much about the Italians! And about the Church and the Vatican! Everything! But in my own way, of course. It is very backward, very oblique." He looks at me anxiously, and I assure him he can be as backward and oblique as he wishes. "You see, everything means something," he goes on. "All my own experience is what I am talking about. So I can't just say . . . this and that . . . about Italy, and walk away to leave a pile of lifeless generalities behind. I have to put myself into it, because that is the way I have learned. For example, I could say the Roman aristocracy is naughty when it is young, and then it grows up and runs the Vatican. (Or part of the Vatican, anyhow.) But what would such a statement mean? I would have to tell you more. I would have to say, for instance, that people always claim they were never really bad, but I admit *I* was. I did terrible things, but they were the usual things. Humiliating girls with instruments — bottles, all that sort of boyish high spirits. They say that's queer, to do that, and they're right insofar as they go. We are all queer when we're young here. And stupid. Do you know that I used to give parties in this house when I was twenty-five, and everyone in Rome would come (you know who I mean by everyone), and we'd all race little cars on the floor. Not slot cars — they weren't around then — but little models with motors in them. We'd scream at them like children, and then we'd go in the bedrooms with the girls and play with each other. Eight hundred years of selective breeding and we were down on the floor playing with the little cars and then we were in the bedrooms playing with the girls. We'd undress them and they'd undress us and we'd all giggle and masturbate together. We couldn't have normal sex with those girls because they were all of the Roman nobility and it wouldn't do if they got pregnant — this was before the pill, of course.

"Anyhow, we liked to masturbate and so did they. So we'd help

[275]

them do and they'd help us (it was very communal), and then we'd all get dressed and go back to eight hundred years of breeding. You could very properly say we were retarded. You could say we *are* retarded, and wonder how we have ever done anything. But here is the point of everything: we have done something. That is where my story, and I myself, begin to curve back to Italy and the Vatican. Young people like we were then grow up to do things. To hold on to our money and position if nothing else. At first, you wonder how any of us can do anything. You look at me or Luchino Visconti and you just can't believe that parade of cardinals and *condottieri* and popes. And yet, here we are. What does it mean? I still have the family acres and the family houses — will it always be that way? It will if what made it possible in the past — the credulity of people — keeps up, and it shows no sign of dropping off. So we shall always have what we have now. And shall always be called on to do something, no matter how ridiculous we are in youth. Or in maturity . . .

"The stupidity of people is a fantastic thing — that's what the Pope must think of when he goes to bed. Otherwise how could he be where he is? That's why all the popes begin to look so tired around the eyes. You see how we have gotten to the Vatican from the little cars and masturbating the girls! It is all connected because it is Italian, that is what I mean. It is even connected to you Americans through me, because it was an American who first told me about the Pope. Can you imagine that? *Me.* An ordinary looking American, I can hardly remember his name — Barry, I think — but he used to be around, years ago. You remember Barry, you were here then. No one else thought he was anything, but I thought he was interesting, instructive. About the Pope, yes, he said to me: 'The Pope is the one man who can't afford to believe in God.' I found it smart-aleck at first, especially because it came from an American. You do understand that to an Italian like me, American men don't exist. American women, yes; American men, no. And most of the time we are right. But this Barry was something else. And the remark kept coming back to me, and finally I could see it was a very religious remark. I was impressed. I had not only learned something about the Pope but also about Americans. There was such a thing as an intelligent American man, there was even such a thing as a religious American."

We go back to work, but he keeps returning to the subject, winding back and forth between the Italians and the Americans, the Vatican and the new society. I tell him that I am writing a book on the subject and would like permission to quote him. He is more than willing.

"An exciting opportunity," he says, "but my identity must be concealed, of course, so that I can say anything I wish." I assure him that it will be. "It is really a marvelous chance," he says, "marvelous. But I have a better idea than talking while you take notes — or try to remember it afterwards. And anyhow, that's too inhibiting. I shall put my thoughts on tape. That way I can marshal them, make them behave . . . you see, what I must do here is make the correct blend of myself and my ideas. But I *shall* do it! You will see. I shall be like Proust, sifting through ladies' hats and ideas until I have it just right. It will be a marvel, it will . . ."

He can hardly be coaxed back to desalinization. During the rest of my stay in Rome he refers to the project constantly, but I leave without an inch of tape. "It is more of a job than I thought," he says. "Science and art — they must be in just the right proportions."

"I would have been happy with a brief résumé," I point out.

"I am trying to make it brief," he says. "I am also trying to make it artistic. I was thinking of Pirandello, how he would have done it. No, don't think I am lazy and looking for an excuse. I am very serious."

Two months later he does send me the tape. It is long for my purposes and I have had to cut it, but have not, of course, tampered with what has been used. I myself find it a valuable, if partial, answer to my own questions cited earlier, and a contribution to any consideration of Italy, the Vatican, Europe and Americanization:

Intelligence, the religious sense, the ability to hate, toughness and dishonesty. Those are the qualities I am probing. They are the great Italian qualities, the qualities which lie at the foundation of the aristocracy and the Church. Especially dishonesty. But this is a very special dishonesty I am discussing. It is not stealing from your employer or telling a lie on your income tax. It is the pleasure derived *from* dishonesty, dishonesty for its own sake, dining with your friend after you have seduced his wife and relishing the dishonesty of the *position*. All Italian history could be written of in terms of this dishonesty. Everything we are and everything we make and do reflects this special dishonesty.

It is a practical quality, too, because the world is evil and he who would rule it must understand evil better than anyone else does while pretending that no such thing exists. We Italians have always been supreme there. That is, until recently, when that supremacy has been challenged successfully. But until now, our knowledge of the human heart has been universally recognized and conceded to be of the first rank. Sometimes the recognition and concession included a shudder, but shudders imply respect.

What we had could be seen in a very special way with the girls we used to amuse ourselves with. I mean the beautiful girls who came to Rome from nowhere and ended up with us — we Romans of family, when we were young, too, and ready to do what we were supposed to do. We passed those girls from hand to hand, we taught them every perversion we knew or could think of, we put them on drugs if we could . . . we did everything to them . . . and then we walked away. After which they went mad or killed themselves or became prostitutes or sank into a lower group for a cruder version of the same. No matter what they did, they were broken for life. Pious people said it was awful, and they were right.

But they also believed in it *because* it was awful. They didn't say that, those pious ones, but we knew it, so it was an incentive for us. It was from the pious people that we gained the knowledge of being right, in some dark psychological way, of catering to the truth in people. We knew that degradation was what people wanted, what they believed in, because it answered their deepest need. That was why the girls came to Rome, and that was why the others looked. The infliction of degradation was, and is, the Roman sport because of its connection with reality and truth, not in spite of it. After all, we have been the center of the world for a very long time. We are extreme, but we have to be. In the case of me and my friends, our uncles were running things across the Tiber and we were torturing girls, and so there was a close relationship between all of us. Otherwise we could never have grown up to follow them in their jobs. Nor could they have carried out those jobs so well had they not, in their day, done what we did. For us, you see, it is only part of the inevitable. It didn't matter where the girl came from, but it was better when she was a foreign girl because in that way we got more of our own back. The control in Rome is based on the hatred of foreigners and it was more pleasurable that way.

We used American girls that way, too, and then we ran into one who showed me that we had lost our monopoly on the understanding of evil. She was a certified American beauty queen and terribly vapid — that should have warned me, but I was young and the game had always worked so well — and she wanted the full Roman experience. (You know, later they came for that experience *because* they had seen *La Dolce Vita* — the exposé acted as a stimulant, not a deterrent!) She was passed from hand to hand and then she came into our tender care — two of my friends and I — and we were, I remember, in a hotel room, somewhere like the Flora, the three of us and her and we got her to strip (she was drunk and spinning, and she'd been spinning for days, for weeks), and the three of us teased her. She was in that condition where she'd do anything, and she wanted all three of us, one after another, because that was what she had been doing for weeks in hotel rooms in Rome, but we were a bit more sadistic and carrying her education a bit farther and we just teased her. We made her do things to herself, promising that if she did what we wanted we'd oblige her later. So she did everything we suggested — bottles, other instruments, everything we could think of — and then we walked out. It had been final, I thought, looking at her very gone face. There was no coming back when they looked like that, crazy eyes, matted hair, emaciated cheeks . . . she was screaming after us as we left and we only laughed together going down the hall.

That should have been the end of it, and I did hear later that she was in other, lesser hands. But a month or so after that she telephoned and asked to see me and the other two who had been there that night. She sounded very calm, very collected, and I was intrigued and arranged the meeting, in her hotel room. She wanted to do it again! All of it! But sober this time. It seemed that she had been discussing her stay in Rome with an American psychiatrist, and out of all her experiences he thought the one with us sounded best for her personal problem, which was losing her inhibitions! I was nonplussed and so were my friends. We really didn't know what to do. She was talking in that flat, deadly serious American voice and peeling off her clothes for an ice-cold orgy, and we were suddenly very awkward. It was four o'clock in the afternoon, hardly our time for such games, and the atmosphere was all wrong, anyhow. So we made our excuses and tiptoed out, leaving her for the second time, only this time she wasn't screaming. Just looking at us rather contemptuously over her uptilted nose and aggressive breasts.

When I analyzed it, I saw that what had happened to her hadn't touched her because she was *different*. She was beyond evil as we understood it, which meant she was beyond us. We couldn't manipulate her because we couldn't reach her. She was more dishonest than we were because she was even less herself. She was no longer a girl at all, she was a monster. She hadn't yet learned how to relish the dishonesty, how to play with others consciously, but she would in time. . . . I had misread that face, I admitted to myself. It hadn't been gone, not completely, but simply preparing its own devilment. We had been a stage in her reaching for power, not she in ours. It was an enlightening comeuppance.

Now this concerns the Vatican because the Vatican knows in general terms what I know in the particular — that its basic dishonesty has been superseded. The Church became necessary in Europe because the basic European unit was a credulous peasant who demanded a Church. The basic European unit is still the peasant, but only barely. Tomorrow it will be the Americanized worker, and there will be no need for the Church. When the Church was real and necessary, it ministered to the peasant's faith, but that didn't mean the Church believed literally in its own words. As Barry said of the pope, it couldn't afford to do that. So in a way, it was dishonest. It was a necessary dishonesty, but all true dishonesties are necessary. Now the Church has had the same experience with the Americans as a whole that we had with the American girl. That includes the American Catholics, who are not Catholics at all, but Americans masquerading as Catholics. The Church has sat with Americans at four in the afternoon, just as we did with the American girl, and had the ground cut from under its feet in the very same way.

So the Vatican's question is: what shall we do? And the answer is: we don't know what to do. My own feeling is that the Church will slide slowly down and out, as we slid out and away from the girl with the uptilted nose lying there on the bed with her hands under her aggressive breasts and her legs defiantly and woodenly spread. . . . The choice is fight or surrender, and there will be no fight so there will be surrender by default.

I have spoken of how Barry, an American friend, showed me that Americans were intelligent and had a religious sense. He also convinced me of the American ability to hate when he gave me his version of the Rossellini-Bergman business. Barry had something to do with the movies, I remember, and was always up too late at night. I ran into him at the Jicky on one of those nights in the early 1950s, and he said, "The hero is Howard Hughes, not Rossellini. Bergman falls in love with Rossellini, or thinks she does, and goes to Hughes to get enough money so she and Rossellini can make a movie together, like a couple of teenagers. Hughes sees she's being taken, but is not stupid enough to argue with her. For his own reasons, he gives her the money and she runs back to the waiting lover with it and they make the movie, *Stromboli*. Rossellini thought he'd outwitted Hughes because he got the money, but Hughes fooled him. He knew when he made the loan that the movie was going to be terrible, so he had it cut secretly in Los Angeles and released it simultaneously all over the United States. Rossellini was furious but Hughes actually made money out of a very poor film. Not only that, he also made a fool of Rossellini, which was what he wanted to do in the first place, when Bergman was standing there like Oliver Twist. To a man like Hughes, wops are to be kicked."

I thought of Barry's story recently, when I saw that Hughes had bought into Las Vegas and trapped Sinatra into making a fool of *him*self. For me, the whole picture was illuminating, because I had had no idea Americans were haters. I thought only Italians and other Europeans were.

. . . As my education progressed, I learned that Americans were superior in everything — intelligence, the religious sense, the ability to hate, toughness, and dishonesty. The dishonesty was the most crucial . . .

Yes, I know the story about Giorgio Vellati and Maury Madder — you told me yourself. Well, I was "anticipated" almost as completely. And when I knew that, I was frightened. The despised Americans had outdone us in every category. But most crushingly in dishonesty. We had been the most dishonest people in the world, the least ourselves, and we were very successful because of that — because dishonesty always triumphs. But now that the Americans have taken over . . . the rest of the world can imagine (I use the word literally, meaning to compare with former champions) how dishonest Americans are, how little themselves. People may not *know* that, but they all have a story to tell, in a bemused way, about the wonderful American who suddenly revealed his fangs and took something precious from them. Go watch the Americans in St. Peter's and try to find one who is affected to the slightest degree under all the pretense of being affected. Conversely, try to find one who does not pretend to be affected.

To be dishonest is to control, to colonize. . . . Americans are a people for world conquest, an entire *people*. In western Europe, *individuals* used to manipulate the lower classes to achieve their dreams of power in Europe and abroad. But Americans move collectively, all in one body. They are more like Asians — or ancient Aztecs or Mayans — in their organization. It is true that the English achieved this to a certain degree — the lower classes becoming a living extension of the *will* of the aristocracy — but the result was nothing compared to what the Americans managed. So American dishonesty is not, as in Europe, the prerogative of the ruling class and the religious leaders. A whole *people* has achieved dishonesty, the first time it has been done, at least in modern times. Think what an insuperable advantage this gives the American over all other nationals. He is not either the conscious perpetrator of a lie nor the conscious victim of a lie (all Europeans are one or the other), but the unconscious carrier of a collective dishonesty that he never has to think about. Thus all Americans are equally dishonest, no more and no less. (The idea that Kennedy was honest and Johnson dishonest, for example, which is held by many Europeans as well as Americans, is sheer fantasy. Or that Nixon is more dishonest than Norman Mailer. Or George Wallace than Arthur Schlesinger. The truth is that no American can afford to be more, or less, dishonest than his fellows.) And that is the real secret of your success. You put our old-fashioned, individual dishonesties to shame. . . .

The entire Mediterranean is a contest of wits, and you have beaten us everywhere. Spain and the rest are not so different from

Italy, just a bit slower. There are people like me everywhere in the Mediterranean, and we are all whining about defeat, because if the Vatican has been beaten by the Americans in this contest of wits we have all been beaten. Even Gianni Agnelli, although he belongs to the second rank, to the people who don't know it yet. But he will know it in the end, and then he will have to come to the old Italy, to Rome, to see what can be done. He will have to come because the economic "miracle" never benefits the workers as much as it does the employers, so the workers become restive. Finally they show signs of getting out of control and the employers become frightened. How to get them back in their cages? Who will know better than the Romans, the Vatican experts who have specialized in this question for nearly two thousand years? Gianni will be in Rome before it is done.

The great question is not whether they will come, but what the Vatican will be able to say. . . . First, I must speak of the Vatican, because it takes some understanding. We all know the clichés: the Vatican is a worldwide business, the oldest in existence, run until very recently entirely by Italians, and even now there are few foreigners at the top. It is run very efficiently, too — an American management survey gave it exceptionally high marks a few years ago. Its presence and reputation for efficiency have always made a deep impression on ambitious Italians outside the Church as well as inside, and all Italians are impressed with its "universal" position. In this way, it is wonderful training for any global business, and directly and indirectly grooms Italians psychologically for the worldwide idea. When we go into world business, we are better prepared than other Europeans.

I don't mean for a moment that we are the best businessmen per se in Europe — any northerners, especially the Dutch, are better — but we have less trouble conceiving the *idea* of a world business. This means, among other things, that we are better able to conceive of a genuine challenge to the Americans. That is even true in America itself, where Italian gangsters have been the most stubbornly unassimilable of all ethnic groups. Even the Jews and Negroes are more integrated. Only the *cosa nostra* Italians have dared to go against the whole weight of American pressure, setting up a permanent, illegal state within the state, even to the extent of speaking Italian in the second and third generations rather than English. Without the model of the Vatican, it is difficult to see how they could have done it, and it is instructive that what they have set up is a perfect replica of Vatican organization. . . .

Then the other side of the Vatican, the obverse of its efficiency — it is oppressive. It is so much the arm of the European aristocracy, so completely concerned with keeping the people down, that it is obsolete in any region where the people have come "free." (The modern freedom is a chimera, of course, but there is no other word.) This weakness makes the Vatican, and us Italians, vulnerable to Americanization. It negates the advantages of efficiency and world view. We are not flexible in meeting the American thrust and we show it. As I have said, the Church rests on the peasant. No peasant, no Church. But also, no Americanization unless peasants are eliminated or transformed. Something has to be sacrificed here. I think it will be the Church, because the peasant is certainly not increasing or holding his own. He is changing and disappearing, and thus the Church is weakening and Americanization is strengthening at just the speed of his change and disappearance. He — the peasant — controls the time, which we first thought would be slow, but now we see it accelerating very rapidly.

The Church is a benefit insofar as it has a world view and teaches respect for organization. From the Church, we Italians learn that if people stick together they can conquer the world. But other peoples have learned that lesson from the Church, too. In fact, the only successful defiances of the Church have come from people who imitated the Church by setting up a counter-Vatican. The English did that in the sixteenth and seventeenth centuries, and you Americans did it in the eighteenth, and Russia did it in the twentieth. Once the people are being offered something they need and want, everyone on the controlling body works to that end, and anyone who fails in his part of the task is sacked. . . . Now the Church is obsolete, but we may be able to graft our group talent onto some new thing the people want throughout the world. You yourself concede that Rome has unified Europe on the two occasions that Europe has been unified, and perhaps it will be Italians rather than French, Germans or English who do it the third time — provided, of course, that Europe really wants to be unified now. Italy may become the European Massachusetts, with Roman Adamses pulling the wires behind German George Washingtons. Stranger things have happened, and we Italians stand ready to serve if called. (Almost indecently ready — too many faces are glistening in greedy anticipation!) . . .

Or we may be the group that brings it all down, if the Vatican goes furiously sour. It is difficult to say which will happen. It comes back to this terrible question of human nature, with which the Church, ironically enough, has always been so concerned. Once the Church had the proper response there: now it doesn't. It has lost its way, and the Americans know more about Europeans (and what they want) than Europeans know about themselves. That is true on the political level as well as the religious: but religion and politics are always the same. Losing the old power of divination is very embarassing to the Church and to the European ruling class in general: now both of them have to choose between going out slowly — being phased out — and telling themselves that they'll find another place to batten on if they remain quiet and watchful; or resisting actively. Personally, I think it will be with the whimper and not the bang, but what if they choose to make the bang? What if embarrassment grows into cold anger, and they decide to do anything to hit back at the Americanization of Europe? After all, that Americanization is not only not to the aristocratic taste esthetically: it also means, in the harshest way, the end of Europe and the end of them. In order to survive, the Church and what is left of the

[286]

aristocracy, shored up by various bourgeois malcontents and as much of the lower class as can be swayed, may decide to fight to keep Europe archaic. In that case, they will need an ally and will turn naturally to Russia, because a Russianized Europe would actually be more like the old Europe than like the Americanized Europe. Russia is still very European — very archaic — and does not actually take as much of the old away from people as the Americans do. You can see this in the occupied countries of east Europe — Hungary, Poland, even East Germany. They function much more as they did before the last war than west Europe does.

People *think* the Russians do away with aristocrats, and so they have in Russia and east Europe, but the arrangement I am talking about would have more control in it. There would never be a formal occupation, just the new balance. You can see how de Gaulle flirted with the idea. When the fact of total Americanization becomes obvious, and the Church and the aristocracy see that there is absolutely no future for their way of life, then they shall begin to think about another arrangement which would not be so absolute. The Russian arrangement, for example, which would be constricting but not absolute. It is the *way* of life I am talking about, remember, not surviving or making money. The Church and the aristocracy can be "worked into" Americanization, and they may both make a lot of money out of it: but the money is no good, because the old life is gone. What good is it to have a Ferrari if the roads are so crowded you can't drive? . . . The modern Russian rulers live closer to the old European aristocratic idea of aloof control than to the modern American intermingling. They are really more sympathetic for the European aristocracy, under all the slogans, because they have the same obsolete ideals of form and behavior.

You can see all this eating at de Gaulle, even at the professional socialists and Communists. I really think all of them are acting from spite and fear and will continue to do so. They see that there is no place for them in the Americanization process, and they go a little bit mad. Those who can, become Americans, as we both see

[287]

Agnelli do, and retain a calm of sorts, but the others are terrified and will do anything. As I said, I don't think they will be able to break out of their ennui, but there is always the possibility they might . . .

The racial differences are significant, even at the Vatican level. Barzini [the author of *The Italians*] has dwelt on our national Achilles heels in such detail that the whole world is familiar with them, but I should add that the cult of the "manly" seems stronger than ever, and that we are, if anything, ever more confused and embarrassed about the military record. The only German who was kind about us as soldiers was Rommel, who said the average Italian soldier wasn't so bad and blamed the officers for the disasters. Well, I was an officer and I was in North Africa, and I think the soldiers were as ludicrous as the officers. We were ludicrous together: it was extremely funny, but we Italians can never laugh at it. . . . When I am in Switzerland or Germany and see the Italian workers from the south and from Sicily, they look like animals to me, something they never do in Italy itself. It must be the northern light. Short to the point of dwarfishness, monkey faces, no more European than Negroes . . . and I can sympathize with the policy that kept us out of Europe for so long. We are capable of bringing a very bad influence to Europe, an African admixture that could prove fatal. When the sirocco blows from Africa, Rome smells like a zoo, and reminds us that we are very close to Africa. When north Europeans say that Europe stops at Milano, they are right. The southern Italians make all Italians seem backward. They are so crude that their Catholicism makes the Church itself seem crude. As an Italian, I myself feel that I must be crude to be connected to such a people and such a country, for I have, alas, inherited my ancestors' contempt for those who work the land — mine and everyone else's. . . . Then I feel that all we Italians are trained, the rich and the poor alike, as monkeys are trained. I am as preposterous as the poorest peasant in the *mezzogiorno* — how else can I explain racing the little cars and masturbating with the girls?

And then going on to do the same with the foreign girls. (We were avoiding maternity with the first group, but what was the excuse with the second? There was none — we had grown to like it!) And the Italian middle class, the huge new middle class, is so noisy, so assertive, so stupid, so like monkeys, again, in their acquisitiveness . . . worse than Jews. There are mornings when being an Italian is too much.

But will the Americans be any better? Or the Americanized Italians, I suppose I should say. Or both. Barzini's thesis, and I agree, is that the Italians are basically unhappy people, and that they are unhappy because of Italy's failures and inadequacies as a country. They compensate for this unhappiness and sense of failure by creating "the Italian way of life," a supposedly charming and delightful facade which is designed to fool all foreigners and most natives. (My primary reason for staying indoors.) Antitheses are not altogether reliable, but could it be that Americans are as secretly dominated by America's success as Italians are by Italy's failure? (And Europe by Europe's failure?) And just as we Italians and Europeans cover over our national failures, you cover over your collective success. It colors all your actions, underlies all your motives, even determines your styles, and it seems to have made you no less unhappy than failure has made us.

Not only do most of the world's non-Americans fail to recognize their leader; very few Americans admit they are the leaders. They pretend they have no real influence, that they are always ineffective bumblers in international affairs, duffers who are always outwitted by other, more "realistic" nationals. If you admitted what you have done, even to yourselves, you might lose your nerve: as it is, you try to retain the innocence of a child in the body of a giant, a special dishonesty that drives the European "realists" quite wild. . . .

Your most touching — and by all odds your most dishonest — national certitude is that you cannot be *defined.* You think Europeans can be placed in categories (for their own good, you are always having to do just that), and Asians and Africans. But not

Americans. Your distaste — almost your hatred — of psychological definition is fed by its implication of boundary, because boundaries mean that the American adventure and the American people do not enjoy infinite expansion. Good Americans deny their existence as social types because they have to believe that whatever type they happen to be at a given moment is only temporary. Despite these avoidances, however, America is a fixed place, and at any given moment Americans are fixed types, no matter what transformations may occur later. In the same way, the success of the country cannot be acknowledged, because that would define and fix it, which would be morally distasteful. Only flux is moral. Definition is immoral, and for a practical reason, like most moralities: if America were firmly placed in time and space, it might collapse. So it has to be deprecated if not denied, privately and publicly. Very clever, we have even achieved it ourselves from time to time, but only in isolated instances, alas, never as a single voice.

Your great source of strength is that you are all alike. Everyone thinks Americans are so diverse, including Americans, but you are peas in the pod. All alike, and the collective genus completely different from any other people. Because you are different from everyone else, other people often make the mistake of thinking you are individually different from each other. For education on the subject, discuss it with an Italian customs officer, who will confirm what I have said. All Americans are different from other nationals in the way they walk and move, and no different from each other. And notwithstanding American denial, the same rules apply for the interior as for the exterior.

Despite the constant American denial of self, the American is nothing but self, and the wants of that self. When I think of the pigginesses of the ones I've met here in Rome! Especially the American young, who think they're so much better than the rest of the world. They never are, but it is interesting that the rest of the world insists they are. (There! That's what Pirandello would have noticed.) . . . Contempt for Americans is difficult to exercise because the object doesn't get it, and wouldn't care if he did. (Remember the impervious beauty queen.) Americans do not believe they can be absurd, wrong, ridiculous or criticized — all the characteristics of the Victorian Englishmen, but devoid, alas, of the knack those gentlemen had for making a harmonious society at the top, no matter how horribly the wretches were squalling down below. The inability (or refusal) to believe in one's weaknesses is mandatory for the conqueror, but it often leads to a very great fall. However, how would the conquered recognize their masters (temporary or lengthy) except by that negation of introspection?

Americans would like to have people believe they just drifted in, but no one can believe that. They didn't drift in any more than the Church did. There is, and always has been, a conscious aim. . . .

Only the memories exist now, because the present is so utterly uninteresting. I mean, of course, the present of Americanization, which is not in the present (a Pirandello point again) but is the result of past happenings. Americanization has given us the present we have, but it itself is not the present at all, which is why it is the most curiously meaningless question ever to have circulation when it is phrased as a present question. It does have a past, though, and that is what we all live in terms of. And why only the memories exist now, and why it is only amusing to ask when Americanization happened and how.

For it did happen, as we are all aware, but in bits and pieces, here and there. And occasionally in formal symbolism, as with Brian Howard in the Excelsior Bar. I go very seldom now, but I remember an evening in 1952 when you and I saw poor Brian there, very dirty, with a hugely bandaged foot, the bandage unwinding. He was sitting with a young boy and complaining about the service — naturally, none of the waiters wanted to come near him. "This used to make servants jump," he said, waving the ends of his Eton tie. "Now it doesn't mean anything, so I won't wear it any more." And he took it off and threw it on the floor. Kirk Douglas was sitting just behind Brian, quite the opposite in every way

— bandbox neat and very undefined, his muzzle properly anticipa-
tory of the great expectations still before him. Brian, of course, had
seen and thought of everything. The tie, the symbol of the lost empire, lay on the floor between their tables, passing the power from
the old world to the new along its soiled length. . . .

And it happened in the comedy of Barry's project. He always had
a project, you must remember that. Always a project and always an
American project, and he always talked about the current project
with great enthusiasm. This time he was determined to get Rossellini to go to Detroit and make a movie. Rossellini is only a memory
now, but then — in 1949 — he was at the top of his fame. The
American public was incensed with their Bergman for having an
affair with him, and furious with him for taking her away, but
Barry claimed the hate would turn to love if he went to Detroit. "If
I can only sign him up," Barry said, "I can raise the money in a
morning. He's that hot now." Barry's interest was not disinterested, you see: he wanted to produce the film. But at the same time,
he was deeply moved by the esthetics of the project.

"My God," he said to me, "you can't imagine what Detroit's like.
You go into a bar and it's two hundred feet long and there's every
race and nationality since Adam drinking there. Poles, Croats,
Slavs, Negroes, Irish, even Jews and Chinese. When they can't
stand it, they have a race riot. When the Negroes take over a bourgeois neighborhood, ten families move into those big old houses
and there are twenty cars on the lawn. The mattresses hang out the
windows and everyone drinks gin all night and fights all day. It's
the most *visual* place in the world. All Rossellini has to do is go
there and he'll come out with a movie. He doesn't work with a script
and he won't need one there. He'll come out with the best movie he
ever made."

So when Rossellini returned from Stromboli, Barry arranged a
quiet dinner at Nino's to discuss the project. They were four:
Barry, Rossellini, Bergman and an interpreter. "Bergman was pregnant then," Barry said later, "but no one knew it. I didn't know it

myself, but I thought it was funny the way she was falling asleep at the table. Like a combination of Brunhilde and that mouse at the tea party. Bad omen for a business conference." *Stromboli* was finished, but Hughes had not yet sprung his surprise, so Rossellini didn't know what was in store for him and could still afford to be as ingenuously full of himself as he pleased.

"I had a hard time getting him to listen to what I had to say," Barry said, "but I plowed ahead. It was a waste of time, of course. He never did *see* the Detroit I was trying to tell him about. And, anyhow, he told me he had other plans — he was going to make a picture about St. Francis. It was his answer to the trouble he was in about Bergman. The Vatican would stick with him if he'd propagandize for them, and he needed help from some corner, or thought he did. What he didn't see, though, was that he could have gone modern with America and Detroit instead of old-fashioned with the Vatican and St. Francis. . . . I went up to Lake Bracciano to see him when he was shooting that St. Francis film a few months later, and there he was sitting talking to a couple of fat cardinals who'd driven up from Rome to give him the word. It was a scene from the fourteenth century, with the artist falling all over his ecclesiastical patrons. What made it really creepy was that the real monks they had for the crowd scenes were playing soccer in their monk outfits between takes, running after the ball in an awkward way, like women, and a lot of those people who hang around artists when they've gone bad were there and gushing over the beauty of everything, especially the awkward monks. I said hello to Roberto and shook hands with the cardinals, but I didn't stick around long. It was a funeral."

Barry was direct, and always in the vernacular, but Barry was right. Rossellini was finished as a director. *St. Francis* was a film so nondescript that very few people remember he ever made it. He did reach for the classic Italian relationship between Church and artist, but, as Barry said, it was too old-fashioned. The complementary strengths were gone. Then Hughes dropped his bombshell,

Bergman left him, and he eked out the rest of his career from the sidelines. He is *our* Malraux, perhaps, but really much more pathetic. It remains a provocative illustration of Americanization, though. Agnelli, who became an American, bet correctly, but he doesn't dramatize the issue as clearly as Rossellini, who remained a European and lost. He had struck at the outside world in the time-honored Italian fashion — the Italian man "ruining" the foreign woman is our oldest gambit, as I have pointed out in examples which include my own sins in the field — and then, in equally traditional Italian form, retreated behind the skirts of the Vatican and stuck out his tongue at those who didn't like what he had done. It would have worked in the old days. The rest of the world would have been so dazzled by Italian wickedness that it would have accepted him as a permanent artist and eaten up everything he had to offer. But the world had already seen through the Italian game by then and only laughed. The woman didn't even stay ruined but walked on into another life as though nothing had happened. It is really a beautiful illustration of *now*. It has everything, even the slow seethe of the Italian who hates the Americanization so much in his secret heart that he would almost rather see Russian grayness. . . .

I have my memories, which explain my present, but I cannot pretend that they permit me to see the future. As I have said, there is the choice between the bang and the whimper, and I think it will be the whimper, but no one can be sure. In any case, the way to stand is with one's behind squarely to the future and one's face pointed resolutely backwards, eyes straining through the fading light to the events which placed us where we are. Proust was right about the past being the only time we can understand, and this present is doubly irrelevant. First, in his sense, because we are living it and so disqualified from understanding it; and secondly, because there is nothing there to understand anyhow. Poor Rossellini trudges the streets with his Indian girl friends, an endless promenade under heavy skies, as dispossessed as any Jew; and his conquerors, the illiterate astronauts, whirl overhead in an equally barren quest. Both camps, winners and losers, are results rather than causes and do not reward the effort to understand them. Only the past is worth the effort, so I avoid looking at the contemporary Rossellini, and think instead of the dinner at Nino's where his younger self (and progenitor) stood at the crossroads . . . where Barry beckons to the future and has no idea *his* nephew will become an astronaut and avoid Detroit as completely through incomprehension as Rossellini ever did from fear, and where, finally, La Bergman's large, lush Scandinavian garden of a body blooms with the child on which the naughty Italian wagers his life. He is sure it will bring her down (and raise himself up accordingly), but he should take heed from the indifference with which she falls asleep in the midst of this laughable business conference. Barry sells, hard but hopelessly; the interpreter interprets; Roberto smiles, La Gioconda without a secret; and Ingrid sleeps, a coil of blonde hair loose in the soft light, secure in her woman's acceptance of the future for her children, unspeakable as it may be. Behind them the sinister Hughes shuffles through his many-mansioned mind, plotting enormous downfalls for pretentious wops everywhere. They are all gathered in the Americanization process, including Hughes, and this is what Americanization *is*. ("What it's all about," Barry would have said in 1969.) That's all there was, there was nothing more than that to it, the rest is detail . . . as, for example, La Bergman's continued affability. The ruined men — for time treated Barry not much better than his fallen prospect, and Hughes not much better than either one of them — may say that her affability is the result of ignorance, and they may be right, but that doesn't change what happened to them. . . .

On he grinds, rather longwinded, but circling his prey — the enigma of control — with intelligent persistence. There are no final answers, but much light is cast, at least for me. I am particularly interested in his analysis of a potential realization of the bond between European aristocracy and Russian bureaucracy, confirming my own feeling that any Europeans, no matter how superficially divergent, have more in common with each other than with any Americans. The Russians are not qualitatively different; their revolution did not produce a mutation. They share common approaches with all Europeans to "culture," formal handshakes, wine and the way the wineglass is held, the form of anecdotes, the places to smile and the places to be serious . . . they remain inside the European net, and all true Europeans are more comfortable with them than with Americans. It is a point of considerable importance.

———————

There is much American comment on Italy — indeed, no other European country seems to draw so much fire — but most of it is familiar. On careful sifting, I can only find two items that rise above the ordinary:

A stout American lady, to her friend as they take an early-morning *negroni* at Doney's:

"They're not supposed to call it spaghetti. They're supposed to call it *pasta,* because there are so many different kinds. Why, ten years ago the word spaghetti was unknown in Italy. Now you say pasta, and the waiter says, 'You mean spaghetti,' and off he goes to get it. But what we call spaghetti is only one kind of pasta. They're doing it all wrong now."

V.J.O., forty-six, ex-priest, now married to Italian girl who works as a secretary. He writes poetry by day and guides American tourists at night. They have a year-old baby, a boy. The topsy-turviness of his life has made him bitter:

"All Americans are crazy — I don't except myself. But that's not the point, either — the point is that the rest of the world puts up with our craziness, like with the Cuban missile crisis. Here in Italy it's the fantasia of the Italians taking us as real. Americans come here with hard eyes, determined to get theirs in Rome or know the reason why. I've been here since the war and I guess I've seen most of them. Dreadful, self-centered people. Remember Mike Stern? The perfect prototype. And the even less appetizing variety, the gangly, gee-whiz American illiterate (like Curtis Bill Pepper) who's determined to get abroad and eat good food and drink good wine. Where do they pick up such a lack of humility, such tremendous plans for themselves? They sit in some lost town on the prairies and dream these dreams. And then make them true, while . . . well, I don't want to sound like sour grapes, but there are some pretty strange things that happen. . . . I quit the Church because of it — because there's nothing the Church won't take from Americans. At first I laughed when Protestants said it was all based on money, but now I don't. I believe it. One of those Kennedys flies into Rome and the Holy Father falls all over himself to accommodate him. Don't think, either, that Jackie would have married Onassis if she hadn't known the Church's condemnations have no meaning any more. The very people the Church has been so anxious to please are, of course, the first to be contemptuous and do what they want. So I thought, if the Church isn't bigger than any of its children it's not big enough for me. You can say the same thing another way: if it's not good enough for Jackie it's not good enough for me. I'm writing a poem now about the whole experience, but I don't know if I'll be able to finish it. This job I have at night is getting me down. They call it a tour guide, but what it really involves is straight pimping. And during the day I have to take care of the baby because Maria is at work. So I just don't have much time to myself. I don't know, either, whether I'll ever be able to get such a poem published. It will be long, kind of like Melville's *Clarel* — the disenchanted pilgrim struggling against his loss of illusion. I don't know — it's a big job. And against odds that I think I can say are pretty tough, even if I'm the one who's saying it."

Pertinent reportage on Italy from various sources:

The dangers ahead for Italy are clearly put below in extracts from two newspaper articles. The first, from UPI, January 12, 1969, warns of possible dictatorship unless the outmoded governmental system is changed very soon. The second, from Robert C. Doty, *New York Times,* also in early 1969, gives details on how the "economic miracle" has not benefited the Italian workers as much as they think it should have, and how the relative prosperity has actually brought on social unrest:

"Premier Mariano Rumor warned politicians yesterday that a dictatorship could come to power unless Italy acts quickly to solve its problems and end the 'credibility gap' between citizen and state. The country faced a new wave of strikes and other agitation as Mr. Rumor's warning appeared in . . . La Stampa. The 53-year-old Christian Democrat, who came to office last month amid nationwide strikes and demonstrations, said Italy is governed by outmoded laws that hold his cabinet ministers 'prisoners,' unable to act efficiently on the problems of a changing society. He said the credibility gap between citizens and the state 'could have a totalitarian outcome' and he warned the present Italian system 'no longer supports the weight' of public demand. He was referring apparently to the possibility of public discontent propelling the powerful Communist party to power, or forcing the left wing into such extreme actions that a right-wing reaction would set in and open the way to a fascist-type dictatorship."

"The Italian economy has something of the air of Scrooge about it — a rich man salting away more and more gold in the safe but keeping his dependents on short rations. The dependents have not been happy about it, and showed it last year in an increasing wave of strikes for better wages and pensions. There is every prospect that this year Scrooge will have to shell out more liberally, both to keep social peace and to safeguard the basic balance of the economy. 'At the present time,' said one economic observer, 'Italy continues to give its resources to the rest of the world — in exchange for money, of course. But it has too many things that need doing at home to continue this policy and the task for this year is stimulation of domestic demand and consumption.' His point was that the nation's continuing phenomenal growth rate — 5.2 percent in 1968, down from 1967's 5.9 percent but still impressive — has been fueled almost exclusively by the striking success of the drive to export. . . .

"For the first nine months of 1968, while imports rose by a modest 4.5 percent over the comparable period of 1967, exports went up by 15.3 percent. In the same period, while gross national product, per capita income, industrial production and most other indicators rose by about 5 percent, private domestic consumption remained out of step, up only 4.4 percent. As a result, Italy's hoard of gold and foreign currency reserves reached a record $568 million, up 5.7 percent in one year. . . .

"It is hoped that [reflationary measures] will help to keep at home and in circulation some of the sums that have been transferred abroad — legally and illegally — in recent years. In the first three quarters of 1968, for example, the net movement of capital abroad was $913 million, a 31 percent increase over the preceding year. Legal transactions of this kind went into foreign stock purchases and other transactions through banks with government approval. Illegal transactions went over the borders in smuggled currency and into numbered Swiss bank investment accounts."

The extent of American influence in Italy:

Chalmers M. Roberts, *Washington Post*, January 4, 1968: "Mr. Reinhardt's [G. Frederick Reinhardt, then U.S. ambassador in Rome] problem arose because he was insistent that Mr. Johnson should not come to Rome to see the pope without a formal call on the top Italian officials. The advance White House party, which reached Rome two days before the President, was told at first not to talk to Mr. Reinhardt but only to the Vatican. Once the President did agree to meet the Italian President and Premier, Mr. Reinhardt was told to arrange the get-together outside of Rome, apparently to avoid Communist pickets. The Italians rejected the idea, saying they saw no reason for meeting Mr. Johnson at President Saragat's summer lodge in the middle of winter. Mr. Reinhardt, however, persuaded President Saragat to reverse his position, but only three hours before Mr. Johnson's plane landed in Rome."

The incident in its entirety is an illuminating revelation of American excitement and European response. President Johnson, it may be recalled, had gone to Vietnam just before Christmas, in 1967, to confer with his military leaders. A few short months later he was to announce that he would not run for a second term, which was to be considered tantamount to admitting that he had been wrong about a military solution in Vietnam. But now he was at the crucial frenzy of the old policy, and lashing out in all directions. The Pope had been critical of the U.S. bombing in Vietnam. Very well, he'd stop at the Vatican and take care of that. But would the Pope be available? More important, would the security measures be adequate in view of threatened demonstrations? A *New York Times* story by Max Frankel from Rome on December 24 details the manic solution: "They [the President's advisers] learned in Thailand only yesterday that they could reach Rome for both governmental and papal conferences, but then they had to await final agreement from those two institutions. . . . The day began for the President before dawn at the Korat, Thailand, air base from which U.S. F–105 Thunderchiefs operate against targets in North Vietnam. The President addressed American airmen on the landing strip there, then flew 700 miles around the fighting zone to Cam Ranh Bay, the huge American base on the easternmost tip of South Vietnam.

"It was shortly after 10 A.M. there (Saturday 0200 GMT) when the President had finished inspecting, saluting and decorating the soldiers. He now doubled back to the west again, his huge blue and white jet racing the sun across Southern Asia. It was 2 P.M. Saturday (0900 GMT) when the presidential plane stopped to refuel at

Karachi, Pakistan, and Mr. Johnson held a one-hour airport conference with President Mohammed Ayub Khan. They said in a joint statement that they had reviewed Pakistan's economic progress, its need for more wheat and vegetable oils and their joint interest in exploring 'every avenue' toward peace in Vietnam.

"At this point a complex tangle of logistics, communications, protocol and security problems that plagued the presidential party throughout the journey put the meeting with the Pope in doubt. Mr. Johnson left Pakistan without knowing where he would land next. The object of heading home westward, an addition of five hours to the flying time from Vietnam to Washington, was to call on the Pope, but as the President approached Europe he was flying on an alternative plan toward refueling in Madrid instead.

"Only as the presidential jet crossed from Iran into Turkey, three hours from Rome, did it finally receive word from Rome that the difficulties of scheduling and protocol could be met and that the President's helicopters, deemed essential for speed and security in the Italian capital, could arrive in time and be cleared for their operations in the area around St. Peter's Cathedral. . . .

"Mr. Johnson's plane landed at Ciampino Airport, a military airport near the Appian Way, and the President flew from there by helicopter to Castel Porziano, a 5,000-acre walled-off hunting preserve that serves as the summer residence for Italian President Guiseppe Saragat. These procedures isolated the President from the demonstrations against him and his policy in Vietnam that were reported to be taking place in various parts of Rome. Mr. Johnson conferred for about twenty minutes with Mr. Saragat, Premier Aldo Moro and Foreign Minister Amintore Fanfani. He then flew to Vatican City, landing in the Vatican area."

After an hour or so with the Pope, the helicopters took President Johnson back to his jet at Ciampino and he flew on to Washington, arriving there in time to spend Christmas Day with his family. Behind him he left a certain amount of colorful debris. There is no question but that the three top men in the Italian government would not have gone to President Saragat's summer lodge in the middle of winter to accommodate any other world figure, including the Pope. And for a twenty-minute conference, barely long enough to shake hands and mumble season's greetings through an interpreter. It was rumored at the time that Ambassador Reinhardt had had to put immense pressure on President Saragat to get him to agree to this ignominious treatment, and one would have thought the ambassador would have been rewarded for successful coercion in the most formidable tradition of Americanization. But not so, according to Chalmers Roberts in his story of January 4, 1968, quoted from above, in which he goes on to say that Ambassador Reinhardt was reportedly dressed down by President Johnson for having insisted on the meeting with Saragat in the first place. And also "over a ten-minute delay in his helicopter flight from the airport to meet the Italians and then the Pope. The delay, however, had been due to bad weather." That didn't help Ambassador Reinhardt, who was relieved of his post a week later, a month before the naming of his successor, Gardner Ackley, had been scheduled.

The scene must have been suitably dramatic. The huge jet on its special runway at Ciampino, seething with confusion and excitement, a Martian spectacle to the Italian children a mile away behind a chain fence. Inside, the telephones ringing, the teletype system clacking with news from everywhere, the communications experts tending their machines; the "man with the bag," the gear needed to set nuclear warfare in motion if needed, drooping from fatigue; the heat, the lights, the crowding, the cursing; the sound of the helicopters dancing overhead in the bad weather, elusively near; the uncomfortable ambassador listening to his President (after a day which had begun before dawn on the other side of the world) venting his displeasure in his quietest, deadliest hound-dog accent . . . Finally the helicopters are ready and the President leaves to see his waiting Italians. First, President Saragat, Premier Moro and Foreign Minister Fanfani, drawn up stiffly before a recently laid fire in the freezing summer lodge, servants scurrying aimlessly about, American security agents from the advance party crashing through the shrubbery and the chilly, deserted rooms. Then the Pope, quiet in the papal library in the Vatican, more dignified but no less obedient. The President of the United States was in town, and woe to the Italian who didn't respond to the outpouring of American adrenaline. This, too, was Americanization, but on the crudest level of intimidation, not a whit different from the technique used by Alexander, Caesar or any other conqueror of antiquity in dealing with subjugated but restless barbarians.

The UPI photograph of President Johnson and Pope Paul bidding each other good-bye is a very fine miniature of this rough but classic Americanization. The President presses the Pope's hands in his own and looks down on the Italian as though to say, "Don't worry, everything will be all right." The Pope seems a bit dazed by this reversal of roles, but responds to it all the same and smiles back up in uncertain gratitude. Jack Kennedy himself could not have been more superbly confident in his patronization, nor more successful in making others — especially the directly patronized — share that confidence.

Nearly a year later, on the eve of the 1968 Presidential election, an AP item shows that in the traditional pattern of conqueror and conquered, humiliation only increases curiosity about the ruler's habits and voodoos: "Italy's state-owned television will broadcast a special program from midnight to dawn to cover the last hours of voting in the American presidential election — the first time an Italian television station has gone on the air in the dead of night."

If the Italian program of no resistance seems futile, the rigid strictures of Spain, the other great Mediterranean-Latin country, are worse than useless. As, for example, in this item from Reuters, January 13, 1969: "Spain acted today to stem the flood of foreign pop music on radio and television, ordering that by March at least 50 percent of all music broadcast must be by Spanish or Latin composers. The measure will affect state radio and television and dozens of commercial stations that broadcast songs by . . . foreign singers. The Information Ministry added that by July 75 percent of all pop songs must be broadcast in Spanish, and 10 percent of broadcasting time must be devoted to classical music."

Such formalism is hopeless in the wake of the encouragement given to American business and American bases, and shows an utter lack of real resistance. Taking from the people what has been already sanctioned (and what they want) only builds to a whiplash reaction in which they will get it all back anyhow, with interest. A few days after this item appeared, Franco imposed martial law on Spain to control rebellious students, separatists and other trouble-makers. His repressive measures could only work if he had another ideology with which to counter produce-and-consume, but he does not, any more than any other world leaders do. On the contrary, he believes in the American way and has not only permitted but assisted it in Spain. His notion that a nation can be selective about the process betrays remarkable ignorance, deeper if anything than de Gaulle's. After his death, the most probable future for Spain is total, unquestioning Americanization. The Spanish-speaking peoples of Central and South America are fascinated with American gadgetry and will trade anything they have — including the so-called cultural background — for the modern-day equivalent of shiny beads, and there is no reason to believe the citizens of the mother country are any different. If Italy and the Vatican cannot stem the tide in the hearts of the Italians, Spain and the Spanish church are not likely to be more successful. Resentment of the American presence may develop, as it has developed in Spanish America, but not of the American technology.

At the other end of the Mediterranean, Greece, the last large country in southern Europe — if Yugoslavia is considered part of eastern rather than western Europe — slides an equally greased chute to Americanization. Juntas know no middle ground and the Greek colonels are resolutely anti-Russian. Increasing American ties — even Jackie's marriage helps — will soften up the present puritanism as it was softened up in Spain, and before too long Greece should be as ripe as any other quasi-banana republic, including Spain itself.

Returning to Italy, the formal business resistance should be noted in these two items:

First, the AP, October 7, 1968, from Rome: "Financial sources said today that two state-owned Italian enterprises have acquired control of Montecatini Edison SPA, the largest chemical company in Italy and the second largest in Europe. . . . The purchasers are Ente Nazionale Idrocarburi, the state oil agency, and Instituto Ricostruzione Industriale, a giant state-run holding concern that already owns or has interests in numerous banks, steel mills, metallurgical and mining companies, shipyards, hotels, supermarkets, shipping lines, the national airline (Alitalia), an auto manufacturer (Alfa Romeo) and many other industrial and financial concerns. . . . The merger created the second largest chemical company in Europe after Britain's Imperial Chemical Industries. . . . The transaction reflects a strong belief in Italy that only through mergers or amalgamations of this type can Italy and ultimately Europe meet the American challenge."

Reuters, January 16, 1969, New York: "Giovanni Agnelli, chairman of Italy's giant Fiat motor company, spoke in favor of a politically united Western Europe last night in a dinner address to the Economic Club of New York. A deep malaise has arisen in Europe, he said. 'The Europeans feel economically strong, but weak and frustrated on the political and military planes.' Mr. Agnelli said European nation-states were continuously tempted by unrealistic unilateral solutions to contemporary problems. Economically, European unity would reduce the scientific and technological gap between the United States and the rest of the world, he said. 'Experience shows that the gap diminishes or disappears in those technical

[305]

or scientific fields where European industry has been able to take global initiatives, and has shown a global mentality,' he explained.

"America's nuclear guarantee was a reality which existed beyond any written pact, he said. Yet, instead of accepting it, Europe suggested solutions such as French President de Gaulle's own nuclear strike force. Unification would strengthen Europe's political voice in relation to the two super powers, Russia and America, he said. But instead of speeding up the process of unification, Europeans complained about the Moscow-Washington dialogue, which they fear may be at their expense. Mr. Agnelli advocated 'a gigantic transfer of political power from the national to the European level.'"

All very tidy, but will it work? There are many forces undermining real unification and real resistance — they are summarized at the end of this book — but for the moment it can be left as an open question. It is incidentally interesting, in view of previous emphasis in this section on the Catholic Church as an Italian creation, that Mr. Agnelli stresses "global" initiative and the "global" mentality.

To summarize, the Italians have shown in their development and maintenance of the Church, Europe's first and greatest global organization (only the British Empire can compare and then solely in the past tense), that they do have a world view and can handle a world system. This inborn ability may mean they are the natural leaders in the unification of Europe. However, there is a problem because of the Church: they can't have two world systems at once. They may think now that they can, but time would force a choice between the two. The competitive power of the Vatican would be intolerable for Italians trying to lead Europe to technological, political and economic unity. It may even prove intolerable for Italian leaders who confine their efforts to sharing the leadership of European unity and carrying out a systematic Americanization of Italy.

For in the dark of its ancient soul, the Church is profoundly against a technological Europe, even though it does not always realize that consciously. And for the simplest and most human of reasons: it has nothing to offer such a Europe. So it is really involved in a life-and-death struggle. As the standard-bearer of the only true resistance, it slowly attracts all those Europeans who wish to avoid total Americanization, Protestants as well as (if not more so than) Catholics. A completely technologized Europe would not mean the Vatican razed to the ground or empty churches. The shell would still be there, but the inner, secret core would be cracked, the psychological power would be gone. The Church in Europe would then be very much like the Church in America. European Catholics would be Europeans first and Catholics second, as American Catholics are Americans first and Catholics second.

This would be a far more traumatic experience for *all* Europeans than most Americans and Europeans can imagine. Europe is grounded on the Church, and even the Protestants are only anti-Catholic. (In America, the Protestants transcended anti-Catholicism by finding a whole new religion in capitalism, one which had nothing to do with Catholicism or Protestantism.) To lose the Church is to lose the primary point of reference. The Americans did it and are confident anyone can, but they did it three thousand miles away, on a new continent, with a selective colonization.

But as traumatic as the experience promises to be, there seems to be no way of avoiding it. The pull of Americanization — whether administered by Americans or Europeans — is stronger now than the pull of the Church, and not likely to weaken. Time is against the Church now, a point well made by Larry, the perceptive Prince Moradonia, at the close of the tape he sent me:

"Everything is time, and that is why time is the most interesting of all subjects. The Vatican has been so successful with time for so long, and has grown so cunning in its use through the practice of so many battles, that it really can't imagine ever losing a contest in which time is the weapon. Whoever has the most time will always

win, and the Church always has the most time. (How *little* time
Communism had, by the way!) It has used time, which no one can
even see, to break the backs of the strongest men and nations and
ideas. It is not arrogant in its assumption of having more time and
thus more strength, because it sees its greater fund of time as a fact
of nature, like the sunrise. 'The Church has always had time on its
side,' it says. 'Thus it is and thus it has always been.' So when it
meets its master, the American social scheme, it can't be blamed for
not knowing it. How could people who look and act as the Americans do have more time than the Church?

"But the Americans do have more time, and they have had right
from the beginning, when they outwaited the British in their revolution. The Church is obvious in its use of time, but the Americans
are not, so they have another advantage there. Also, people think
the Americans are always in a hurry, but it is only a nice trick because they are never in a hurry, really. When they get involved in
the orient, the Asians naturally think they can outwait such clumsy,
hasty people. They believe their own propaganda, which tells them
that orientals are patient and westerners are not. But they are mistaken. And we Europeans have been even more mistaken. Especially the leaders of the Church.

"The Church has always been able to outwait, and this is what it
tried with the Americanization. But the Americanization doesn't go
away and it can't be assimilated. Now it even sucks in those Italians
who used to fight it. The end is very near, but the Church doesn't
know that. She sits like one of those pathetic women in a play by
Tennessee Williams, waiting for the doorbell to ring, for something
to happen to save her, as it always has. But this time it isn't going to
happen that way, and so the Church will go like any other old
woman whose time has run out. Not even a whimper, just those
poor old eyes staring at the door and the tendoned hands twitching
and the rouged cheeks standing out against the terrible pallor. Her
end will be the end of Europe, because they are the same thing, the
same person — an old woman dying in a shabby room with quiver-

ing lips, her soul skewered on time like a butterfly on a pin. From then, you shall be able to see her under glass, because she is an important specimen, but no one will ever know again what it was like in her room when she was alive. . . ."

4

THE GERMAN-SPEAKING WORLD

THE Germans are supposed to be the most Americanized people in Europe: on the surface, they certainly seem to be. Right down to subtle details. The non-German European family on vacation, for example, is American in that the father drives and the wife sits next to him and the children are in the rear seat and the roof rack is loaded. There are still differences, though. The parents are neater than Americans; there is less junk floating about the car; and the children are upright and surprisingly well behaved. But the German family can achieve authentic American disorder. When they pull into Garmisch after a hard day on the autobahns, the parents are shattered, the car is a mess, and the children are in corkscrew positions in the rear, which they have turned into a garbage pit.

As the American divorcée quoted in the section on France said, the French bourgeoisie models itself on the jet set, and the German middle class has used the world of the *Ladies' Home Journal* and *Better Homes and Gardens.* Germany is flooded with magazines built on those formats, and German wives (and husbands) learn from them how to build the ideal American home and community. An American woman long resident in Germany has told me that these magazines are the strongest single agent of Americanization in Germany, more potent than the presence of the Army, the movies, or the music.

(It can be pointed out that it doesn't really take. There is the outward American form, but never the American grace. No one wears old clothes on Saturday morning, no one puts his feet up, no one is ever entirely at ease. The German home, with its tensions just below the surface, is a caricature of its model. As Bill Coleman, the American trumpeter who has lived in Europe for twenty years, says: "I'll tell you, though, I do miss certain things here, the feeling musicians have when they work together. You get it so much more over there than you do here. Here they can only play two ways — slow or fast. It's that in-between feeling I miss, that something that American musicians have." Only slow or fast, without the in-between feeling — the distinction goes beyond jazz and can serve, in poetic extension, as a definitive comment on all differences between Europeans and Americans; especially between Germans and Americans, where the similarities are more pronounced. But if the essential message doesn't get through, the form does, and Germany remains the most ardent American disciple on the Continent and the yardstick against which the others are measured.)

Although the Germans are more Americanized than, for example, the French or the Italians or the Danes, one is less conscious of the process having exposed weaknesses and destroyed self-respect. Americanization seems to crush and depress the rest of Europe in varying degree; the Germans have taken to it quite naturally. Losing the war prepared them for retribution, of course, and facing the fact that the rest of the world didn't want to do things their way prepared them to do things someone else's way. Americanization has come to other European countries in a rather underhanded fashion, working through unacknowledged weaknesses. But in Germany the arrangement has been comparatively aboveboard. After losing two wars and being branded as outlaws, the Germans had to stand naked at the bar, admit their way didn't work and accept suggestions. They had to try another way, and what other way was there except that of the prime conqueror, the one country that could have beaten them singlehanded? Having been politically and

militarily wrong was the German humiliation, not being Americanized afterwards. This differs sharply from the experience of the rest
of Europe, where the Americanization is the humiliation. What the
Germans had — what they were and what they believed in — was
wiped out in 1918 and 1945. They tried to impose German control
on the world and failed, which meant they had to accept the victor's terms — a very different position from the rest of Europe,
which didn't try anything and was eaten anyhow. The Americans
didn't really take anything from the Germans, because the Germans had already lost everything on their own.

The distinction is apparent on the individual level. The usual
European businessman is uncertain with Americans, not knowing
whether to fawn or attempt patronization. Because his position is
undefined — in the process of becoming — he doesn't know who he
is or how to behave. The German, on the other hand, can look the
American in the eye because he knows where he is relative to the
official conqueror. There are also psychological distinctions. Social
or business intercourse with Germans is not at all as it is with Englishmen or Frenchmen, because the Germans are not children.
(They may be capable of monstrous actions, but their wickedness
is mature, not petty.) They are social and business equals, and
commercial arrangements with them do not follow the English pattern, for example, where an American has to be left in charge like a
wet nurse.

In the teeth of the deserved German reputation for efficiency,
hard work and business acumen, it is odd to find that it is in Germany (and in Switzerland) that the essential frivolity of Europe
makes its strongest impression. This is frivolity in a rather technical
sense — the inversion of the American calendar according to which
the year is composed of days on which one works, less holidays.
With the five-day week, plus holidays and vacations, Americans
work somewhat less than two-thirds of the year; and when the
promised four- and three-day work weeks arrive, this will drop to
half and perhaps only a third of the year. But the psychological

view will remain the same. The year will still be work less leisure, as it is now, which accounts for the inbred awkwardness of the American when he is not working, no matter how much free time he has. The European, on the other hand, thinks of the year as leisure less work, even when he works a six-day week (as he still does in many cases). He is most natural on holiday: it is when he is most himself.

That this is as true — or truer — of the Germans as of any other Europeans would seem to contradict the German reputation. But the Germans are most efficient, most hard-working, and have the most business acumen when they work in the holiday spirit, when they bring to their labors a sense of fun and the day's work is done as pleasure, with the pleasure carried over from the most recent holiday. Ideally, work is no more than an extension of the holiday, not the other way round. Even war, in the classic German view, was fun first and work afterwards.

The German word for holiday is *Ferien,* and the number per year is extraordinary. Sunday, of course, and Saturday except for a few shops and stores. A dozen or more days off for religious reasons, which does not include special or regional religious celebrations and commemorations. Then national holidays, a two- to three-week vacation in summer and a "skiing week" with the entire family sometime in the winter. Shops are closed one afternoon a week in many Swiss and German towns, and no one is around the office much from December 21 until the second week in January, after the feast day of Drei Koenige. From then until Lent, there is Fasching, six solid weeks of merrymaking. Easter signals the imminence of summer, which is unalloyed *Ferien,* and after summer there is fall, rather slow but a good time to prepare for winter sports and activities. After all, a few weeks have to be set aside for rest!

Conversation with a proper American is grounded on his work and his prospects; a proper European discusses the holiday he has just been on and the one he is planning. Leisure is a distraction for the American; work is an interruption for the European, no matter how conscientious he is about it. A Swiss banker whom I know quite well has never talked to me of business with the profound interest he brings to vacations in Morocco, weekends at Klosters, the road conditions in Italy last year, and so on. His sense of time is forever relative to *Ferien*, not to the bank. This is not to imply that he shirks his work. On the contrary, like all Swiss bankers he is industrious, efficient, dependable and knowledgeable. But if he had to choose between giving up a weekend at Klosters and working through Saturday and Sunday in some emergency which might be to his advantage later, in terms of money or career or both, he would choose Klosters without hesitation. It is basically a religious matter. As noted earlier, Europe did not substitute the abstract attractions of capitalism for deceased Christianity, as America did, but chose to worship materialism in the raw, stripped of moral imperatives and self-imposed duties. All holidays were once dedicated to God. The Americans substituted work (the holiday as rest for more labor), and the Europeans a good time for its own sake.

Whether the European position is better depends on the point of view. That an increasing number of Americans find it healthier is not so pertinent to a consideration of Americanization as the fact that Europe would not be full of Americans had not their immediate forebears held the other view. Even today, the American indifference to leisure commitments, the readiness to break all engagements and work straight through a weekend, gives the American businessman obvious advantages. Hour for hour and day for day, the Swiss and the German are his equals if not his superiors, but his total availability opens a small but significant lead.

It is known that the English are tremendous loafers, along with the French, the Italians and the rest of southern Europe. It comes as a surprise that the Swiss and the Germans are equally committed to the worship of *Ferien*. Not loafers, perhaps, but certainly devotees in their off-hours; and their participation changes one's conception of all Europe. It is not only the known seekers after pleasure who are bent on enjoying themselves — from Narvik to

Palermo and from Vigo to the Urals it is one great yearning for fun! That middle and central Europe are dour, and much of eastern Europe dismal, does not change the picture in the heart. Over 400 million people see life as pleasure (whether individually realized or not) interrupted by work. Even the poorest European lives for his moment in the café, his seat in the park, his trip to the museum — *not* for the satisfaction of the job well done. Up a level, it is the Sunday stroll with his wife, the sports with his friends, and the formal holiday. From there, the spiral climbs to the combination of full dedication and ample money: expensive restaurants; attendance at plays, operas and other musical events; boats; ski-ing; summer and winter vacations in the ever-changing centers of fashion . . . but never for the satisfaction of the job well done.

The American who is long resident in Europe finally develops an empathy with what is going on, whether he wishes to or not, and becomes quite conscious of the passion of the collective heartbeat. He doesn't need to actually see the great mass movements from place to place, the five million pairs of skis lashed atop the frantic cars, the detailed planning over maps and schedules — he knows it is happening because it is in the air. And even the most insensitive American realizes that although much the same thing happens in his own country every day, it is different because the emphasis is different. He knows further, especially if he is in business, that the difference in emphasis gives him much of his leverage, and America much of its basis for colonization. His Swiss and German colleagues can and do take care of their own affairs, but that does not invalidate the overriding importance of the *Ferien* psychology, nor the advantage it gives him.

(Consideration of western Russia as a European country is beyond the scope of this book, but even there the *Ferien* instinct, long dormant, is showing signs of life. Western Russians are more European than anything else — presuming that Americans are qualitatively different — and in time may come to the same scale of values as the rest of Europe. If so, 587-plus million neo-hedonists will be on the loose in greater Europe. Without Russia, the number is 429-plus million, and even without eastern Europe it is 312-plus million, still an impressive figure.)

Germany also makes one conscious of Europe's dreaminess. Not only in matters of the soul, but in the practical business of life. American well-being starts with a large, rich, nearly self-sufficient continent, easily able to feed itself and supply basic material wants. (America now goes abroad for certain items — oil, iron ore, special metals, and so on — but even if these were cut off the country could survive.) But Europe cannot begin to feed itself or supply its own basic material needs. Its whole economy is based on turning imported raw materials into finished goods to be sold abroad to pay for the importation of food and other necessities. It is a dangerous position in American eyes, because if the world market for finished European goods should enter a decline — either because the presently backward countries start their own manufacturing or through unbeatable competition from non-European countries like Japan — the whole European economy might well collapse. Somewhere between 300 and 430 million people (Russia, with its huge land mass, is safe from such a fate) could find themselves reduced to a standard of living not much better than that of contemporary India. Indeed, if only arable land and natural resources are considered, Africa and Asia and South America are in a stronger longterm position than Europe. If those continents ever do start making their own finished goods, Europe will collapse, and many economists see the independence of the undeveloped regions as inevitable. This would mean that Europe's prosperity is merely temporary, and has been since the seventeenth century, when the exportation of finished goods began.

No American could live securely in such temporariness; he would have to "do" something about it. The Europeans, however, not only live in it, but find it perfectly natural. To do so, though, requires that they be able to avoid thinking about certain realities. The avoidance leads on to the dreaminess, the quality one sees in the faces of English girls, Latin laborers, and, surprisingly enough, German businessmen. Americans, more puritan and more observant, do not dream as much and so present the bills rather than receive them. To put it coarsely, they win.

If one is surprised to find the Germans economically dreamy under their surface hardness and realism (one almost expects a certain dreaminess from other Europeans), one is equally amazed to find them softly, disconcertingly confused about all speculative matters. A Swiss friend, a textile manufacturer, gives a personal explanation: "The Germans are really in a straitjacket. They are so convinced they have a guilt for the war that they are paralyzed. Outsiders notice they won't talk about the war or concede guilt, and so they think the Germans don't care. But they do care, and the not talking about it only means they take it much more seriously than if they did talk about it. They are literally paralyzed with guilt, especially about the Jews. They have the economic miracle, but they are political dwarfs, as they say themselves, because they are afraid to take a step. Psychologically, they allow themselves to be pushed around. I give you an example: Sammy Davis, Jr. He is supposed to be a very popular entertainer in West Germany — but why, because he is not what you call the German's ordinary cup of tea, is he? I tell you. The crazy combination he is — Negro and Jew and American — is all three in one what the Germans think they were wrong about, and so in their clumsy way they welcome him and make a fuss over him (you see photographs of him in the newspapers with the mayor of Berlin — believe it?) because it is symbolic to them of now doing right what they did wrong, of what Hitler was against. It it so extreme in Germany that many very bad Jews have gone back there to run businesses that are on the edge of illegal if not outright illegal because they know the Germans are afraid to prosecute them and be called anti-Semitic. Jews like that Jack Ruby was in America, men who run sex nightclubs all over Germany, perfectly safe because the Germans are so paralyzed. The richest man in Frankfurt is a Jew who runs the prostitutes there. Cornfeld [the head of Investors Overseas Services] could never have gotten away with the methods he used to sell mutual funds if he hadn't been a Jew. . . . No, the Germans have bent over so far backwards that they can't tell up from down any more."

In January and February, 1969, I spend some weeks in Munich, working with an American businessman who is putting together a heavy machinery merger with a German concern and needs outside participation. We reach a certain point and can go no farther without an unofficial insight into the feelings of the government. We need to talk to a man who is that well connected in Germany, preferably a non-German, and inquiries lead me to George Hitchcock (not his real name, of course), who lives in Salzburg, an hour from Munich on the autobahn. Mr. Hitchcock is seventy-one, very elegant, and has a lovely house overlooking the Salzach. "I like to be close to Germany, but not too close," he says. "Austria is silly, but very predictable and it suits my purposes." Mr. Hitchcock is a rather mysterious figure — former lawyer, former OSS stalwart, former husband of two women with fortunes. But above all a former American diplomat whose German connections are excellent.

He receives me graciously (we have had an exchange of letters to arrange an appointment), and we discuss his influence in German government circles. "There's no need for me to be shy about it," he says. "The people who referred you are people I trust, so let's be frank. My fee is high, but I can deliver." He has Averell Harriman's ever-youthful urbanity, but with strong undertones of piracy. "I was not born a rich man," he says. "Very social, but no money. I have had to work for everything, and I still can't bring myself to do anything without charging for it."

We talk about the business in hand, and he says he needs time to think about it. "Not more than a few hours — I'll have to make a call or two." I am staying at the Goldener Hirsch and go back there for a nap. It is Saturday afternoon and the old part of the city is very quiet. Everything is closed — shops, stores, everything except restaurants and cafés. I return to his house at four and we start again. At six he suggests a bottle of champagne ("So much better than cocktails!") and the butler brings in a lovely old silver double cooler with the necks of two bottles sticking out at opposite ends.

"What do you think of the Germans?" Mr. Hitchcock asks me abruptly as we enjoy the first glass.

"I don't know them that well," I answer quite truthfully. "I have a few ideas, but I'd like to know more."

"Funny people," he says, "very confusing. Think of this . . . leave the morality aside and consider the practical aspects of being German — how you, as a German, handle the carryover from the war. What I mean is: think of yourself — or any American — as a German, and try to figure out how you'd handle the problems they meet today. They're intelligent people, but the first thing you find out is that they don't know what they're up against. They have no idea, for example, that the English-American-French world has been running the Germans down since . . . well, since the year one, I suppose, but most emphatically since 1871. That was when the Germans beat up the French and made it plain they were going to have their share of world markets or else. Such a lack of feeling for the status quo naturally provoked a reaction, but the Germans have never understood how profound the reaction was.

"I lived abroad before Hitler came to power, and there was just as much anti-German talk in Boston and London and Paris in 1927 as there was after this last war and the atrocities came out. It's all based on the proposition, carefully cultivated by the French, English and American upper classes, that the Germans are barbarians. I know what I'm talking about because as a member of the American upper class, I have been privy to what has been said. (My American pedigree goes back to the 1600s on both sides, and I might add that it has no Germans in it — I'm unusually clean!) When I was a boy in New York and my father — who was in banking — would have German business friends to dinner, there was always a submerged derision in the air. The German was a Hun and who could tell what he might do? Eat with his feet? No one would have been surprised. That none of those Germans — all rigidly trained in the social customs of the day — did anything awful made no difference. The propaganda, which was openly based by then on English and French fears of German competition, was insistent and everyone believed it against the evidence of their eyes. The Germans could be rather stiff and boring, of course, but so could most of the native products. The slightest German stiffness, though, was pointed out as evidence of the correctness of the entire indictment. What struck me most — and this was before World War I, remember — was that the Germans never knew they were being laughed at and despised. It was extraordinary how obtuse they were. As a people, their lives depended on what other people thought of them — it was an indication of how far they'd go against them — but they never seemed to understand how important it was to find out . . . so inefficient of them, despite all their talk of efficiency.

"Then came World War I and they were the official villains, and the propaganda began to have some basis in fact. I say *some* — there wasn't all that much to choose between them and the Allies. But even after that war they still didn't understand that they were disliked socially. They just don't comprehend the snicker at the boy in the wrong trousers, the laugh behind the hand that English and American boys of good family have always been taught in boarding schools, and which becomes their social manner with the Germans when they grow up. Jews have always known what went on behind their backs, and the Negroes are famous for their intuitive sensitivity. But the Germans never seem to twig. It's not a barbarian insensitivity, either, but a sort of innocent inability to understand dismissal on such frivolous grounds. They can't comprehend the casual, hidden evil of Anglo-American life (German sins are always serious and obvious), which is really much more barbaric than German life — who but barbarians could be so easily propagandized?

"So, because they don't understand what they're up against, they've never been able to fight back effectively. Even in two wars they weren't fighting their real enemy — the ancient propaganda that had the entire populations of three powerful countries against them — but an abstraction. . . . I was in Bonn last November when the Germans were host to the financial meeting called to do something about the franc. The rudeness of the British and American delegations to the Germans was simply extraordinary — money troubles always bring out reality, even faster than war or sex. Roy Jenkins, the Chancellor of the Exchequer in England, and Henry Fowler, our own Treasury Secretary, went completely wild. Jenkins screamed at the German Finance Minister like a fishwife — the Germans say he was drunk. Wilson is supposed to have sent Chancellor Kiesinger a message saying the British would pull out their Army of the Rhine and such protection as they give West Berlin unless the Germans revalued the mark. That was what all the trouble was about. The British and the Americans and the French wanted the Germans to revalue the mark upwards rather than have the French put the franc down.

"Wilson even got the West German ambassador in London out of bed and over to Downing Street where he and Jenkins and Michael Stewart, the Foreign Secretary, tried to bully the German into doing what they wanted. They did everything they could, but the Germans refused to cooperate, so the French had to agree to devalue. Then, after the meeting, the French reneged on their promise. And Johnson cabled his congratulations to de Gaulle!

"It was all very ordinary at bottom, of course. America and Britain and France couldn't stand the idea of Germany becoming so strong again, and that is not an unreasonable fear. Even their rudeness was comprehensible if they were sincerely frightened of Germany after two horrible wars. But what amazes me is that no German with whom I discussed the scenes understood that they were all grounded on an acquired anti-German prejudice, as deep and rank as any other in the world. If the Germans think about it at all, they think such a prejudice stems from the Kaiser and Hitler and the concentration camps. They don't understand that it predates all those disasters and would be just as strong if they had never occurred. The overt anti-Germanism would be less, but the unspoken prejudice would be the same. When Americans and English screech at Germans, they are not thinking of Hitler and Dachau at that moment — they are acting off the nursery training that taught them Germans are comic . . . to be yelled at with no more compunction than sheep or donkeys. The 'serious' condemnation of Germans is reserved for quieter reflection . . . stress brings back the lessons of childhood."

(A young American Jew, a very talented musician who has spent much time in Germany in the past ten years, makes somewhat the same point in another way in a later conversation: "As a Jew, when I first came here to Germany I didn't think much about them except in terms of what they had done to us Jews. And to their other victims, of course. But you can't think about that forever, and so I began to see them in the present. I can never forget what they did in the past, but I can see the present, too. And do you know that what gets me is — and don't let me shock you — how it never occurs to them that they might have been right. There's a lack of logic there, and they're supposed to be such logical people. But if you are logical, you have to consider all possibilities, and you'd think that a people who had committed so many murders over such a length of time would wonder whether it hadn't been justified. Or at least some of them. I mean, in America we exterminated the Indians and everyone knows it was wrong, but at least we admit we did it, and defend it by saying we had to have the land.

"But the Germans can't face anything. If they were right about Hitler, then they ought to hold up their heads and say so. If they were wrong, they ought to admit it. But they don't do either one. They stay in some sort of middle ground. I don't mean they don't take certain *actions*. They pay Israel reparations and a lot of young Germans go there to work. But you feel it doesn't really come from inside them at all. Where the thing is, they're turned off. I tell you, if a German said to me: 'So what! We killed six million Jews and I'd do it again because I'm an anti-Semite and I believe in Hitler's final solution,' I'd despise him for holding such an opinion, but I'd see him as an entity, as part of a dialogue, no matter how degrading. Or if a German said: 'Yes, we did terrible things and I personally have a deep and horrible sense of shame about it,' and he really meant it, then I'd see him as part of a dialogue, too. But they won't do either one. They all say: 'I don't know anything about it.' It's not logical, it's not intelligent, it's not anything you can do anything with. They can't do anything with it themselves.

"If they were one way or the other, they'd have a position from which to evaluate everything else. But they keep their heads in the sand and they're nowhere. If they really, honestly saw their own guilt, for example, they'd be able to draw the line at the way other people exploit that guilt. Like when Bill Manchester does a book on the Krupps. Well, everyone except a German knows that Manchester isn't after the Krupps, he's after the Germans. He didn't do a book on the French Krupps or the English Krupps or the American Krupps. And no one else will either, because when you say Krupp you've got every Jew and every liberal in the United States standing there with his ten dollars, ready and waiting to read what they know they're going to get — a book about how awful the Germans are. I think a lot of unscrupulous Jews have exploited the Germans in the same way, but at least they have an excuse. Manchester is pure exploitation, but no German is in a position to say so and make it stick because no German has the thing straight in his own mind. And as long as they keep acting like ostriches, they're going to go on being exploited. . . . You see the Fasching parades in Frankfurt and all the kids — and plenty of the adults — are dressed in cowboy-and-Indian outfits. Colorful old German traditions! But it's no more than they deserve.")

"You can't get anyone to admit that there is and always has been an anti-German prejudice that has nothing to do with German militarism and atrocities," Mr. Hitchcock adds. "But it's there and it's always being fed. When I was a little boy, I went with my parents to Europe in 1910, and I can still remember how my mother told me France was so lovely, and so it was. And when our train crossed the German border at Aachen — we were on our way to the Rhine — she wrinkled up her nose and said now we'd have to put up with those fatnecked Germans. Well, we saw some fatnecked Germans, but as a people I didn't think they were any more fatnecked or unattractive, in any class, than the French or the Italians. They seemed *better* than the English, and the idea of the English complaining about German manners has always seemed hilarious to me, anyhow. Now, since the wars, the Germans can be legally painted in movies and books as unrelievedly gross, and so we have raised a whole new generation more violently prejudiced than the last. Well, I suppose the Germans had that coming. But they didn't have the original prejudice coming, and it's unfortunate that people can't distinguish between the two — the real objections and the unfair prejudice."

The champagne is finished and I ask Mr. Hitchcock if he will have dinner with me. "I'd love to," he says, "if I may bring my brother." I have no objections and ask where we should dine. "Your hotel," he says promptly, "the Goldener Hirsch — there's really nothing better in Salzburg. This isn't Paris, you know."

He and his brother meet me there at eight-thirty. The brother, Jerome Hitchcock, is fifteen years younger than George Hitchcock — in his mid-fifties — but not nearly so fit. He seems an invalid, in fact, and his long, gray-white, rather dirty hair flaps dismally around his emaciated face. His eyes burn disquietingly; he recalls John Carradine as a religious fanatic.

"George tells me you were talking about Germans," he says to me with sly pugnacity.

"*I* was talking about Germans," Mr. Hitchcock says firmly, helping himself to the *Getrüffelte Gansleberpastete "Lacroix."* "He was listening."

"I could tell you a lot about Germans," the younger brother says. "I was in Germany all during the war. Interned, but with a lot of rope. Do you know Berchtesgaden?" he finishes off disconcertingly.

"No."

"If I were a guidebook, I'd say, *Berchtesgaden is a small thumb of Germany projecting into Austria, a hilly bowl surrounded by mountains.* And I'd be telling the truth. It's important that you have it straight, because you have to see it if you're going to understand about Germany."

"You don't have to explain it," Mr. Hitchcock says. "We can drive over there tomorrow. It's only fifteen miles from here," he says to me in explanation.

"No!" says Jerome Hitchcock. "I can explain it better than anyone can see it. I was there so long. It's the old Berchtesgaden I want to explain, anyhow, not the new one. The new one is all sports facilities and new vacation chalets for Germans from Munich and Dusseldorf and Hanover. That has all happened since the end of the war. Before that it was *very* quiet, except for Hitler's compound at Obersalzberg, which is a little hamlet five hundred meters above the town of Berchtesgaden. Hitler had his own chalet there, the Berghof, and there were other houses for other top Nazis — nice fellows like Bormann and Goering. And later there was an elaborate system of barracks and underground tunnels for the SS troops who guarded them. In the late 1930s, Bormann (who was secretary of the Party) had the Eagle's Nest — the teahouse on the Kehlstein — built as a birthday present for Hitler. That was on top of a mountain about eight hundred meters above Obersalzberg itself, and you could only get up there by elevator. It cost about ten million, which was a lot of money in 1938, and even more expensive when you realize that Hitler only went up there two or three times. People think he was up there all the time, staring out over the Alps with his patented madman look and thinking up new devilments, but he really spent ninety-nine per cent of his Berchtesgaden time in the chalet in the compound, much more earthbound. . . .

"Hitler had always loved Berchtesgaden — he started coming there just after the First War, when he was just an unknown little agitator. There was only small *Pension* in Obersalzberg then, and he stayed in a tiny stone hut near it and walked out every morning and thumped that little chest of his and then disappeared back inside to plot more trouble. He was planning the Munich *Putsch* then, and after that failed he was jailed and started to write *Mein Kampf*. When he was let out in 1923, he hotfooted it right back to the little stone hut in the mountains and finished up his book. It's some picture, isn't it — the little corporal with the crazy moustache writing away in the little stone hut in the mountains just like any other penniless author working on the book that he hopes will make him famous? Very much the same, except that it was going to be so different.

"From then until he got in, in 1933, Obersalzberg was his home, insofar as he had one. His half-sister, Angela Raubal, and her two daughters were with him there. He was so jealous of one of them, Geli, that she killed herself. Later Eva Braun came down from Munich. After he became chancellor, Obersalzberg was his vacation place, and the compound was built. It was fantastic, you know — all the furniture in all the houses was middle-class German Alpine, and there's nothing more overpoweringly cute than German Alpine. But there they were — Bormann, Goering, Hitler himself — plotting to take over the world in German Alpine. Hitler's first house was the Wachenfeld; the Berghof, with the famous picture window (he had one of the first picture windows) facing the Untersberg, dated from 1939. It . . ."

"Jerry," Mr. Hitchcock says, "we know all that."

"I didn't," I say. "I think it's very interesting."

"I have to explain it this way," Jerome Hitchcock says to his brother. "The background has to be there for what I'm going to say about the Germans."

"Very well," Mr. Hitchcock says. We are now on the *Kalbsmédaillons Orloff* and the *Rehfilets Chasseur*, washing it down with local Austrian wine, young and rather fiery.

"You've got to see it in your mind's eye," Jerome Hitchcock says, fixing me with his own unsettling eyes, his bony hands clutching the tableware tightly, "the way I saw it from the side of the road in 1938. I was on a walking tour and in Berchtesgaden when the great man arrived for a weekend. The people lining the roads, the flowers, the *love* for him — it was amazing. And then the motorcycle riders, covered with dust, and the enormous Mercedeses grinding along those narrow roads, and finally one of them with the peculiar god in the rear. He flapped his arm and accepted flowers from a little girl. It was history. You knew that immediately, if you didn't know anything else.

"When the war came, the Germans turned the hotel they had built at Obersalzberg — the Platterhof, on the site of the old *Pension,* and right in the middle of the compound — into an army hospital. The place was only bombed once and nothing much was damaged. The liberation honors fell to the Americans. Over the next few years everything at Obersalzberg was dynamited out of existence — no shrines, according to official policy — except the hotel and the teahouse on the Kehlstein. They were spared, to become the nucleus of a rest center for American troops on duty in Germany. The teahouse, which the Americans called the Eagle's Nest, was turned into a tourist attraction; and the hotel was renovated, enlarged and christened the General Walker, after the officer who led the airborne troops into Berchtesgaden and was later killed in Korea. It has three hundred rooms, a motion picture theater, a bowling alley and a nightclub called the Skyline Room, built in 1955. Nearby are a golf course and ski runs.

"At first it seems that they can have their cake and eat it," Jerome goes on, becoming more intense. "Hitler's traces wiped out and all that beautiful snow. But it's harder than that to get rid of the old lunatic. He keeps coming back. It's almost as though there's a curse on the place. It's something you can almost feel . . . no, you *can* feel it. It's . . ."

"Now, Jerry," Mr. Hitchcock says, admonishing his brother cheerfully but firmly.

"I'm not exaggerating," Jerome Hitchcock says, his eyes widening and the long hair more agitated. I am to learn later that he is considered very odd by his immediate relatives, although completely harmless. He was interned in Germany for four years under mysterious circumstances — now in a camp, now on a farm, now interpretating and translating, now back to the camp. "After the war, after he was found by our troops near Regensburg," Mr. Hitchcock tells me later, "I wondered if he hadn't been a collaborator. But not a scrap of evidence to show that has ever turned up. His story is vague and contradictory, but we presume now that he never did anything questionable. We have tried to get him to return to America, but he won't go. He has a little income, and he just wanders around Germany like a lost dog. Whatever it is that he's misplaced, it's in Germany, you see . . . Germany, always Germany. He won't leave Germany, that's what it amounts to. He comes to see me two or three times a year, and stays a few days and then I don't see him or hear from him for months. Always polite, though, and never stays too long. I love to spring him on people." Not knowing all this at the time, though, I had no idea what the Hitchcock brothers were up to, and could only wait for enlightenment.

"I'm not exaggerating," Jerome Hitchcock was saying, then, with his eyes widening and his hair more agitated and one understood he was approaching the point of his discourse. "The power of the dead is very strange. I know, because I spend a lot of time around there. I go to the Skyline Room at night and sit there and have a drink and it's very strange what is in the air. It's a huge place, with ghastly gray-mauve walls and an enormous high ceiling. It's a nightclub, but a peculiar one because the soldiers don't have to wear coats and ties. They're all in civilian clothes anyhow, of course, but they can wear what they please, so the result is a hodgepodge. Sport shirts hanging out, sleeves rolled up, sweaters — and all mixed up with the serious couples who *have* dressed for the occasion. But so many of those couples have brought their children that they only add to the confusion. When the place is full, with about four or five hundred people in it, it looks like nothing you've ever imagined. That special American mess, as though the people aren't part of anything — not a country, not an idea, nothing. The mouths all slack, the bodies so unwieldy, the utter meaninglessness of the faces . . .

"And I sit there and I remember that Hitler said the Third Reich would last a thousand years and that the Germans would be the world's master race, and it lasted twelve years and the Germans are nowhere. So he seems to have been quite wrong, but then it seems he was only wrong about who was who. It's America that looks like lasting forever, and the Americans are the master race. I look around me and they're the most forlorn bunch of mongrels you've ever seen and they're the master race.

"Then the entertainment starts — a Bavarian folk show, with the dancers in costume. The men in *Lederhosen* and the women in *Trachten*, with their hair in high, tight coils on their heads. And the men have those fine legs that the alpine Bavarians always seem to have, still brown from summer even in January, and the women are pretty, and all of them full of vitality. Especially when you look from them to the audience, the shattered dumplings watching them. The Germans are the conquered and these doughfaced American zombies are the conquerors. What does it mean? It's supposed to mean Hitler was wrong, but does it? A hundred yards from where I'm sitting is where he wrote *Mein Kampf*, and then he lost the war so it's supposed to be all wrong. What doesn't work must be wrong, that's the American test. Hitler said master race and the Germans lost, so no master race. No such thing as a master race. But in practical fact, there is a master race — us. We Americans. It wasn't the Germans, it was us. How's that for a surprise? We look as though we can't put one foot in front of another, but we're the master race. Hitler said it would be the strong, but it turned out to be the weak, just as Christ predicted. There they sit on Hitler's grave to prove it. They and their unbelievable children have taken the world.

"And the Germans, who sincerely believe now that the whole idea of master race was immoral as well as unworkable, don't understand that there is a master race after all, only it's the weak instead of the strong. Hitler said conquer or be conquered, and we said that was wrong and we made everyone believe it was wrong, and then we proved it was right when we conquered him and the Germans and finally the rest of the world. Just as we are now being conquered by the weakest among ourselves. It's all very scientific, exactly as the crazy dictator said it was. He had it backwards, but quite right, and because he was right, his spirit still has power, still hangs in the air, still dominates the atmosphere up there at Obersalzberg.

"I saw a terrible American child out in the snow there one day, yelling and screaming in that way they have, not playing but fighting against play, against nature, against the serenity of the landscape, its awful face distorted into pure hate against the beauty of the fields and the mountains behind, and just as it opened its mouth for another scream and moved its arms back for another swipe at the snow, it stopped. It stopped and looked up and over at where the Berghof had been, although it couldn't have known the significance of one place in that landscape from another, and the face was screwed up as though it saw something, as though it heard a voice telling it something . . ."

Jerome Hitchcock is a rather provocative, if peculiar, dinner companion — certainly an unusual one. His brother is effortlessly bland with him, and, because we are both rather tired, it seems a relief when Jerome finally winds down. The next day Mr. Hitchcock and I finish our business, and the eccentric Jerome is nowhere to be seen. Mr. Hitchcock tells me he has gone to Berchtesgaden, "to moon around and glare at the American children. What must they think when they see that wild face grimacing at them! No wonder they shut up and gaze into the middle distance. I would myself — wouldn't you?" I decide to drive back to Munich in the late afternoon, and it is just after I clear the border checkpoint at Walserberg, a few miles outside Salzburg, that I start to think, quite accidentally, of what Jerome Hitchcock was saying. Not the disconnected complaints, but the sum effect, particularly the esthetic results of Americanism.

In most of Europe, the fact of Americanization provides a tidy boundary to speculation: in Germany, for some reason — probably because the Americanization is so advanced — one must go further and wonder what Americanization actually means. Popular fancy sees it as the adoption of certain mechanical appliances and methods, but that is far too superficial. Americanization, one discovers in Germany, means much more than that. It means the remaking of people in the American image. In America itself it is often difficult to understand that this has happened, that it was a necessity, but in Europe — especially in Germany — the mechanics and demands of the process become painfully apparent.

In the course of several weeks in Munich, I discovered that one can always tell American servicemen and their wives by their clothes, which are invariably cheaper and shabbier than what the Germans wear. They are paid far more than German white-collar workers, though, and one would presume they could easily build up a civilian wardrobe adequate enough for an occasional holiday. But they appear in threadbare blue jeans, battered windbreakers, frayed trench coats . . . The children are particularly shabby, and large families utterly woebegone. In view of the announced benefits of the produce-and-consume society, it seems impossible that they should look like beggars on European streets, but they do. We know that produce-and-consume ruins natural resources, the air, the environment and general health, but we have paid the price in the certainty that it brought material affluence. Is there, in final, sardonic joke, a last assessment? The affluence itself?

An even more sinister question is whether such shabbiness lies

ahead for Europeans. On paper, Americans have money and resources. In actuality, the produce-and-consume society breaks
down the individual spirit until an inner despair botches and bun-
gles the individual and, finally, the way he looks and what he
wears. The men aren't comfortable in their jackets, the women
can't get their lipstick on straight, the little girls are unable to put a
hair bow where it should go. One must concede to Jerome Hitchcock the disorder of the American appearance, especially the appearance of American children.

It can be claimed that lower-class and lower-middle-class American children are not typical of all American children. That is partially true; the American lower-class child, for example, looks worse
compared with the European lower-class child than the American
upper-class child looks next to the European upper-class child. But
in degree, *all* American children are ill-mannered and badly turned
out compared with European children, and compared with those
from any period in the American past. The lower class used to imitate the upper in America; now the upper imitates the lower, and
the upper-class child, along with the upper-class adult, is already
defiantly tawdry and will become increasingly so.

In any appraisal of Americanization, there is no dodging the fact
that we Americans have suffered a severe loss of individual pride
and spirit as the price of produce-and-consume. We have been reduced to the position of market geese, feet nailed down and force-
fed as the price of keeping the machine going. When all the apolo-
gies in all their provincial sophistry have been made, there is no
more to it than that. That is what has happened, that is all that has
happened, that is what Americanization means, and the Americanization of Europe means no more than that Europeans will soon look
as pathetic and drained as we do. Behind all the shrilly cocky Herman Kahn-Hudson Institute talk of "post-industrial societies . . .
computer information centers . . . exciting new communications
. . ." looms the dismal harbinger of what is really coming: the
pale, unhealthy, bewildered, profoundly uneducable face of the

American child, as dreary a portent as can be imagined. It is for this future, for this nothingness, that Europeans are abandoning their ancient vitalities and marching into their gilded tomorrows with such pathetic docility.

Once understood, the degrees of difference in Americanization come down to microscopic shadings of very little importance — how Americans look and act in one country as compared with another, minute variations in native reactions and times of ultimate surrender, and so on. It is quite final, and quite sad.

The finality and sadness come home with special emphasis in Germany, I think, because one wonders if even the Germans — the only people unanimously condemned in our time by the rest of the world — deserve such a fate. If they don't, how much less does the rest of Europe?

But the sympathetic mood passes quickly. If disaster to the human spirit were of any significance any more, there would be cause for concern, but the definition of catastrophe has changed; and no one — least of all an American! — is in a position to enjoy the luxury of sympathizing with what doesn't exist. What was, not so long ago, a prime human motor (and trigger of innumerable revolutions) has disappeared and will not be coming back.

The Germans themselves seem blissfully unaware of what lies ahead for them. "They have fantastic nerves," a Swiss tells me. "They are caught between the Russians and the Americans in such a way that there is no real security possible, but they act as though everything is all right. The uncertainties would drive any other people crazy, but not the Germans. They must know that in the end they can't win — not even in terms of the economic strength they have earned — because the Russians won't let them keep anything. They can only lose, but they play anyhow. Their very existence keeps showing Russia up as a barbaric society that can't build or maintain anything, and that brings the Russians down on their head, but they can't help it. They have to keep going."

He is right. Germany is not a country, nothing is settled, and the

Germans have had to learn to live without security as astronauts have to learn to do without gravity. But they keep going. One must also agree that of all Europeans, only the Germans could have accepted such conditions and built on sand with such fervor. To paraphrase Mr. Hitchcock, they either know something no one else does, or they are as stupid as their detractors have always claimed.

Switzerland is the only country in Europe that arouses a genuine interest in the average American because it is the only country he has to acknowledge as equal or superior to his own United States. Not primarily because of the organization and efficiency — as superior as Switzerland is in those fields, Germany and several of the North Sea countries are as much or more so — but because of the inborn pride of the Swiss themselves. They have weighed the Americans and find themselves just as good: no other people in Europe can say the same. Those who think themselves equal (or better), like the Austrians, have not thought the matter through; those who have thought it through, like the English, think themselves inferior. Or, like the Germans, not possessed of the talisman.

There is no superstition in the Swiss attitude. They look through the American as well as at him, and their "Let's get down to business" punctures the cloud of voodoo in which American businessmen are accustomed to envelop themselves as quickly as those same businessmen usually puncture other national clouds with the same remark. The Swiss beat them to it.

There are exceptions to all generalities, but as a rule the Swiss are not rude, flappable or off-balance, business advantages which the Americans like to think of as their own strongest points. It comes as a surprise to them to find the Swiss more so. It is only after these psychological nuances have sunk in that Americans discover, and don't forget, that the Swiss telephone system is superior to their own.

The Swiss see Americans and Americanization as a people and a way of life to be used and controlled, as they have used and controlled everything else that has come to Switzerland in the past seven hundred years. More, perhaps, than any other people, the Swiss understand that everything has its price, and they are always willing to pay for what they want, which must make them the most honest people in the world. If they adopt certain features of Americanization, they expect to pay for them. First in the weakening of Swiss life, and then in a tithe of some sort to the Americans themselves, ranging from the right to throw gum wrappers on the quay at Lucerne up and through the more exotic licenses.

Foreigners think of the Swiss as being unable to raise their eyes from their bankbooks, but in my personal experience they are more attuned to the sensitive, the unspoken, the unseen but potent side of all human relationships than any other nationals I have known. (I refer to German-speaking Switzerland, Catholic and Protestant, by far the largest segment in terms of land and population. Only twenty per cent of the Swiss are French-speaking, a fact which comes as a surprise to most visitors who know Geneva and its lake better than the rest of the country. Everything we find original in the Swiss character — the passion for freedom, the unparalleled physical and moral courage, the ability to think and the familiarity with paradox — comes from German-speaking Switzerland. Geneva was an exception to this, but that was years ago: its day is long since gone and it is now only a pleasure-dome such as can be found anywhere. Ethnologists hesitate to call the German-speaking Swiss Germans, despite the related dialect, because of the uncertainty of migration patterns, and the Swiss themselves are fervently anti-German.) They see the world as a dangerous and fickle place, and try to anticipate the dangers and save themselves and their overwhelmingly lovely country. Rather than mean and grasping, such dedication seems gallant and highhearted, and the Swiss the most interestingly positive of people.

They can deny and discipline themselves to the degree that they love life, and in their case that is a good distance. The Swiss state, to which everything is subordinated that touches on survival, depends on the willingness of the individual subordination. A proper Swiss is thus a Swiss first and a person second. The arrangement may be restrictive for the individual, but it is marvelous for the state-as-a-work-of-art, for what makes Switzerland all of a piece, dependable and harmonious. The Swiss are the first to admit that their system puts restrictions on the individual, but they insist that man is better off with a few restrictions.

They know, too, that no city or state in history has achieved harmony or beauty without restrictions. To them, unchecked permissiveness is synonymous with disorder and ugliness, and they are aware that modern America is their strongest argument.

But the key to the Swiss state is that it was not imposed by a man or an oligarchy, but was deliberately chosen by free men who could have repudiated it at any time in the past seven hundred years. It is voluntary, and the Swiss will not permit it to be manipulated into an instrument for imposing controls for which there are no practical or esthetic reasons. (The esthetic and the practical are actually one in the Swiss mind. One meets hardheaded businessmen in Zurich whose manner suggests they would be as casually indifferent to conservation, for example, as their American counterparts. But they are not. And why? Because they consider the weekend walk in the hills as a vital part of their lives. They keep Switzerland as it is for their own purposes, and so their children can grow up, not to "enjoy" the beauties of the country in the sentimental American sense, but to go to them on Saturday and Sunday for the revitalization needed to put the whole man back in shape for the Monday-morning struggle at the office.) No Hitler or de Gaulle could ever impose on the Swiss — they are not fools and have no unsatisfied longings on which a clever "leader" can play. The antipathy to humbug is so complete that there are no political personalities in Switzerland in the fashion of the rest of the world.

The Swiss edifice is firm but not rigid. It is very supple when it chooses to be, and well aware that the rest of the world is not up to its standard. It refuses to be blackmailed — Hitler wasn't allowed in, and Cornfeld, the head of Investors Overseas Services, was put out when he refused to observe government restrictions on the importation of foreign personnel — but it is careful to compromise whenever possible, because it doesn't want to go past the point of no return. Unlike most peoples, the Swiss draw the line at living under certain conditions, and although they don't relish the idea of national suicide they are capable of it. Being so capable, they have to watch themselves as closely as they watch others.

All in all, an informed, intelligent, even thrilling effort to deal with life, and yet . . . I don't think it will work. Against it is the terrible weight of the modern world, especially the thrust of Americanization. Against the Swiss tranquility and cohesion of family and state are pitted the American nervousness and insistence on fragmentation. Americans discovered they could not have cohesion of family and state *and* produce-and-consume, so they gave up family and state. Nor could they have tranquility, so they gave that up, too. They don't see how any other people or country can become Americanized without having to give up what they have had to give up, and they are probably right. The Swiss are aware of the dangers, but they think they can effect one of their compromises.

But can they in this case? If the Swiss have a weakness, it is their certainty that their willingness to pay is synonymous with the ability to pay. As shrewd as they are about the cost of Americanization, they don't go so far as to admit that the bill may be beyond their resources. And this bill — or compromise — may be just that.

I was brought to this conclusion by a number of factors, among them the opportunity of witnessing an experiment in Americanization under nearly perfect laboratory conditions. The small Swiss village overlooking Lake Lucerne in which I had a chalet in 1967–1968 had never known resident Americans. I was the first, but I was not the test because I was not an active missionary. That distinction fell to an American boy of fourteen who arrived in June, 1968, to stay with his grandparents for three months. His mother, born in the village, had left after the war to become a translator in Geneva, where she met and married an American restaurant owner and moved to New Jersey. Chuck, as I shall call the boy, was her son and this was his first visit to Switzerland. His grandfather was the village carpenter, and a man whom I occasionally employed. "Chuck will be here next week," he said to me in early June. "We shall go to Zurich to meet the plane."

I was away for a time and had forgotten about Chuck's arrival when I returned. But it came back as soon as I saw the strange boy in the village — pale, hunched, awkward, slightly effeminate, such a contrast to the strong young Swiss. He spoke to me immediately with the American lack of preamble. "Say, I'm an American, too — how do you stand it here? My grandparents talk to me and I can hardly understand them even when they talk American. My own grandparents! . . . There's nothing to do at night. And I'm supposed to be here until September. I think I'll go crazy or have a nervous breakdown or something." His face was framed against the brilliant green of a Swiss mountainside in summer, a far-off glacier perched above his lifeless hair. The background gave special emphasis to the sallow meaninglessness of his skin and the raw lack of intelligence in his eyes. In America, this supermarket face was only one of millions and only background itself — here he seemed so wrenched from context that one could almost sympathize with his personal awareness of dangerous dislocation. He could only be comfortable (normal, in a sense) in an irreversibly neurotic atmosphere: here he was not only uncomfortable but obviously abnormal.

A visitor unfamiliar with the hierarchic structure of the western world, watching him flapping and careening about, would have dismissed him as the village idiot. And without the consciousness that he was backed and supported by the most powerful nation on earth, Chuck would have slid into that role on his own. But because he was an American, he had to put his position to work. It seemed to me that his only chance was to make the Swiss feel that he was normal and they abnormal, and that was precisely the course he took. What made it so very interesting was that he had had no advice or warning before coming, and received none during his stay in Switzerland. Yet he instinctively adopted the traditional American stance on his own, which would seem to show that the appetite and ability to Americanize is inherited and not acquired.

He had to make the Swiss boys his own age shift from belief in their own way of life, which involved belief in themselves, their families and Switzerland, to belief in him and in the American way, which meant giving up everything they held dear. It seemed impossible, but he did it.

He started with simple destructiveness. Before he came, there was no idle throwing of apples, rocks and other objects. In a week, following his example, it was epidemic. He began with stones, picking them up from along the sides of the village streets and heaving them at fence posts. It was a very artistic performance, because when the other boys stopped to stare, he didn't acknowledge their presence, but kept on throwing. After a few days, a couple of the watching boys joined him. At the end of a week, they were all throwing. The initiation accomplished, he led them on to more exciting targets: cows, the sides of houses, car tires . . . Bruises and breakage accumulated and parents began to chastise their sons, which drove them back to Chuck with redoubled avidity.

He was not a genuine rowdy, which would not have seemed so sinister, but diffident, almost girlish. He did not throw rocks decisively, but lobbed them indifferently. He was not a tough off New York's East Side, but a listless blob. Yet he was more effective than a truly nasty boy would have been: and more representative, because the truly nasty boy has almost disappeared. (He was a loner: today's nasty American boys run in packs.) The village boys were already in blue jeans, of course, and already softened up through the mass media. They were ready to give homage to their first American for what they had received to date. Getting Chuck was the luck of the draw, but it wouldn't have been qualitatively different in any case, for he was *not* atypical.

Chuck was more like a clever girl than a mean boy, and in this lay much of his irresistibility. He started his working morning on a bench in the little village square, sitting listlessly in the bracing morning air and eating a peanut butter sandwich. (Warned that peanut butter was difficult to get in Switzerland, he had brought a dozen jars with him and seemed to live off it. "I can't stand this Swiss food," he said to me. "And the bread! It's so hard I feel like my teeth are falling out.") The sandwiches finished, he would start bending or twisting something with the nervous hands that were never still. Soon the village boys who didn't have to go to the fields would drift along to him and the progress of the day would start. First, a litany of complaints in his whining, adenoidal American (the boys all understood a little English, from school, and Chuck, of course, never learned a word of *Schwyzerdütsch*), to which they listened very solemnly, looking for all the world like a group of men with a single, shrewish wife; and then the movement to the day's first troublemaking.

(Along with the hints of polyandry, there was the strong flavor of the old frontier gone sour. Everything Huck Finn feared in Tom Sawyer — and Tom was dangerously clever with other boys — has come true. All American boys are Tom Sawyers now — the handful of Hucks didn't survive World War II.)

Under his guidance, they chased animals, overturned haycocks, let the air out of tires, misplaced equipment, wrote on walls, broke glass, insulted girls, stayed out at night and got tipsy, became insolent to their elders . . . and all in a bored, quite indifferent way. By the end of July, the village was a different place and the parents had had enough. A delegation came to see me, headed by the carpenter grandfather.

"We have put up with Chuck because we did not wish to be impolite," he said. "But he has too much influence here now and we can't permit him to go on. We wish you to understand that, and to know that we realize he is not a typical American boy."

It would have been too cruel to disillusion them, and I could only nod and ask what they proposed to do.

"Keep him indoors," the old carpenter said grimly. "He can't go back to America for another month, so he will stay indoors at our house until then."

And he did, more docilely than I would have thought possible. As I passed one day a week later, he stuck his sickly face out an upstairs window and hailed me wanly.

"I didn't know you were allowed to call to passers-by," I said.

"Huh?" he replied. "Oh, you mean people walking by. No, I'm not, but you're an American, too, so it's different. They think it's such a big deal, keeping me inside, but I don't care. Inside, outside, it's all the same here — lousy — so I don't care where I am. Only three more weeks and then I'll be back in Trenton, and I'll never have to come back here again."

"Do let me know if there's anything I can do," I said.

"I wish I had some food I could eat," he said. "That's all."

"It won't be long," I said.

"I don't see how you stand it," he said. "Why do you stay here?"

"I have to," I said. "For business reasons."

"Can't you get transferred?"

"I'm working on it, but it takes time."

He looked at me with faded, unsympathetic eyes. "I hope you make it."

"I hope so, too," I said. "And the best of luck to you."

"Thanks," he said. "But a lot of other people need it worse than I do."

On the surface, Chuck had become himself. Even if as village troublemaker rather than village idiot (although the two were not unrelated), he seemed more in character in watchful familial custody than running loose. That evening, thumbing through *Life* and *Time*, looking at the advertisements in the *New Yorker*, I couldn't help wondering how a photograph of Chuck behind bars, locked up as a menace to ordinary living, would strike one were it suddenly to appear between the automobiles and the whiskies. For Chuck was nothing if not the end result of the total effort, and a jailed Chuck undermined the whole semiconductor-transistor-printed-circuit dream. If the heir to the future was so comically taken out of circulation, the future was equally comical, not at all what the computers and the private institutes predicted.

Even to his former comrades, incarceration seemed Chuck's natural state, and they quite forgot him and the orgy they had enjoyed under his tutelage. They returned to their normal pursuits and the village resumed its quiet ways. The prisoner in the carpenter's house was only remembered by the older citizens, who seemed not at all surprised that it had become necessary to lock up an American teenager. But very little does surprise a Swiss.

It would have been reassuring to believe that the controlled Chuck was symbolic of a possible control over all Americans and Americanization itself, but I could not believe that. The comedy of Chuck in custody was real, and his relation to the future comedy of the American dream was real, but he had no meaning for the intermediate steps. The day had been saved by the old folks; the young had shown little or no resistance. In a few years, the old would be gone and these same young would be in charge. Well-Americanized themselves by that time, they would not move against the final touches on their own children when the future Chuck(s) arrived. I could only see the incident in that context as an indication of Chuck's power, not of Swiss character. The first was on the rise, the second declining. As splendid and sympathetic as the Swiss were, it was extremely doubtful they could hold out against the neurasthenic aspects of Americanism. It was only a matter of time.

(Of parenthetical interest, in addition to the light cast on the American and Swiss futures, comic and grim by turns, Chuck's activities were informative on the very nature of Americanization. In the cliché, it is the abstract introduction to various goods and services, but the more definite underlying reason is a form of behaviorist seduction, an inducement to take up the anti-esthetic, the atonal, the destructive, etc. American businessmen, athletes, housewives, tourists, artists, students, movie stars . . . they all have some Chuck in them, and they all take something out of foreign atmospheres and peoples as they imprint themselves and their national customs. There are really no exceptions.)

In Zurich business circles, I found more criticism of the ruthlessness of American business than elsewhere in Europe, but very little objective analysis of Americans themselves. The tacit assumption that business methods exist in a vacuum, that they are not an extension of personality, seemed naïve and vulnerable to me, yet another clue to eventual Swiss surrender.

For example, the head of a large Swiss transport company had no qualms about telling me "what bastards you Americans are in business. Take 3–M, Minnesota Mining and Manufacturing. They set up a Swiss company here in Zurich to sell their products under license, and when the company did well they refused to renew the contract and came in and opened their own subsidiary under their own name. The first arrangement was only a pilot company, but the Swiss who built it up weren't told that was a possibility when they started. They were given the impression that it was theirs for as long as they wanted it. Big American companies do that all the time. Everything is a pilot company to them, even when they pretend it isn't. The minute they find out you're making money they take it away from you. And if something they control doesn't make money, they close it down like that — bang! — with no mercy for the staff or the workers. Bastards, that's what you are, worse than Jews, worse than Germans, worse than anyone!"

"We can't help it," I say. "It's the way we're brought up."

He can't accept that. "You're no different from us," he says, suddenly solemn. "It's just that the pressure is so intense in American life that you've all forgotten your ethics."

"You think we'd get them back if the pressure dropped?"

"Of course you would."

"You don't think the point of no return has been passed? That we're qualitatively different?"

"I don't believe in those racial theories. Here in Europe, we don't believe in people being different any more. The Germans gave us a lesson in that."

Despite reservations concerning Swiss answers to the larger generalities, no one can fault them on specifics. Ask the average European a question about why something is handled the way it is, and one receives, ninety-nine times out of a hundred, either an evasion or erroneous information. (European ignorance of local and national mechanics, how things work in their own communities and countries, is a very grave weakness vis-à-vis Americanization.) Ask a Swiss and one receives a plausible answer or an admission that he doesn't know.

For example, I was curious as to why the Swiss, with their highly developed pharmaceutical industry, couldn't have the lion's share of their own toothpaste market. Swiss-made toothpaste is available in Switzerland, and is cheaper than the American brands produced under license, but it is heavily outsold by the latter. I put the question to H. G. A. Meili, general manager of the American Chamber of Commerce in Switzerland, a Swiss who has spent much time in the United States.

"Snobbism," he replied without hesitation. "The Swiss believe that certain American articles are the best in the world — cigarettes, hair cream, toothpaste, and many others — and that if you can't afford to have those things your friends will think it is because you are not very well off. Why do the Swiss believe American products are the best? Well, the cigarettes are a matter of personal experiment — the rest have been sold to them as part of the image. Through brand-name advertising, yes, but not altogether. It is almost more because they are part of the American image as a whole. The fact that they are more expensive is part of that image, too."

"Is that as true for the rest of Europe as it is for Switzerland?"

"I think so. It is all snobbism. I don't think the Americans planned it that way: it just happened. But once the market was apparent, of course, American companies moved very fast to capitalize on it."

"In a supermarket in a very small Swiss town on Lake Lucerne, I find frozen chickens from Georgia for sale, and they are cheaper than the frozen European chickens. With shipping costs and duty, how is that possible?"

"I don't know," Mr. Meili said. "But in that instance, I think it is the price and not the snobbism that leads people to buy."

———

Austria is the least Americanized country of the German-speaking trio, and quite possibly the least Americanized country in Europe. This is not due to character, but is the result of a formidably protective innocence. The Austrians are united in a dream, the aftermath of the Empire, in which everyone still has his place. It starts at the top, with the extraordinarily numerous aristocracy, unique in modern Europe for still having the power to awe and control the middle class and the peasantry. The middle class is not very extensive, either, so the important relationship is the one between the aristocracy and the peasantry, and that remains surprisingly close to what it was before World War I. The aristocratic principle can only function if the peasantry believes its rulers to be qualitatively different, if it is sure, in the vulgar but vivid phrase of an American diplomat in Vienna, "that their shit smells sweeter." If this belief is in force, as it is in Austria, the rest of the program flows smoothly from the first premise, and the entire country remains gathered up in an endless minuet.

Of course, in the not too distant future Austria will suddenly wake from the dance and break the dream and become like everywhere else. But as of now, the dream is still strong enough to prevent true awareness of the rest of the world. Uncharitable persons find the Austrians smug, and it is a fact that they are remarkably full of themselves, but in such a vague, unaggressive way that the grossness of the official Teutonic self-satisfaction is lacking.

The Austrians live in public, like the Latins but unlike the Germans and Swiss. The latter prefer to have their own ways and their own comforts in relative privacy; the Austrians are concerned about the figure they cut in the parade. It is difficult to determine how the fine feathers are paid for. Austria is supposed to be a cheap country, but with the exception of rent it is no less expensive than Germany or Switzerland; and all imported items are actually more expensive, because Austria is not in the Common Market.

If prices are not less, wages most emphatically are: an Austrian secretary makes about one hundred dollars a month, compared to two hundred and fifty in Switzerland and Germany. This must mean that Austria is a very poor country, so at first one is baffled by the apparent affluence. Austrians are always well dressed and seem to have plenty of money for vacations, restaurants and pastry shops. They are also the most handsome people in Europe, and the sum effect is of easy prosperity. But how do they do it on salaries below those of field hands in the American South, in a country where nothing costs less than it does in the United States and most things cost more?

The answer seems to be selective buying. An Austrian girl may have only three outfits, but she takes remarkable care of them and they always look new. She lives at home until she marries and then she and her husband take a tiny apartment and eat potatoes all month so they can buy him a leather coat so he can look like a count when they take their Sunday *Spaziergang*. They simply don't have the mass of goods that other nationals do. Living is stripped to the bone, as it must be when their combined salaries are two hundred and fifty dollars a month, and the emphasis is all on the *bella figura*. (The Germans claim the Austrians are more Italian than

[346]

Teutonic in all habits and characteristics, "sneaky and untrustworthy, always dressing up like peacocks." But the Germans love to visit Austria, as they do Italy, and seem to enjoy the slight inferiority complex which they find in themselves in those countries.)

Although Austria is a Catholic country, families are carefully planned — in one village near Salzburg, nearly forty per cent of the primary school enrollment consists of only children. Everything is planned, cut, scrimped and saved for.

Initiation into the dream starts for Austrian children when they are very young. They are taught that the Austrian Empire was the highest achievement of man on earth to date, and that it is the duty of all Austrians to keep the traditions alive. Culture is heavily plugged, and the Americanization of other countries is cited as a warning of how swiftly a country can lose its cultural heritage once the discipline relaxes. "We try to keep our traditions," a Salzburg shopkeeper will say. "Our music, our memory of Mozart, our appreciation of social protocol." There is no sense of irony: the shopkeeper has no idea what the "our" sounds like in a post-Marxian world that sees him (even the capitalist Americans agree here) as the pathetic dupe of a cynical aristocracy that gives him culture instead of a decent wage. "They all look backwards here," says Arthur Glover, resident director of the Salzburg Seminar in American Studies. "They don't care about the present at all. If they can have their coffee and cake in the afternoon in a café, they don't care that their houses are badly heated."

It is *Ferien* sustained at the highest possible pitch, but the price is terrific on the negative side of the balance sheet. The average Austrian city — including Vienna — is fifty years behind the rest of middle and northern Europe in the organization of the produce-and-consume process. "There are *no* supermarkets in Salzburg," a German woman claims. "A city of one hundred thousand, and not one supermarket. I ask why and they say the Austrians don't like them. But I notice they will drive over to Bad Reichenhall [a German spa ten miles from Salzburg] to shop. It isn't that they don't like supermarkets. It's that the people who run Austria won't let the Austrians have them."

"What I don't understand is the illogic," an American woman in the textile business in Austria says. "It's what I used to call in England the get-your-Kotex-at-the-ironmonger's. I've forgotten just where you did go in England to get your Kotex, but it wasn't where you thought it would be, and you ended up in some place as improbable as an ironmonger's. I suppose they have it ironed (that word again!) out there now — this was fifteen years ago — but they don't have anything ironed out in Austria.

"Sewing things, for instance. In America, you can get patterns and needles and thread in the same store in which you buy the material. Not in Austria. Only materials in the material store. You have to go elsewhere for everything else — not to one other shop but to several. And no one in the material store knows where the other items are sold. 'But you must know,' you say. No, they don't, because no one has ever asked before. The Austrian women all *know* where to go. Hasn't there ever been one who didn't know, who asked where to buy a needle? No. But you yourself, don't you sew? Of course, but my sister buys my needles for me. Where is she? In St. Anton, skiing.

"You go out on the street and accost likely-looking housewives. Finally you get the needles in this shop, the thread in that, and the patterns in, of all places, a bookstore. That's where the patterns are, but they don't carry what one needs with the patterns — the special paper that goes under the material and the little toothed wheel that one pushes along the material to make the special paper mark the material for cutting. Where does one find the wheel and the special paper? No one in the bookstore knows. It is as though a stationery store sold paper but not pens and ink, and didn't know where they were to be had. After several more inquiries, the wheel is located in a crafts shop and the paper in an office furniture store. (I could never find any of those places again in a million years.)

[348]

Even for an Austrian who knew where everything was, it would have taken hours, so why not have put it all in the materials store in the first place? No answer from anyone on that — I suspect it's because it would infringe on the articles allocated by custom to the smaller shops. My being put out is only personal, of course — what is important is that the whole country is always putting itself out. . . . All this talk of an Americanized Europe is nonsense, because every country in Europe is confused like that, to a certain extent. Austria is the prize, but all the other countries have enough of it so that you don't see how they will ever change in the end. It's too ingrained."

Another American woman: "In Austria, the children can't buy their books in school. The school doesn't sell books. The parents have to buy the books in a bookstore. Not all at once, in the fall, of course — that would be too easy. One at a time over several weeks — and there are dozens. Also, if the parent gets the wrong book at the bookstore and tries to return it, the bookstore refuses to take it."

An American man, husband of the second American woman above, based in Austria for business reasons: "I could give endless examples, but I'll limit myself to one: the car. When I brought my car into Austria, it still had German 'Z' plates, meaning it was still in customs, because I want to take it back to the States. I got an extension of the customs status here, but had to put on special Austrian plates. When I got the insurance for the car, the agent told me that he would arrange those plates, and that there was nothing I had to do. We went over that point several times, and he was sure of it.

"The next day I got a call from the plate-issuing office telling me I had to have the car inspected before they could issue the plates. I went and had it inspected — I didn't mind, that seemed reasonable — and got the plates. But out of curiosity, I went back to the insurance agent and asked him why he hadn't told me I'd have to have an inspection. 'But there is always an inspection with a foreign car,' he said. 'Fair enough,' I said, 'but why didn't you tell me that?' 'I thought you knew,' he said. 'How could I have known?' I asked, and although he couldn't answer that one he was still convinced I should have known. And that I was really complaining about the inspection, not just trying to get some information from him. Very bushy, as they say in the West Indies, and Austria is a lot like the West Indies once you scratch the surface. They know the name of everything, but no idea of where it comes from or how to handle it if there's a change in plans.

"The plates I bought were supposed to run from October, 1968, to October, 1969, and the issuing office told me that I wouldn't need new plates in 1969. I was a little concerned about that because they said '68 on them and I could hardly believe they would be good in 1969. 'No,' said the police officer in that department, 'this is a mere technicality. You have paid from October, 1968, to October, 1969, and you have a written receipt to that effect. Should anyone stop you — although no one will because there is a directive out to all patrols saying that all plates which read '68 are good in '69 if accompanied by the proper receipt — you simply produce that written receipt and all will be well.'

"I was stopped six times in the first four weeks of January, 1969, and had a tremendous struggle each time. The police officers who stopped me said I should have 1969 plates. I said another department had told me I didn't need them. They said that department didn't know what it was talking about. I went back to the original department, and they said the patrol police were all wrong. I begged for 1969 plates, but they said they were unnecessary. Three days later I came back to my parked car in downtown Salzburg to find the plates gone and a card telling me to call for them at a certain station house. In the meantime, said the notice, I was not to drive the car. I took a taxi to that station house, but the plates were not there, they had been transferred to another station house, a remote one, I couldn't find a taxi and had to walk the two miles there. It was now eight o'clock at night and snowing.

"The police at the second station house were polite and gave me back the plates immediately when I produced the written receipt. I explained yet again what the issuing office had said. 'They are wrong,' the officer in charge said. 'You can see that for yourself. We are under orders to remove all '68 plates now that it is 1969. You must go back to the issuing department and insist that they give you 1969 plates. They have them.' The next morning I did go back and I was given the 1969 plates, after three hours of wrangling. 'Here they are,' that officer said when he finally handed them over. 'They are unnecessary, but we do this to please you.'

"From this experience I formulated certain theories. First: no arm of the bureaucracy in Austria — and in most other European countries — ever knows what any other arm is doing. The situation is aggravated in Austria because they have inherited the full bureaucratic apparatus of the old Empire, which used to rule most of central Europe and was very large. Now Austria is a fraction of the old Empire in size and population, but the bureaucracy tries to stay the same size, so the situation is rather wild. Whatever you are told in one office will be contradicted in another, so you can never get the answer to anything. It is an iron law, as true for Austrians as for foreigners. The Austrians are used to it, though, and foreigners never do get that far. But used to it or not, no country can function properly under such a handicap. Ergo, Austria does not function.

"Second: private industry functions no better than the public services. Efficiency — Americanization, if that is the operative synonym — depends on dependability. Everyone in the producing chain, from raw materials to finished products, has to know what his job is and what he can expect from those in the links on either side of his link. In Austria, however, no one knows what is going on in his own link, or what the previous and next steps are, and so no one knows what to expect and doesn't understand what he's doing or what anyone else is doing. Talk to people here who have to import and export if you want some real stories.

"The chaos is why they have no amenities in the American definition — no central heating, and there's not even any hot water except at certain intervals during the day. So much would have to be done here — and undone! — before they could have just the fundamentals that it staggers you to think about it."

Surprisingly enough, it seems to be in Austria, supposedly more organized than Spain or Italy, that many Americans begin to wonder if Americanization will ever work in Europe. The Austrians have the knack of puncturing the biggest optimists' smallest balloons. The unattached observer can hardly find it unamusing. Austria is a great joke, perhaps, but so are the despairing Americans.

Personally, I am very fond of Austria. Not only because of the talent for balloon-puncturing, but because the Austrians have much of value that is in short supply elsewhere, more than enough to compensate for the so-called lack of efficiency. In addition to being the most handsome people in Europe, they are also the most polite. It is not a superficial politeness, either, but integral; not used to beguile others, but in the service of their own desire for harmony. Social intercourse is difficult without politeness, without some sort of manner, without a certain amount of charm — as the residents of France, Germany, England and the United States often find. (The Swiss are polite but wooden; there is no manner.) Austrian children must be the most pleasant in the modern world. The parents are firm, the schools are good, and the result can be coped with. Austrian cities have great appeal — Vienna remains the most livable of all large European cities, and perhaps the most attractive. If Austria is a minuet, it is a well-done minuet, and the world will be less when the American jaws finally bite through and meet.

Lastly, a cynical Austrian says, "The descendants of the Salzburgers who were so cruel to Mozart still run Salzburg, and even though they make a great deal of money out of the festivals in his memory, they'd do it to him all over again if he reappeared." The pragmatic American, even more cynical, although not deliberately so, replies, "The Mozart legend wouldn't be what it is if he hadn't been mistreated. You'd think they'd realize that. Maybe the mean

Salzburgers do realize it, and know that bigger festivals can be built on the memory of penniless geniuses. The more penniless the genius, the bigger the festival. You can't blame them for knowing it. And at least *someone* is getting something here. I was really worried for a while."

In a way, poor Mozart is the perfect symbol of the Germanic passion for *Ferien,* for perpetual pleasure. As tirelessly as any seamstress sewing Fasching costumes for the vacuous aristocracy in Vienna and Salzburg, or for the big-bellied funlovers in Munich and the Ruhr Valley, he turned out the stuff of careless amusement. As sublime as his music is, its primary purpose was to entertain, to feed the insatiable Danube-Rhine appetite for pleasure. If one had never been to that part of the world, careful attention to Mozart would almost paint the full picture. The "immortal strains" of *Don Giovanni* take on a morbid depth when set against the details of the harassed life, and the two combined give a very accurate picture of the crowd that sat to listen and of its descendants.

5

NORTHERN EUROPE

In its broadest definition, northern Europe embraces all the non-Communist maritime countries which border on the North and Baltic Seas — Belgium, Holland, Denmark, Norway, Sweden, and Finland. The United Kingdom qualifies, but it has been discussed separately, as has Germany, which is not primarily a maritime country anyhow. As a group, these six countries are better organized to compete with America technologically than any other region of Europe. (Switzerland can compete, too, but it is geographically and psychologically isolated from the north. The iron hand of the past hampers Germany.) And they do compete. The Dutch have an aptitude for big business unmatched in Europe — Philips, Shell and Unilever are among the largest companies in the world, and more such international giants are being planned. The Belgians are equally adroit, although antiquated methods have begun to catch up with them lately.

All these countries have been Americanized, in varying degree, but there are more different attitudes in north Europe toward the process, and toward America itself, than in the rest of the Continent. They are not only different, but also more extreme, ranging from frank admiration and emulation to intense dislike and contempt.

In Holland, a very successful Dutch businessman says: "We have learned much from America and we are grateful. But I can tell you now that we are able to stand on our own feet, and in ten years we shall have passed you. It is because of the internal problems that you have that we do not. I mean the racial troubles first, of course, although there are others. You have been what you call the front runner in the technology race, but I really think your days are numbered as leader. The native intelligence of our peoples here in Europe is higher and we shall pass you as soon as we make a real federation. What is holding us back *does* have a solution, but your troubles do not."

I have encountered this view many times in the past few years from men who make their livings from their decisions, and are not given to cocktail talk. It has a certain chill in it, and the climate gets even colder as one goes north into Norway and Sweden, where the pessimism about America and Americanization is often untempered by the Dutch idea that someone is going to derive benefit from leading the technology race. The countries that produced Ibsen and Strindberg have the stomach for the jaundiced view, and many Norwegians and Swedes take a bitter pride in their unspoken certainty that on the whole they are a more advanced society technologically and sociologically than America is, and that they are a more civilized people, and that they are the first to know it doesn't mean anything anyhow. Because they think they entered the twentieth century earlier than the Americans did, and have gone a greater distance since, they feel they can see farther into the future, and they don't like what they see. I had expected to find the apocalyptic view at peak in Sweden, the country of Gunnar Myrdal and Ingmar Bergman, of official sanctuary for American deserters, and of rampant anti-Americanism and antimaterialism, but it was actually in Norway that I was fed the strongest and most persuasive dose.

An elderly Norwegian shipowner, retired to a beautiful house near Trondheim, has been advising me on the selection of a shipping firm to carry certain materials from the African Gold Coast. It is an area he knows well, and his suggestions are valuable. It is difficult to imagine him — tall, with finespun white hair and veined, large-knuckled hands — in Accra, but he spent many years there and speaks of it as familiarly as Oslo. The snow is brilliant in the winter sun, which cuts through the clear windowpanes of his library and falls lightly on both of us, and the steaming coast of Africa seems very far away to me if not to him.

"I loved Africa," he says. "It was so primitive that I could think there. I had real thoughts. I never do here, not in the same way."

He tells me how he hated Norway as a boy, and although he likes living there now, he could not do it had he never been outside the country. "We are so rigid," he says. "Worse now than before."

Americanization comes inevitably into the conversation and I encourage him to tell me what he thinks of it.

"I can never hear the word without equating it with failure," he says. "To me, Americanization and failure are synonymous and I am always mildly surprised that more people do not see it that way. I have traveled widely in the United States and I consider it a literal hell. The landscape is ruined and the people are ruined. It is death, and there is no use pretending it is anything else. Among ourselves, of course, although I have known many Americans who were as aware of the true situation as any European could be.

"Now we have here in Scandinavia a growing idea that the 'American adventure' may not be the direction to take. Some of us here see the nightmare — especially the blacks and the young white people wild in the streets — and we appreciate that total Americanization means total trouble. We think we should draw back. What do you think?"

"I think it's too late."

"No, you are wrong. It is not too late if *everyone* does something. . . . The sociologists think it is a social problem, naturally, but I think it is a business problem. In America the demand for markets for goods means the establishment of buyers at any cost. The young and the blacks represented such buyers, and so they were fully franchised to buy; they were given money to that end. That gave

[356]

them the freedom to do what they want, and so they are tearing the fabric of the society apart. But business prevents their being taken in hand because business cannot lose that market. It is not the young and the blacks who are the villains — it is the businessmen. They won't give up a single dollar, even if it is the last one they earn before the end.

"That is what we must stop here — business getting so powerful that it will permit anything in order to make sales. It is a fatally shortsighted view, because once the fabric of society starts to go, it will go very fast and there will be no markets of any kind left anywhere. We must stop it here — don't you agree?"

"You don't think it's too late?"

"I can't believe that — I won't. . . . America will also collapse because the American generation now growing up will not be able to keep such a complicated country going. The young American whites and the blacks have either been allowed to get so wild that they can't be put into harness again, or they are turned into such robots that they will not be able to function in the coming emergencies. In neither case are they probably prepared to work as efficient custodians of the American machine. America is maintenance, as your man Eric Hoffer has said, and the maintenance will not be sufficient in the future. The whole trouble comes from the greed for markets, of course, but also from a sentimentalization about young people. Young people have to be controlled, there is no other choice. No society has ever let them loose and survived, because they are naturally destructive. Americans have always been permissive with their children because of the guilt, and now they have permitted past the point of no return.

"I don't know if we can put our young back under control or if they are too far gone. Yes, you would say too late — perhaps you are right. Certainly they are like the American young very much already. If you watch them closely, you see that they are deadened, they never *look* at anything. Even when they are outdoors, they never look at the mountains or the sea — only at the skis and the motorboats. They come here in the summers, and sit and talk to each other like old people. Like the old painters one used to see in Paris, old Bohemians. But even those old painters had some life left — now the young touch everything with paralysis, and everything they say is abstract. They think they are living, but they aren't — as they call their most petrified art 'action painting' . . . But I talk too much. Tell me what you think."

"I'd rather listen to you."

"No, tell me what you think. Am I right or wrong?"

"I don't know. The modern young are awful one minute, and not so bad the next . . ." I tell him about Chuck being locked up in Switzerland, and he is amused. Then I tell him about Ingrid Thulin, the Swedish actress who has starred in many of Ingmar Bergman's films, saying: "The Swedish public is more enthusiastic for American films. I went to my hometown for Midsummer Night and they were all dressed like cowboys," and he is not amused.

"That's what I mean," he says.

"My own feeling is that they were dressed like cowboys because of an inherent weakness in Scandinavian life."

"No! They have been . . . ah . . . temporarily talked into acting against their backgrounds. But it is only temporary!"

"I don't think so."

"Let me explain . . . what do you think the weakness is?"

"Oh, they probably think it means more freedom."

"Freedom!" He leans forward at me, the big hands opening and moving forward with a faint tremble, but the blue Norse eyes — the eyes that see the Gold Coast when they look down into the fjords — clear and steady. "Freedom is an illusion! We all live like the Czechs, really, although we don't know it. We are controlled by A-bombs, the threat of biological warfare, and worse. We are none of us free, and can never be and never were. This is the basic, basic fallacy in the American gospel. This is the terrible falsehood the Americans have taught their children from generation to generation until it has ruined them and is on its way to ruining what is left

[358]

of Europe. Now we sit in Europe and see the horrible American faces built on this delusion coming at us like ghouls in a nightmare. One doesn't think the next face will dare go farther than the last, but it does . . . Modern life is a dance of death, and the Americans are only the leaders in it. . . . A disaster lies ahead that is so enormous one can only marvel at it, unless there is a change of heart.

"The only freedom is the realization that there is no freedom. Only then can men have some something to themselves, some privacy, something that could be called freedom. That was the unpalatable truth that Hitler illustrated, and if he had not been the wrong man his message would have succeeded. But none of us understood that then. We all saw that he was mad and so we were all good little anti-Nazis. But now . . . if he should ever be cursed for anything it would be for making it impossible for the truth ever to show its face again after what he did to it . . .

"The United States proves him right because in complete permissiveness the weakest and most degenerate finally take over and humanity has lost its chance. Now the future belongs, no matter how brief it is, to the lunatics and the robots, the degenerates and the astronauts, both sides of the same coin. It is finished for you, and it is very close to being finished for us. We might yet save ourselves. But you can't. Because it is finished for you! If we do save ourselves, we would have to give you up as an example for anything. For *anything*, do you understand?!"

It is his high point, and I am not sure he can survive it. His hands shake openly now, his lips quiver and his eyes are filmed with tears of rage and excitement. I offer some small talk and in a few minutes he starts back to normal. Ten minutes later he is calm, and tells me about his grandchildren. In the evening his daughter-in-law, a fine-looking woman of thirty who has come for the weekend with two of those grandchildren, tells me she worries about the old man.

"He is so preoccupied with the dangers of living today," she says, "that he does not see the duty to make more of what is pleasant. I know — we all know — that these times are difficult, but we can only do something if we make more of what is pleasant."

In the doorway behind her, young Nils, seven, takes careful aim with his forefinger at the portrait of an ancestor, a stern nineteenth-century Norwegian with a beard. His mother wants me to reassure her that her father-in-law's fears are groundless, and I do so as well as I can, trying not to seem too namby-pamby. Even here the atmosphere of invitational weakness, the door opened to Americanization, is strong, too strong for candor.

Later in the next week I am in Stockholm, and hear more iconoclastic talk from two Swedish businessmen, one an executive of Bofors and the other a timber magnate. The timber magnate is quite specific in his criticisms, delivered at the Kellaren, the beautifully designed restaurant in the opera house.

"I am as lazy as any businessman when it comes to taking stock of what is really important," he says, "and I have only realized very slowly what has been happening. . . . There is this American way of making people think they are failures if they don't have everything, which has wrecked the United States as much as anything else, and which is pernicious enough to wreck the world without any help from any other perversity. It is a psychological nerve gas which produces terrible unhappiness, because naturally there is not enough for everyone to have everything: so to allow such an idea to get around, especially among simple people, is fomenting revolution. And that is why violence and revolution always come in the wake of you Americans. You always bring that idea with you, and it always ends with blood in the streets. Even here in Scandinavia, where people have more and can have more in the future than most of the rest of Europe, the impossibility of this idea has already created dangerous unrest.

"Because the more people get, the more they want, and the more they want the more neurotic they become. America is already too neurotic to recover, but we still have a chance and we don't want to get that sick. We had a highly organized civilization before you did, and we value it deeply and don't want to lose it. What has happened in America frightens us, and we don't want your ways to take over here. Your heartlessness toward each other in all business and social questions has stamped a look on your faces that we don't want on ours. Especially the look that is in the faces of your poor and dispossessed. Because once that look comes on the faces of the poor, it comes also on the faces of the wealthy. It destroys the nation from top to bottom. The poor and the dispossessed in America are not just those who are hungry or jobless or badly housed. They are everyone who does not have what a Kennedy or a Rockefeller has, because everyone there knows that to have less than everything is to have failed. So less than one per cent have succeeded, and ninety-nine per cent have failed, and you can see it in their faces. We don't want it to happen here, but it is what will happen if we don't draw the line."

He sticks out his jaw aggressively, but I wonder how the line will actually be drawn. It's a bit late for that, isn't it? I mean, if the line *could* be drawn there wouldn't be any need to draw it because the situation wouldn't have gotten that far out of hand.

I am assailed on all sides in Sweden, and feel quite battered at the end of a week. Only in the company of a-motion picture producer and his gorgeous mistress do the dark clouds lift, but the producer and his mistress have other, more pressing problems.

"Americans are very naughty," the producer says. "They like naughty movies and naughty books and naughty photographs, and we have made an industry here in Sweden out of that appetite."

"There is Copenhagen, too," the gorgeous Sigrid reminds him. We are in her apartment, and she lies on a chaise longue with a huge teddy bear. It is two in the morning, but she is very fresh and her smile has lost none of its brilliance.

"Yes, but they made a mistake coming out into the open," the producer says, and then explains it to me. "The Danish government now lets anything be printed in Denmark. *Anything,* and it has cut into pornographic book sales there by as much as eighty per cent.

They had a huge business in dirty books in English when it was under the counter, and now that they can sell in the open it's gone way down. In Sweden, we're still under the counter and we're booming. A dirty book in English that won't sell over there when they have it in the open will sell here from under the counter. Isn't that amazing? But I am worried, frankly, about what will happen to the movie industry when they can do anything in Denmark, because it looks as if the government there is going to take that step next. What will it mean when they can show anything? *Anything!* Do you know what it will mean to our industry here in Sweden if the Danes can show, let's say, the complete act of intercourse? To say nothing of the perversions. Think of masturbation! Fellatio! Cunnilinctus! Sodomy! Tribadism! All in detail! All we can do here in Sweden is breasts and behinds and heavy breathing. I don't think it will be like the books. I think it will boom for the Danes in the movies. And put us out of business."

The vision he has conjured up disturbs him and he chews his nails nervously.

"Why don't you go to Denmark and produce there?" Sigrid asks languidly, one beautiful arm, more naked than a body, draped around the teddy bear.

He waves his hand impatiently. "Those Danes will keep it all for themselves. No outsiders. And if they do let any in, there'll be so many producers lined up . . . ah, it'll be like a bus queue. But the real fight will come when they try to show that stuff in the United States. You can buy a dirty book and keep it to yourself, or take it back to America and it never gets into the public view. But a movie is different. It has to be shown in a public place, and so the authorities have to approve it. Will the Americans go that far? Will they call an all-out movie art, I mean? Can they? That's what everyone will be waiting to see."

"That's what you'll be waiting to see," Sigrid says.

"That's what half of Stockholm will be waiting for," he says. "Say, there's one for those investors of yours. Risky, but no riskier than a lot of other futures. Don't you know some people who might want to take a flyer on the American end?"

"Not at the moment, but you never know."

"All the world loves a dirty movie," he says, and gives me details.

"He's worried about the Dutch, too," Sigrid says.

"Queers are legal there now," he says. "Amsterdam is the queer capital of the world, and I figure that once the barriers start down, they'll come all the way. Some of those queers in Holland — or even some straight Dutch — will be making all-out movies there before we do here. We're very advanced in some ways, but the Swedes have a lot of Puritan in them, and we can't let go the way the Danes and the Dutch can when they start rolling. I think we're going to be losers in the next ten years."

"Don't worry," Sigrid says, "you'll always have me."

Even she laughs as she says that, and he snorts bitterly. "How long do you think she'd stay with me if I wasn't making money? She'll be down in Copenhagen with some Dane the minute I can't give her what she wants."

"I don't like Danes," Sigrid says. "I like you."

"But you have to go where the action is," he says.

"That's true," she admits. "I have to go where the action is. But that's healthier than having to go where the art is."

"She's right," he says gloomily. "Action beats art every time."

In fabled Copenhagen, the market in pornographic books, with and without photographs, is wide open and mainly for tourists. "Especially for American tourists," says Count Laber, a fussy little man who claims to know. He has huge investments in Swiss chemicals and wishes to get together with my Dutch precious metals friends. The count lives a very odd life in a vast old house just off the Vestervoldgade, taking care of his respectable little financial empire from a completely modernized suite, and pursuing a random and eccentric life in the rest of the place. The business suite could pass muster in New York — all glass and synthetics, modern art on the walls, gleaming filing cabinets, two nylon secretaries, complicated telephone system with direct lines, news tapes, the works — but when one goes through the door into the rest of the house one enters the late nineteenth century. Empty rooms filled with baroque furniture and covered with the faint dust of decades succeed each other along endless corridors. The count is a bibliophile, and even the enormous library is not large enough for his acquisitions, which have overflowed into the rest of the mansion.

"I am a schizophrenic," he says cheerfully as we pick our way through the maze. "One life over there," he gestures back toward the business suite, "and another here. I am what you call a nut. Yes, yes, I am. I really am."

We come to his private study, a comfortable room of the early 1900s, sunless, with heavy furniture and large-shaded lamps. He seats himself at his desk and rubs his cherubic face. We talk of this and that and I tell him a bit about the pessimisms of the Norwegian shipowner and the Swedish timber tycoon.

"Premature senility!" Count Laber cries jubilantly. "The Scandinavian disease. What do I tell you? All old men who cannot see their hands before their faces. They don't understand we have to go through the future, always — like a looking glass. What do those old fools know of America? Nothing. Everything they say are mere bagatelles. Mere bagatelles, I say . . . People are such fools about everything. Americanization! What is Americanization except this: the American Revolution created a new type, or was created by a new type, and this type finally took over the world because it was superior . . ."

His voice drones on and one's own mind picks up the familiar argument and carries it forward. Superior, yes, in the Baconian sense. So very simple, and no one understands it. The great story of our time and no one noticed it. Not even Marx. Without America, the French and Russian revolutions would have gone nowhere, because they did not create a new type, without which no revolt can be permanent. Only America supplied the new type and broke the old system, which was back in France by 1800 and in Russia by

1927. Only America caused the old systems trouble and made them change, and now makes Russia change. America made everything old-fashioned . . .

Clothilde said that, in her way, in her maturely youthful way, with the dead Europe lying behind her exquisite profile as she said things that seemed so new to her but were commonplaces to any American. She had been listened to because of her vitality, the tantalizing sense of life that Americans have lost and which they are always trying to buy back at a price below market value — far below . . .

The count goes on, carrying the argument, which seems so advanced to him, on a lower level than it came into one's own mind so long ago, when it first occurred. As he speaks, in that forgotten rococo room, one's ears take it in and reword it in one's own version, like simultaneous translation at the United Nations. He thinks he dares, this professionally eccentric little count. How surprised he would be to find that he has been wholly anticipated.

. . . So nothing could have changed without the American Revolution. And nothing which has changed has changed from any other cause. Americans are a new breed, and so they have created a new society and everyone who imitates them is automatically less. (Those who don't imitate can be equal in a way, but they must resign themselves to living in the past.) It is not that Americans are the same as other people and just a bit more energetic. They are intrinsically different (although not necessarily better) and hence the true, the long-awaited master race, the forebears of the not-to-be-denied *Übermensch*. As stupid as they look, that is what they are. . . .

The differences, the differences — the difference between the English going to the top of Everest for the Queen and the Americans going to the moon for . . . what? Old-style men could climb Everest, but it takes new men to go to the moon. Only the Americans can do it in the public view. Russian cosmonauts have had more trouble with space sickness than Americans: the Russians are still Europeans. Americans are the most evolved of the earth's peoples, although — disconcerting thought — the evolution may be backwards, and one explanation of their unattractiveness. And of the unattractiveness of their direction.

Backwards evolution?! Yes, a definite possibility. But even if true, they are still humanity's leaders. Unattractive to a degree . . . indeed, viewed from the standpoint of unevolved peoples (which includes all non-Americans, as well as those Americans who can't make it or take it), they are horrible. But they are the future if there is one, and the young all over the world know it. Naturally — to say nothing of scientifically and esthetically — this does not mean they are better. We must think of it as measurement against a fixed standard, like the one-hundred-yard dash, where the ability to produce-and-consume and otherwise prance in the approved Baconian styles is the race. There is no way to measure except against a rigid and arbitrary standard, and unless we are prepared to abandon measurement altogether we have no choice except to use such a yardstick. It is only fair to point out that once that standard is generally adopted, there is no time for anything but produce-and-consume, but what alternative is there? Our time only knows one system, and if we are to measure everyone we have to measure them inside and against that system.

Americanization, then, is not what we think it is — the girl with the impeccable armpits handing a Coca-Cola to the boy with the extra pills in his pocket — but pure, old-fashioned evolution, part of the endless process from somewhere to somewhere. And, now started, it will continue with or without America until a more important bend or dip diverts the present direction.

Without America, nothing of modern Europe would exist, so it is American to a larger degree than commonly supposed. Imitation of America without the American presence is still Americanization. Even if America goes down, disappears as finally as Atlantis, or even if Europe surpasses it in the next forty years, Europe will still be American in all details and directions. Its present, past and future, its beginning and end — all will be facets of Americanization. The new Protestant world of the 1500s is a parallel. It forced the Catholics to change. Without its lead, change would have been fractional; the earth would still go around the sun. . . .

To be educated, in the modern sense of the word, is to understand about America; to understand that it has been America's world since 1775, and that the only things that have happened are those things America has done. Everything else has been imitative or extraneous, of no evolutionary importance in either case. That these facts have been singularly unrecognized in the past two centuries is squarely within the tradition according to which humanity never recognizes anything until long after it is over. Now it is over, and the Americans stand revealed as the chosen people, the anointed of the Lord. Not the British, not the French, not Europe as a whole, not the Russians, not even the Jews. In classic perfection, the other aspirants showed the sublime indifference to America that the hare showed to the tortoise — no, more than indifference, a sublime ignorance of the presence of the Americans as rivals at all.

The Americans themselves stayed in character and shared that ignorance and were as stunned as everyone else when the cup was presented. They knew they were the latest thing, always, but they thought that was rather *déclassé* in certain contexts, like nylon lingerie as opposed to silk. They were afraid they were no more permanent than the Hula-Hoop, Cracker Jack or the latest subdivision, and had no idea that they were expressing the deepest yearnings of the Life Force. But the unseen powers reassured them and the world that even their throwaways were a clue to the grand design of Providence, and at last they understood, too. Ma said "Land-o'Goshen!", Pa shook his head in facetious disbelief, their middle-aged children looked solemn and thought about all the martinis and steaks, and their teenaged grandchildren didn't get it at all. But they didn't have to: they were on the other side of the wall; they were the realization of the dream.

The count finishes his speech as the tones of the more personal original fade out. Mistaking the fixed stare on the face of his listener for stunned admiration, he launches into yet another unwitting plagiarization, but this time the automatic mechanism does not take over. Instead, the mind drifts altogether away from him, out and beyond to Europe itself, lying sullenly in the seas of its confusion. Not even in the great clean massif of the Bernese Alps, rising sheer from the floor of lesser ridges, can the realities of this colonization be avoided. It has happened and the backbiting is now familial, the bickering of sibling states already trussed into one. The reaction against it by any — the old, the young, even the colonizers themselves — becomes part of the process, predictable and on time. A true rebellion would look very different.

Superimposed on the count's earnest but unlovely face is that of the Norwegian shipowner, the tears still in his eyes, the tremble on his lips. He and the count, incomplete themselves, make a forceful whole and what the colonizer would call a balanced picture. The spare old man's impotent rage and the chubby count's bland, sophistic apologia meet and merge in cogent presentation.

Cogent, but not really significant. Pro and con, they think they have something to offer, these thinking Europeans, but they don't. They imagine they can discuss America, Americans and Americanization, but they are deeper in the net than they know, and they are not in a position to shed any light whatsoever. The American world is not distinct from them but all around them, enveloping them from inside as well as from out. They are surrounded and impregnated, without a chink left. This, then, is why they fatigue one so, even at their best, why one can never receive what they are so sure they give, but which never exists . . . why one is always so tired when they talk.

But if there are no ideas behind them — the process doesn't seem to be an idea or give rise to ideas, even for Americans — they are still real as people, and one remembers them as people, the splendid, doomed people of Europe who have been known. Clothilde, de

Renville, Larry (an omen so ostentatious there as to wither its ve-
racity), and the myriad others known, seen, guessed at.

The shades gather, and the count's preposterous study is an appropriate place for one's European education to crest, even to ter-
minate. Can there be anything left to learn, here at the northern
extremity of the continent? Outside is Copenhagen, low and porno-
graphically oriented on its watery spits, the sea birds and the memory of Hans Christian Andersen and the magic of the old city not at
all sufficing, as such talismen do not suffice anywhere any more, but
reminding the idle watcher that . . . once it was different.

The count smiles amiably and preens himself on his schizophre-
nia, implying that it is sensible to be so, to have a foot in both
worlds, to be able to pass from the heartless pastels of his modern
office suite to this evocative old European room without going outdoors. Perhaps he is right, perhaps he is healthy in his eccentricity.
After all, there could have been footfalls here from persons of
meaning, somber old gentlemen with muttonchop whiskers and top
hats, and coldly beautiful Danish women in long dresses with ten-
drils of blonde hair lying along their elegant cheekbones, and such
footfalls may have a symbolic echo. Whereas, in the office, no one
ever comes and nothing of consequence ever happens and there are
no echoes, symbolic or otherwise.

That is what the count believes, that is what they all believe,
whether they know it or not, and that is why Clothilde killed herself. The American has to flinch from their version of his works,
either in the comic crouch of the perfected Babbitt or the heroi-
cally gentle disagreement of the Hudson River tycoon turned diplomat who produces an astronaut out of his capacious pocket and
plays him wordlessly as the last trump, hoping the foreigners are
convinced even if he himself isn't entirely sure.

("In paraphrase of Keats," my American scholar says, "my most
visual memory of a boy's America was the repeated sight of men
looking down and into automobile engines. The driver stepped
from his dilapidated Chevrolet in the service station of the 1930s,

threw up the hood and peered inside. He was immediately joined by everyone in the vicinity, and they all looked in, too, frozen in a posture of reverence. Their necks were bent at a certain angle, and they could hold the pose indefinitely. They weren't America in themselves, but they were when joined with the mechanical artifact. The engine, or any other formed thing, was the indispensable catalyst, the other half of the dialogue. The frieze multiplied by millions was the country, and now it has become the world. The American discovery that looking at inanimate things — preferably down and in — is universally and uniquely irresistible has made us masters of the globe.")

The mighty European dead are dispossessed with pious regret, but the treatment is so inclusive as to bundle off trios as mixed as Charlemagne, Calvin and Joyce in fraternal vagabondage. In the thin Copenhagen air, the experience of it comes at last. This is what it *means,* this is what it *means,* this is what the raw truths of colonization and surrender look like when they happen to people, when they impose themselves on living beings, when they tunnel into the soft wet channels of the mind, when they get into what can't be seen as well as what can.

Its feet may have been anchored in pre-Marxian mud of unmeasurable viscosity, but Europe was a rainbow in its day. Europe was a crescent of hope compared to the new outline against the sky, the imported high-low profile, ubiquitous and shameful in a hurried, hangdog way. Slow-speaking termites with first pipes from Dunhill and first suits from Savile Row and first ducks from the Tour d'Argent are borne complacently to Cannes on fast trains and eat up the other passengers in the dining car with direct, unselfconscious stares. No amount of applied urbanity can deter the chomping jaws, lined with rows of razor-sharp teeth, that guide those bulging, froglike eyes.

Finally, the surrender is literal and indifferent. The female body lies on the medical examination table, the flesh delicately chilled by the leatherette beneath and the lifeless air above, the knees up, the heels in the metal sockets, the thighs spread wide. The unscrupulous physician pokes about with feigned scientific interest, toys with the nipples and the slack labia, makes a few invented notations on a chart, and then, as if the idea were occurring for the first time, arches clumsily atop the still patient, whose eyes stay fixed on the ceiling. The unethical doctor's feet remain on the linoleum floor, and his shoes slip against the awkward pressure, much like — exactly like — the horny toes of a tortoise trying to scale a tiled ramp.

The body is violated and the woman will swear that the violation is complete; she will deny any memory of ever having been anything except what she now is. But women are not all that accurate, even when they wish to be, and the doctor, now a bit mad, will always wonder if he triumphed after all. (Wasn't it odd that she didn't resist, that she knew what he was going to do?) It is essential that she forget what she once was, and he can never be altogether sure she has. In time, even he hears the faint, pathetic scratching of his shoes and realizes he cannot move. All must come to him because he can't move. They come now, but will they stay? What will happen when they find out he is immobile?

They — the ghosts of the old Europe — hurry along stone passageways in white dresses and black cloaks, their fine-boned faces pitted with plague and their clear eyes fixed on peculiar visions. Faster! Faster! Through medieval archways, down along ancient stone colonnades, running now to meet, to cry out, to sink in exhaustion . . . to surrender.

It would seem to be the end, but is it? If it is, then how explain the appetite of these northerners for the apocalyptic vision, their stomach for disaster? How explain the unchanging existence of the Baltic Sea itself, old and gray and shallow, the low brown land rising reluctantly, the mottled white of the country houses, the lined faces of the fading aristocrats, the intelligence of their elegant, spidery minds? How explain even the count himself?

"We shall have a good dinner," he says now. "There is no point in dining badly. We Danes love good food, you know, all of us. We

[371]

are very Gothic, but we love good food. Even my relative Karen Blixen, who wrote under the name Isak Dinesen — perhaps you have read some of her books — loved good food, although her feeling for the Gothic left nothing to be desired. Nothing to chance and nothing to be desired."

We leave the study and stroll back through the house, passing again the great stacks of books, looming like dolmens in a druid forest.

"But now we shall work," the count says as we near the door to the business suite, and smiles in anticipation as he turns the handle. The two secretaries look up from their typewriters like chipmunks, and then look back again. We step across the threshold, leaving behind the talk, the reveries, the questions, and plunge into the enchanted world of precious metals. In ten minutes the telephones are humming with calls to Amsterdam, Zurich and Johannesburg. The count's cigar is cold in its heavy glass ashtray and he speaks into his telephones with increasing emphasis. Outside, the birds are visible but they don't seem as real as when they were imagined from the shuttered study. During one lull, the count covers a telephone mouthpiece with his plump hand and says, "We shall go to a nightclub after dinner. A wonderful place where you are quite at home. Not like the usual nightclub at all. But then, I am at home anywhere — at least, I try to be."

IV
EASTERN EUROPE
Diary of an Impression

I N March, 1969, Jim Carter and I drive up to Prague from Austria. (As in previous sections, names have been changed where necessary.) It is not a business trip. I am going to have a look, and Jim goes along for the ride and what hunting he can get in. We'll stay in Prague awhile, then drive to Budapest via Brno and Bratislava, and return to Austria. I have some introductions to Czech and Hungarian party officials and managers, and Jim has some hunting connections. It will be a brief look at eastern Europe, but not a restricted one, and it has become apparent to me that no consideration of Americanization in Europe as a whole can be complete without an appraisal of the east.

It is fifty-eight kilometers from Linz to the border crossing at Wullowitz and the country is hilly and rather grim. The stone farm buildings are not inviting — there is little of the Austrian charm here and no consciousness of its lack.

The Austrian border guard comes out of a small, neat station and asks if we have visas. (Since the Russians moved in, they must be obtained before entering Czechoslovakia; prior to August, 1968, they were available at the border.) We assure him we do and he waves us on. The road is flat on the two-kilometer stretch from the Austrian station to the Czech, and there is a good view of the formidable fence which now bisects Europe, all trees and brush cut back several hundred feet on each side. A young soldier in a cubicle, loutish in an ill-fitting uniform, presses a button and the barrier slides back.

The Czech border station is a portent of things to come. Large, aimless buildings painted in livid colors, unswept sidewalks, men and women in shabby uniforms, an atmosphere of ineradicable incompetence. Inside, the personnel wander aimlessly around, pleasant but slovenly. Two men in neat suits and with shined shoes, probably Russian plainclothesmen, stand out by comparison. A young man in garish civilian clothes, reeking of schnapps, asks if we will take him to Prague. We say we aren't going that way. When we get back in the car we notice a long kennel back to one side, filled with ferocious German shepherds, evidently for patrol duty.

"What does this place look like?" Jim asks as we leave.

"An abandoned amusement park on the Maryland shore."

"Not bad, but I think you've missed a few nuances."

"Let's have them."

"How about a CCC youth center that was painted by the kids themselves back in the thirties, and hasn't been used since the war?"

"You win."

It is forty kilometers to České Budějovice, the capital of southern Bohemia, and I drive slowly because the road is pitted. We have a deliberately plain car — a two-door Chevrolet Impala — with Austrian plates, but everyone notices it. There are lots of trucks on the road but very few passenger cars.

The first few villages are dismal. Except for the main road through their centers, nothing is paved, and the views up the muddy side streets are from another time.

"Georgia in the late twenties," Jim says. "I can remember going down there to a relative's plantation when I was a kid. Only this is more rundown than Georgia was then. What gets me is the pile of rubble in front of *every* building."

We are to find that the rubble is static, part of the *décor*, like ornamental shrubbery in the west.

The people are poorly dressed in clothes from which the life seems drained. I learn later that this comes from weaving used material into the new goods. The women all seem to be in ski pants with very baggy knees, with which they wear low shoes or white plastic boots, not the most attractive choices.

As we approach Česke Budějovice, the villages get progressively grimmer.

"The Germans had all this once," Jim says. "They were here for hundreds of years, but now you don't see a trace of kraut. No sturdy farmhouses, no decent buildings in the towns. They couldn't have all been bombed. What happened to them?"

Česke Budějovice is fantastic. The side streets are Kafkaesque nightmares, with figures dressed like ragpickers trudging slowly through the mud, slogging around the piles of rubble. The buildings are uniformly dark and dreary.

"It makes Harlem look like heaven," Jim says. "I can't believe it."

It is even worse where attempts have been made to brighten facades on the main streets by painting them over with ill-matched pastels. Our guidebook says that the main square is one of the largest in Europe. The size gives full scope to the horror.

"It isn't happening," Jim says. "Stop the car. I want to remember this."

I stop and a couple of dozen idle youths immediately crowd around to ogle the car. "Gives them something to do, anyhow," Jim says. The vast square dwarfs the pedestrians, who trudge through it as though unwilling to reach the other side. The middle-aged and elderly are somber and crushed. The young are crude and vulgar. All the younger women seem to have dyed red hair, a vibrant, screaming red not often seen in the west.

"It's the maid's night out gone mad," Jim says. "It's . . . how could you say all the things it is? . . . You know, the Germans called this place Budweis, and when the Busches wanted to let the other krauts in St. Louis know they were getting a good beer, they called it Budweiser because Budweis, back in the old country, was famous for its beer. If you were in South St. Louis in 1875, you bought Budweiser because it made you think of beautiful Budweis, with the big square and the fine beer and the easy prosperity. I wonder what they'd think of it now. Let's go."

The youths have been staring at Jim openmouthed through the car window. His six feet, five inches of socialite confidence, his Palm Beach tan, his expensive clothes . . . the cumulative effect is much too much for latterday Budweis.

It is a lovely afternoon, with a warm winter sun, but the weather can't do anything for the rest of the trip to Prague. Improbable village succeeds improbable village without mercy. One thinks of how far down it is from what it was before the war, from what it would be if the Russians had never come. There don't even seem to be any bars or decent restaurants in the towns, no provision for social life of any kind. We'd like a beer, but such cafés as do exist are too forbidding.

"I've never drawn the line anywhere," Jim says. "The wilds of Mexico, Africa, even New Guinea — always went anywhere. But this is different."

One's education does not cease on the highway. The old Skoda passenger cars limp along slowly, the drivers cautious about pushing them over forty. The trucks are all old, too, and spew thick black exhausts which hang so heavily that it's often difficult to see the road.

"I guess all the new trucks go to Russia," Jim says.

When we go through Tábor, he says, "I can't look at it seriously any more. From now on, I'm going to see it the way a Russian does. Imagine a Russian VIP in the back of a limousine going along this road. He sees a particularly awful town and turns to the Czech next to him and beams. 'Gold star,' he says. 'This place really has it.'

Then he sees a pulled-together house — a rarity, but they do exist — and the brows knit. Storm clouds on the heavy face. 'Get your notebook out, Dubček,' he says to the Czech, 'and take down that address, and send someone out there with a few yards of rubble and some Bill Blass fuchsia paint and fix that place up!' Isn't it that crazy? I mean, don't they see it that backwards? Don't they have to, to keep it up this way?"

"I don't know . . . I guess they must."

"They have to, there's no other explanation. And so does the visitor. From now on, I'm wearing reverse glasses." He finds the suburbs of Prague sensational.

We are staying at the Alcron, a couple of blocks off Wenceslas Square, and that area is quite presentable.

"Not bad," Jim says.

"I thought you were wearing your reverse glasses."

"You take them off when you roll up to your first-class hotel in your satellite's capital city," he says. "Party theory is one thing, but personal comfort is important, too. Say, the Alcron looks pretty good."

It is very comfortable, as good as any but the best hotels in the west. When east Europe decides to do anything properly, it can, using the model of 1939. The result has period charm, and is actually more pleasant than the present tense in the west.

We have a Pilsner at the bar in the corner of the lobby and it is excellent.

"My God, that's good beer," Jim says. "That's the best beer I've ever tasted. I've had it in Germany, but it didn't taste like this."

"They keep the best at home."

"This is heavier."

"It's pre-1939."

"You're right. Everything is. It's like being young again, going back in a time machine."

The central public room is filled with foreigners — businessmen, reporters, spies — and domestic whores. The foreigners are an unprepossessing lot, and the whores good-natured but dumpy. They sit together in groups of three, waiting.

"Those are rough-looking hookers," Jim says, "and very definitely pre-1939."

We have a late lunch and then go out to take a walk, splitting up at Wenceslas Square.

"You go your way and I'll go mine," Jim says. "We'll compare notes later."

Wenceslas Square — actually a very wide street — is filled with long-haired young, as vacuous as any on view in the west. The people, although poorly dressed, have a hard, animal energy. There are a lot of misshapen faces, violent hennas, and curious combinations of clothes — fur hats with cloth overcoats and tennis shoes, moth-eaten fur coats with ski pants. An elderly man in rags carries a silver-headed cane. A woman in a careless yellow turban is holding an empty cigarette holder between her teeth. The atmosphere is of Bryant Park, in New York, also of sections of Second Avenue and even of the Bowery — with touches of old-clothes day in private day schools.

The shopwindows promise goods, but the stocks inside are low and far below western quality. Hordes of uncertain clerks tend unpainted wooden shelves barely covered with their pitiful supplies. The shoppers look more often than they buy, and look with a passion which suggests that full produce-and-consume would be heaven.

I have arranged to meet Karel Bendl, an engineer and an old friend, in a small restaurant near the foot of Wenceslas Square. From there we take a taxi to Malá Strana, the "Lesser Town" under the Castle. Here were the baroque palaces of the nobility of the Austrian Empire — the Wallensteins, Ledebours, Furstenbergs, Auersbergs, and some two hundred others. They are still there, turned into offices, theaters and other necessities of the state, and fairly well cared for. Workmen are busy at the Wallenstein Palace, but we are able to go into the famous gardens, and there we stroll and talk.

Like all Czechs, Karel has only one topic — the Russian invasion and control — but his view is not exactly what I expected. "We can say we were brutally taken over, but it is not quite that simple," he says. "The Russians do have some points. When they insist that our 'liberalization' here was being fostered by America, that may not be literally true. But it is true that the liberalization process in any socialist country tends to move that country into the American camp. There are no alternative solutions for countries like Czechoslovakia, because we are not capable of developing an 'alternative' to produce-and-consume socialism other than produce-and-consume capitalism. So we can't leave the Russian orbit except to enter the American orbit. The noise on the surface — the argument over 'repression' versus 'democracy' — may seem important outside Czechoslovakia as well as inside, but it is mostly a fantasy. We can't be truly independent; we can only be under the Russian thumb or the American thumb.

"East Europe is the fight, it is the focal point of the American-Russian struggle. If you start with the Americanization of Europe, then you see that it has to keep going east. In the Russian view, they have to see east Europe and then themselves taken over or they have to fight it. It could ultimately mean war, you see. . . . America works through West Germany, with or without knowing it. The Germans are rich, they wish to become richer, they push against our borders with the American message. And the Russians push back, so we are really an American-Russian background. That is the story through east Europe, and there is no other story. On one side of the fence are the Germans with their Mercedes cars and money and goods, and on the other side here we are with very little or nothing. That fence is the white-hot focal point of the confrontation. Can it last forever? Can it keep the Germans (and the Americans) out forever? That is what the Russians keep asking themselves. That is what we — or some of us — keep asking our-selves.

"I don't mean to defend the Russians — God knows they do noth-ing but plunder us. If we didn't have to sell them everything we make, and for ridiculous prices, we'd be rich. They are nothing now but czarist imperialism all over again. There is no Communist thought left, we all know that. But to deal with them at all, we must understand what worries them, and we must grant them a point when they have one. They saw our reforms as leading no-where except to the German and American presences throughout Czechoslovakia, and we touch the Russian border. So they saw the American orbit extended to the Ukraine, and they were right. Even Tibor Szamuely [the British Kremlinologist] conceded that when he said: 'Russia is perfectly correct in interpreting the Czechoslovak experiment as something that will lead that country into a non-Communist democracy. The Soviet empire in eastern Europe is at stake.' You understand that 'non-Communist democracy' is the western euphemism for American orbit. . . . Yes, I know that peo-ple say that Yugoslavia has been free of direct Russian dominance for twenty years and is not in the American orbit. But that may be only temporary, because Yugoslavia is no more than a passed pawn — can I say that? — yes, a passed pawn in the American-Russian contest. And in time Yugoslavia will probably become American, if she is left alone by Russia. Remember that Russia can afford to ignore Yugoslavia where she can't ignore us, because we are so cen-tral to Europe.

"And is America what we really want? Is it what we would want if we knew it, I should ask. Many of us are not at all sure that it is. We see now, too, that much of the reform program was in the hands of men who didn't care what the outcome was in terms of western infiltration. They refused to *see* that we have to be in one orbit or the other. . . . Dubček was a figurehead in many ways, and there is concern about the role of the Zionists. To us, Zionism is synonymous with Americanism, because America is the Zionist base. When a Czech Jew becomes very high in the government, we are afraid that he has nothing on his mind, really, except Zionism — every Jew in the world seems to place his first loyalty there — and we suspect that he will have more in common with an American Zionist than with any non-Jewish Czech.

"It is true that from the start of the reform, in early 1968, Prague was full of American Jews. They were drawn here like flies — that I saw with my own eyes. The Russians claim that American Jews work for American hegemony in Europe in return for American support of Israel. Silly, you non-Jewish Americans say, but are you so sure what goes on in your government? I don't see how you can be positive about anything, or in a position to deny that such-and-such could or could not take place. . . . The Russians also insist that any Jew in a high place today is dangerous because of the Zionist passion, and their suspicions may not be misplaced. This is not anti-Semitism, no matter what the Jews say, but a matter of national interests. It is not reassuring to see a national program being taken over by men whose primary interest is not national but vested in a country which has nothing to do with Czechoslovakia. From my own experience in speaking with western Jews — especially newspaper correspondents — and some highly placed Czechoslovak Jews, I find that the Zionist hysteria blinds them to all other considerations. I give the Russians that point. If I were a Russian — or even a Czech government official before the Russians came — I would be concerned about the reliability of Zionists in high places. To call such concern anti-Semitism is in itself very suspicious. . . .

"I would not leave for good. Perhaps it is weakness. But I have a nice job and I love my country. We still think we can make something here. Perhaps we are wrong, but we have to try.

"There is much about the reform program and the subsequent events that is unexplained. The liberalization people here are very dogmatic, you know, and if one criticizes them in any way, they make threats. It is not as nice as you think. . . . The western journalists are always delighted to find representational painters who hide their beloved abstract art in their closets and take it out to show to westerners. Now the shoe here is a bit on the other foot. We ex-liberals in Prague meet in the dead of the night to complain to each other, and to speak candidly to old friends from the west. You see, I am taking out *my* abstract art for you now . . ."

In our walk we approach a wall of the palace covered with a gray-black material, thick and viscid, plastered over several hundred square feet.

"In the old days, the peasants came here and made a mixture of fresh eggs and ashes and spread it on the wall," Karel explains. "It was a form of fealty. At least we don't have that any more."

He is so sure it is better now on that count, that the absence of such customs outweighs all the rest they have to put up with. But does it? Could feudalism have been worse than what Jim and I saw today? Hardly. Then there was, at bare minimum, a sense of form — national dress and a gold watch for the men and silver combs for the women, and perhaps nothing else, but there was unity in the dress and the few precious possessions and the relationship with the lord and the king and the deity. Now there is absolutely nothing. Pure chaos and total dissonance. Poverty made permanent, made legal, without a moment of dignity or amusement. The national dress and the gold watches and the silver combs traded for sleazy ski pants and ball-point pens and plastic raincoats.

Looking at Karel, standing thin and intense before the egg-ash wall, I can think of nothing except what a creature of abstraction he is. The abstract socialist world has made the abstract man, and he is more abstract than the most bloodless AT&T executive. The Czechoslovak past was real here — it is not difficult to imagine the long-moustached peasants in this garden, streaming up to the wall with their strong-legged, brightly costumed wives, eggs and ashes in hand — but this present is unreal. There is nothing here except abstract rationalization. No materialism at all, really: material is precisely what it is not.

Karel has to go to a meeting now and I return to the Alcron. Jim, who resembles the late Errol Flynn and has the same attraction for women, is having a drink at the bar with a handsome Czech girl.

"She's a figure skater," he says, "and she's been telling me how hard she works."

"It is very difficult," she says.

"How was your afternoon?" Jim asks.

"Not bad. And yours?"

"Nothing to talk about. I have a new slogan: the only thing worse than capitalism is Communism."

"That's very good," says a large, rumpled man on the seat next to Jim. He speaks Akim Tamiroff English, fluent but heavily accented, and seems drunk.

"It's not really that good," Jim says. "So obvious."

"I'm a Russian and I should know," the rumpled man says. "The obvious is often overlooked."

"You're not a Russian," Jim says. "Where are your tanks?"

"About thirty miles from here." He speaks with aplomb, and there is a gambler's amused indifference in his disarming smile.

"You should not talk of such things," the Czech girl says.

"The fiery nationalist," the Russian says. "All these Czechs are ready to argue at the drop of a shoe."

"You can hardly blame them," Jim says. "By the way, it's 'drop of a hat.' You've got it mixed up with 'waiting for the other shoe to drop.' "

It takes a while to straighten out these American folk phrases, and then the Czech girl returns to the attack.

"We didn't ask you here," she says to the Russian.

"Of course you didn't," he says.

"You invaded us," she says. "There is no other way to look at it."

"Of course not," the Russian says. He is in his late fifties or early sixties, with a big, intelligent head and very fine — although very bloodshot — eyes. He speaks so distinctly, if slowly, that one questions his drunkenness. But the eyes and the livid, purplish-red complexion can have no other source. His iron-gray hair is cut long, like that of a few Russian diplomats, and he is extraordinarily at ease — with himself as much as with others. He does not have a Russian tailor: his dark flannel suit is rumpled but the material is good and the cut is English.

The Czech girl is disconcerted by his amiable agreements, but decides to go one step farther.

"Doing it for our good!" she says scornfully. "You do it for your own good. You wish to keep us as slaves working for you!"

"But naturally," the Russian says. "Wouldn't you, if you were us? We're a clumsy, incompetent people — if we can enslave efficient workers like you to do our jobs for us, then it's a good business. Too good to give up." He smiles very widely, revealing large, stained teeth with a number of gold crowns.

The girl is too stunned to go on. We are all taken aback, in fact.

"Listen, fella," Jim says, looking over his shoulder facetiously and lowering his voice, "isn't it a little risky for you to talk like that?"

"Not at all," the Russian says. "I am a colonel of intelligence. I can say what I please — who knows but what I am merely trapping others?"

"You're too intelligent to be in intelligence," Jim says. "You must be drunk."

"Perhaps."

"If they come for you, we'll say you were only drunk," Jim says. "You'll be the drunken colonel."

"Very well," says the drunken colonel. "Let's have a drink."

No one knows what to make of him, least of all the Czech girl, but we join him in a drink. He drinks straight Scotch, very large slugs poured by the bartender, who seems to know his wants.

Political matters are the inevitable topic, and Jim tells the drunken colonel about his reverse glasses.

"That's very good," the D.C. says, "and very close to the truth.

Because everything is geared, you see, to the woman in the babushka. You know the babushka, the head scarf our Russian peasant women wear. . . . In Russia, those women are the economic common denominator. They look just as they did in 1917, perhaps a bit dowdier. They mean we have not progressed at all in fifty years. They also mean that we cannot allow any of the countries in our empire to advance beyond the level of the common Russian denominator — the woman in the babushka. Never forget the woman in the babushka, my friends, because she is the ruler. No one can get ahead of us . . . no one can be allowed to get ahead of us, because that would make us look bad. If she looks bad, we look bad. So, naturally, when we inspect conditions in Czechoslovakia or Hungary or Poland we have to keep that in mind, and we judge what we see exactly as you do with your reverse glasses."

"Is there anything you won't agree with?" Jim asks him.

"We are in deep trouble in Russia," the D.C. says. "You should be more sympathetic. This occupation of Czechoslovakia is a giveaway of the condition we have. Even we begin to suspect now that we are not socialists, that we are not even state capitalists, that we have returned to czarist bureaucratic administration. It is all very artificial, and if it is not changed we may go bankrupt soon and drag down our empire with us. Can't you shed a tear? Some of my best friends are seeing that the czarist mentality is apparent in all our foreign relations now. In fifty years, we have failed to find the change in human nature that Marx thought would come in a socialist state. The ladies in the babushkas are still there, still threatening us — doesn't the idea of men unable to sleep in the Kremlin because of the pictures dancing through their heads of those women coming after them touch your heart? . . . We have given up and returned to the czarist, pre-1917 conditions. Now we only play to increase Russian territory and control, and we are bankrupt ideologically today, and perhaps economically tomorrow. We no longer have an idea of any kind — we are only a power. And we shall try to keep our empire together as the other countries with empires did.

We are the last of the great colonial powers — no more than that, now — slowly sinking into the setting suns. It is very sad: you should weep for us."

"And then what will happen?" the Czech girl asks. "After you collapse, then what?"

"As fast as we are falling apart, the rest of the world is falling apart even faster," the D.C. says. "Our position is very bad absolutely, but very strong relatively."

"I'm interested in the extent of Americanization in eastern Europe," Jim says, appropriating my identity in confused gallantry. "Sort of a hobby of mine. Any comments there?"

The D.C. goes off into a long, rambling discourse, the point of which seems to be that Russia is quite Americanized in a negative way. Says they long ago accepted the American idea that production and consumption are the point of life on the national as well as the individual level. "Don't forget that we learned how to build dams from you," he says "We went farther. We learned from you what they were for." He laughs at his own joke. "Electric light in the country, electric light to tie the babushka on with . . . Aswan . . . we would never have been able to perform those miracles without you. Of course we're Americanized." He concedes that Russia is still bound to carry out the production-consumption idea by theoretically anticapitalist methods, but that is of no more significance than that America is still theoretically bound to function capitalistically. In actual fact, the factories hum and the workers buy the products and fall into bed in both countries "with equally dirty feet — no, whose feet could be as dirty as a Russian's?", and Russia is completely Americanized in that sense.

He claims that it makes no difference that Russia has achieved such actual (as distinguished from theoretical) Americanism as it has without using American capital and American supervisors. "We have the independence the west Europeans say they want, but what difference does it make?" Resistance to Americanism in Russia may continue on several levels — most importantly, the inertial incompetence — but the idea itself is triumphant.

In comparing western and eastern Europe in terms of resistance to America, there can be "confusion for the smaller minds" because eastern Europe is organized to keep American capital and control out physically and western Europe isn't. But despite the barriers, eastern resistance is largely mythical because physical exclusion is not what matters. What matters is — more to the point, what mattered was — whether Russia and the rest of eastern Europe could find in Communism an alternative idea to the American produce-and-consume. They could not, and so had to adopt the American answer.

The current goal of the Communist bloc ("As you know, we are very fond of goals: we would rather have a goal than reach one") is to become more proficient at produce-and-consume than America. But even if this could be done "— and it is the thinnest of fat chances . . . we can only imagine how the sainted Lenin would have winced in the mouth at the bankruptcy of the imitation — it would not be real resistance, but merely the extension of America through the American idea." He jabs at the air with a long, fine-boned forefinger. "I ask you yet again, my friends, what difference does it make? What difference does it make to these people — and to my people — where it comes from? The reality is whether America-as-idea, as you yourselves call yourselves so modestly, has taken over. And to what degree. Not whether America-as-idea comes from Russia, or America, or Germany . . . or even from Albania."

He wheezes with laughter at the last idea. He appears drunker now, but his speech remains clear. He seems to be speaking because he must; I have the impression that an intolerable pressure is finally too strong. He must speak, and he doesn't care to whom.

"You're not a Russian," Jim says to him now. "You're putting us on. You're a German."

The Czech girl agrees: he can't be a Russian.

The D.C. only smiles, revealing all his stains and gold. We leave him at the bar, still drinking, still smiling.

Upstairs, I shower and nap for an hour. Jim comes in while I'm dressing and we have a drink together.

"The drunken colonel can't be a Russian," Jim says. "Milo doesn't think he's a Russian."

"He's an odd one, all right. Who is Milo?"

"My little figure skater. Funny name, isn't it — but very Czech, she says. She thinks I should report the D.C. to what she touchingly calls 'your government.' 'For what?' I asked her. He hasn't done anything."

"No, he hasn't."

"I think he's CIA, anyhow. Just sounding us out."

"There's an idea."

"Report him and you only make a fool of yourself. Besides, isn't he grist for your mill?"

"Anything seems to be."

We dine at U Mecenáše, an elegant little restaurant in the Malá Strana, fitted out like a sitting room in one of the nearby palaces in the old days. The place is filled with what we take to be Germans, but Milo, who is still with us, says no.

"They are all Russians. Listen to the way they speak German — the accents. It is barely intelligible. They are under orders not to speak Russian here in Prague so we won't know how many there are in the city. But we know."

"If you don't know *some* German, what do you do?" Jim asks her. "Sit in the barracks?"

"I suppose so," she says, not particularly interested in the small questions.

Milo has studied in the United States and was rather disappointed. "The students there seemed so immature," she says. "Here we are not trying to destroy the establishment. We are one with our establishment, which is fighting with us to try to be independent. We are Communists, so we don't want capitalism. We just want to make our country work. We don't want to destroy everything, the way the leftist students do in America. I had nothing in common with them. I thought I would, and they thought they would have a bond with me, but there was nothing."

We have caviar, moussaka and Hungarian wine, all quite passable. The thinly disguised Russians around us spend a lot of time over their menus and there is much discussion of the tableware, furniture and *décor*. When their food arrives, they eat slowly and seriously, holding their knives and forks in familiarly awkward American lower-class positions.

"Who says they're not Americanized?" Jim asks. "They're all fertilizer salesmen from Oklahoma and this is Le Pavillon. No, I'm wrong. Our modern American fertilizer salesmen are more knowing. These are fertilizer salesmen from fifty years ago — 1920 Babbitts. But that's still in the national tradition."

The drunken colonel enters in grand style with an extremely good-looking woman, and winks at us as he sits. He orders in his very good English, and the fertilizer Russians gape at him shamelessly.

"Czechoslovakia is wonderful," Jim says to Milo, "but why not *really* resist?"

"They would kill us all," she says.

"I don't think so," he says. "But what if they did? What difference would that make?"

"Then we wouldn't have a country," she says.

"You don't understand," Jim says. He turns to me. "If they were Americans, they'd do something. Can you imagine a bunch of Texans in this situation? Why didn't that Dubček shoot himself when he got the news? Why should the students kill themselves if the leaders don't? Why do the leaders go along with it? What if they all shot themselves? What if they all took a member of the Russian Politbureau with one shot and themselves with the second? Don't tell me it wouldn't give the Russians fits."

"It would not be practical," Milo says primly.

"It might be more practical than you think," Jim says. "And that crazy wall between you and west Europe. Why not get rid of it?"

"How can we get rid of it?" she asks. "It is defended by our own soldiers as well as with Russian troops."

"If twelve million people decided to get rid of it, they could do it in a single night," Jim says. "If you don't like it here, you could all tear it down and get out. Even before that, you could down tools and refuse to work. You could, if you wanted, wreck the Russian game completely. But you're too nice, you won't do anything that extreme."

"It is not practical to destroy," Milo says. "We are trying to build, not destroy."

"That's a sucker's game," Jim says. "Don't you see? They're playing on your belief in order, the fact that you won't go all the way, that you'll always be European in the way you think and act."

"You are not practical," Milo says.

"I'm more practical than you realize," Jim says. "I'm nothing *but* practical. That's what American means. If you aren't getting what you want, don't play the game until you do. Tear everything down if you have to, because it's easier to build it back than you realize. But don't go on living on terms you don't like."

Milo remains sturdily unconvinced. When she leaves us momentarily after dinner, Jim grunts sardonically. "If Americanization is your specialty, how can you call these people at all Americanized with the attitude they have? Aren't they Europeans first, last and always?"

"You've put your finger on the heart of the matter. But she's rather admirable in her way, too."

"So stupid, though."

"Pretty girls often are."

"So are the ugly ones, I've found. . . . She is attractive, though, isn't she. You know, when I was walking around this afternoon, I didn't see a single pretty girl, and I was thinking that it was because they have no upper class here. You need leisure for looks.

[392]

. . . And then I saw her in a bookstore and she started talking to me, asking me if she could be of any help to the lost foreigner, and I was wondering why she was an exception — pretty — and it fell into place when she told me she was a figure skater. They treat their athletes so well that a sort of leisure class develops there."

"I didn't know upper-class Czech figure skaters allowed themselves to be picked up so easily."

"Our bond is sport. When I explained my interest in skiing and sailing, and told her I was here on a hunting trip, she saw that we had a great deal in common. I also overcame my natural shyness and told her I was so besieged with local tarts that I'd appreciate the company of a decent girl to ward them off. She was only too anxious to uphold the national reputation for assisting foreigners. . . . What the hell, she's a nice kid. I only wish she was a little smarter for herself."

We leave, exchanging nods with the drunken colonel, and go to the Bibita, a slow and nearly empty cabaret. The band plays old American songs. When they play "In September" Jim smiles at Milo and says, "We could be at the Del Monte Hotel in Monterey in 1939."

"Was it very nice?" she asks.

"It was a period," Jim says. "It didn't seem so much then, but it seems very nice when you look back from now."

He and I sit in forty-five-year-old serenity, and Milo, equally serene, drifts with us.

"They do have something to offer here," Jim says. "The going back to the former time. I've never had such a sensation. I was thinking of how we used to drive down from San Francisco to the Pebble Beach house before the war, and how clean it smelled on the Monterey Peninsula, and then those actual smells came to me. I was smelling the hot pines and the water and I was there, sixteen years old and helping the butler take the tennis rackets out of the trunk. . . . Doesn't the literary set call that the Proustian experience?"

[393]

"Whatever it's called, it's supposed to be rare, but here it's an orgy."

"That's because it *is* 1939 here. All the time. Nothing has moved since. The rest of the world has, but it hasn't here, so when you're here it's 1939 in San Francisco, too — and everywhere else."

"You may be right."

"I might become an addict. Stay in Prague for the rest of my life and relive my glorious youth."

Even the stripper — a very serious girl who looks like a violin student — contributes to the mood. She enters with candles and veils and is supposed to be bringing Saharan sensuality. But the seriousness, the determination to take her clothes off if that will help the state earn foreign currencies, turns the performance into something else.

From the Bibita we go to the Lucerne, a large, crowded night-club filled with Czechs as well as foreigners. A band with electronic amplification thunders out, and the air is thick with smoke. The drunken colonel and his lady are there and he beckons us to his table. We accept, and the D.C. orders more champagne. He is a bit more rumpled and runs his hands through his hair with impatience, but seems no drunker than at the cocktail hour.

"How did you like your dinner?" he asks over the din.

"Very good," we say.

"So many Russians," he says. "Too many for me."

"Nice, quiet fellows, though," Jim says. "Seemed to be grateful for everything."

"The manner is annoying if you are used to it," the D.C. says. "I've been to too many frank and comradely meetings and dinners. They have such a shopgirl idea of correct social behavior. Modern Russians playing at being civilized are as funny as chimps dressed for a tea party in a zoo. Grotesque. But you wouldn't know."

"Don't be too sure," Jim says. "Come down to Houston the next time you're in the States and I'll have the gang over for a cookout and you can make your own comparisons. Or better yet, come to New York and we'll all go to Lincoln Center."

The D.C. does not introduce his lady and she sits with her impeccable face turned resolutely toward the stage. The band has left and a floorshow is going on. A man balances himself on his fingertips atop a stand. Then on one finger, to wild applause.

Jim tells the D.C. about using westernized entertainment in socialist capitals to go back in American time. The D.C. is properly impressed with this decadence.

"The older I get myself," he says vaguely, "the more I feel like someone from a former time. Probably an aristocrat from the nineteenth century, in what we then called so innocently 'the troubled time of Mother Russia.' Turgenev, Chekhov, even Dostoevski . . . they didn't know what troubles were. I can see myself in green carpet slippers and a fez, pottering around a country estate and being too kind to my serfs. . . ."

Milo screws up her courage and asks him his name. He waves his hand negligently. "I have so many names — I couldn't tell you. I have a name for this, a name for that. The drunken colonel is as good as any."

The Saharan stripper from the Bibita appears on the stage and does her number again.

"Now if I were an author, that's what I'd call a significant detail," Jim says to me. "One stripper for the whole city."

I am later to learn that the Bibita and the Lucerne are under the same management and use each other's acts. Still, it *is* significant. The Saharan departs and another stripper, also a Czech, comes on. This one, more professional, is supposed to be an Indian, and temple bells, purportedly Hindu, clang on a tape. She is also very young and very serious, another violin student building socialism.

At the table before us, a group of male Czech students make a point of paying no attention to this stripping. It is necessary for foreigners and decadent Czechs, they say in their stiffness, but not for true socialists. They have a political bond with the strippers, quite the opposite of the usual relationship.

". . . tougher," Jim is saying to the D.C. "Why, that Wenceslas Square is full of hippies. This city has more hippies than San Francisco. If I were a Russian and I had the tanks, I'd get rid of them. I thought you were supposed to be so tough. How come you let them run around?"

"We're softhearted," the D.C. says. "But with a reason."

"Sheep as a lamb," Jim says. "If you're going to have a reputation for brutality, you might as well be brutal. Everyone thinks you have the lid on here, but the place is full of hippies."

The D.C. shrugs his shoulders. "We're really not very efficient," he says.

"This is a sloppy occupation," Jim says.

"You have no idea," the D.C. says.

The star of the show comes on, a short plump women of fifty who sings. She is professional, and can belt in the Merman-Piaf style. She prances from one end of the stage to the other, pounding out songs in several languages. She is a great favorite with the Prague crowd, and the applause is lavish. The students who wouldn't look at the strippers are overcome with enthusiasm now. This is what they came for, and they have had to wait a long time. There is an undercurrent of excitement as she launches into her final number: from the tenseness of the students, one senses that something is going to happen.

The song is "Those Were the Days," sung in English. She is not through the opening bar before the crowd realizes the political meaning she is giving the lyrics; and as they respond, she responds back with ironic smiles and stresses to certain words. There is genuine frenzy in the air — three-quarters of the crowd is standing, singing with her. "Those were the days, my friends," she chants, and they chant with her, powerfully and without sentimentality. "We thought they'd never end . . . We'd fight and never lose . . ." We are all standing now, even the D.C. and his lady. If there are Russians in the hall, they are not going to draw attention by remaining seated. Milo turns a radiant face to Jim — this is what she meant by resistance — and he nods to her. His own eyes are filmed with tears, whether for the lost tea dances of his youth in Burlingame and San Mateo or for the Czechs. "We are older but no wiser. In our hearts the dreams are still the same . . ." The emotion crests, and the big, packed two-story room sways to the final stanza. "Those were the days!" they cry out, and the singer leads them to the climax.

She bows and is gone. There is an afterbuzz of conversation as everyone sits down, spent.

"Do you see what I mean?" Milo asks Jim. "We are united."

"That was something," Jim says. "You hear about it, but you can't believe it until you see it."

"Very moving," the D.C. says.

At two in the morning, the D.C. and I are in his suite at the Alcron having a nightcap. Jim and Milo have gone on, and the D.C.'s lady has retired.

"I am always delighted to meet a writer," the D.C. says. "Especially a writer on Americanization. Do send me a copy of what you write — I look forward to reading it."

"I'll do better than that — I'll put you in it, if you don't mind."

"I don't mind at all. Why should I mind?"

"I wouldn't know that in detail. But I was under the impression that a Russian colonel, drunk or not, might very much mind being quoted if he said things as unorthodox as the things you say. Wouldn't your superiors care?"

"Russian colonel? What's this about a Russian colonel?"

"You said you were Russian and in intelligence. We assumed you couldn't be less than a colonel in rank."

"A Russian colonel of intelligence," he says meditatively. "Well, so I am, so I am . . . I do a lot of talking, don't I? Why don't you do some talking? You're the expert on Americanization, aren't you? Why don't you tell me all about it?"

"I don't know that much about it in east Europe. I was hoping you'd tell me."

"That's not fair — I think you're tricky — but I'll talk anyhow. I have the talking vice." He has put away an immense amount, but if anything he seems soberer that when we first met him. "No, I won't talk. I mean I won't talk until you tell me something. Make a tithe, that's not asking too much."

"All right. Henry Adams said over sixty years ago that America would be stopped in Asia by the Chinese-Russian inertia and would have to turn to Europe. He also predicted that east Europe and European Russia would, in time, have to become part of the western system. It seems to me that those two prophecies are sound, and that they are the completed generalities on the Americanization of eastern Europe. Russia can choose not to become part of the western system, but only at terrible cost now, at such a price that I don't think it would invalidate Adams's prediction, which was based on the assumption that rational self-interest would finally prevail. I think that Adams's remarks are the kernel of the Americanization process in east Europe. Everything else that has been said and seen — including one's own observations — is window dressing."

"Not badly put," the D.C. says. "Good enough, but of course we know Adams. We study him. It would surprise you to know how much we study. . . . There is nothing in the world now but Americanization — we know that. Eastern Europe is completely Americanized. Not on the surface, but underneath. Even on the surface, we have young people in Poland, Hungary, Czechoslovakia, as silly as anything you have. The western magnet continues to draw, and it will not stop. Nowhere, not even in Russia. Look at Sakharov's simpleminded essay on co-existence. Officially, we wince at the blatant Americanism there. I wish I could say that we wince incorrectly, that Sakharov is a terribly nice and interesting man, but the sad truth that he is neither. All writers are peculiar, though, and only to be trusted when they are humble. That is a theory of mine. I hope it does not bore you. All our great Russian writers had humility, especially Turgenev and Dostoevski. Tolstoi yes and no. All the great European and American writers, too. Dickens, Twain, James — yes, James, I am very fond there — it is always the characteristic. But now who do we adore in east Europe? Who is the most popular writer? Hemingway . . . all arrogance . . . sanctified destructiveness and so sanctified Americanism.

"Despite appearances, you resist us nationally and economically, but not ideologically. We resist you ideologically, but not nationally and economically, not with our hearts. You have the best of the bargain, as any fool can see. Your fat old women with thousands of shares of General Motors think of those shares when they think of Russia. To them, Communism is not an idea but a Russian soldier blowing the door off the safe and pulling out those shares and using them to wipe his behind after he has eaten all the steaks in the deep freeze and then burning them to keep warm after he has broken the central heating. They don't care about the *idea* of Communism at all, and they are right. They know it isn't an idea that threatens those shares, but the drunken hordes off the steppes. Ideas don't mean anything any more, and we are wasting time to be afraid of you as an idea when you are appealing to our people in their entrails." He taps his own abdomen firmly. "That's where the fight is, not here," and he points to his head.

". . . So they say eastern Europe is darkening now under our esteemed leadership, with its increasing return to Stalinism. For example, these Czechs want to make loans from the west, to become independent. But we can't let them do that. We have to reduce them to our level and hold them there. Whether their economy sags down or not, that is what we have to do. No matter how fascinated they become with America in east Europe, we have to stop it. But we can't stop it, so we lose."

He looks at me intently, swirling the brandy in his snifter. His color is not good, and his eyes bulge ominously, the whites dirty and yellowed. But his tongue is still nimble enough and his words only faintly slurred.

"You do?" I say.

"Don't we? Don't we *have* to lose because we are the last gasp of Europe? Formal socialism is a European idea, if you remember your history, and its last idea. The Communist-capitalist, east Europe-west Europe struggle is part of the 'European' story — the last act. In the finale, we are stealing everything we can, but that is only in the best tradition. We do that because we don't have the answer, we can't win the minds of the people, our own included, the way you can, east or west. So we're going to lose. We can't raise up the woman in the babushka. We've had fifty years and we can't move her. She has moved us — we have had to bring everything down to her level — but we can't move her. *You* could move her — you even move her a little already — but we can't. So we lose."

He pauses again, and I don't say anything. "Isn't that right?" he asks.

"If you say so."

"How can it be otherwise? Russian socialism is European confusion and inefficiency pushed to the final end. Everything to the level of the woman in the babushka. Barbarian. And wherever we go, into all the other countries of our empire, we have to take her as the yardstick. We are really the triumph of the old Europe, the peasant Europe, with nothing of the future about us at all. The victory of the greatest inefficiency! But at the exact moment of triumph we are faced with defeat from another quarter. We can conquer Europe, but Europe is already conquered by America, by Americanism, by efficient materialism. If only America didn't exist! We could keep Europe European forever. But now . . . we are only transitional. We must lose, yes?"

"You seem awfully anxious to have me agree with you."

"Yes, because I have a surprise for you. Just for the fun of it, agree with me that we lose. Say yes."

"You lose."

"Aha! Aha! But we don't lose!"

He crosses the sitting room with decision, and pulls a large, leather-bound book or notebook from a briefcase, and returns to wave it under my nose.

"What do you see?" he asks.

"I'm terrible at games."

"Answer me that question and I am done asking."

"A book."

"A book of sorts," he agrees. "But there is no title stamped on the outside. And for a very good reason, because this is . . ." He pauses dramatically. "What do you think?"

"You said no more questions."

"Yes, of course. I forgot. . . . This, my friend, is *The Pushkin Report.*" He weighs it in his hand. "Nothing to do with Pushkin at all, of course. Merely a code name for what it really is, and I think you'll agree when you understand. Very sardonic, you will see. *The Pushkin Report,* I will have you know, is a report on the United States of America, prepared by a team of Russian experts, including your humble servant. It is the result of five years of intensive work, a very new kind of work, because I can assure you that it was not done in the usual way, and is not at all like the usual Russian report. We absolutely did not work in the old style, starting from preconceptions and trying to work the facts into them, what I call putting the raisins in the pudding. We started with our eyes open, working from elaborate field reports, from all American publication sources, and, most of all . . . from our own common sense. For once.

"Our conclusions are interesting. We are quite sure now that you are very close to your end. I don't need to apologize because I know you understand this is not at all personal. As bad off as we are, you are worse, so there will not be, finally, an Americanization problem. There won't be one in eastern Europe; there won't even be one in western Europe. You will be gone down, finished before then, before the Americanization is so fastened on that it can't slip off. As you collapse, your image and tentacles will fade and drop off, and we shall take charge in our inimitably slowfooted but irreversible manner. So I repeat, there is no *true* Americanization problem in Europe."

"That *is* very interesting."

"You do not believe me. Very well." He adjusts gold-rimmed, rather incongruous pince-nez, opens *The Pushkin Report,* and reads with slightly mock portentousness: " 'America, like all societies, capitalist as well as socialist, is merely a proposition in control. It does not matter if those who are controlled are willing or unwilling. . . . Those who are controlled work, and those who control supervise them. The economic aspects — the organization of production, the presence or non-presence of huge profits — are of great interest and importance to professional socialists, but of none to social analysts. To the social analyst, human history is the story of succeeding controls. We may begin with the Egyptians and see that it was an old story at the time of the pyramids. Old *then,* and no different now. The trappings have changed, but nothing else. Now there are better wages and more willingness, based on the illusion that anyone (and thus everyone) can get from the slave to the master status . . . But no real change . . .'

" 'The American problem, then, is no different from that of any other historical society. From the standpoint of those who control, the slaves must be kept working and given enough diversion to keep them working as happily as possible. American controllers carried out their historical task adequately enough until after World War II, when they began to permit excesses. Now the diversion has gotten out of hand, has approached chaos, and the workers will not be able to withstand the external pressures much longer. . . . To go to the root, the lack of control means that there is serious trouble among the controllers themselves. They have suffered a disastrous loss of will, and are allowing events to dominate them completely. Even the Negroes sense this when they say that white men will now put up with anything from them, the Negroes. The American controllers have lost the desire to control and the faith in their ability to control. The chaos follows *from* that psychological state: it does not precede it, nor does it have a parallel life. The young, the Jews, the Negroes — all dissident minorities get out of control *after* there has been psychological collapse at the top, among the controllers. The dissidents have no independent life as such: they are only symptoms, never first causes. They only reflect a state of collapse on the part of the controllers: they have no other existence or role. When and if control is re-established, incidentally, they are the first to recognize it, and to resume their natural functions. . . . Their only meaningful existence now is as visible evidence of a suicide wish on the part of those who have let them loose, not only the leading controllers, but all those down to the beginnings of the symptomatic dissenters. We may thus be confident, in view of the rapidly increasing dissenters, that there is a profound death wish on the part of American society, from the top to the near bottom.' "

He looks up over the reading glasses with anticipation. "Mainly my hand there — you can't imagine what a struggle. How do you like it?"

"Very interesting. Are you translating as you read, or is it in English?"

"It is in English. We have it now in all languages."

"But what are you going to do with it? Make it public?"

"Of course not."

"Then why are you letting me in on it?"

"You are a professional writer, an analyst of the Americanization process in Europe. I am enlightening you."

"What if I print what you've told me?"

"It will not be entirely credited, perhaps. But if it is, what can that matter? It will only accelerate the process already in effect. Either way, it makes no difference to me or to us."

"Then you don't mind if I use it?"

"Do whatever you please."

We continue for another two hours, and it is nearly five when I totter down to my room, my head filled with what I have been offered of *The Pushkin Report*. The D.C. reads from it, adds asides and details, and often thrusts it into my hands so that I can see for myself, always reminding me that if *The Report* is correct — "And how can it be wrong?" — there can be no Americanization problem.

From the premise that "American controllers" have lost the appetite and the will for control, it proceeds to lengthy analyses of "the continuing breakdown." Below I have combined the D.C.'s readings, my own, and his comments into an informal summary which offers an interesting, if specialized, view of Americanization:

We can see that Rome, among the older societies, also lost its faith in its ability to control and in the appetite for control, and gave in to the stronger appetites of the controlled, those appetites increasing in direct proportion to the loss of control. With their greed for diversions unchecked, the controlled got completely out of control. This is not an exact parallel for America, but comparable in many ways.

Authority is the only answer for any human problem. There was formerly authority (control) in the United States — what is now denigrated as WASP control. It ran from coast to coast and interlocked. It was, of course, a conspiracy, because all authority is a conspiracy on the part of the controllers. "When the controllers are strong, they don't mind being conspirators," the D.C. says. "They are not frightened by words like that. But as they grow weaker, someone says 'conspiracy' and they lose their nerve. They become concerned with questions of abstract morality, forgetting that all control is crime if you want to look at it that way, or the highest service if you want to look at it another way, a truer way. . . . At the present time, for example, the American Zionist Jews, who are certainly a cabal and thus a conspiracy, are the only controllers in America. They represent the only *order*. Very little, but there is no other."

Sensing the loss of faith and loss of appetite on the part of the controllers, the three most potent minority groups — the young, the Jews and the Negroes — reacted predictably. We see the three of them as the same in this reference. They do not revolt, technically speaking, but react to loss of direction from above. It is the entrance into the abhorred vacuum. . . . Nor are they technically important. When a physician sees the signs of leprosy, he does not say, "I see a case of thickening skin, of leonine features," and so forth. He says, "I see a case of leprosy." In this case, we do not say that we see Jews, Negroes and young Americans taking over the United States. We say that we see the controllers of the United States giving up.

"If we have done anything original," the D.C. says, "it is on that point. We don't think the young, the Jews and the Negroes mean anything in and of themselves, as other analysts do. We always see their enlarged presence as symptom, never as cause. We look for the meaning behind their presence, we never waste time looking at them. When we have to consider them in various contexts — economic, social and political — we do, and very exhaustively, as you shall see. But we don't lose sight of the first cause, we never put them first. This is, I think, our largest step."

We have had not a little to do with the present condition of the United States. By preventing the outbreak of war, we have driven the controllers to face themselves. War would have been a screen behind which they could have kept control even with loss of faith and appetite, because war provides a darkness in which many things can be done secretly and hence cheaply. But the lack of war put all events in the United States into a sharp white light. Now those who controlled could not control without being seen. They had to take the penalties as well as the rewards. In this choice, they showed the great lesions to inner strength that had taken place. They could not, for example, control the Negroes without losing the support of so-called world opinion. Very well, they did not have the courage to be socially unacceptable, so they gave in to the Negroes. They would have given in anyhow, of course, but the lack of war made it happen very much more swiftly. In the new white light, they could no longer be called a "democracy" if they controlled in the necessary way. Faced with a choice, they settled for the fiction, like a man who would abandon his family rather than be seen in the wrong sort of suit.

Once the controllers realized their lack of courage they were frightened. Once they were frightened, they made greater and greater concessions to the groups which closed in on them like hyenas, sensing the fear. That fear has now grown to the point where they are all running, very frightened and only trying to protect what they have. There is no dignity and no future. "The things we know about what they do in Switzerland and South America," says the D.C., grinning widely. "Talk about rats and the sinking ship!"

The decline of the controllers has psychological roots which are not the concern of *The Report* except in certain relations. One such strand is the subconscious conviction that the weak are to be given full license because they are weak, a very special American idea. The scenario begins with permissiveness to the young, who are weak because they are children. Then the next "children," even weaker, are the Jews, to be pitied because of what they have suffered at the hands of all non-Jews from Hitler down. Their chronic complaining must indicate great weakness, the American reasons, without knowing he so reasons, and so he responds in parental degree to the constant, neurasthenic dramatization of these children's troubles. Then the Negroes, surely the weakest "children" of the entire family, because there is not social or intellectual parity. The retarded must be the ultimate pets. . . .

As we know from individual as well as national experience, once the strong bow to the weak, the weak become more tyrannical toward the strong than the strong ever were to them. By definition, one side of weakness *is* a lust for tyranny over others. (There is a great distinction between control and tyranny.) Thus the privileged, indulged weak strike back against the former strong. (There is never a transposition. The weak do not become strong, even in later generations.) We also know that this striking back masks a deep desire for the return of control, for the return of the strong, for the recognition of their weakness and the taking of appropriate steps. This fact is becoming widely disseminated in the case of the dissident young. It will soon be general knowledge in the cases of the Negroes and the Jews.

"It is almost a law of nature that the weak set up a noise when they sniff collapse at the top," the D.C. says. "They are frightened — and correctly so — at the dangers implicit in being left without leadership and protection. There is nothing improper about what they do. The villain is always the abdicating controller."

The indulgence and permissiveness shown each weak group leads to feedback with the others. Thus the Jews take the young one step beyond where they have already gone, and the Negroes take the young and the Jews yet another step. By the laws of the process, the weakest must triumph in the end, so succeeding weaknesses devour the former. "You can see this very clearly at your educational institutions," the D.C. says. "At Harvard, for example. First the petulant young; then the unhappy Jews; finally the 'militant' blacks. Each time a greater weakness absorbs a lesser, until now Harvard resembles a 'university' in the poorest part of Africa more than it does the Harvard of thirty years ago. The chaos is academic as well as social, despite denials."

The ascendancy of the least gifted Negroes over other Negroes is also part of the process, which ends with the transformation of all Americans into the lowest social Negro denomination. This will happen faster on the cultural level than with actual interbreeding, but the cultural transformation is no less disastrous for a technological power, perhaps more so. "It is a long slide toward the lowest common denominator," the D.C. says, "but we see no signs that you are capable of arresting it. Our woman in the babushka is the counterpart of your Negro, and we admit she has certain economic and social powers over us, but we have resisted her to the best of our ability. We are still controllers to the extent that we prevent her taking over *all* life."

Fear leads to increasing blindness. When a world power sinks to the condition of uncontrolled crime in the streets, it means the leaders — the controllers — are out of control. The streets mirror *their* condition. "It is ridiculous as well as serious," the D.C. says. "I have always claimed that if *we* can't see the humor in it we will make the mistake of taking it seriously. We must remember that these examples are all pants-wettings. A rapidly rising crime rate means wet trousers at the top. We cannot afford to forget that. Even in our own case, I am sorry to say."

There can be no protest of any kind on any level against the young-Jewish-Negro excesses, because to protest at all is to protest entirely. And to protest entirely is to promote civil war, because the "genii" can't be put back in the bottle without severe measures. Thus crime cannot be stopped on the streets of Washington because to stop crime the Negroes would have to be controlled, and to control the Negroes would lead to national chaos. "National, but temporary," the D.C. says. "The current trend is creating permanent chaos. However, it is easier for small men to permit foreign diplomats to be mugged than to have a civil war." The lack of protest is partially the result of the American certainty that everything unpleasant will go away if it is not discussed.

("To play the devil's advocate," the D.C. says, "I pretend that I am a rich American of the best family. I wish to keep what I have and I think that by making concessions to the young, the Jews and the Negroes I can do that, whereas if I take a firm hand I lose everything. That is the way those people think. I know. So I sell my business to a Jew, my daughter marries a Negro, my son becomes a hippie, and I sit on Park Avenue — or the Main Lines, in Philadelphia — still hugging what I have and thinking I am still what I was and have what I had. I will continue to think so, too, when everything has been taken. I will totter up to Harvard for reunion in my old coat, clutching what is left of my depreciated stock shares, knocked down by Negroes whenever I get in their way, and I will say, 'I am still the ruler.' People go very crazy when they get like your former controllers are now. You can read about them in Chekhov.")

Great reservoirs of material strength were built up in two hundred years. They are now being spent to avoid facing facts — i.e., moving out of the cities rather than remaining and cleaning them up. "Even in Russia," the D.C. says, "we have protests against the hooligan young, like Solzhenitsyn's *The Easter Procession.* But an American writer does not have such freedom. When he sees Negroes rioting like animals he cannot say the truth about it. One word might touch off the conflagration and wipe out his share — two cars and the little stock portfolio. All America is a conspiracy of silence — vaster than any we have ever had in Russia — with everyone leaning against everyone else, the most delicately balanced and dangerous house of cards."

The moment we wait for is when Americans discover that the unpleasant won't go away and that silence doesn't work. Then the realization that things have gone too far will make a hydrogen bomb of the spirit. The stock market, the consumer process, the fabric of daily life . . . all will go up in a moment. It is not Russia that will send over bombs. We don't need to. The bomb will come from inside. It is already activated and ticking. . . .

There is ineradicable hostility between the Negroes and the whites, and between the Jews (more accurately, the non-Arab Semites) and all non-Jewish and non-Negro Americans. (Although the Jews will finally turn on the Negroes, too, which the Negroes already realize.) The hatred of the Jews and Negroes for other Americans is the hatred of the destructive for the constructive. The Jews and Negroes are both ultra-destructive, and their aim, now almost as conscious as unconscious, is to bring the United States

[409]

down. In the words of Eldridge Cleaver, who has spoken of "my delight in violating what I conceived of as white men's laws, and my delight in defiling white women." The Jews are less obviously destructive than the Negroes, but they are a powerfully parasitic people who can only take from the host country. Jews do not create in the economy, but take control of what has already been created, by artificial manipulation of stocks, etc. It is significant that so many of the conglomerate companies are controlled by Jews. . . . The power of the Jews in the American economy is potentially so disastrous that it would suffice in itself to bring America down.

In their long history, the Jews have never had as much power in a host country as they have in the modern United States. They are power-mad, and by now controlling the strongest country in the world they control everything. It should be sufficient. But they are not real controllers, not able to use power constructively. If they were, they could re-establish true control over the United States. But they cannot do that, because they are parasitic and destructive. They cannot rest; they must go on, like Hitler.

Also, they all have the Israel virus. When a relatively uninfected Jew, like Henry Kissinger, comes into a high office, he is so badgered and harassed by important Zionist Jews that he becomes like them. The ultimate Jewish aim is not proper and constructive control in the United States, but the ruination of the United States by making the country serve Zionist interests, subordinating the United States to Israel. It is an extreme inversion of values, not really in the interest of American Jews. But the Jews are not a practical people, they prefer the sensational. Israel does not exist except in aggrandizement: a peaceful Israel is very dull, even to the Jews. It must fight, conquer, keep everyone in an uproar.

We think there is a very good chance it may end with the Jews forcing America into a Hitler-type adventure on behalf of Israel. They will force the United States to attack, and we shall defend.

"We have researched this very carefully," the D.C. says. "Because I lived many years in America, I am considered an expert in deduction from small contemporary signs. We find these every-where and anywhere, even in obvious places. . . . Did I tell you we call *Time Pravda?* We read your publications backwards, too, not for what they think they're saying, but for what they give away. . . . Everything is a barometer, of course — as in the fields of art, where the fact of tomorrow is put as a tentative contemporary as-sertion. For example, I point out that Norman Mailer, in *Armies of the Night,* in writing, 'Brood on that country who expresses our will. She is America, once a beauty of magnificence unparalleled, now a beauty with a leprous skin,' tests the non-Semites very strongly. For the leper to cry leprous there can be no motive except to see if there exists yet any will whatsoever to contradiction. He and those like him test for us, in fact — and more accurately than we could test for ourselves. When the symptom presents itself as analyst and is not questioned, we know where the hands of the clock are pointed, what you call the lateness of the hour, very well indeed."

I say: "I thought you said you never waste time looking at the 'symptoms.' "

"I said we never make the mistake of thinking the situation origi-nates with them: we don't confuse the symptoms with the cause, the breakdown at the top. However, I added that we consider the symptoms exhaustively in certain contexts when we have to. One such context is the theory of the controllers that the dissident young, the Jews and the Negroes can be made part of the American technological society and work constructively within it. Although we feel the controllers make such decisions from fear and wishful thinking, there is always the possibility, scientifically speaking, that they might be right. The theories of frightened men *tend* to be wrong, but to make sure we have to test the theory itself. We have to ask if the dissident young, the Jews and the Negroes can be con-structive, and to make an answer we have to think of them from all sides. Our conclusion is that they cannot. In the case of the dissi-dent young, not a great deal needs to be said because they are already much taken over and telescoped into . . . Jews and Negroes. I have shown you something of the material on the Jews. Lastly now, the Negroes, perhaps the most important group of the three, because if the weakest does have ultimate power, then the Negroes will make the final form of American life, even by indirection."

The Negroes, of course, are more obviously inferior and destructive than the Jews. There can be no Negro aim except to bring all non-Negro life to the Negro level, which means a level at which the American economy cannot function.

"When we say the Negroes are 'inferior and destructive,' we mean in the present context. The Negro can be somewhat constructive in a controlled society, but is invariably destructive in an uncontrolled society. The confusion is too much for him and leads to panic and violence. . . . The difference can be seen in time. I should explain, to give you an idea of our work, that we have graphs of the decline according to years. We can see, from a distillation of all available evidence, that thirty-five years ago — to pick a date — the American Negro was far less destructive than he is now. He was even constructive within his limits. This was based on his greater respect for whites and thus his greater self-respect. It is not degrading for a Negro to work for a responsible white, but it is when the white is irresponsible. . . . Then, as the Negro began to realize the accelerating white collapse, his destructiveness increased. The graph is steady, showing a constant decline. No one could claim, for example, that there is not a descent from Richard Wright and Langston Hughes to LeRoi Jones, or from Louis Armstrong to the modern Negro 'entertainers,' from relative self-reliance to total dependence. The laws of the process demand that the Negro level drop at the same speed as the white level. . . ."

Recent tests in the United States show the inferiority of the Negro for technological living. Even more important are the practical results. Where Negroes are not controlled in the educational system, for example, they drag it down to their level. The Negroes in Africa have a frightful history of barbaric cruelty toward each other. This course was arrested among those slaves taken to the western hemisphere. Now it is being re-activated. The Negro "level," the natural level to which the least civilized Negroes will go when unsupervised and to which they will take all other Negroes, is, first, one of destructive hostility to all non-Negro persons and institutions, and, second, the same hostility to all Negroes and Negro institutions as have been made permanent in a given time and place. The idea that Negroes can be integrated socially or economically into an uncontrolled environment is entirely wishful. The lack of control literally — and rather reasonably — drives him mad, and he tries to destroy that which is causing the pain, again rather reasonably. The more the impossible "integration" is attempted, the more driven the Negro will be to destroy that to which he is given access.

Thus the Negro cannot be a part of a technological economy in an uncontrolled society. It is beyond him. He cannot hold a job, maintain a home, etc., in chaos the way a white can. In a controlled society, he can make a contribution, however simple. Uncontrolled, he can do nothing. Entirely uncontrolled, he can only destroy. This is evident in the cities he has taken over — i.e., Newark, New Jersey — and the pattern is the same for the entire United States. "The Negro is a very expensive tax for you in your present condition," the D.C. says. "He cannot contribute; he must be carried. In any job except physical labor now, he will always have to have a white sustaining him, which means doubling production costs as well as demoralizing the whites."

In a controlled technological society, all citizens must act in terms of the society. Because the society is conceived and executed by whites, this means the Negroes must act in terms of a white society. When that society goes out of control, the Negroes are allowed to insist that the whites with whom they deal adopt their non-white, non-technological, essentially primitive social patterns. Thus more and more American whites, especially among the young, act and talk like Negroes. In a relatively short time, the

[413]

United States will become one vast Newark, the immense machinery of production and habitation in shreds, the whole population living like Negroes in an enormous shanty town.

If the Jews have never had such power, neither have the Negroes. "The idea of Negroes taking over a developed country is so fantastic that we could hardly credit our conclusions. At first, we ourselves were misled by the semantic confusion. 'Take over' implies visible appearance at the controls. But this taking over is not like that at all, quite the opposite, in fact, although no less complete than if in the classical form. . . . As is so often the case, we can learn from prophetical art, in this instance American literature. In *Benito Cereno*, the modern conditions are all anticipated. The captain of the ship must be weak before Babo, the Negro, can take over. And even after he has taken over, the fact is hidden from the world. . . . Now you have an inverse Mississippi, with the white men stepping off the sidewalks, and permitting a dual standard. The white can be insulted — be called 'honkie,' for example — without being able to retaliate with epithets of his own, just as the Negro could not retaliate before. . . . In the end, it will be either your Negroes or your entire society. You can't have both. The fact that your leaders can think so is a clue to how extreme they are."

Some Americans — primarily workers — dimly understand that the situation is out of control. They see the Negro and Jewish excesses, and find them distasteful. But they are not strong enough or well enough organized for real resistance. They fall into the trap of hating the Jews and Negroes, of not seeing that the situation did not originate with the symptoms, but with the national leaders who have so callously betrayed them and let the wolves loose on them. As capitalists, however small, they wish to hold on to what they have, and so they can always be talked out of genuine resistance, which would have to be prepared for insurrection.

("A number of conservative Jews begin to sniff the waterfalls," the D.C. says. "They see that there will be no pocketbook and no Israel if the present trends continue. In our research, we find a beginning criticism in some popular Jewish figures — Norman Mailer of the Negroes, Art Buchwald and Al Capp of the young — and we know this means that many conservative Jews are starting to worry in private. This bears out our theory that the Jews, although ultimately destructive, do not have the same short-term suicide wish as the non-Jewish Americans — all of whom remain very quiet — and so will increase their criticisms and become the only group trying to put the brakes on the process. They will be unsuccessful, but they will try in increasing degree.")

We feel that sensuality has a great deal to do with the present state. It is sensual to be in control, the sensuality of the full play of capability. But there is also a depraved sensuality whereby the declining controller actually enjoys the sensation of being taken over by his inferiors. It is a perversion, closely related to masochism. In that state, the controller actually wants to be humiliated by Negroes and Jews. He *wants* to see his daughters violated by Negroes and his sons talking like them. . . . The Chinese and the Koreans have found with American prisoners of war that there is a definite desire for total humiliation — America is not so innocent, even in the working classes. . . .

The sickness of the non-Jewish, non-Negro American leaders is the extent to which they have let this happen. The prominent statesmen who use Negro jargon such as 'cool it,' and permit their daughters to marry Negroes, cannot be realistic about social realities or the responsibilities of their jobs. Educated men who assure threatening Negroes that they will 'tell it like it is' are showing their fear. The debasement of language into the Negro form is an accurate gauge of the extent of the surrender to inferiors.

"It starts with men like Harriman and Rockefeller," the D.C. says. "They are born to control, and then lose faith. Harriman I have often observed on official business, and I know much about his background. He is the perfect example of the lost controller, starting with, in all innocence, the croquet playing with Swope and his nest of Zionists. Disenchanted with the crudity and brutality of the world into which he was born, he allowed himself to believe that the liberals, Jews and Negroes were 'better,' and so make the steps down one by one. Also, to forget that control is always a necessity. First there creeps in with such people the insidious idea that a world without control is desirable and possible. They actually believe that if they give up control it will disappear. They don't realize it will only pass to another group. It is a wishful thought coming from personal inadequacies. . . . And to think it all became manifest over croquet! . . . Roosevelt, Kennedy, the 'intellectual community,' all began from much the same personal inadequacy.

"To me, the most interesting detail is that it is so complete. In any European country, even in Russia, there is always a minority ready to protest a given policy. In America, the commitment at the top, in all fields, is interlocked and powerful, which naturally discourages the American who dissents, but that does not explain the perfection of the silence. The lack of American analysis and comment on the dominant trend — for the most American 'story' of the past twenty-five years is the collapse at the top — speaks many volumes about all Americans, and is very important to us in all estimates. A national conspiracy of silence on such a scale is a strength in one way, but also a great weakness when the time runs out. Then there is no preparation for bending: there must be breakage."

The decadent controller encourages everything, finally, that will destroy the state. In addition to Negroes and Jews and his dissident young, there is modern art, homosexuality . . . the list is a long one. The perversion takes delight in the debasement of the country, of the young, of the economy. In recapitulation: the young are encouraged in their insolence, which only means they are begging for control to be re-established. The plea falls on deaf ears. The indulgence given to Negroes and Jews started, after all, with indulgence to those very children, and then spread, on the premise that the most destructive "children" were the most desirable. Thus the Jews, and then the Negroes, became more desirable than their own children because they were more destructive. . . .

So the leadership has collapsed to the degree to which it has permitted the young, the Jews and the Negroes to take over, and the national life is being rapidly dragged to those inferior levels. It is a mistake to take the symptoms seriously. The sickness of the young, the Jews and the Negroes does not exist except as a subsidiary of the sickness of the leadership which has failed in its responsibility. Instead of controlling the above groups, as all controllers have had to do since the dawn of history, they let them loose. This has driven them to the present excesses. To have done such an irresponsible thing indicates that the controllers have a death wish.

If things are that bad, how does the United States continue to function? Delayed realization. It is already over, but the reality has not been faced. "It is the man walking around after the automobile accident and saying, 'I'm just fine.' Five minutes later he is dead. Our phrase is 'when the Negroes get to the stock market,' by which we mean that when the stock market investors in the United States suddenly realize the true domestic situation, there will be financial panic and collapse. A firm or rising stock market is based on the expectation of continuing or rising purchasing power. But the increasing chaos means that there will be less purchasers, not more. This means less markets for goods, lower production levels. When this becomes apparent, there will be stock market collapse."

The American adventure is collapsing because of leadership abdication many years ago. This primary cause, working through the Jewish adventures superimposed, and the Negro inefficiency underfoot, will bring the economy down, either in war or peace. This will trigger the general world collapse. Africa, South America and India, with the thinnest of civilized and technological veneers, won't last a year after the American demise. Then Europe will be strangled without the foreign markets. The house of cards will be in ruins.

The D.C. raises his hand majestically, grave and impressive, a latterday Jeremiah with a mighty message, drunk or sober: "When the United States collapses, the rest of the so-called free world will collapse with it. We shall be the only great power left intact. And we shall, then, be the natural controllers of the world, taking over the chaos and trying to straighten it out as best we can. As unworthy as we are, we shall be in charge. The Americanization will stop. There will be no Americanization. . . .

"If men cannot achieve heaven on earth, they would rather have hell than anything in between. And we *can* offer hell. That is the Russian message, if you please; that is the basic, binding fact of centuries of pan-Slavism, the great truth that Koba understood. You could always see it in his eyes, in everything he did. . . . Hell is equal to heaven; it has to be by the very nature of the division, perfectly equal on the other side. If you don't believe that, ask our famous Solzhenitsyn, our beloved Pasternak. They wouldn't want to live anywhere except in Russia, or write about anything else. All Russians have a touch of religion, and will always desire one extreme or the other. Also a touch of cruelty. If you think any Russian will lay flowers on your grave, you are very mistaken. They prefer to be triumphant, even the liberals. . . .

"So, in a strange way, Marx will come true after all. The lack of war will eventually drive the capitalists mad and sink them, if not through direct competition then by rot from within. And after that . . . us. I could say we wish we could bring heaven rather than hell, but that would not be true. It would not be in harmony with our destiny, our passion, what all our history leads to. Nor is hell a small offering — remember that it is as precious and marvelous as any other completely unique gift. . . . That is all, and it is really so very simple."

It is the end of the exposition and I am expected to offer a comment. "Simple, yes," I say, "but I don't think it's going to turn out as you think."

"You don't?"

"No."

[418]

"And where do you disagree with our analysis, with the findings of our little *Pushkin Report?*"

"Well, I rather hate to say it, but I think you're going to fall apart before we do."

"Impossible!"

"It's only one man's opinion."

"Wishful thinking."

"Perhaps."

"Bourgeois patriotism."

"I doubt that."

"But *The Report* . . ."

"*The Report* is impressive, but that doesn't mean it's right. I was taken, though, with your last claim — that you can provide hell where we can't provide heaven, putting you closer to the divine will."

"You like that? But it's merely a personal notion — not very scientific."

"It seemed exceptionally scientific to me."

"How kind of you to say so. Now, one last whisky and . . ."

"No, it's already far past my bedtime. I must go."

"If you insist."

As I leave, he is busy making notes on a pad, his bushy head bent over his work, a large brandy at hand. I think of the "years in America," the endless days of watching, thinking, the endless nights writing up the day's material. Such dedication, such service in such a cause . . .

———

The next morning I hire a guide-driver and take a tour of the city. We concentrate on the Prague Castle, a truly remarkable series of connected buildings. Inside the royal palace is the Vladislav Hall, a marvelously proportioned room nearly two hundred feet long, fifty wide and forty high. The style is Gothic, dating from

[419]

the late 1400s, a weightless Gothic with light streaming in the near floor-to-ceiling Renaissance windows overlooking the Vltava. The floor is wood — long, ancient planks with a deep, lambent finish — the kind of wood that makes one want to walk on it barefoot. It is a very beautiful room, one of the most evocative in Europe, but also curiously modern. Absolutely empty, it could be a barn in a celestial dream, the granary of unknown gods.

Below, the earlier royal suite, laid out as an archeological site, with signs and exhibits, has immense dignity and charm. Here, before the Hapsburgs came, the gifted and cultivated kings of Bohemia pursued their pleasures and left the legacy of a unique taste. Even the later, gilded rooms elsewhere in the castle — such as the Spanish Hall and the Gallery, in seventeenth-century Baroque — have unusual distinction and beauty. The whole is a finished monument to the Czech sense of proportion. No more need be said.

"The kings were all here once," the guide says to me enigmatically. "Now just the people."

They move about us in sad clumps — mostly peasants from the country come to see what now belongs to them and which they allow their high comrades in the government to use in part. They look at the empty rooms with equally empty faces. They have been told that this all belonged to the kings in the old days, which was inequitable. Now it is theirs, which is as it should be, but the message has left them unsatisfied. Perhaps there remains in the collective race memory a realization that when it was the king's it was everyone's, and now it is no one's. "You never really own anything until you give it away," Ernest Hemingway once said, and for these people the inverse is painfully true. They are learning that a castle without a king is useless.

And Kafka, the excluded resident who looked up at this castle and made something of it because he was excluded — could he have done anything with it now? One doubts it; the ease of access and lack of mystery leave nothing for the touchy imagination. He didn't like it then, but one wonders how much more he'd dislike it now.

Once this was the center of Prague the Golden, surely the most glamorous place in middle Europe. Now it is nothing, except as a clue to the past. But the past is stronger here than the present. It is the pathetic peasant-owners who are not real; the ghosts of Wenceslas, Charles and Vladislav are still terribly here, supported and extended by the sound and vision of the wonderful music and the exotic ladies of their courts. In the inner rooms, the dances never stop, and perhaps the peasants know that now, too.

My guide is intensely political, and amusing about the Russians, who are also around us in strength.

"All soldiers in civilian clothes," he says. They are serious yokels who line up dutifully in large groups to listen to endless lectures, staring solemnly at the object of interest.

My guide is even more interested in the material than the political, though, and tells me proudly how he manages to dress so smartly.

"Everything I wear is German," he says. "Whenever you see a decent coat or suit or pair of shoes here, it comes from outside. Friends bring them in, and there are other ways. We buy ourselves in Germany. And there is also Tuzex, a government store system for foreign currency. I show you."

He drives me to one — there are a dozen or more Tuzex stores in Prague — and shows me in with pride. Tuzex has Czech wares for tourists with foreign monies, at rates slightly below what the same articles cost in ordinary stores. But most of the goods are foreign-made — home appliances, special foods — and the main business is with Czechs. Relatives in the United States buy Tuzex coupons for dollars and send them to the old country, where they are redeemed for the foreign goods. The government's passion for foreign currency was originally confined to that which the tourists brought in, but the overseas market turned out to be so much bigger. The national currency must be very weak indeed if there is such a need for foreign money that it overbalances (with full Russian approval, presumably) the flooding of the country with American and German goods and admitting they are so much more desirable than the domestic production.

"My sister sent me enough coupons to buy a car," the guide tells me. "So now I have a German car. We Czechs have so many relatives in the States, and they are all generous, so half the country lives by Tuzex."

Half must be a wild exaggeration, but on any scale this is Americanization if the term has any meaning whatsoever. The idea of having to depend on a relative handful of hardworking Czechs and Slovaks in Pennsylvania and Illinois if you are going to live above the subsistence level in a people's democracy seems a definitively sardonic example of the economic side of the process, at any rate.

As we drive back to the Alcron, the driver points out the site of the new Hilton hotel with far more civic interest than he has shown for the monuments of the past. The Hiltons, surely part of the wedge, are allowed in for the same foreign currency reasons.

Back at the Alcron, Jim and the D.C. are having an aperitif before lunch. The D.C. seems calm and looks rested.

"We're having a frank and comradely martini," Jim says.

"Very frank," the D.C. says with a smile.

"Very comradely," Jim says. "I was telling the D.C. how we won the war. These Russians never understand how little they had to do with it. They don't realize that all their matériel came from America. Without what we sent, they wouldn't have lasted through 1943 against the Germans."

"I know that," the D.C. says, "but not everyone does."

"It's very comradely of you to say that," Jim says.

"And very frank," the D.C. says.

"The unbeatable combination," Jim says. "May I ask you a personal question?"

"Do."

"When the leaders of the Communist parties in the western countries come here and see what a mess it is — how can they go back and advocate the same thing in their own countries with straight faces?"

"They don't see what you do," the D.C. says. "They are still believers. Dedicated Communists see Communism as American liberals see American Negroes. Despite the present imperfections, everything will be all right because they wish it to be so. We don't have a monopoly on madness, you know, even if Communist cities do look exactly like Negro suburbs."

"Very frankly put, comrade," Jim says. "But how are you ever going to get Americanized with such goofy leaders? What I mean is — the infinitesimal amount of Americanization that you have is, all the same, *all* you have. You don't have anything else. You don't have any future except more Americanization. But how is that future going to be realized if the people who are in charge now stay in charge, when they're so over the hill?"

"Perhaps we could pension the present leadership off and leave the field free for the Americans. We could hire our leaders from American industry."

"I don't think that's so impractical," Jim says. "Isn't that what all your top men want anyhow? A dacha in the country, or whatever you call it, and two hundred grand a year? It might be the cheapest solution all the way around."

"The D.C. thinks America is going to crack up before Russia does." I say.

"It would be nice to think so," Jim says, "but I think your side is going to win that race."

"We don't."

"Well, that just shows you how wrong even smart Russians can be," Jim says. "But look, that's not what matters anyhow. You seem like a sensible man, so you know it's not the big things that matter. It's the little things. We don't care about the big questions, like whether the breakdown in Prague is the preview of the breakdown of everything in the Russian empire, or whether the breakdown in New York is the preview of the breakdown of everything in the American empire. We can't do anything about all that, so we forget it. We care about the little things — the comradely martini, the comradely duck shoot, the comradely girls in their comradely sleeping bags. Am I right?"

"No, you are altogether wrong," the D.C. says without hesitation. "I give you an example. If western Europe went Communist, we would insist that the Dutch, for instance, work for us, and that they be reduced to the level of the woman in the babushka. Holland, to put your reverse glasses back on, would have to become beautiful and organized instead of being as ugly and disorganized as it now is. But let's take those glasses off, and look at it as it would be after we had been there ten or fifteen years. A complete mess, and we would say it had to be that way because we could not afford to have a competitor to the woman in the babushka, and that would be true. But only partially true, because in addition to the economic and political considerations, there is the deeper fact that we *like* it that way, as certain animals like certain surroundings that are rather . . . different from green grass, shall we say? In that atmosphere, the . . . ah . . . strangeness of the 'big questions,' as you put it, becomes far more real and important than the little questions. They are a necessary complement to the transposition of values that has taken place. . . . We are not and never again could be interested in the pleasant little things of life. It has gone too far for that. If we lasted a thousand years, and ruled the world with complete authority, and had nothing to fear, we could still not enjoy the little things, nor could we ever permit them to be enjoyed by anyone else in the world, our own people included. We have crossed over. We cannot come back. . . . I hope I have explained it. Am I clear?"

"I guess you are," Jim says. "It's quite a message."

"Yes," says the D.C., "it is."

There is a constrained silence, which the D.C. considerately breaks by asking Jim about his hunting plans.

"Sam Reynolds and Bob Reilly have been telling me for years about this capercailzie shooting here," Jim says. "That's the big European grouse — season from March to May. They have everything arranged and the three of us are taking off for the back country as soon as they get here. Tomorrow, I think."

There is more desultory talk about hunting, and then Jim says, in answer to some query from the D.C., "That *is* my profession. You're a socialist and I'm a socialite. You talk and I hunt. And I probably work harder — at other things besides the hunting, too — than you do."

"I believe you," the D.C. says.

"I hope so," Jim says rather defensively. "A lot of people think socialites don't work, and so they don't have the right to opinions. Well, I *do* have just as much right as anyone else because I've put just as much in seeing the world and thinking about it as . . ."

Jim and I lunch in the Alcron dining room and bring each other up to date. I give him a brief description of *The Pushkin Report*, and he tells me he and Milo were even later.

"We saw every nightclub in Prague," he says. "Wondering if they all had the same stripper. It was like a dare. . . . No, the Sahara one wasn't everywhere, but they all looked like her sister. And the same smart crowd in each place. Germans, and Russian Germans. Talk about a small world. . . . I had no idea until we got back here, and found one of the downstairs tarts in my room. 'I'm Elena,' she said, sitting there in the chill dawn. 'I've been waiting.' I told her there'd been a mistake, I hadn't ordered her. We had a time getting her out. They're so serious, like Southern mill girls on their first crack at it. And so hardheaded. Someone had told her she was to go to my room, and she couldn't get it canceled in her mind. It wasn't you, was it?"

"No."

"Might have been the D.C."

"More likely a simple mistake."

"Yes, they make so many. But I kind of like Prague. There's something about the place. On the other hand — I won't mind getting out in the field for a few days. I guess you'll have plenty to do here."

"Enough people and places to keep me very busy."

"And when I get back, we'll drive to Budapest."

"Right."

"I'll probably be leaving tomorrow, so let's have a quiet dinner tonight. Just you and me and Milo."

"You and Milo have a quiet dinner — I'm having one with Karel Bendl and his wife."

"We could join forces."

"No, I'm going to their place."

"Well, have a drink with us about six."

"All right."

"Without the D.C.?"

"All right."

"I like him, but he stirs things up so."

The food at the Alcron is good, and the waiters are excellent. They hover over us seriously as we eat and one wonders why they are so dedicated. There is not the future in the field there once was, but also, as Jim puts it, "You don't have the feeling a lot of fat shareholders are getting fatter off them, and they probably feel the relief, too."

After lunch, my lack of sleep — I had less than two hours — begins to tell, and I nap through most of what is left of the afternoon. At six, Jim and Milo and I have the arranged drink. She is a bit stunned at what the last few days have brought. Not only Jim, but everything he implies. Her square, strong hands have just a suggestion of tremble in them, and her eyes are uncertain. Jim is not untouched, either. He has reached the uneasy emotional plateau of the man who is accustomed to getting what he wants and has gotten it. What does he do now? They are faintly uncomfortable with each other — the relationship shows many of the strains of classic Americanization.

How different Karel Bendl and his wife are in their cocoon-like apartment. They have two well-mannered children, a boy six and a girl four, in four rooms which are remarkably cheerful and neat. There is the atmosphere, as there is in so many European families, of all working to a common purpose without the rasping crosscurrents and lack of direction so common to the American household. If the ideal is merely a smoother materialism, it is not made worse by being badly done.

Vera Bendl is prim and serious and listens gravely as Karel and I chat over a Scotch, my present. We have an excellent dinner — small beef filets in the Czech manner — and I fear they have splurged. They are so civilized, so ready to do their bit to hold society together, and so unaware of how outnumbered they are, of how many there are everywhere in the world who don't care at all what happens, even when they pretend to. There are also decent, simple people like this everywhere in the world, but their simplicity is a handicap because they are always in the minority. They can't credit human weakness when they see it; in consequence, they are often eaten. They are invariably eaten, in fact, and the eating is often as ludicrous as it is touching. They are the cornerstone of any successful society, and well worth the first attention and protection of any statesman. But they can't survive without that protection, and there is something sickly about their dependent hope for a better tomorrow here in Prague. Stronger people would not be able to hide the truth about the present and future from themselves so easily.

"The Russians are a small people," Vera says, her finely cut mouth shaping the words decisively. "And they have a small way of doing things. I agree with my husband that the point of contact with the west is Germany. Now there are two opposed economies, one rich and the other poor, and they are too close to each other. It will have to break one way or the other."

"You mean that either the Germans and the Americans will move in or the Russians will occupy Germany?" I ask her.

"No, not quite." She shies away from such a summary of what she has been saying. She can't face the finalities, she clings to the comforting sound of her own voice, the familiar arguments . . . "In any case, it can't be bottled up. It is bound to come to some sort of decision."

"But what kind?"

"A definite one."

"If not Americans in Prague or Russians in Munich, then *what?*"

"I don't know."

"I was recently told that the Negro problem in the United States was very much the same, an either-or situation in which the whites would eat up the Negroes or vice versa. Whether I agree or not, I can see the two extremes, I can imagine either one happening. Can you in your case? I mean, can you *see* the Americans in Prague or the Russians in Munich?"

She disdains that question and nibbles at the more interesting tangent of racial disturbances. "They say you Americans are fascistic toward your minority groups," she says.

"Not at all," Karel says warmly. "Americans are very patient in this matter. I know from experience, from the sessions last year at the Salzburg Seminar in American Studies, from all the Americans I saw in Salzburg on that trip. The Jews and Negroes took great liberties in what they said, and the white Americans turned the other cheek. Morbidly forebearing, I would say. It is not healthy never to contradict people who insult you."

"I don't know," Vera says carefully. "There are so many conflicting reports. I believe my husband, of course, but even he can't explain things like the police brutality in Chicago."

"Yes," Karel says. "Now *that* was terrible. We saw it on television. Vera is right. I don't know how the decent Americans can put up with that sort of thing."

How to explain? Not the Chicago riots, but the odd position of talking to people concerned about events in Chicago when those people are in much more danger and have much less than anyone in Chicago, black or white. They do more with what they have, the Bendls, but they start with less, and it makes a common understanding difficult.

After flailing around inconclusively in Chicago, we return to the omnipresent Russians.

"We are all agreed, I think," says Karel, "that the Americanization process is perhaps spearheaded in east Europe by the Germans more than by the Americans, at least in the countries very close to Germany, as we are."

"But the Germans are not Americans," his wife says softly.

"No, but as I have explained, they are Americanized to the point that they are Americans in their message, so it is the same thing."

"Then when the Russians call the Germans agents of the Americans, you agree with them?" she asks him.

"No," he says with the air of a man who loves his wife and doesn't mind explaining things to her. "Not agents like spies, not espionage agents. The proponents of a certain economic system, and one which still out-produces us, I might add." They straighten it out, and he returns to me. "But the big Americanizations are still done by the Americans. The Hilton hotel here, and the one in Budapest. And the Pan American hotel in Budapest."

"I'm surprised they let us in."

He spreads his hands. "Foreign currency. They think they can control the operation so that they get the currency but not the Americans."

"I would doubt that."

"So do I. But the Russians can be very shortsighted at times."

Karel is called to the telephone later, and Vera says, "We would have so much if we didn't have to sell everything to Russia for so little. It is imperialism, if you use the big word, but to the Prague housewife it is easier to understand in simple words — doing without."

When I leave we all shake hands and say nice things to each other. I like them very much, and I respect the effort they make, but there is the descent down the three battered flights of stairs and the walk along the depressing street. "We are not allowed ourselves to do anything about the stairs," Vera said. "We can only make our own apartment as we choose. The stairs are the responsibility of the building committee, and nothing is ever done by committee." There is no explanation of the street. There couldn't be; they can't afford to think about it. They are very decent people, but there is so much they can't afford to think about.

It is eleven o'clock when I get back to the Alcron, and Jim is sitting disconsolately in the lobby with his sister Grace, a formidable woman a few years younger than he.

"The hunting is off," Jim says unhappily. "Everything is off. I have to go to Munich."

"But you'll be back in time to go to Budapest, I hope."

"We may get everything straightened out by then," Grace says.

She leaves us shortly, and Jim explains. "It's that damned Kay, my wife, the one I divorced ten years ago. She's tried to kill herself in Milan and the kids are stranded in Munich — I don't see how they got separated, but they did — and Grace was in London so she came down and took charge, and then flew over here to get me. She was too smart to call, she knew I'd shake her. We go back on the nine o'clock plane. . . . If there's anything I hate, it's that kind of mess. It's not just missing the hunting — would you believe that Grace found Sam and Bob and told them I couldn't make it? — it's the bloody, endless, damned mess of it. . . . I gave plenty to get rid of Kay — I never wanted to see her or those kids again, and I don't see why I have to."

"Why can't Grace take care of it for you?"

"She could. But she won't. She's a damned sadist, and she's got the whip hand, for reasons I don't want to go into. . . . Jesus, *Kay*. Did you ever meet her? Of course you did, but you didn't know what she was like. No one did, except me. She read stuff like *Peanuts* and those books about the Hobbits or whatever you call them — all that cute stuff, and she'd talk about it when she was drunk until I thought I'd go out of my mind. Then when she was sober, she'd swear like a trooper and try to kill one of us . . . or both of us."

It takes a while before he calms down. "It was embarrassing as hell about Milo," he says glumly before he turns in. "Grace came storming right into the room. She's always been like that."

Poor Milo, if she was dazed before, what is she now? Americanization at such a pace — Grace was supposed to be the end of the education, not the beginning — might well turn out to be too rich to keep down.

In the morning I start on my rounds, and in the next week plow dutifully through my introductions. I meet half a hundred Czechs and other eastern Europeans who hold responsible positions and not one can tell me anything new about Americanization, directly or indirectly. It seems that the subjects, those on whom the process is working, can't be objective. Only non-Europeans can see it with any clarity. One can watch it fermenting in them, but one can do that in the street or informally — there is no need for this legwork.

Although I don't find anything new on Americanization, I do stumble on a crusty factory manager who is amusingly scathing about the Russians and also about his fellow Czechs. "Russia is doomed," he says. "In so many different ways. Take the very good chance of war with China. If they have that war, east Europe will not be a good friend behind them, so they will have trouble on two fronts, always fatal. The Chinese have such a huge population, with hundreds of millions along the Russian border, and there are not many Russians in that part of Asia. But *two* fronts! With the Germans behind us! A very dangerous situation for them. They should make a peace with east Europe now, but they can't because they are so greedy to have everything. . . . The Russians are completely crazy, that is the truth, completely. When you get to know them, you see they are crazy because they believe their own lies and never remember how they started. Like all lunatics, they will end in great trouble. Watch. Remember what I say. They are much crazier than Hitler ever was. . . .

"I spit on the Czech leadership. Dubček and Smrkovský and the rest are such trained Communists that they can't stop believing in maneuvering. Maneuvering! What is needed is a direct push against the Russians! A total national strike, where we refuse to do anything until they leave. So they occupy the cities, so we starve — so what? In the end, we win. The people are ready for this, but the leaders don't understand. They are Communists first. . . . There is a Communist high-up atmosphere. They get in a room and hypnotize each other. Like rabbits. It is disgusting.

"And they allow the Russians to hypnotize them, too, because they can't admit to themselves that Russian Communism is completely crazy. They can't admit — Dubček and Smrkovský can't admit — that all those years of working with the Russians was pointless. . . . The Russians can control them because they, the Russians, are so awful, and our leadership can't admit they were taken in for so long. The Russians are very repulsive in their barbarity. If you are near them, and I have had to be near them a great deal, you develop an antipathy. It is like working with apes. They are not human in the European sense. They are animals."

I see the D.C. occasionally in the evenings, and we have a few quiet conversations. He elaborates on his beloved *Pushkin Report,* and I record my doubts. The reactions become automatic.

Jim wires to say he will be back at noon the next day, and that evening I see the D.C. in the lobby and he tells me he is leaving the next morning. His lady, who has not been in evidence for several days, is with him, and we have a last drink together.

We chat idly, the conversation devoid of politics. The D.C. is alert and his mysterious companion is revealed as a cultivated and informed woman who is especially knowledgeable about ballet. The D.C. is a student of Slavonic folk music and has a fund of amusing anecdotes about his travels in strange corners of the Balkans. She has stories from the Bolshoi, Sadlers Wells, the National City. They have both been in the Arctic, and I offer what I can recall from a trip to Baffin Bay. For an hour, we might be a trio of bona fide tourists, and then it is twelve and I must get to bed. We make our farewells, and the D.C.'s lady smiles charmingly as she says good-bye. The D.C. himself, ponderous but confident, is on his large feet and gives me his large hand. "It has been very pleasant," he says, with no other hints on his affable face. "Very frank and comradely, as your friend Jim would say. Do tell him how much I enjoyed that."

"I shall."

He bows very slightly, smiles blandly, and we part.

Jim arrives next day on schedule, happy to be out of Munich but not so sure about being in Prague again.

"I hope I didn't keep you waiting," he says.

"Not at all."

"When do we leave for Budapest?"

"How about tomorrow morning?"

"Good. Bob Reilly had to go to Morocco, but Sam Reynolds and I have arranged to go on a boar hunt in the Mátra — that's the mountain range east of Budapest — for a few days. You and I drive down, see the Budapest sights, and then Bob and I take off, leaving you to your labors, O.K.?"

"Sounds fine."

"What's new?"

"Not much. The D.C. left, passing along salutations to you."

"It was awful in Munich, but I won't bore you with the details. Kay was beyond belief, but Grace was worse. And the damned kids."

He gets in touch with Milo, and I see them having a drink in the bar in the early evening, but do not join them. Jim is telling her something very earnestly, and she nods her head rapidly and me-

chanically. She is pale and seems even more uncertain and confused than when they were last together.

———————

We leave at eight next morning and Jim is not in good spirits,
although he pretends to be.

"You have to say good-bye to Prague in a friendly sort of way,"
he says. "Just like you said hello. It's that kind of city."

It is a sunny morning, but the drive from the heart of the city to
the outskirts is not cheerful. The endlessly grimy buildings, the
endlessly dehumanized people.

"It's almost as good as Sixth Avenue," Jim says. "No, out toward
Riverside Drive, deep in those West Side pockets where you really
have to love New York to stay on."

"I thought of New York, too, but over on the East Side — Second
Avenue and the Bowery."

"It doesn't matter. East Side, West Side . . . only New York can
compare. But at its best it's a poor second to this, let's face it."

Later he says, "Sorry I missed the D.C. I was thinking that he's
not what they meant when they used to say 'swell people,' and
that's in his favor. Or what Frank O'Connor used to call 'a willing
mixer and a credit to his race.' But my God, what can you do with a
man who doesn't exist?"

"He seemed real enough."

"Milo went to the desk and tried to find out who he was, and they
said he wasn't staying in the hotel even after she pointed him out.
Then she asked who was staying in his suite — she had the number
— and they said no one. So I still ask how you can take a man
seriously when he doesn't exist."

"He must be more important than I thought."

"Too important for me. I'm just a country boy — can't stay the
pace with these mysterious strangers. Anyhow, after what Milo
told me about the Russians here I think they're a bunch of bastards

and I'm not drinking with any of them from now on no matter how charming they are."

For Milo herself the hardened philanderer could have no sympathy, but her stories of third-person oppression have opened his heart. It is very American, very much in the grain of the process.

Jim has the guidebook and says we should take a look at Kutná Hora, forty miles from Prague. " 'Kutná Hora is an ancient town with preserved medieval and baroque houses,' " he reads. "The Cathedral of St. Barbara is the star attraction, surrounded by a lot of other stuff. It's only four kilometers off the main road and the most important collection of buildings we'll be passing all day."

"I didn't know you were interested."

"I'll try anything once, including tourism."

We turn off at the appointed sign and drive along a straggling country road to the hilly little town. It is very grim.

"Jesus Christ!" Jim says. "It's too much."

If we are passing preserved medieval and baroque houses, they can't compete with their own dirt and the shabby grotesques of the contemporary scene.

"Let's get out of here," Jim says.

"What about the Cathedral of St. Barbara?"

"Don't torture me. Let's go."

We retrace our route in silence.

"Do you realize that's the first place we've seen off this main road?" Jim says when we are aimed for Brno again. "I thought what you saw from this road was the end, but after that peek I wonder what it's really like back in the boondocks."

"The dishonesty of these guidebooks!" he blurts out a little later. "And how about the dishonesty of our own guidebooks — and the *National Geographic* sort of article on the beauties of Bohemia! Even the professional anti-Communists never dare to say how bad it is. I tell you, what the Russians have done to these people is worse than anything and everything the Nazis did. How those jerk

American correspondents can celebrate Leningrad and Stalingrad without talking about how the same people wrecked half of Europe is beyond me . . ."

He rants on for a full ten minutes before subsiding, and then we drive in silence for quite a while, passing through empty, lovely country. The rolling farmland and woods spread off to the horizon and there is still snow on the uplands.

"When you think what it was . . ." Jim begins once, but doesn't go on.

The country is still the same; it is the human condition that has deteriorated. A stretch of beautiful country only intensifies one's consciousness of the rest, as it did just now with Jim.

At half-past ten we come into Jihlava, an appallingly rundown market town of thirty-six thousand inhabitants where we are going to buy bread and cheese to eat as we drive. "You can't go into a restaurant except in a city anyhow," Jim says glumly. There is snow and ice in the main square and the usual hundreds of people milling aimlessly about. "You wonder if anyone ever works," Jim grumbles. We park near a store and are immediately surrounded by two or three dozen louts who peer anxiously into the car.

Jim's promenade in Jihlava is memorable — I wish there were a motion picture record of it. The residents have seen foreigners, they have even seen Americans, but never one like this. Magnificently shod, overcoated, shirted and tanned, all six-feet-five of him moves toward the sad little store, the most opulent of Gullivers among the most disreputable of Lilliputians. They gape at him unreservedly, staggered before this, the perfection of materialism. How many thousands of years will pass before they can hope to attain to such a state? Even to its imitation?

I lock the car and follow the procession into the store, where the crowd is equally overcome. All other activity stops as the god selects bread and cheese and pays. When he favors the cashier (this is a supermarket in intention if not in execution) with a full American smile, revealing several square inches of dazzling teeth, there is a faint but perceptible falling back, the kind of voluptuous shudder reserved, in the old days, for special Church festivals and the advent of kings. It seems the ultimate in religious Americanization: the fleshpots of western Europe are grossly indifferent in comparison.

"How did I get into that?" Jim asks as we drive off.

"Cortez arriving in Mexico preceded by the legend."

"Cut it out — it was damned uncomfortable."

The experience cheers him up, though, and an hour later, as we approach Brno, he is himself again.

"My God," he says, "look at that hill."

To the left is a hill covered with tiny houses, all in different colors. Where farming is cooperative, there are no incidental dwellings in the country, and we are at a momentary loss to explain this isolated patch.

"I've got it," Jim says. "You live in Brno, and if you're rich you have your country place out on this hill."

"No, they're toolsheds. You have your garden plot out here."

"Take another look. Those are villas. One-room villas, but still villas."

He is right. They *are* supposed to be villas. Like so many Communist imitations of western living, the original idea has been so scaled down and so indifferently executed that the resultant daub bears very little resemblance to the model. It is touching, it is pathetic . . . but it is also comic.

"Think of Cary Grant stuck on that hill for the rest of his life," Jim says with a laugh, and then laughs some more. "What can you do except laugh?" he asks. "It's all so goddamned crazy. How about Jim Kimberly in Kutná Hora on a permanent basis? How about Jim Carter in Jihlava forever?" He guffaws immoderately. "I haven't laughed like that in years," he says when the bout is over. "But what else can you do?"

Fortunately we don't have to go through Brno, but turn right and south to Bratislava before getting into the city.

[437]

Jim expounds as we have our bread and cheese, both of which are good. "The Russians have been awful, but I have to admit that's only part of it. The class question is very big — this whole mess is the triumph of the lower classes — and so the strongest argument for aristocracy you could make. But isn't it strange that no one has ever defined it that way? You know, like Evelyn Waugh. No one has ever taken a look and then written about it as just plain funny. You see the colors of their clothes, and what they paint their houses — those roses and greens and yellows and . . ." He searches for the word.

"Don't forget the pistachios."

"That's the one. All the chalky colors that go gray so nicely. All lower-class selections, what you might call antibeautiful, like all of Communism, right down to the smallest detail, the religion of beauty backwards. When the lower classes get in charge, with those peasant mentalities — some of them are retarded, too, like that bunch looking at me in that town where we got the cheese — they're egomaniacs. You've got to be an egomaniac to believe in this. They're worse than any other ruling class anywhere in the world, and that includes Africa. But why is it they're such egomaniacs?"

"Is the question rhetorical, or do you want my considered opinion?"

"I want your considered opinion."

"It's because they have no sense of the past. It's been wiped out by their system and their leaders, deliberately and efficiently. With no sense of the past, they have no standards of comparison; and with no standards of comparison they have no taste. So the socialist adventure is really an exercise in tastelessness.

"And all from no sense of the past — right, professor?"

"Right."

"Then *I* was right — these countries *are* the greatest case for the old aristocracy that could be made. I wonder, though, if it could have worked if there had been taste at the top — a sort of Communist aristocracy."

"Maybe. It would have been an interesting try, anyhow."

"And one last question — why doesn't anyone write the truth about it? Why isn't any writer funny about it?"

"For several reasons, I think. The American and western European theory is that the Communist system is all wrong, but the people in the Communist countries are all right. Perhaps they have it just backwards — Communism is not a bad idea, but the people are no good, particularly when stripped of their aristocratic bellwethers. Americans in Prague say, 'Such lovely people, isn't it unfortunate they have to live this way.' But perhaps it would be more accurate to say, 'Such poor stock — they've only gotten what they had coming.' Accurate or not, though, nothing like that can be said because the weak cannot be criticized in modern American and western European life. The fashionable prejudice against being honest about the weak is too formidable, and nothing can be written about them which is 'funny' or truthful in any other way."

"That's a pretty good explanation."

"Thanks."

"Don't mention it. . . . I don't know, the people here are so incomprehensible. So grateful for getting now what they must have had before anyhow. It's as though America went broke and then started to get back on its feet and people who could remember the old days were given — razors, let's say — and they jumped up and down and said, 'Razors! Can you imagine that! What a marvelous system we have now!' But Americans wouldn't do that. They'd look at the razors and say, 'Big deal,' and walk off."

"Don't be too sure."

"What do you mean?"

"People change, you know. Especially in prison camps. They can sink very fast. And forget very fast."

"Yes, I suppose so."

In Bratislava we stop at the Carlton Hotel for a beer. It is presentable from the outside, and the lobby and main dining room are picked up, but the men's room in Dostoevskian underground. Old paint and moisture drip down the high walls of a huge enclosure, filled with cracked and stained urinals. Old men stand about reading newspapers and an ancient crone hobbles after tips.

"Never saw a woman working in a men's can before," Jim says.

"She's very old."

"I thought they got rid of those old European customs."

"I'm beginning to think they perpetuate them."

"But why didn't they fix the can up while they were doing the rest of the hotel? Don't bother answering — that *is* a rhetorical question."

The hotel is filled with Russians who make no effort to conceal their presence. The lobby rings with the language, and the manner is rather pushy. If concealment is the order of the day in Prague, there are other directives for Bratislava. The stares we receive are insolent, and as we enter the dining room a Russian on his way out rashly tries to elbow the approaching Jim aside. But one of the heaviest linemen in Yale history is not all that easy to handle. Jim does not elbow back, just keeps going, and does not look back at the angry Russian on the floor. We sit, and the angry Russian is immediately with us, yelling and gesticulating.

"What the hell," Jim says.

"You've evidently breached the lower-class sense of decorum."

Jim stands up slowly, towers over the Russian for a suitable moment, then takes him by the lapels and lifts him clear of the floor, movie strongman style.

"Listen, you lesbian son-of-a-bitch, beat it or I'll call the cops," Jim says, with ample spaces between each word. "Nov schmoz ka pop?"

The Russian is so undone that he walks off quietly when replaced. The dining room, filled with his compatriots, sits in awed silence.

Jim sits down with admirable composure and we have our beer.

"It's enough to make you want the D.C. back again. Where do they get these?"

"The smoothies go to Prague, I guess, and Bratislava gets the bottom of the barrel."

"But why so many here? What's the attraction?"

"I don't know. It's only thirty miles from Vienna — maybe they like to be close to the shopping."

"What a bunch."

"The real joke is that they think they're carrying the torch of civilization — if they could talk, they'd all tell you they have a brother in the Leningrad Symphony. They've got nothing on their minds but art and culture."

"I hope I did the right thing."

"You were splendid. The veneers peeled off like onionskins. Shostakovich's Seventh turned into the embarrassing Star-Spangled Banner and put everyone back on the manure spreader."

"I guess the moral is that you should never educate a peasant."

"That's what the D.C. would say."

"What about Marx and Lenin?"

"I think you could count them in. Stalin, too."

"Philistine culture, and they try to knock you down."

"They're only jealous."

When we leave, the stares are still intense but the insolence has gone.

"When you think what the D.C. has to put up with, you get kind of fond of the old rascal again," Jim says as we get into the car.

"He wasn't bad."

"He wasn't very frank, but he certainly was comradely," Jim says. The expenditure of physical energy has put him in the best of spirits. "You know, he was very clever when you think about it. Saying all that stuff and still able to stay at the top. But the rest of them are such goons. They think they're so hot and have the answer to everything. But there's a comeuppance for people like that.

What happens to them when they find out they've been wrong all this time? Talk about Americanization! They'll be the easiest pickings in history when the light goes on. . . . The better I get to know these Russians the plainer it becomes — to me, anyhow — that they just don't have it. They probably never have had it, and when the time comes they'll cave in. All the way."

"That's what a factory manager I met in Prague said."

Bratislava is very warm in the afternoon sun, and the muddy Danube is very wide as we cross the bridge. The streets are correctly messy, to use Jim's reverse terminology, and the *de rigueur* piles of rubble stand near each building.

"Those are very good piles, Dubček," Jim says. "You will begin the repairs in 1975. Until then, nothing is to be touched."

We cross the border into Hungary some ten miles from Bratislava, at Rusovce-Rajka. Czech and Hungarian customs are in the same building, and the Hungarians are noticeably gentler and more urbane.

In the late afternoon sun, the wide, flat Hungarian landscape is appealing. The farm buildings are neater than in Czechoslovakia and golden in the slanting sun. The villages are poor, but in better taste and the people look better. They also ride bicycles, which they avoid doing in Czechoslovakia. One has the impression that a bicycle is beneath a Czech's dignity because it is symbolic of the old days. As a thoroughly forward-looking socialist, the Czech will have an automobile or nothing. He would rather walk than compromise that principle. The Hungarians, less touchy about the ignominious days before full socialism, are able to ride and enjoy it.

The repair piles are present, but not in the Czech depth. Jim notes, in his phrase, that "arc lights are big here, too." The poorest villages in east Europe often boast the sort of expensive arched highway lights that one associates with American urban freeways. The extravagance only serves to point up the poverty and the delusion of material progress.

It is just over a hundred miles from the border crossing to Budapest, and we shall be there by six. The dreary towns succeed each other — Györ, Komárom, Tata, Tatabánya — and then the Buda hills appear in the gathering dusk, old and gray, like elephant hide. There is a ten-mile stretch of four-lane highway going into the city and we are in the outskirts just at dusk. The first impression is that it is far more attractive than Prague, seedy but not startlingly so. The people seem much calmer, and are better dressed.

The Hotel Gellert, where we are staying, is on the Danube near the Liberty Bridge, and we have rooms overlooking the river, wide and gleaming in the early evening. As with the Alcron, in Prague, there is a feeling of the past at the Gellert, although in a different way. The Alcron is 1939-urban, the Gellert 1939-resort. The Gellert Baths, next to the hotel and as large, carry out the resort theme with an equally wide stone facade from another day. Budapest has over a hundred medicinal springs within the city, dozens of which are housed in elaborate, prewar buildings, and these spas are the main tourist attraction even today.

We call Luther Attenborough, a connection of Jim's who is with the American Foreign Service and travels east Europe. A friend of Jim's has insisted that Jim look him up, and he says he has been awaiting Jim's arrival with great impatience.

We dine at Mátyás Pince, loud and touristy, although the food is good, particularly the Hungarian fish soup. Attenborough is thin and nervous and giggles at everything his wife says. She is in her thirties, ten years younger than her husband, attractive, and American by birth, the daughter of White Russian aristocrats who fled to California after the revolution. Her parents had Hungarian relatives, and she knows the country well from that viewpoint. She can even speak some Hungarian, a rare accomplishment for a non-Hungarian, and she is pleasantly condescending with the help. She is also mildly amusing about the great socialist experiment, but not nearly so witty as her husband thinks she is. Conversation is diffi-

[443]

cult because of the gypsy music, not bad but incessant and too loud. Only one person can talk at a time, and she is the obvious choice, so we listen to her.

"I can't understand why we worry about the Russian nuclear bombs," she says. "Like everything else Russian, they probably don't work."

Attenborough giggles furiously at this, and Jim and I smile dutifully. After dinner we go nightclubbing, the inevitable activity for strangers thrown together in a foreign city. We go to the Casanova, Fortuna and Alabárdos, and they are predictable.

Attenborough's wife talks about the exchange rates and titled friends in Vienna. Attenborough himself giggles, and Jim looks at him with affable disapproval.

"What do you think of the 'socialist' countries?" Attenborough's wife asks Jim.

He can't resist teasing her. "If I were in my twenties, I'd move here," he says.

"You would? What on earth for?"

"I think there's a great future here after socialism caves in," Jim says. "Right now it's like America fifty years ago. Think of the money you could make when they start to go modern."

She is still European enough not to like this a bit. The soft sneer at Communism is acceptable, even mandatory, but applied Babbittry, realistic under its bromides, hints at that other world which the true European must ever resist. The vision of Communist collapse is always wishful, an article of faith but not to be taken literally. When it is propounded as an actual possibility, and one probably not much more attractive than the present condition, the hackles rise.

"Oh, isn't that just like an American," she says. "To think of the money, I mean. But you are wrong. Eastern Europe will never become American, even if the Russian empire collapses."

"It's already American," Jim says flatly. "All they want is washing machines, so they're Americanized."

"I think you will find that they are not so materialistic," she says frostily. "There is an interest here in culture that you . . . may not appreciate."

"Culture is what they kill the time with until they can have the all-electric home," Jim says. "Culture won't last when the fun starts, any more than it has in Germany."

"And you approve?"

"I don't approve or disapprove. It's just a fact that you have to face like any other fact."

She smothers her exasperation, and we talk of other things. Attenborough doesn't like anything that ruffles his wife's feathers, and permits himself a tiny glare at Jim. If Jim weren't so rich and socially impeccable, he would do more, but he is too typically American to fight with his betters. Even the adored wife can't compete with the social laws he learned at Hotchkiss.

Jim went through the same mill, but he is different. Not only because he has so much more money and rank, but because he would be somewhat the same without those attributes. He is rather an old-fashioned American — careless, rude, brutal on occasion — but also honest after his fashion, even about himself. He can't help but observe and compare, the essence of the intellectual approach; Attenborough, only a servant, believes what he is told and doesn't — can't — ask questions. Jim *is* Americanization, he Americanizes everything he touches, and there is pathos as well as style in the way he does it. He Americanized Milo, but he didn't know what to do with her when the job was done, and could only press on to the next girl. Self-sufficient and reliable, he is also restless, rootless and weak in a final, personal way. Able to deal with anything foreign, he quails before domestic tyranny — Grace can bring him to heel with a word. It is sobering to realize that even with his drawbacks he represents what is left of what was best in the national character; and more sobering to realize that he is a disappearing species, like the buffalo. Not very many today, and there will be less tomorrow. Looking at him now, through the hazy nightclub air, I think of the D.C. and his graphs of declining controllers. Jim never was a controller; he was even more representative, and even harder to replace.

The White Russian woman with the American passport doesn't understand his strengths or his weaknesses and writes him off according to a preconception. She is awed by the American rich, and she concedes they have it on a Romanov, but she thinks it happened by accident and that it is unfair. She is not capable of Jim's intellectual doggedness, which, if the roles were reversed, would make him say to himself: "These people have taken the world, so they must have something and I'm going to think about it until I figure out what it is." Jim, only the great-grandson of an American Civil War fortune, is capable of mental effort. She, the result of six hundred years of selective breeding and money, isn't, and so must live in his world.

There is harsh evidence of this dependence in the morning. Jim joins me in the dining room for breakfast with the news that Mrs. Attenborough arrived at his room an hour after we left them. "She wanted to continue our conversation," he says. "I asked if her spouse wouldn't object, and she only smiled. Frankly, she was one hell of a lay once she got her clothes off and forgot about how bright she's supposed to be. . . . She didn't leave until seven this morning."

At nine, we go on a tour of the city with a car and driver, and guide from Ibusz, the state tourist office. We have a serious young girl, quite pretty, who shakes hands with us formally before we start out. "I am Bláthy Róza," she says, reversing the Christian and family names in the Hungarian style.

It is another fine day — we have had marvelous luck with the weather — and Budapest turns out to be very appealing. We see everything — the new stadium; the City Park, where they are still skating outdoors, in front of the strange replicas of medieval buildings; Heroes' Square, with the wonderful monument commemorating the one thousandth year of the Magyar conquest, the sculpted

Magyar chiefs looking like Vikings; the staggering Parliament House, a lifesize copy of London's; Margaret Island; Castle Hill; and on and on.

The boulevards, public buildings and apartment houses in the center are all generous, and the strongest impression is of solidity and prosperity. The prosperity is belied by the human shabbiness, not extreme but definitely noticeable, whereas the solidity is untouched. The superb buildings of modern Budapest were built in a nationalistic surge in the last half of the nineteenth century, long after the other great cities of Europe were more or less completed. After the Austrian control was thrown off, Hungary came alive and created this city in less than fifty years. So when Bláthy Róza tells us the city was almost destroyed in the fighting between the Germans and the Russians at the end of World War II, we don't understand. "But the buildings are still here," Jim says. "We have rebuilt them," she says. "The effort has been expensive, but we Hungarians want our city back as it was. So Budapest has been built twice in one hundred years."

Even the enormous Royal Palace is being reconstructed exactly as it was, and there is a very complicated restoration going on inside St. Matthias' Church, where the ancient kings of Hungary were crowned. The preservation of the past is a morbid business in Prague, but there is genuine pleasure in it in Budapest. The Hungarians are more pragmatic than the Czechs and Slovaks, and also more subtly knowing. When a Czech says, "We want our city back as it was," one is tempted to ask where the former people will come from; but when Hungarians say the same thing, as Bláthy Róza did, one feels they don't mean it that literally. They know that only the buildings will be the same; they have thought it through. As Jim puts it: "You never know *what* these Hungarians are thinking, but you do know they're always thinking. It must be that oriental streak."

When we leave St. Matthias' Church, Bláthy Róza points to some building activity behind it. "There will be the new Hilton hotel," she says. "It will be built to conform to the architecture of the rest of the buildings here. Only three stories high, and not many rooms. Like a cloister."

"I'll bet," Jim says.

"It is agreed in a contract," says the imperturbable Bláthy Róza. "The new Pan American hotel, on the other side of the river, in Pest, can be as big as it wishes, but this hotel must be as agreed."

"Budapest is a wonderful-looking place," Jim says. "One of the most beautiful cities I've ever seen. What it must have been like in the old days."

"We had capitalist exploitation then," Bláthy Róza says gently. She is very feminine, but firm on the socialist line.

Jim is very nice with her. "Was it really so awful?" he asks.

"I was not born then, of course," she says, "so I never saw with my own eyes. But it is well known that there was very bad exploitation."

"So the war was a blessing in a way?"

"Yes, in a way. It was terrible, but it led to the end of the bourgeois state. After the Red Army arrived, we were able to build the socialist democracy, so if there had not been a war . . . who knows?"

She seems perfectly sincere as she speaks, and yet — can she be? As a tourist guide, she has to be careful, but does she really believe the old days were that bad? Or that these days are so good?

"You wouldn't have gotten the Red Army without a war, that's certain," Jim says. "But think how close it was. The Americans were heading this way too, you know. What if they had gotten here first?"

She laughs in a girlish but well-bred way. "Then I imagine we would still be capitalist. But it didn't happen that way, and that is what is important."

"You're right," Jim sighs. "Yes, it's better this way. Imagine how it would look if we'd taken over — Hilton hotels next to the churches, Pan American hotels along the river, Americans everywhere . . ." He pauses artistically to give her time. It only takes a moment — her face lights up and her smile is radiant.

"Yes," she says. "Isn't it fortunate that didn't happen!"

We have a good lunch at the Gellert, served in the usual ultra-polite Communist fashion, and head over to the Gellert Baths at three o'clock. The baths were once managed by the hotel but are now an entirely separate and completely proletariat operation. When the hotel was a capitalist spa, fat old ladies and gentlemen went down to the baths in a special elevator in their dressing gowns. The lift is still there and still operating, but it is grimy and the paint on the ironwork is peeling. At the bottom, one debouches into a room the size, shape, color and general odor of both Grand Central waiting rooms combined. Hundreds of drably dressed citizens of both sexes sit on benches, evidently waiting to see physicians on the upper floors. We pay nine forints (about twenty-five cents) apiece for entrance to the baths and a massage. For this, we are also given individual dressing rooms, loincloths, and towels. We start with the hot rooms, then steam, then an icy dip, and then an hour in the baths themselves, wonderfully tepid waters ("moderately radioactive, containing hydrocarbonate . . . beneficial in rheumatic and arthritic troubles, neuralgia and the diseases of the respiratory organs"), in a terraced Romanesque chamber in semi-darkness. The only light comes from an enormous skylight, and we sit in the watery twilight with a couple of hundred silent citizens, strangely at ease.

"It's as comfortable as Skid Row," Jim says. "No worries, no responsibilities. With their cradle to grave security, it does come to a sort of Skid Row. No incentive, as my father used to say . . . but it isn't so bad when the tramps take over, if you're honest about it. There's really a better atmosphere here than in the Everglades or the Pacific Union — a lot less bullshit. And they're in much better shape."

The relative fitness is a surprise. Without their gray clothes, the Hungarians of all ages do look remarkably healthy.

"They take better care of themselves than most people," Jim says. "That's why they do so well in the Olympics."

We finish off with a proletariat massage (rinsed with a hose on a slippery table just vacated, then soaped and kneaded for ten minutes), shower, change, and go back up to the Gellert.

"Not bad," Jim says. "This is not bad. And remember lunch today here . . . the place wasn't crowded, the food was good, the service was excellent — you can't find that anywhere in America any more. You can't even find it in West Europe. There's always some repulsive creep at the next table. Here there's no one. It's all for *you*, the capitalist pig with the desirable currency."

In the early evening, Jim comes in to tell me that Attenborough has called to tell him they can't make it for dinner as planned.

"He wasn't frosty, though," Jim says. "Actually very friendly. Said he felt the flu coming on. Mrs. A. — Irene — was not mentioned. Wonder if that means another visit tonight?"

"That flu can be pretty contagious."

"I hope it is — I'm bushed. . . . Attenborough says he's sending one of his staff to fill in for him. I tried to talk him out of that but he insisted. The substitute will meet us downstairs."

Mr. Lennox turns out to be an insipid young American who fancies himself as a man of the world. Over a drink in the bar he is soon telling us where to buy gloves, where to go in France in July, how to have cars shipped "home" . . .

"Let's ditch him," Jim says as we prepare to leave.

"How?"

"Jesus, I don't know. Let's surely get rid of him after dinner, though."

In the limousine he has brought with him, Mr. Lennox, upon being addressed as Mr. Lennox by Jim, says, "Call me Bill, Jim."

"Nobody calls me Jim unless I've known them for at least five years," Jim growls, and Mr. Lennox beats a hasty and unaccustomed retreat, his in-flight social manner deflated, if only temporarily.

[450]

We go to Régi Országház, the Old Parliament, near the Royal Palace, an attractive place with several rooms, each decorated differently. In the cellar is a proletariat wine cellar lit with candles, a spot Mr. Lennox insists on showing us and explaining. He would like a glass of wine there, but Jim says it's too smoky.

Dinner is good, although there is the usual high-volume gypsy music, and Mr. Lennox has an unnecessary altercation with the head waiter. Jim is furious at that and after making Mr. Lennox apologize to the waiter says to me: "Isn't it extraordinary the number of illiterate Americans you see abroad! Spiritually illiterate as well as literally. People you never see in America appear here and have all the responsible jobs. Illiterate Ph.D's who say, 'Mrs. Bendix and I certainly enjoyed the view.' I can't imagine what the Europeans think of us."

Mr. Lennox colors, but he is unstoppable. He discourses on Hungary under Communism and says, "Do you realize these people never have any money the way you and I do? I mean, they don't have life insurance or real estate ɔr stocks. They don't even have the beginnings of a portfolio — it's an unusual Hungarian who has more than five or six hundred dollars at any specified time. They live from day to day and hand to hand."

"Hand to mouth," Jim says, but Mr. Lennox doesn't know what he's talking about.

Over coffee, Mr. Lennox gives us the contents of the current *Time,* and a panegyric to *Peanuts.*

"I guess you can find just about every philosophy expressed in *Peanuts,*" he says. "It's so deep, but also so frothy and charming."

Jim looks at him with undisguised fascination. "How about the Hobbits?" he asks. "Don't you go for them, too?"

"J. R. Tolkien!" cries Mr. Lennox. "Just about the most amusing and cutting books ever written. I've read *The Lord of the Rings* — that's the complete trilogy — three times."

"I knew it," Jim mutters. "They always go together. When they have one, they have the other. That's the way Kay was."

We finally do shake Mr. Lennox and go to the Casanova. Some pleasant Hungarians next to us strike up a conversation, and tell us that the young Hungarians are very Americanized. "They all wear the Levi trousers," a young woman says. "Just like in the west."

"That's all it takes," Jim says. "A pair of Levi's and you're baptized."

These Hungarians visit the west often, but tell us that visas are increasingly uncertain. "We never know now whether we get it or not," they say.

"Then you should stay out when you get out," Jim says.

"But our work is here," they say.

"Then you ought to forget about trips to the west," Jim says.

"We don't like to do that," they say. "It is very amusing to go to Vienna and Paris."

"I give up," Jim says.

When we get back to the Gellert, a German businessman in our corridor asks us to have a drink with him and his friends, and we find an old-fashioned wild party in progress. Connecting doors are open, drink is flowing and nude girls (brought from Germany) prance through the rooms.

A German with no shirt on offers French champagne. "You don't see parties like this very often, do you?" he asks in all seriousness.

"Oh, I don't know," Jim says. "I can remember stumbling into a Shriners' convention in Kansas City that had a close resemblance."

"Shriners?" the German asks, and insists on an explanation. He gets a rather farfetched one which seems to satisfy, and then he tells us that "all the rooms at the Gellert are bugged. We give them interesting tape tonight."

Unharmonized singing breaks out shortly and we leave.

The next morning Jim tells me that Mrs. Attenborough — Irene — did not appear. Much to his relief, he claims.

Sam Reynolds arrives in the early afternoon, and he and Jim leave for the Mátra and the wild boars. They are gone for five days, and I apply myself to the introductions again. As in Czechoslovakia, I learn nothing new from those in whom and on whom the process is working, although I do sense a difference between Czechs and Hungarians insofar as Americanization is concerned. The Czechs are so uncritically committed to the new that they would become perfect Americans if they could. That the Russians will not allow them to do so does not negate the direction of the natural bent. If the Russian harness is ever removed — even after many more years — the desire to be American will still be fresh and ready to sprout.

The Hungarians are less idealistic and have a clearer memory of a pleasant past. If they could get rid of the Russians, they would really prefer to have 1939 back, the vintage year for Budapest, before doing anything else. Washing machines and refrigerators would be nice, but they don't take precedence by any means.

Also, as contemptuous as the Czechs are of the Russians, the Hungarians outdo them. The Czechs see modern Russia as a return to czarism. The Hungarians go further back in time and see the present Russian expansion as merely a recurrence of the historical westward drive of the oriental barbarians.

"Here in Hungary we have had the Huns and the Mongols, and now we have the Russians," a mild Hungarian bureaucrat tells me. "That is all there is to it. If you try to think of it as any more than that, you make a mistake. . . . We ourselves are not oriental, despite some theories. The Magyars were a Finnish-Ugric people, not at all oriental, and since then we are so intermingled with Austrians and other western Europeans that we are far more western than eastern. The Russians are not — they are oriental, as they have always been, and they have rolled to their high point in Europe here, as the Huns and Mongols did, and someday they will roll back, we hope."

This is a popular theory in Hungary, and one hears it often.

A high Hungarian army officer serves up even stiffer fare: "Russia today is a military dictatorship. The central committee of the party has been set aside completely, and the empire is being run by Grechko, Yakubovsky and Brezhnev — two army marshals and a civilian, and the civilian is the weakest of the three. This is absolute violation of the Marxist principle that the army must be kept under strict party control. I am a soldier myself, but I do not believe in the military taking over. Now there is Bonapartism in the Soviet Union, and a strong appetite for adventures. The marshals will push for small actions everywhere, and finally a big one: war with America. There is no other way now. The party will never come back into control, and so we enter the final phase of the revolution — the Napoleonic catastrophe. Win or lose on the battlefield, they lose as people, as a country, everything now."

It occurs to me that a military dictatorship in Russia would be a convincing testimonial to the Americanization of Europe. With the west converted, the pressure on the east becomes unbearable. The civilian government in Moscow — the party — can't cope, and the military are called in to hold the line in a deteriorating situation.

Most Europeans would call a Russian military dictatorship the natural finale for Asiatic Communism, but the Russians aren't all that oriental, and one suspects they might have avoided the military takeover if it had not been for the Americanization threat.

When the boar hunters return, they have three massive, stinking heads which are immediately turned over to a taxidermist.

"It was very nice," Jim says in his room at the Gellert. He and Sam are still in their elaborate hunting outfits, and the floor is littered with knapsacks and their contents. "Real country and we slogged through the woods — and the snow — all day every day, and slept in cold inns at night. The guide knew his job, the wine was very good, and there were no political overtones. We might have been anywhere."

"Small mountains, but they can wear you out," Sam adds. "We saw a couple of pretty girls at the place we stayed in the night before last, but I couldn't move. Not Jim, though . . ."

"That'll do," Jim says. He and Sam are tired. They can hardly get their boots off, and when they do they sleep for fourteen hours.

The next day they are recovered and full of nervous energy. Jim and I are to start for Vienna — an easy three-hour drive — after lunch. Sam won't come with us.

"You may not believe it," he says, "but I'm about cars the way some people are about planes. Can't stand them. I'm headed for London anyhow, and I'll have to get in the air sooner or later so it might as well be sooner."

He spends the morning at the taxidermist's, arranging shipping details on the boars' heads. "I got two and Jim got one," he explains to me. "And Jim says I can have the one he got, so I'm going to put all three in the Maryland house. I've got a perfect place for them, all three together. Not in a row, the one in the middle will be higher. It'll be a unique mounting, especially on wild *Communist* pig. There's only one question — getting them out of here. The paperwork! You'd think I was exporting Lenin's tomb."

"Don't you ever think about anything but hunting?" Jim asks him.

"What else is there?" Sam rebuts, and Jim shakes his head.

He leaves for the airport and we have lunch at the hotel. Attenborough appears unexpectedly, recovered from the flu.

"Knew you were leaving today," he says, "and just wanted to make sure everything is all right."

"Couldn't be better," Jim says.

"Bill Lennox says you dispensed with him early the other night."

"He's too good to waste," Jim says. "We wanted to save him."

"That's what they send us now," Attenborough says. Without Mrs. A. he is rather good company. He likes Budapest, too, and knows it well. "We have a very pleasant apartment," he says, "It's not a bad place to live."

"I can see that," Jim says. "It grows on you. I can see why Jack Johnson loved it."

Attenborough makes a dignified departure after lunch, and we have our bags brought down and put in the car. The doorman is whisking our car with a feather duster and Jim gives him a generous tip.

"You know," Jim says as we start out of the city, "when I was young, I wanted to be someone like Phil Sheridan, or Sherman, standing at the top of the Shenandoah Valley or outside Atlanta, my saber in my hand and twenty thousand men behind me and a winning campaign in front. The only thing is, there's no campaign any more. Even in the war — I was in Europe — there was no campaign like that. Patton thought he had it, but those tanks are too noisy. . . . When we were after those boars in the Mátra I was thinking that if you do it now, you have to do it in your head, there's no other place left, and that's where this Communism gets interesting. Why would it be so bad if order came back everywhere? As the D.C. said to you, if you can't have heaven, hell is the next best thing, so what about a little of it? And that's what Sherman did, didn't he? Spread a little hell around — and don't tell me the Southerners didn't enjoy it, too. They're still talking about it, I notice. . . .

"Imagine everything in order again in America — and I don't mean the kind of order the politicians talk about when they say 'law and order.' I mean order, period. No law to it, just straight Communist order. Think what America would be like — everyone polite again, the way they are here, no one able to beat you on a technicality . . . no stock market, no instant millionaires . . . no TV commercials. Not even any TV if you wanted to go that far. Imagine all the snot taken out of American life — no more muggings, no more aggressive nightclub comedians, no more singers who can't sing being paid a half million a year, no more lip from anyone on anything . . ."

"And where would you fit in?"

"Probably at the bottom, but that's the chance you'd have to take. And you can't get what you want at the top any more, so maybe a spot at the bottom in a polite society — just think, no more Lennoxes — would be better. I might be a crane operator, something like that, and loll around Hot Springs on my vacations with the rest of the workers, just like the Gellert."

He seems to be in earnest, but his large, tended socialite head and movie star good looks undermine his text.

"You forget the mess."

"Well, I'm presuming that we Americans could do a better job than they do here. On those terms, it might not be at all bad to have some Red order."

"I think Budapest and the Mátra went to your head."

"Maybe they did. But on the other hand, maybe I'm right."

The farther we get from Budapest, though, the more doubtful that seems to him. Hungarian workers, dressed in filthy quilted jackets and trousers, gather at the factory entrances, and in Győr the dismal apartment buildings seem to stretch forever. It occurs to me that Communism is not only European confusion and inefficiency pushed to the logical end, but also the final extension of American mess. It contains, rather miraculously, the worst features of several continents and systems. In western Europe, a picnic by a river is usually free from outlandish interruption; in eastern Europe, one is sure that a dozen workers would come along in a wheezing truck and park within ten yards. *Dreck* is everywhere and at all times and no one notices it. Western Europe is anti-efficient, but not altogether anti-esthetic. America is anti-esthetic, but not altogether anti-efficient. Eastern Europe is wholly anti-esthetic and wholly anti-efficient. They have managed the worst of all possible worlds.

"I guess Budapest did go to my head," Jim says as we approach the border. "But it was nice there for a minute. What I was thinking about the last hour was how you could never try to fix up your own end of anything here because no one else ever does anything. You know the old American saying — 'As pathetic as painting your half of a double house' — here everything is that pathetic. The little improvements that you do see should never have been made, and you can't figure out how anyone could be so insensitive as to try. If you cared at all, or if you had any memory of what living was like, you wouldn't try anything — you'd just quit. . . ."

We have come up behind a new car with Hungarian plates, driven by a man with a certain porkiness to the back of his head and neck. The car is small, and would attract no attention in the rest of the industrialized world. Here it marks the driver as a man of importance — he is probably a party or agricultural functionary — and he is not unconscious of that importance.

"It takes so little here," Jim says, nodding toward that self-satisfied neck. "They settled for so little. But isn't it interesting to wonder what they could have done if they'd done it right — if there had been any taste at the top?"

At the border, a man with a flashlight examines the under side of the car to make sure there are no Hungarians hanging there. He also looks under the seats. Five minutes later we are in Austria and heading for Vienna.

"Well," Jim says, "did you learn anything about Americanization?"

"Quite a bit."

"That's good."

And almost more from Jim than any other source, as he came, saw, conquered and was conquered, and ended up muddled as to how he felt and what it meant. There had been cultural and intellectual cross-pollination between him and those he met, more than would have been possible in west Europe because east Europe has an alternative idea; west Europe has none. The idea is not carried out — indeed, it is grotesquely inversed — but the traveler can't help but wonder how it would look if executed by Americans. Jim and I have been equally intrigued there, and I think all Americans are, whether they admit it or not.

In Vienna, the material well-being, the shops and the well-dressed people, come as a physical shock after what we have seen. There seems to be no question as to which side comes off better in that comparison. But later, at the Sacher Hotel, as we dine surrounded by Americans and Europeans, their complacency appears gross, even moribund, in comparison to what we have just left.

"Very padded," Jim says, "but neither frank nor comradely."

V
IN SUM

I N this book, what used to be called the "point of departure" has
been the assumption that all Europe is Americanized and going
to become more so. (Students of the present as past will note that if
the phrase "point of departure," once as sensually pleasing to the
American tongue as the current "charisma," "viable," and "confrontation," had been written of as mortal twenty years ago, public incredulity would have been as great as if "dialogue" were similarly
treated today.) The surrender is complete. On the basis of visible
evidence and experience, it would seem to be a valid assumption.

With a clearer understanding now of what underlies newspaper
features, a report such as Tad Szulc's in the *New York Times* (part
of which was quoted earlier in the section on England) assumes
genuine meaning:

"From the Iberian Peninsula to Scandinavia and from the British
Isles to Italy, Western Europe is becoming Americanized in its
consumer habits. Western Europe imports a steadily growing volume of United States goods, along with industrial licenses, capital,
techniques and managerial talent to reproduce American products.

"It consumes in increasing quantity foods packaged the American way and bought at the 'super-marchés' and 'super-mercados.' It
spends 'les weekends' at 'les picnics' and 'campings.' It dresses its
children in Levi's and cowboy shirts and it uses credit cards more
and more. It smokes American cigarettes, for taste and for status,
and it watches 'The Man from U.N.C.L.E.' (as 'El Agente de Cipol'

in Spain and as 'Agents Très Spéciaux' in France) on television, as it drinks a pop-top can of locally brewed Schlitz beer.

"This process of everyday Americanization in Western Europe is directly related to the mounting influx of United States private capital — an estimated $10-billion in new investments since 1958 — and management. Jean-Jacques Servan-Schreiber . . . has concluded in . . . 'The American Challenge' that an Americanized Europe will become the world's third industrial force after the United States and the Soviet Union. A survey by correspondents of the *New York Times* in 10 European capitals and a recent leisurely tour of Western Europe have produced the picture of a multilingual and multicultural European society that is Americanizing itself along strikingly uniform lines. . . .

"The critics of American policy do not take out their anti-Washington attitudes on American products. In Rome a correspondent reported that Coca-Cola (known in Italy as Koka) 'is sold at most Communist rallies.' Elsewhere, the United States finds itself berated for Vietnam or for rioting in Newark or Detroit while its critics smoke Kent cigarettes — produced locally under license, imported or smuggled — and drink Coke, 7-Up or Fanta, a popular orange soft drink produced by the Coca-Cola concern. The soft drink symbolizes, in a sense, this phenomenon of Americanization. The European landscape is fairly covered with billboards and posters advertising in various languages 'the pause that refreshes.' European airwaves carry the message of Pepsi Cola and whether Europeans think young or old they have to live with American jingles translated from English into their own languages. Trucks with posters proclaiming 'Tutto va meglio con Coca-Cola' speed down the Italian highways from Naples to Milan, and there is no intimate little bar between the Adriatic coast and the Aosta valley where a thirsty Italian or a foreign tourist may not find his Koka or Pepsi. What this avidity for American-brand soft drinks, bottled by local companies, does to wine consumption in Europe, is impossible to

measure. The producers in the main European wine-drinking countries — France, Italy, Spain, Portugal, Greece and Germany — de-
plore the fact that people sometimes seem to prefer a sweet carbon-
ated drink to the nobility of wine. But they have not produced
comprehensive statistics.

"Perhaps the clearest explanation for the momentum of this advancing revolution in Made-in-America tastes, habits and manners
lies in the sentiment that Europeans are Americanizing themselves
not out of any conscious identification with the United States, but
simply because American ways and products 'are the best,' or are
the most fashionable. A Spanish Government official explained that
he smoked American cigarettes because 'they taste better' (most
Spaniards stick to their own 'black' cigarettes) and that he had just
purchased an American washing machine for his wife because it
was 'the best thing on the market.' The American cigarette, in
demand since the liberation days of World War II, tends to be overwhelmingly a status item. With a pack of 'legal' American cigarettes selling between the postdevaluation equivalent of 42 American cents in Spain and 85 cents in Britain, it is not infrequent for
Europeans to carry two packs — the American brand for smoking
in public and the local brand for when they are alone. In most
countries, smuggled American cigarettes cost one-half the official
price. At least one American brand, Kent, is manufactured in Switzerland for 'legal' European consumption. The same advertising
techniques exist here as in the United States. Hence there is 'Marl-
boro country' in Europe.

"Such intense propagandizing of other American products ranging from detergents to cosmetics is a leitmotif of European merchandising. . . . American-imported goods usually cost more than
similar local products. Custom duties, often designed to discourage
luxury items, make it so. Locally produced American brand name
products have to be competitive with the local name goods.
Canned juices or soups produced in Europe by large American

companies often undersell the independent domestic producer because of the volume in which the United States owned corporations deal.

"Fundamentally, the correspondents found, the phenomenon of Americanization is fed by the rising living standard in Western Europe. The postwar economic and sociological changes in Europe — larger family incomes, women increasingly at work, the gradual disappearance of the household servant and the creation of mass-consumer markets — have made traditional American solutions to daily problems not only desirable but also necessary. The sociological change in the European home has created an immense market for refrigerators, blenders and dishwashers, as well as for frozen and canned foods. Until not long ago, these precooked foods were regarded as 'barbaric American inventions,' but now even servants press their employers to open a can of Campbell's soup (very popular in Europe) instead of preparing soup the old-fashioned way.

"Supermarkets, indistinguishable from the American kind and complete with piped-in music and air-conditioning, have wrought their own revolution in food tastes, merchandising and frozen foods, started in the United States, forced European producers and packagers to modernize. Even American ideas such as paper napkins and plates, once frowned on, have made their appearance. Ten years ago, it would have been unthinkable for the proud Spaniard to do the family shopping, but today he pushes his shopping cart down the aisle of a 'super mercado' with no loss of dignity. Therefore, Señor Rodriguez (Mr. Smith of Spain) may fill his cart with frozen fish, a novelty here, a bottle of Scotch, College Inn vegetable juice from the United States and a box of Ajax detergent.

"In most European cities, the Americanization includes the 'lavamats' and 'laundromatos,' now an accepted institution. As personal checking accounts are becoming increasingly popular — and as downtown traffic jams mount — even Madrid and Lisbon have provided drive-in banking services. The development of these and other American tastes in Western Europe stems from a variety of sources. But the correspondents believe that the lengthy postwar presence of United States military personnel — notably in West Germany but also in France, Italy and Britain — played a major role in introducing American products and ideas to Europe. American tourists and American movies, television and publications are another constant fountainhead of United States influence.

"Since it is generally assumed in Europe that the process of Americanization will keep gaining, rather than losing momentum . . . the steadily mounting presence of American tourists in Western Europe is certain to accelerate the process, because the tourists set in motion a chain reaction. To attract dollar-bearing tourists, the European city fathers and hotel and store owners are busy developing styles and facilities attractive to the visitors. But once the European customer discovers these facilities, he often seeks them himself. The beginning of 'jumbo' trans-Atlantic flights in the nineteen-seventies is expected to increase the American tourist presence and, therefore, to heighten the socioeconomic and cultural cross-fertilization that has been operating in the last decade.

"Inevitably, a social or cultural synthesis implies a two-way traffic. The American visiting Europe does go home with new ideas and they may range from the sudden discovery that a Chateau Mouton Rothschild wine or a Spanish Riscal merits being served in an American home to the notion that there may be something to be said for the European obsession with bidets. It may also go deeper and encourage an American who toured the Louvre to return home and visit New York's Metropolitan Museum or Washington's National Gallery. Yet, the visible trend today is for the everyday American influence to assert itself to a much greater extent in Europe than for European ways to make an impact on America. As an Italian intellectual remarked recently, the 'Western wind is blowing stronger.'"

The obvious could not be put more simply, but it is not invalid because it is either obvious or simple. (Or because it appeared in

November, 1967. If anything, the surface Americanization has increased since then.) As was pointed out earlier, once the psychological basis of the surrender and the colonization is comprehended, the physical results can be understood and appreciated. The accumulated data then assumes multidimensional meaning, and, within limits, can be informative and helpful.

———

Against the fact of Americanization, there are two general conscious and intellectual forces at work: active resistance, and the threat of American collapse.

Effective resistance is confined to the aristocracy (Protestant as well as Catholic) and the Vatican, and such of the middle and lower classes as those bodies can enlist. The reasons for this resistance — mainly personal comfort — are given in detail in the section on Italy. But as was noted, time is not on the side of the resisters. Nor are the Communists, especially in western Europe.

In fact, because Communism is not capable of resistance, it is difficult to see how either eastern or western Europe can draw the line at any aspect of Americanization, at least in the near future. No true resistance can really come in either area until the full Americanization process has been gone through, so it is a question of which side can get that over with first. Western Europe has greater innate sophistication with regard to the material, but eastern Europe is less chained by the past, at least on the conscious level. However, as noted earlier, it is in America itself that the Americanization process will be completed long before it can be elsewhere, so probability favors internal American resistance far antedating its appearance in any part of Europe. The aristocratic-Vatican-Gaullist reluctance is not a genuine resistance, being ignorant of the true nature of Americanization and already on the decline.

The hypothetical internal resistance in America is synonymous with the threat of internal collapse, for it is difficult to see how there can be a native American movement against Americanization without an American collapse. In western Europe — especially in the northern countries — there is a desire for as well as an apprehension of this collapse. The great majority do not want it, but the minority is less subjective and more prepared for the consequences.

The majority want it even less in east Europe, but it would obviously be of enormous interest to the hierarchy. The drunken colonel's *Report* was no more than an attempt to show how and when the pressure of Americanization would come off Europe, west as well as east. As he had said at the end: "When the United States collapses, the rest of the so-called free world will collapse with it. We shall then be the only great power left intact. And we shall, then, be the natural controllers of the world, taking over the chaos and trying to straighten it out as best we can. As unworthy as we are, we shall be in charge. The Americanization will stop. There will be no Americanization."

America may collapse, but until it does, Americanization will continue. The collapse is problematical, the Americanization is a current fact. Also, as pointed out, it is doubtful that the decline of America, whether from internal collapse or external attack, would spell the end of the Americanization process. Modern Europe could not have come into being if America had never been, so the consumer-society Europe of the future, east or west, does not depend on continued American existence any more than European Christianity in the Dark Ages depended on the continued existence of Rome. If America is overturned, Russia might fill the power vacuum by taking over: but unless Russia substitutes some other idea-method for the American philosophy of increasing material consumption as the apex of human evolution, America would rule from the grave. And what other idea-method could be substituted? One can hardly think of another, and the D.C.'s notion that Americanization would disappear with America begins to seem untenable.

Perhaps he had a presentiment of that himself when he claimed earlier, to Jim and Milo and me, in the Alcron bar, that it makes no difference that Russia has achieved such actual (as distinguished from theoretical) Americanization as it has without using American capital and American supervisors. "We have the independence the west Europeans say they want, but what difference does it make?" he had asked. "Resistance to Americanism in the east may continue on several levels — the inertial incompetence is the most important — but the idea itself is triumphant. Even if we could become more proficient at produce-and-consume than you, it would not be real resistance, but merely the extension of America through the American idea. . . . What difference does it make where it comes from? The reality is whether America-as-idea has taken over. And to what degree. Not whether America-as-idea comes from Russia, or America, or Germany . . . or even from Albania."

He had contradicted that view with his summary of his *Report,* but in later sessions he had returned to his earlier position: "Tipping is now allowed in the Soviet Union again," he said. "After fifty years — isn't that the handwriting on the wall?" And: "We have such hopeful people. They think that because they can say the CIA runs half the countries in the world and would like to run the other half, they have solved the problem. When you tell them, 'No, that isn't important. What matters is that the American Negro has a higher per capita income than an Englishman, to say nothing of an east European,' or, 'The United States is widening its lead in science research and application over Europe, again to say nothing of east Europe,' they only take out their notebooks confidently and tell you that the new U.S. immigration laws have ended the 'brain drain' from west Europe, so the United States can't go on. Of course the United States can't go on, but not for those ridiculous reasons. What can you do with such people?"

"Make Americans out of them," Jim Carter would have said, and that solution seems unavoidable. Whether the United States goes on as a political-economic entity or disappears, Americanism — the dedication to produce-and-consume — will last until the millennium, provided it is not unhorsed by a greater idea or a universal catastrophe. Barring the last two possibilities, there would seem to be no appeal from the ultimate Americanization of the world, whether under the auspices of Americans or their disciples.

That would seem to settle the question, and so it does, on the active, conscious and intellectual level. If that were the only level, Europe would be a perfect carbon copy of America by now. But it is not, and so there must be a block on some other level preventing completion of the metamorphosis.

Under the extensive surface Americanization, there is another force at work. It is certainly not conscious, because the desire of Europeans to be Americans — the intellectual commitment — is total. If there were nothing more to it than that commitment and the willingness of the Americans to supply the educational "know-how," the carbon copy would have been achieved. Because it has not been achieved, the diagnosis must be modified. Europe is Americanized . . . and Europe is also not Americanized.

The preventive factors are subconscious, but there are physical symptoms. From the American point of view, the symptoms are all different and yet all the same. The American first notices . . . anything. Any examples are as good as any others, as in this random list:

— Europeans drive differently from the way Americans do. The American goes from one place to another in his car, the European is having an adventure at the wheel. He imitates the former climate of European motoring, when it was dominated by the European aristocrat and the racing driver (often one and the same). When he comes up behind another car in his toy Fiat, he is Prince Scipio Borghese and Tazio Nuvolari in a Type 41 Bugatti (La Royale), and so he feels perfectly free to come too close to the rear of the car ahead, and to pass on a blind curve and cut back in savagely to avoid a collision with an oncoming truck. In certain ways — a feeling for the road and for what his car will do — he is often a better driver than the American. But in terms of what the road and the car are there for, he is much inferior because he drives in the past rather than the present.

— Europeans can't delegate financial responsibility. The restaurant owner has his sister acting as cashier, and she oversees every penny. The same arrangement might exist in America, but if the sister were sick or on vacation, another employee would be allowed to substitute. In Europe, the help can't touch cash because they can't be trusted. The owner is positive they would steal given half a chance, and it is always amazing to an American who penetrates the inner workings of a great French restaurant or English store or German financial house to see the antiquated safeguards at work. In the great restaurant, everything funnels through the stout lady in the ancient black dress who sits in the tiny cubicle just out of public sight. To her come the ancient waiters like schoolboys, and no matter how long they have been working there her suspicions are never allayed.

In most European banks, only a few employees handle money. The ordinary tellers, who in America have their own cash drawers, are merely allowed to take care of the paperwork of the transaction, after which the customer is given a numbered slip corresponding to one which is turned into the cashier's cage, and the cashier hands over the funds if the numbers match.

Many thoughtful Europeans claim the greatest American strength is the trust reposed in employees by employers, but the American employer who permits numbers of his employees near company funds isn't trusting them at his own expense. He has simply discovered that it is cheaper to insure against loss than to give himself ulcers trying to watch everyone. (Even if he were not insured, he would rather write off theft — and often does — then resort to the archaic European system, or perpetrate it when he is in business in Europe.) And not only cheaper, but better for morale and absolutely necessary for expansion. The European passion for watching everything in the business means many small businesses, because family watchdog concerns can't grow beyond a few hundred employees. Even in large European corporations — even in large American-owned European corporations — the old customs are often in effect under the new, making a joke of the whole structure.

Lastly, and most important in the long run, the atmosphere of suspicion and mistrust not only inflames the very conditions it guards against, but also leaves the labor force permanently stunted insofar as assuming responsibility, and hence a shaky base for the nation's industry. Employer mistrust is responsible for much of the pall that hangs everywhere in Europe.

— The curious lack of correct information. The European never seems to know what is happening, or when, or how many kilometers it is to the next village.

— On Sunday, the big trucks pile up at the customs stations on the trunk highways. The customs agents who handle large shipments don't work on Sundays, so the truckers have to wait until eight o'clock Monday morning. The trucks — from east as well as west Europe — line the autobahn at the German-Austrian border near Salzburg, and the overwhelming weight of European red tape is as literal as the Alps in the near distance.

— The inability of the European to really absorb the American way, even when the institution is a direct imitation:

(1) The large automobile service center, complete with service managers in smocks, seems a faithful copy of the American prototype, but a European feeling about money prevails. In America, if a service can't be performed, there is no charge for time consumed — i.e., if the clutch can't be repaired because the necessary part is not in stock, there is generally no charge for having pulled the engine to get at the clutch. The lack of parts is the garage's fault, not the customer's, and the garage has to bear the financial loss. This is not true in Europe, where labor must be paid for if expended, no matter if the expenditure was irresponsible. Also, if work is inadequately done, by admission of the garage, it still can-

not be corrected free of charge as it would be in America. This is not to say that American garages are not often inefficient and dishonest, but that they operate on a different theory. In Europe, the new form is always infected with the old mentality, so that it becomes panic-stricken and farcical under pressure.

(2) In many European supermarkets, goods are not in the same place each week, and items are stocked erratically, undermining many gleaming new stores in two of their major arguments for existence and often sending exasperated buyers back to the old-fashioned shops.

(3) Before direct dialing came in, the Austrian telephone service used to provide collect and person-to-person calls. Now both amenities are impossible with the new system. Company officials spread their hands helplessly when asked how AT&T can offer direct dialing *and* the other services. This stripped system is now the rule for most of Europe, and only in those countries or parts of countries where direct dialing has not been installed can the caller enjoy the former luxuries. How was the mistake in imitation made? The American model was so clear, so accessible. How could it have been copied in part but not in whole? The answer seems to be in a false sense of economy, the classic European failing, taking over and reducing the desired system to farce again.

(4) Even in Berne, the capital of Switzerland, electric current for the washing machine is shut off during peak load hours. The custom exists all over Europe, and usually includes the hot water tank as well. Not even the Swiss can explain precisely why, but evidently there isn't enough power to cook and wash at the same time. But the culture that has to wait to wash is not contemporary; or, as an American woman puts it, "What's the point of having a washing machine if you can't use it when you want?"

— The European schools, endlessly educating the children in terms of a vanished world.

— The Italian family with the apartment in Rome. It is old-fashioned but huge, and they haven't been able to rent it for years because they are asking too much. A well-heeled young American couple find it tempting, and make an offer of two-thirds of the asking price. There is a meeting between the couple and six members of the family and the family lawyer. It lasts for hours. The Italians won't budge on the rent. The American offer creeps up until it is ninety per cent of what is being asked. "I won't go any higher," the American says. "This place has been empty for four years. The furniture is all out of date. I'd have to pay a lot to put it in shape. The only attractions are the size and the location. You must understand that, or it wouldn't have been empty for four years in a city as crowded as Rome. I've gone as high as I can. You'll have to come down that last ten per cent." The family, all in best black, lean forward. They want to rent the apartment, they are *dying* to rent it. But the price is inflexible. It is the price they agreed on among themselves and they will not come down. "Think of the money you're losing," the American says. "Think of the money you've lost over the last four years. You could have taken twenty-five per cent off the asking price four years ago and you would have rented it easily and you'd have made over fifteen thousand dollars. By being so stubborn, you've made nothing." They lean forward, but they can't come down. The lost fifteen thousand and the further thousands they will lose now don't matter as much as remaining European. This was always the family apartment; this is where they were born; they have their price. "It was unbelievable," the young American says later. "There was no *give* in it. They'd rather rot with what they have than change. They had a look on their faces . . . I can't describe it. It was from another way of life so complete . . . you could get closer to an Australian bushman with a boomerang to sell."

— There is no escape from noise and the presence of other people in Europe, and the European's unconscious but complete acceptance of noise and the human presence limits him.

— Europeans sell stocks when the market is down. The *New York Times*, March 24, 1969, reports that "John Wright, the

Bridgeport, Conn., publisher of Wright Advisory Reports, says that although foreigners may be sophisticated in some areas of finance they are among the worst handicappers of the American stock market. 'Foreign investors have repeatedly demonstrated a positive genius for selling when they should be buying,' he commented. 'During the last three "bear market declines" foreigners sold American common stocks most heavily just when stock market prices were bottoming out.' "

— American girl of socialite background goes to work for German kennel owner and veterinary to learn about care of small animals. She does menial chores, putting in long days doing work for which he formerly hired a Yugoslav woman. He pays her what he paid Yugoslav, which is all right with her because she's not in it for the money. She speaks very good German and is popular with his German customers. She has connections with American kennel owners, and decides to invest her own money in setting up a business to export dogs to America. She proposes to the German that his kennel act as European depot. He is so stunned that an employee could reverse roles and hire him — the un-Europeanness of it — that he not only refuses, but asks girl to leave. And looks for new Yugoslav — less efficient, not as good for his business, but predictable! Most of Europe would rather stick with the predictable than change, despite all talk to the contrary.

— The French play basketball, but in the French fashion, not the American. In a Paris *Herald-Tribune* story by reporter Mike Brandt in March, 1969, he quotes Leroy Johnson, an American Negro who played at Indiana University and was then with the French team at Caen, as saying: "Last week only two or three of those guys came to practice. They just don't care. . . . Frenchmen are a funny sort. They are very modest during their first three drinks but then they start saying, 'Hey, we can do this, we can do that, we can beat the world.' But it's just talk. They never do anything about it." Joe Galbo, who played with the San Francisco Warriors and is now a player-coach with Paris's Club Stade Francais, calls the French dreamers. "I see them," he says, "as a people who say, 'I want change, but only when I'm ready for it, and then I want it all at once.'" The stories Johnson and Galbo and other American basketball players in France tell of their teammates' egotism, pettiness and temper tantrums are endless; and one suspects that the same little volcano bubbles under all the veneers on all imported Americanisms.

— Archbishops blessing new highways in Italy, bulldozers in Germany, drugstores in France, supermarkets in France. The Church tries, and often successfully, to enwrap the new in the old.

— Tribal customs, fixed notions that defy change. The inside of the front door in many European dwellings, especially in the Latin countries, is a network of chains, locks and bars. Not to keep out burglars, but against invasions and riots, the sort of civil insurrection which hasn't occurred for decades and against which all the locks in the world can't prevail.

In European apartments, the heating begins on October 15 and is turned off on April 15. It doesn't matter if it's hot in October and snowing in mid-April, and the custom is unchanged in the newest apartments. The change in clothes follows the same rigid schedule. The European puts off his winter clothes and assumes his spring outfit on April 15, no matter the weather. And he wouldn't dream of doing so earlier, no matter the weather. Thus, one can see Europeans sweltering in heavy overcoats on a warm April 10, and freezing in spring suits on a cold and snowy April 20. German women who have taken courses in achieving the perfect sex life, women whose apartments contain shelves full of the latest sex literature, devices and creams, put three and four pairs of underpants on their children despite the fact that they now live in heated apartments. Such customs come from a much older and unheated Europe and have no relationship to the present, but are carried along into the new life because of the inflexible atavism.

(The archaic is, of course, even stronger in east Europe and Russia, as per this Reuters item, May 5, 1969: "Spring has come to

[477]

Moscow and Russian grandmothers are once again on the warpath — against wicked Western women who risk their children's health and lives by dressing them in spring clothes. A Western mother who takes her child for a stroll in the spring sunshine — and Moscow temperatures are now averaging 64 degrees Fahrenheit — begins to run into a barrage of hostile glares and remarks as soon as she comes out onto the street. Russians — most of whom still swaddle their infants — consider it the height of cruelty to allow a small child out-of-doors before late June or July in anything less than woolen leggings, sweaters, a thick topcoat, and preferably a balaclava covering most of the head and neck. A typical East-West confrontation on this topic goes like this: Russian woman, in heavy overcoat, gloves and fur hat or head scarf, stops to stare disapprovingly at approaching Western woman, clad in short skirt, blouse and cardigan, with her small, barelegged child rejoicing in the freedom after months of wearing heavy winter clothes. Russian woman quickly bends down to touch child's legs and then declares accusingly: 'This child is freezing. Have you no conscience?' Western mother, if she speaks Russian: 'She (or he) is quite warm enough. It's very warm today.' Russian woman, probably by now supported by one or two others: 'It's quite clear that you have no conscience at all. People like you should not have children. What sort of mother are you?' And so it continues."

In addition to serving as a prime illustration of the archaic in the midst of aspirant modernity, the above example also gives strong support to the drunken colonel's claim that the old women in the babushkas still run Russia.)

What price — what use — the new apartment houses, east as well as west, if they are inhabited by people with such primitive baggage? One could hardly find a clearer example of anti-Baconism than dressing children according to the calendar rather than the weather, and the flaw is present in all the north European countries, eastern and western. There are still strong pockets of the heresy in Britain, where mothers and nannies unite to defy American pragmatism in children's clothes and some other domestic details while using it avidly most of the time.

— Many European service stations and large garages, despite complete surface Americanization, do not repair flat tires. The oasis turns into a mirage for the stricken motorist, and he is advised to find a tire repair service.

— One enters a European hardware store and asks the clerk for a screwdriver, or a hinge, or a kind of screw, or a putty knife. Instead of reaching for the item, he consults another clerk, and more often than not both of them trot off to find the store owner, who has to drop what he is doing and show them where it is. Then no one — not even the owner — knows what the price is, and it has to be looked up in a catalogue. The whole transaction takes twenty minutes instead of five.

Eric Hoffer says America is maintenance, but it is also the vast reservoir of knowledgeable clerks. In an American hardware store, the clerks — at least the older clerks — carry the location and price of thousands of items in their heads. By comparison, the organization of the modern European store is crude, belying and making sport of the contemporary contents.

— Gillette Super razor blades made in England under American license and sold throughout Europe are much inferior to the American originals.

— The poor telephone service all over Europe. This is poor *service*, as distinguished from the comforts that direct dialing has eliminated, as noted above. France is particularly poor, and notorious, but not alone. In France, the price for connection is one hundred and twenty dollars — compared to five dollars in New York — after an average wait of one and one-half years. People have waited as long as ten years. Once installed, the subscriber finds he often has to wait two hours for a dial tone, and even longer to make a call to a village twenty miles away.

— To be finally American, Europeans would have to have homes in something like the American percentage. Not tiny apartments, but homes. Real "homes," with garages and garbage disposals and deep freezes and utility rooms and oil heat and yards and barbecue pits and riding-rotary mowers and swimming pools. England is the only country in Europe that can offer homes in any quantity, but its average homes are Navajo hogans compared with the ordinary American article. The problem begins with space — homes alone require much more land area per family than apartments, and when yards are added there isn't enough room in Europe. There wouldn't be enough room if everything was bulldozed flat and the Continent rebuilt from scratch.

And even if there were enough room, there wouldn't be enough money to build and equip homes in such number. Cars and vacations and stock shares are cheap — it is the home that is expensive. And because it is forever impossible, Europe can never really know the full flavor of Americanization. The surface crust of amenities — and most of those poorly done — is the best that can ever be managed. That crust may satisfy the natives, but the American will always have to recognize it as a mere hors d'oeuvre.

As his own collection of observed symptoms mounts, the American is finally struck with the great truth: it is not so important that Europe is inefficient; what matters is that Europe can't be efficient when it tries. It isn't that the telephone system doesn't work; it's that it doesn't work after all the effort to create a telephone system. In the African bush, one wouldn't expect efficiency and one wouldn't care; in Europe, one does expect and there is disappointment and frustration when the European effort doesn't function properly.

The reaction is perfectly illustrated in this item from the "People" column in the Paris *Herald-Tribune*, April 22, 1969: "MIFFED AND MOVING: American actor William Holden, who couldn't put through a telephone call from Nice to his broker in New York. 'This mess cost me more than $100,000,' he said. 'I wanted to get in touch with my New York broker to get a stock deal started, but it was impossible to telephone him. I don't want to risk this happening again and I refuse to work in France anymore despite the quality of the artists and technicians here.' He's off to Rome to finish the film he had started in Nice."

Holden later denied the story — which had been released by Agence France Presse — but it could very well have happened, to someone else if not to him, and stands as a definitive example of the basic conflict between European inefficiency and Americans. It was not that he couldn't get through to New York that enraged — or could have enraged — Holden, but that he thought he could get through because he was in Nice, France. After all the talk about Americanization, it comes as a shock to find it can fail at the crucial moment.

"When Frenchmen sit around the table," Clothilde had said, "it is not that they could be sensible if they chose . . . but that their egos keep them from doing anything together." The inability extends throughout Europe. Even after a decision has been made, it is difficult to carry it through inside a country, and nearly impossible to enforce it throughout Europe. In his head, the European wants to be an American, but subconsciously he also wants the old European albatrosses, the atavistic weights. When the two desires clash, only one can survive. Sometimes it is the American, sometimes the European — each instance is different. The result is a delicate balance between complete Americanization, east and west, and *no* Americanization.

If America is arbitrarily pegged at zero, the inefficiency ranges from minus values in certain fields in north Europe and Switzerland through generous figures for England, France, Spain and the rest of west Europe, and ends in astronomical numbers for east Europe, where the inefficiency becomes Russian and sufficient in itself to block almost anything.

But as with the specific characteristics — English silliness, French egotism, German pleasure-seeking, and so on — the inefficiency is only a symptom. It is not that the Europeans won't, but that they can't. They are enamoured of America, but can't be finally Americanized, can't want it with their hearts as well as with their minds. The possibility of failure begins to occur to the most sanguine colonists.

In addition to the physical symptoms of preventive subconscious factors, as discussed above, there are non-physical symptoms. They are more diffused, not always apparent to the casual observer, and essentially abstract. But they are equally significant.

Two — nationalism-tribalism, and the inability to break with the past — are of special interest.

Despite all the talk of European federation, European nationalism is on the rise, as evidenced by the reports below:

James Reston, *New York Times,* November, 1968: "Europe is still struggling, 50 years after the end of the First World War, to learn the lessons of that tragic conflict. . . . the spirit of nationalism, which produced this frightful disaster, is rising again five decades later. . . . The pride of nationalism, and the glorification of military arms go on, and the ideal of a United States of Europe, so bright and hopeful even a few short years ago, has declined . . . Even Jean Monnet, the father of the post-war movement for European political unity, and still at 80 the most optimistic statesman on this continent, is alarmed by the drift of Europe's political leaders back to the old nationalism."

Eric Wentworth, *Washington Post,* January, 1969: "At first glance, the record wave of mergers, partial takeovers, cooperation agreements, joint ventures and other forms of industrial cross-fertilization in which companies of Western Europe have been indulging this past year suggests they are finally rising to the challenge of American competition.

"But despite the flurry of activity, skeptics note for one thing that the actual mergers, and many of the less-ambitious hookups, are occurring within the boundaries of single nations. This phenomenon appears to result from the influence of national interests among the companies involved as well as their governments, and from the absence within the Common Market of a 'European company law' or harmonization of the currently conflicting laws and policies of the six member nations.

"Enthusiasts of the present trend view the building of larger industrial entities even inside a single country as an encouraging first step toward eventually having true, transnational 'European companies.' But skeptics, eyeing the continuing domination of nationalism, are concerned whether the much-desired second step will necessarily follow. And unless it does, they fear European industry may fail by and large to gain the economies, efficiencies, flexibilities, expanded resources and overall muscle needed to compete successfully with major U.S. corporations.

"Politics so far has frustrated the Common Market goal of clearing away some of the big technical obstacles to cross-boundary mergers. . . . As things stand, there are a number of crucial differences between laws of individual Common Market members that make mergers across national boundaries a potential nightmare. Among these are conflicting accounting and taxation systems. Related variants include the West German law about participation of labor unions in management decision making and an Italian one requiring disclosure of shareholder names. Because of these and other problems, only one corporate marriage that comes close to a true European-company merger has occurred in recent years — between West Germany's AGFA and Belgium's Gevaert, which joined hands in 1964 against competition from such giants as Kodak in the photographic field. . . .

"The threat posed by nationalistic attitudes was raised by Vice-President Alcon C. Copisarow of the management consulting firm McKinsey and Co., in connection with the need for what he called 'a new type of technological management.' 'It is, however, improbable,' Mr. Copisarow said, 'that such increases in efficiency will be offered to the fullest extent in the European market since national-

[483]

ism remains strong in the more important countries of Western Europe. It is therefore unlikely that efficiency will be the governing criterion for corporate management. The more probable development is the establishment of large national companies which will eventually become European monopolies . . . a major deviation away from the major increases in efficiency which the international corporation promises to provide.'

"National interests can also intervene where something short of outright merger is proposed. Perhaps the most celebrated example this past year came when Italy's Fiat — number one auto maker in Europe — sought to gain a substantial foothold in the number two French producer, Citroën. The French government, with backing from labor unions, insisted Citroën's autonomy be preserved and barred any arrangements that might allow taking jobs away from the French workers or upsetting the French car market. The companies eventually agreed to a compromise scheme that met these conditions. Though their establishment of a joint organization to coordinate research, production, sales and other activities should prove beneficial, the companies presumably are prevented from closing down any inefficient operations in France however desirable such steps might be. Thus the larger corporate size attained through merging may simply mean pooling inefficiencies that plagued the individual merger partners beforehand."

(In fact, such incomplete and inadequate mergers may only provide fresh opportunities for American competition, the pooled inefficiencies creating greater weaknesses than when they were individual — a geometric rather than an arithmetic increase.)

C. L. Sulzberger, *New York Times,* January, 1969, in a feature entitled "The Tribes of Europe": "An odd feature of this epoch is the parallel drive for bigger supranational organizations such as the Common Market or what Moscow fondly calls its 'socialist commonwealth' and that for smaller tribal groupings. One must view currently riotous Northern Ireland against this paradoxical background. . . . Resurgence of tribalism in contemporary Europe is an unexpected but widespread development. Britain is infected by North Irish, Scottish and Welsh nationalism. If all varieties of clan dynamism were to succeed, one could foresee a day when border peoples would paint themselves blue and create a Pict Republic.

"This trend isn't limited to the Continent's offshore island . . . In Spain, Catalonian and Basque nationalism simmer. French Basques are less restive but Breton nationalists conspire. Belgium is riven by the Walloon-Flemish dispute. A small group of Swiss in the Jura mountains wants autonomy from Bern. The Teutonic peoples, willy-nilly, are divided into West and East Germany and Austria. In Italy there is a Sicilian nationalist movement. As if it didn't have trouble enough, Czechoslovakia has just divided into two autonomous Czech and Slovak halves. Yugoslavia made a concession to its various elements by creating six separate subrepublics; now the Albanian minority asserts new claims with riots. And the differing 'nationalist' movements in European Russia are renowned — Latvians, Lithuanians, Estonians, Ukrainians: in the Asiatic U.S.S.R. the problem multiplies.

"The origins of European tribalism are involved. They derive from the tribes who once scrambled out of Asia and dug themselves into this continent's forests and swamps. Their inherited differences are often rendered tangible by the persistence of vestigial languages like Basque, Welsh or (may Saint Patrick forgive me) Gaelic. Most of these clan societies — the various groups of Goths, Syths, Vandals, Lombards and Celts — were slowly hammered together into nation states by time and tough rulers. Only thus did the various Alemans, Teutons, Nemtsi and Franks become what we now call Germans. But atavism runs strong in the human mind and the melting pot process never fully encompassed Europe. Furthermore, it was complicated by dynastic rivalries and religious differences which often preached war in the name of peace. Tribal influences were further stimulated when the dynamism ran out of

Europe. Great empires dissolved and central governments were exposed as weaker than tradition had supposed. . . . Areas unwilling to become bigger and stronger by centralized union seem fated to become smaller, weaker and more quarrelsome by disunion."

The smaller subdivisions which Sulzberger mentions underlie the grand nationalisms — France, Spain, Germany, England — and give a far more chilling picture of where nationalism may eventually end. When the insoluble threatens the individual human, he instinctively takes the fetal position. When it threatens the federation, there is a desire to return to the nation. When it threatens the nation, there is a desire to return to the tribe. Among other things, the current desire is a symptom of fear of large-nation disintegration. As prophecy, it may be correct or not, but its continuing presence will put increasing pressure (subtle as well as overt) against organization and survival and for just that disintegration and elimination it fears.

European tribalism is not literal and immediate. Europe is not going to dissolve into tribes tomorrow and be living in skins the day after. It is slow and poetic. The tribalism does not threaten federation and nationalism per se, but is a sign of innate opposition and disenchantment, and Europe may end in skins as a result. And not only Europe but the world. As Sulzberger points out, the rise in tribalism is worldwide and includes the black-white division in the United States. Instead of bringing the glories predicted by Herman Kahn, the year 2000 may be quite a comedown, materially speaking.

The inability to break with the past is shown by the inability to get rid of the totemic anachronisms: the English monarchy, the Papacy, the aristocracy, Gaullism if not de Gaulle, Russian neoczarism. Europeans no longer need nor believe in any of those trappings, but they can't bring themselves to eliminate them. They rationalize their reluctance by saying, "What difference does it make. The Queen is no longer a political force, but we prefer to keep her for the pageantry and the sense of history, and the tours she can take for British business. The aristocrats don't mean anything any more, so who cares how they play with their titles and customs. The Pope is very good for the Italian economy, and what a vacuum he would leave." It seems reasonable: Europe can have its archaic icons and be Americanized, too. But it doesn't work out that way. Retention of the ancient totems means there has been no final break with them. At bottom, they do mean more than anything else; that is why they have been retained. The man who can't bring himself to get rid of the mistress whom he says now bores him must be still interested, even if he doesn't know it.

Europeans are probably honest when they say they don't think the totems have meaning, that their existence is purely decorative. When an American tells them that forms are important, and that a change in form means a change in substance, they can't believe it.

"They saw that nothing changed in France after the monarchy was done away with," the American scholar in Paris quoted earlier says, "so they are reluctant to try anything like that again. Naturally, the point is that they didn't go far enough, but it is impossible for them to think that way."

Of course, the man who would change form has to be himself already changed, so it is not so simple.

Americans have changed the forms, cut through the old ways and come out on another side, the only people to do so since the 1500s. To date, the results are debatable. On the one hand, there is the technological way of life; on the other, the awesome unattractiveness of that life and of Americans themselves. Because of the unattractiveness, the current American position must be regarded as temporary. Americans are now in between the old and the new, and the process is nowhere near completed. They must go on, or succumb to the reflected horror of the unattractiveness. But whatever happens, they preview the end of the old form for Europeans.

As awful as the results of the American direction have been so far, there is no active choice for Europe except to follow it as blindly as the Americans have.

The two examples above — nationalism and the inability to break with the past — are, again, instances of the fact that it is not that they won't follow it but that they can't.

They can't because they are imprisoned in the past. This is the basic affliction to which all the symptoms, physical and non-physical, finally lead. This is where Europeans are decisively different from Americans and it is in this shadowy but vital area that they are *not* Americanized. If they are not ultimately Americanized here, however, the surface Americanization may come to nothing, so it is a question of considerable importance. There is frustration for the dedicated American in their situation, because this final Americanization can't come from outside.

America and Europe are now in the position of the cinema father and the cinema son when the cinema father says: "I've taught you all *I* know about tracking bear, Steve — you'll have to go after one on your own." The final commitment has to be interior and personal, and the Americans may find, as the Romans did with those barbarians who became Roman citizens in name only, that the veneer comes off very swiftly and ungracefully under pressure.

It should be emphasized that imprisonment in the past does not imply an understanding of the past. The imprisonment precludes an understanding, in fact. And as savagely and proudly ignorant as most Americans are about the past, their own as well as that of the rest of the world, individual Americans are capable, when they wish to be, of understanding the common past far more accurately than Europeans. There is something of this in Eliot's comment on James: "It is the final consummation of an American to become, not an Englishman, but a European — something no born European, no person of European nationality can become." And in Auden's comment on that comment, in his preface to James's *The American*

Scene: "It is from American critics like James and Eliot that we Europeans have learned to understand our social and literary traditions in a way that we could never have learned by ourselves, for they, with natural ease, look at our past, as it is extremely difficult for us to look, with contemporary eyes."

The American break with the past has, in general, also meant forgetting the past, which is profoundly unfortunate for Americans and explains much, if not all, of the horror of American life. But given a choice between living in the past as Europeans do, with no real comprehension of either past, present or future, and living in the present with no comprehension of the past and very little of the future, as Americans do, the American outlook is preferable as the lesser of two evils because there is a certain feeling for the present.

The desirable break with the past — the break which never forgets what went before — is, perhaps, impossible for the majority. In Shaw's *Caesar and Cleopatra*, Theodotus, Ptolemy's tutor, comes to Caesar to beg for help in putting out the fire ravaging the library at Alexandria, which he calls "the first of the seven wonders of the world." "What is burning there is the memory of mankind," Theodotus says, and Caesar answers, "A shameful memory. Let it burn." Then Theodotus asks wildly, "Will you destroy the past?" And Caesar replies, "Ay, and build the future with its ruins." No one could seriously believe that Caesar was less civilized than Theodotus, because people understand instinctively that Caesar didn't need the library — everything in it had become part of him. Theodotus, on the other side of the fence, in the past, was not so fortunate and wanted the library because he felt unreal without it.

Because Europeans are trapped in the past relative to Americans, there is an ineradicable if hidden hostility between them. The two systems run on different clocks, and in the end this will be intolerable. One or the other will have to become standard. In the Roman experience, the barbarian notion of time triumphed over their own: the Americans may well have a like experience. Particularly when all parties realize that western European time is closer to Russian than American time. At that revelation, the great European land mass could easily become one in the past to oppose the American present.

Until then, Americans are left to contemplate the narrow but bottomless abyss which separates them from Europeans. They look across the time differential and see . . . what they have to see, people who are unbridgably different from themselves, imprisoned in a former time and hence pathetic as well as unreachable. The pathos of Europe, the sadness, becomes the overpowering emotional response, piling up until the American is quite bathed in it. It doesn't matter where he goes or whom or what he sees, it always ends in pathos.

As in a dream, as in Joyce's soft, endless snowfall, the American reaction to Europe can't stop any more than sexual fantasy, once started, can stop. The American reactions are as uncontrolled, as terrifying, perhaps, as any others which occur when the individual is frank with himself about the unpleasantly moving, and they often come out in spoken lapses, partially bowdlerized, as in these by Americans of all ages and backgrounds:

— No American is as empty as a European.

— Europe was prepared, before the Americans came, to go on repeating European life forever . . . the little joke, the little smile. There was no craving for another form.

— The endless sadness, and then the comparison of Roman Spain, the urbane proconsuls sheltered from the blazing sun in cool, well-built offices and villas. . . . freshly shaved and toga-ed, but always thinking of Rome, the reality, where fellow patricians were waiting to welcome them home with knowing smiles, the expectation that had carried them through many a Spanish summer, and that carries, in lesser but comparable degree, the American counterpart through the same exile in much the same way.

— If America was a willingness of the heart, says the young American girl who looks like Ali MacGraw and talks like Gloria

Steinem, then the Europeans have never been willing. Or have no heart. . . . When I went to see a doctor in Vienna — about something else — he went to pieces over my feet. "They are like the feet of the beautiful bird," he said, "and only Americans have feet like that. European feet are like stumps next to them." So I walk the old earth of Europe with these swan-like feet, and the game I play with myself is mirror, mirror on the wall, who's the unfairest of us all, because when any of my lovely European lovers are quiet next to me I could weep for them, not only because I have the beautiful feet and the *way*, but because they don't know it. . . . Don't know it, don't know it. I am the bird with the beautiful feet and they are the earthbound ducklings with the stumps, but they don't know it. They feel it, they act off it, they look up at me with passing awe, but they just don't know it. Boys or girls, they just don't know it. And I could cry for them. I could, but I won't, because they don't deserve it, do they . . .

— Europeans in sidewalk cafés watching other people — logic would insist that a truly new face was never going to come along, but they can observe the old ones forever in just that hope. The fabulous appetite for repetition. . . .

— No American can have a true and lasting relationship with any European.

— It never stops skiing in Europe, and skiing is as perfectly mindless as *discothèque* dancing, up the hill and down, up the hill and down. Millions of pairs of hands putting millions of pairs of skis on millions of car roofs on millions of four o'clock Saturday mornings — this time we will be early — and driving to the mountains. Parking and discovering that everyone else had the same idea. The two-hour wait for the big cable cars to the top, standing with thousands of others in the black cold. Then up on the lesser lifts and down the slope — thirty, forty, fifty times, then lunch, then another fifty. Then the two-hour wait for the cable car down. Then the drive home, arriving at ten at night. Eighteen hours, not of sport, but of waiting and mindless repetition, as on assembly line work. Americans, proud of their own mindlessness, think they can match it, but they wilt and find the last ten hours distinctly unpleasant.

— Optical tests show that dogs see the physical world differently than humans do. People look larger to them than they really are, or than they look to the human eye. And the American feels the European sees things so differently than he does, and that he appears larger to the European than he really is.

— The bland faces of the European girls going about their business, more brave-new-world than the most nylon Americans. A little Bach here, a little coffee there, a little love affair down the street, a tidy purchase of material for the new curtains, the dream that never ends, no questions asked.

— The poverty and paucity of their lives, which often comes out as perpetual social combat. Did you ever notice that if you're having a certain kind of endless fight with anyone in an apartment house in America, it usually turns out that they were born here in Europe? They like to have a situation to hate — the neighbor whose tree obscures the view from the kitchen window — and hate it forever. They become what they dislike, they couldn't live without it.

— The sheer difficulty of life in Europe. Physical, social, any kind. The impossibility of ease on any level, always so stiff.

— The good-looking American boy of twenty who came to Europe for one reason, to sleep with European girls, and enjoyed nearly four hundred in two years and then quit. It was so depressing, he said, to be doing it and be thinking at the same time of them doing it all over Europe, millions and millions of them, all the same, and doing it forever just because they had always done it. They were so available, and so much the same that it got you down in the end. In America there's a zig instead of a zag once in a while. This way you might as well be pulling yourself off ad infinitum.

— Any American, even the most ignorant, knows things no European does, even the most intelligent, even the Nabokovs.

—What is it about England? Ladrick asked recently. I came around the corner in Florence and there were one thousand English schoolchildren filling up a square. Once upon a time, one thousand English schoolchildren were not too bad, surmountable at least. But now, a lower-class nightmare, and they all thought they were so beautiful. The hideous voices, the hideous faces, the hideous legs revealed by the hideous mini-skirts up to the hideous crotches. The terrible deprived of the nineteenth century dressed up for the twentieth, so sure they were acceptable and so determined to make it their own. It was a scene from science fiction. . . . *Cavalcade* made contemporary, Harlech being pelted with pies by the Rolling Stones at a party and saying he liked it, poor Sarah Churchill singing at a nightclub in Rome . . . The Liverpudlians are our Negroes, and in great demand for the same masochistic wallowing. . . . Around Americans the English are like poor people at a big party given by their betters. They look, they copy, but they try to pretend they aren't there. What they do and what they think they do are in watertight compartments. Very English, very cheap . . . The quality of the smile of the English woman trying to patronize the American and yet file away the latter's style for future imitation. That smile in a painting would be worth everything ever written or said on the subject. . . . England is so sad, the very saddest. Eliot wrote, "I have gone at dusk through narrow streets and watched the smoke that rises from the pipes of lonely men in shirtsleeves, leaning out of windows," and that is what I thought of when I saw those children in Florence. Those old men were their grandfathers, and they were sad, and the grandchildren are sadder. It doesn't diminish, it increases.

If the great European land mass does become one in the past, a single clock from the Atlantic to the Urals, then all European pathos would be united as well. The sadness of east Europe, the most piercing of all European sadnesses, would become standard. The drunken colonel said the Russian leaders would never enjoy the "little things" again, and never allow anyone else to, even if they lasted a thousand years. If all Europe became like east Europe, and like Russia, the sadness would not be primarily in the shattered appearance of people and things, but in the belief of generations of Russians, and then east Europeans, and then west Europeans, that it would be different tomorrow.

"The present condition is permanent," the D.C. had said. "We would never change it. Not if there were no exterior struggle, not if we had ten million United States dollars for every man, woman and child in the world." And it would be the inability to *see,* the inability to break with the past, that would keep all Europe in the permanent, grotesquely bathetic position of eternal hope and eternal postponement. Today, east Europeans can't break the Russian form because they can't break any form with which the past is sufficiently entangled, because that would necessitate breaking with the past as well. When Jim said to Milo, "Why not *really* resist?" he put the American view quite clearly. But the current eastern dilemma is genetic and/or subconscious rather than intellectual and political, and it could eventually be the problem of all Europe.

Because such a possibility exists, the special quality of Russian sadness is worth examination. In April, 1969, excerpts from a letter written by Ivan Yakhimovich, former chairman of a collective farm, were published in the west. Yakhimovich — who had been cited in 1964 as a model Soviet citizen — was dismissed from his position after he wrote to the Politbureau to protest the trial of Soviet intellectuals. Now, a few hours before his own arrest, he wrote a letter which was circulated in Moscow in typewritten copies. The text is from the *New York Times:*

"The days of my liberty are numbered. On the eve of imprisonment I appeal to people whose names are sealed in my memory and heart — hear me out! . . .

"I am compelled to talk about myself because soon a flood of lies and hypocrisy will come out of the court. I am compelled to talk about myself because my fate is the fate of my people and their honor is my honor.

"I am accused under Article 133 of the criminal code of Latvia of spreading false fabrications deliberately slandering the Soviet state and social position. The maximum sentence is three years' deprivation of freedom . . .

"Bertrand Russell: You are a philosopher, so perhaps you can see more quickly what the accusations are founded on . . . What laws have I broken? The Constitution of the Latvian Soviet Socialist Republic and the Declaration of Human Rights allow one to write and distribute things, and to demonstrate, etc. . . . Whom does my freedom threaten, and why is it essential to take it away from me?

"Comrade Alexander Dubček [the party leader of Czechoslovakia]: When seven people went out into Red Square on Aug. 25 with the slogan 'Hands Off Czechoslovakia,' and 'For Your Freedom and Ours,' they were beaten until they were bleeding, they were called 'anti-Soviet slanderers,' 'Yids' and the like. I could not be with them but I was on your side and I shall always be on your side as long as you serve your people honestly. 'Remain firm, the sun will rise again . . .'

"Aleksandr Isayevich [Solzhenitsyn, the dissident Soviet novelist]: I am happy that I had the opportunity to read your works. May 'the gift of the heart and the wine' be yours. Pavel [Litvinov] and Larisa [Daniel, participants in the Red Square demonstration, sentenced to exile in Siberia]: We welcomed your gladiator-like courage: 'Hail, Caesar, we who are about to die salute thee.' We are proud of you . . .

"Peasants of the Young Guard Collective Farm: I worked with you for eight years. That is long enough to get to know a person. judge for yourselves and may your judgment serve the truth. Don't let yourself be deceived.

"Workers of Leningrad, Moscow and Riga. Dockers of Odessa, Liepai and Tallinn: To save the honor of his class, the worker Vladimir Dremlyuga went onto Red Square to say 'No' to the occupiers of Czechoslovakia. He was thrown into jail. . . . Who will help a worker if not another worker?

"Comrade [Pyotr G.] Grigorenko, Comrade [Pyotr I.] Yakir [other protesters against the Czechoslovak invasion]: You are hardened fighters for truth. May life preserve you for the just cause! . . .

". . . Watch carefully the fate of everyone deprived of freedom for political reasons.

"Academician [Andrei D.] Sakharov [a nuclear physicist, author of an essay on intellectual freedom circulating clandestinely in the Soviet Union and published in the West]: I heard your 'Reflections.' I regret that I did not manage to write to you. The debt is mine.

"Communists of all countries, Communists of the Soviet Union: You have one lord, one sovereign — the people. But the people is made up of living persons, of real lives. When human rights are violated, especially in the name of socialism and Marxism, there can be no two positions. Then your conscience and your honor must command.

"Communists to the fore! Communists to the fore!"

The style, the childish picture of the western world (where the quickwitted Bertrand Russell lives) as well as his own, are amazing in a seasoned bureaucrat. How can a man who has seen such a system from the inside be so naïve? Are they all so innocent? Is it all held together because of such a staggering lack of imagination and intelligence? Are such people the last word in the process? Are they all forever swallowed up, like poor Yakhimovich, in the preposterous labyrinth of "frank and comradely?"

He is not an exception, as one discovers in visits to east Europe, and the strongest indictment against Russian Communism would seem to be that it has turned the Russians and east Europeans into extremely ignorant persons. Yakhimovich's father could have written a more intelligent letter, certainly a far more literate one. But

Yakhimovich and his contemporaries have been reduced to thinking and speaking and writing in such a sub-basic collection of awkward clichés that even their dissent is tragically primitive. Getting rid of a political system they don't like is the least of their problems, because they would then be up against the far more difficult tyranny of their own condition. They would have to be completely re-educated as human beings, a task of fabulous dimensions. (This is in addition to the physical problems, and in a recent series of ten articles, published in the *International Herald-Tribune* in June, 1969, Anatole Shub, former *Washington Post* correspondent in Moscow, claims that Russian living conditions are below the pre-1914 level in many departments. "Before the 'great October Socialist Revolution [of 1917],'" he writes, ". . . admittedly backward Russia fed half of Europe . . . and — as Svetlana Alliluyeva quietly noted — her father met her mother in 1917 in her worker-revolutionary grandfather's seven-room apartment. Russians also used to be a tall people, like the Swedes and Montenegrins, before the Communists began their agricultural experiments." Physical improvements are supposed to be the only excuse for the past fifty years, and if they turn out to be nonexistent the bubble begins to tremble alarmingly. Especially in east Europe where the knowledge that it was better before 1914 is only kept unspoken by the assumption that there is still hope if Russia has improved.)

Even the best Russian writers don't seem to be able to *see*. They write of people who are nothing — who can be anything under such circumstances? — as though they have ideas, plans, substance. Because of their impotence, reality can't be faced on any level. "We walked to Boris's house," reads an apocryphal passage from any current Russian novel, "speaking of Sartre and Camus, and when we got there, Natasha came running out to Boris. His face lit up, for she had in her hand a copy of the manifesto he had drafted the night before and lost. She had found it at Pavel's. There had been much excited talk, and it had been misplaced in Pavel's papers, which always overflow his desk and he takes them up and

waves them vehemently to make his points. Now we read it together, Boris and Natasha and I, sitting on the grass in front of the
little cabin, the birch shadows almost reaching us from the edge of
the wood. The setting was so idyllic, so charming, that I wanted to
lie back and look at it, paint it on my memory forever. . . ." But to
non-Russian, non-European eyes, it is not that. Natasha, Boris's
mistress and inspiration, has a dreadful tic on the left side of her
face and is slovenly in her personal habits. To Boris, she is the Natasha to whom he wrote the famous poetry, but she was never that
Natasha. She was always as she is now, and the cabin was always
just as filthy and the dishes piled just as high in the kitchen. Even
the birch shadows are thin, and the three figures huddled over the
manifesto seem as forlorn as the sparse trees and the ragged turf.
The novel would never be published in the west were it not for the
political competition. And if the Russian censors permitted themselves humor, they could explain repression on the grounds of
artistic inadequacy: "It is worse than subversive; it is badly written."

Jim Carter would say that it is not a time for poetry and talk and
love and manifestos and novels, but for revolt or death . . . but
that is the American as opposed to the European view. There can
be no revolt because there is no appreciation of the reality. The
enemy isn't the Politbureau, and the problem wouldn't be solved if
the intellectuals were allowed to publish what they want. The
problem — and the sadness — is what they themselves are.

"Of all that is missing," the drunken colonel said in our last session, "the greatest lack is the absence of an understanding of reality. No Russian seems to be able to know who he is or what is going
on. Against the evidence of the physical senses, we have been calling our failure a success for over fifty years now. You westerners
think we are hypocrites, but I can tell you that it is much worse
than that — we can believe what we choose to believe and ignore
everything that doesn't fit what we have decided to believe. This is
the profound Russian weakness, the great madness, and we all

[498]

suffer from it. Even the *émigrés* have the disease — you can see it very strongly in Nabokov, for example."

In the present, Europe has surrendered to conscious Americanization with utter voluptuousness, and demands more. But the European subconscious is dominated by the past and not Americanized.

The future offers many possibilities. Europeans can either federate, remain nationalistic or dissolve into tribes. They can continue, stop, increase or diminish conscious Americanization. They can remain dominated by the past or break with it, in which case they would become totally American. Western and eastern Europe can continue as two variants of the domination by the past, or they can merge as one, which would then be dominated by east Europe, the more primitive. There are also more complex possibilities involving combinations of the simpler ones.

And there is always the immense influence of the American future itself. Americanization can continue long after the collapse of America, but such a collapse would naturally have a great effect on Europe, as would an America climbing on to more dazzling technological heights.

Not only does no one know what is going to happen — no one can even make a convincing guess, especially a guess restricted to the next thirty to forty years. "We are all reduced to speculation," Larry Moradonia, the Italian prince quoted earlier, wrote to me recently, "and I always wonder if speculation is worth it, just as I always insist that you see the present and the future by looking to the past. . . . As I have told you so often and so tediously, the point never was that Rossellini was atypical. All Italians have some Rossellini in them, just as we all have something of the Pope in us and the Pope has something of us in him. Rossellini looked wonderful when he was on top, just as Agnelli does now, and was just as glamorous to the public. And he looked just as pathetic when he hit bottom, and I leave the rest of the sentence to you. . . . On Easter Sunday [1969], there was much activity in Rome, as usual, but I didn't go out, also as usual. My gloomy old palazzo seems more real to me than Via Veneto ever did, and while the church bells were pealing their debatable message I was working on my theory that everything in a nation rises from personal characteristics, even its science. We think science is so impersonal, but it isn't. There are Italian physics, French physics, even American physics. Every discriminatory theory starts as a joke, but we know that every joke is an earnest in the womb of time. Pirandello didn't say that, but he would be proud of me all the same. . . . We don't believe in restrictive theory today, but we will see it all in time. We will see it as the Pope sees the great crowd in St. Peter's Square when he comes to his little window. The little man in the little window, and there are many men below who are more intelligent — certainly more infallible — than he, but he has the sublime advantage of being above and looking down. That is all done by a trick, the past used as a ladder to the sky, but it is an effective trick and a very old one. And one from which we can learn, too. We must also conquer the past, make it our own, and then we, too, will be able to climb it to the top, to the place where the sky becomes very dark and from where we shall be able to look back to earth as the Pope looks, only from much higher and from much more outside. . . . Then we shall see what really happened with old Europe and older America, the two old dancers in the deserted ballroom . . ."